WHO BELONGS

Who Belongs

*White Christian Nationalism
and the Roberts Court*

Stephen M. Feldman

New York University Press

New York

NEW YORK UNIVERSITY PRESS
New York
www.nyupress.org

Library of Congress Cataloging-in-Publication Data
Names: Feldman, Stephen M., 1955–   author.
Title: Who belongs : white Christian nationalism and the Roberts Court /
Stephen M. Feldman.
Description: New York : New York University Press, 2026. |
Includes bibliographical references and index.
Identifiers: LCCN 2025016558 (print) | LCCN 2025016559 (ebook) |
ISBN 9781479841141 (hardback) | ISBN 9781479841165 (paperback) |
ISBN 9781479841172 (ebook) | ISBN 9781479841202 (ebook other)
Subjects: LCSH: Political questions and judicial power—United States—History. |
Freedom of religion—Political aspects—United States—History. |
White nationalism—Political aspects—United States—History. |
Christian conservatism—Political aspects—United States—History. |
Pluralism—Political aspects—United States. | Democracy—United States—History. |
United States. Supreme Court. | Warren, Earl, 1891–1974. | Roberts, John G., Jr., 1955–
Classification: LCC KF4783 .F45 2026 (print) | LCC KF4783 (ebook) |
DDC 342.7308/52—dc23/eng/20250407
LC record available at https://lccn.loc.gov/2025016558
LC ebook record available at https://lccn.loc.gov/2025016559

This book is printed on acid-free paper, and its binding materials are chosen for strength
and durability. We strive to use environmentally responsible suppliers and materials to
the greatest extent possible in publishing our books.

The manufacturer's authorized representative in the EU for product safety is Mare
Nostrum Group B.V., Mauritskade 21D, 1091 GC Amsterdam, The Netherlands.
Email: gpsr@mare-nostrum.co.uk.

Manufactured in the United States of America

10 9 8 7 6 5 4 3 2 1

Also available as an ebook

As always, to my partner, Laura

CONTENTS

1. We the People   1

PART I. HISTORY AND POLITICS

2. Republican Democracy: Inclusive or Exclusive?   17

3. Pluralist Democracy: Emergence and Development   42

4. Conservative Reactions to Pluralist Democracy and the Warren Court   60

5. White Christian Nationalism Enters the Political Mainstream   70

PART II. THE ROBERTS COURT: WHO BELONGS?

6. The Roberts Court's Disdain for Pluralist Democracy   101

7. Religious Freedom at the Early Roberts Court   111

8. Non-Christians Do Not Fully Belong: The Later Roberts Court Solidifies the Transformation of Religious Freedom   125

9. Who Fully Belongs? Not People of Color, Women, or LGBTQ+ Individuals   149

PART III. CONCLUSION

10. Toward a Fully Realized Democracy   175

Acknowledgments   189

Notes   191

Index   253

About the Author   269

1

We the People

Who belongs to "We the People of the United States"?[1] The conservative justices on the Roberts Court view white, Christian, heterosexual men as the truest Americans—the Americans whose constitutional rights should be most fully recognized and protected (being wealthy helps, too).[2] The Court simultaneously has narrowed and diminished the rights of non-Christians, women, people of color, and LGBTQ+ individuals. From the Court's perspective, they do not fully belong to the People.[3] The Roberts Court, it seems, is engaged in the purposeful contraction of the People. That contraction, rather than any particular interpretive methodology, such as originalism, unifies the Court's decisions.

The first words in the Constitution, "We the People," are provocatively ambiguous. Those words appear to create a People who are dynamic, who can act and grow.[4] This People is welcoming and inclusive. Yet, those same words also appear to acknowledge a preexisting People—a People with a recognizable identity. This People is exclusive: The Constitution merely "announced their presence."[5] The ambiguity of the constitutional People has generated an inveterate conflict: "[The] basic American struggle is over who is an insider and who an outsider—who comes within the most fundamental 'we': We the People."[6]

The Roberts Court justices, then, are participating in an ongoing multi-century battle over the meaning of the People. The framing and ratification of the Constitution as well as the early years of nationhood bubbled with tensions over the nature of American government and the People. Many framers were political elitists who feared democratic excesses. They conceived of the government as a republican democracy that was exclusive, inegalitarian, and hierarchical. Virtuous citizens and government officials were to pursue the common good, with only a sliver of the population directly participating. Concurrently, however, many Americans envisioned a government that was more inclusive and egalitarian, and the constitutional framework allowed them to continue to press for greater participatory rights. Even so, throughout the ebbs and flows of American history, the forces of exclusion have more often predominated over the forces of inclusion. For the most part, white, Christian (heterosexual) men, particularly wealthy ones, have controlled the levers of power in both the public and private spheres.[7]

During the 1930s, though, the forces of inclusion gained the upper hand for a variety of reasons. Under President Franklin Delano Roosevelt (FDR) and the New Dealers, American government became more egalitarian, more of a participatory pluralist democracy, open to societal groups that had previously been excluded or suppressed. A conservative Supreme Court resisted these changes. Partly for that reason, the Court invalidated numerous New Deal statutes. Then, in 1937, after FDR had been reelected in a landslide, the Court succumbed to political pressure (and then changes in personnel) and acquiesced to the new form of government, pluralist democracy.[8]

This 1937 transition rippled throughout constitutional jurisprudence. The Court not only deferred to Congress while upholding New Deal statutes but also began to elaborate the pluralist democratic process. To promote this inclusive, egalitarian, and participatory democracy, the Court, for the most part, invigorated the individual rights of religious freedom, free expression, and equal protection, rights that had been relatively toothless before 1937. The pre-1937 Court had allowed the predominant political and cultural forces in American society—again, in control of (wealthy) white, Christian (heterosexual) men—to hold sway, mostly without constitutional interference, and sometimes with constitutional support. But in a pluralist democratic world, protection of these individual rights became central to the acceptance of diverse interests and values and the expression of those interests and values in the democratic arena. When Earl Warren became Chief Justice in 1953, the Court intensified its enforcement of individual rights and liberties while deepening its protection of pluralist democratic processes.[9]

During the years after 1937, conservative reactions to pluralist democracy and the Warren Court varied, depending on political possibilities and opportunities.[10] Eventually, though, conservatives focused on the Court's 1937 transformation as a catastrophic mistake that had corrupted the Constitution. Justice Clarence Thomas, for instance, proclaimed that the Court took a "wrong turn" in 1937.[11] Indeed, Thomas and the other conservative justices on the Roberts Court now seem intent on undoing the 1937 transformation. The conservative justices in *Dobbs v. Jackson Women's Health Organization* did not merely overrule *Roe v. Wade* and eliminate a woman's right to choose whether to have an abortion; they declared that *Roe* "was egregiously wrong from the start."[12] From their perspective, *Roe* had perverted the true Constitution. In *Dobbs* and numerous other cases, the justices invoked originalism to legitimate their decisions—they were purportedly following the original meaning of the Constitution, a meaning that is supposedly objective, apolitical, and preceded the corruptions of 1937.[13] But apart from the justices' questionable assertions about originalism, what is their vision of the lost or exiled Constitution? In other words, what do they intend to accomplish as they undo the so-called mistakes of 1937?

Recent Supreme Court decisions suggest the conservative justices are largely uninterested in returning to the constitutional principles invoked before 1937, which revolved around the virtuous pursuit of the common good. Instead, the justices often invoke principles and rights recognized and strengthened during the post-1937 era—rights to free speech, religious freedom, and equal protection—but they are reinterpreting those principles and rights to protect and empower a narrow segment of the American people, namely white, Christian, heterosexual men. The Court's individual rights cases therefore go hand-in-hand with multiple decisions more directly undermining pluralist democratic government—for example, decisions narrowly construing congressional power.[14] Quite simply, the Court is returning the nation to a more exclusive, inegalitarian, and hierarchical form of constitutional democracy. The current conservative justices act in service of minority rule—hence, the contraction of We the People. They aim to resurrect a pre-1937 version of the Constitution, but to them, that Constitution embodies the political and cultural privileging of white, Christian, heterosexual men. People of color, non-Christians, women, and LGBTQ+ individuals are, in a sense, lesser Americans.[15]

* * *

Many legal scholars and political scientists acknowledge that the Supreme Court decides cases based on neither pure law nor pure politics.

Rather, the justices' votes and the Court's decisions arise from an uncertain amalgam of law and political values (defined capaciously)—call it a law-politics dynamic.[16] In most cases, perhaps, the justices sincerely interpret the relevant legal texts—the Constitution, statutes, executive orders, and so on—but interpretation is never mechanical. No algorithmic method reveals the correct meaning of the text; constitutional interpretation, in particular, is never merely two plus two equals four. The justices' interpretive horizons always influence their understandings of the texts—where interpretive horizons arise from cultural values, religious orientations, political ideologies, and so forth. For this reason, the justices' legal interpretations and conclusions typically coincide with their respective political values or preferences (again, where politics is defined broadly, extending beyond mere partisanship).[17]

Given the normal political characterizations of the justices, the Roberts Court predictably and consistently hands down conservative decisions. Empirical studies underscore the political tilt of the Court.[18] Ever since the conservative Clarence Thomas replaced the liberal Thurgood Marshall in 1991, conservative blocs of justices have controlled the Rehnquist and Roberts Courts. These conservative justices have interpreted (and continue to interpret) the Constitution and other legal texts from within their conservative political horizons. On the Rehnquist Court, running from 1986 to 2005, the bloc of Chief Justice William Rehnquist and Justices Antonin Scalia, Sandra Day O'Connor, Anthony Kennedy, and Thomas (after his appointment) often voted together and handed down conservative decisions.[19] The early Roberts Court, beginning in the fall of 2005, with the appointments of Chief Justice John Roberts and Justice Samuel Alito, hardened the Court's conservative tilt, as Roberts and Alito consistently voted with Justices Scalia, Thomas, and Kennedy.[20]

On both the Rehnquist and early Roberts Courts, though, at least one conservative justice could occasionally be persuaded to vote with the progressive justices, even in politically salient cases. O'Connor and Kennedy were moderate conservatives who joined their progressive colleagues to form majorities in some important cases. Most prominently, O'Connor and Kennedy, joined by Justice David Souter, authored the joint opinion for the Court in *Planned Parenthood v. Casey*, which reaffirmed that women have a right to choose whether to have an abortion before viability.[21] Kennedy also wrote the majority opinions in two cases protecting LGBTQ+ rights: *Lawrence v. Texas* held that due process encompasses a right to engage in homosexual conduct (O'Connor concurred in the judgment without joining Kennedy's opinion),[22] while *Obergefell v. Hodges* extended the right to protect same-sex marriage.[23]

Regardless, during the years of Donald Trump's first presidency, because of justices' deaths and retirements—and the Republican-controlled Senate's maneuverings—the Roberts Court became more conservative. Justice Neil Gorsuch replaced Scalia, Justice Brett Kavanaugh replaced Kennedy, and Justice Amy Coney Barrett replaced Justice Ruth Bader Ginsburg. At that point, after Ginsburg's death in the fall of 2020 and the rushed nomination and confirmation of Barrett, the *later* Roberts Court truly starts, with an ultraconservative bloc of six justices in control.[24] The current conservative justices hold their six-to-three supermajority, it should be emphasized, though the Democrats have won the popular vote in seven out of the last nine presidential elections. In fact, since Earl Warren retired as Chief Justice in 1968, Republican presidential candidates have won a majority of the popular vote in only six of the 15 elections (in 2024, Trump won a plurality), yet Republican presidents have nominated 15 of the 20 confirmed justices. Gorsuch, Kavanaugh, and Barrett nonetheless are historically unique, being the only justices in history both nominated by a president, Trump, who lost the popular vote (in 2016), and confirmed by senators representing a minority of the people.[25]

To be sure, changes in the Court's personnel affect the politics of the Court's decisions. Moving from a liberal icon, like Marshall, to an ultraconservative, like Thomas, will inevitably change the politics of Supreme Court adjudication. The same can be said about the more recent transition from Ginsburg to Barrett. Still, one should not overlook the importance of less extreme transitions, such as the replacement of the moderately conservative O'Connor with the ultraconservative Alito. Regardless, given that a conservative bloc has controlled the Court for more than 30 years, an analysis of the Roberts Court requires an understanding not only of the politics of individual justices but also the broader trends in conservative politics. And conservative politics has unequivocally not been static. The conservative politics of 1990 is not the same as the conservative politics of 2024, including in relation to judicial decision-making.[26] Of course, just as conservatism has changed significantly over recent decades, so too has liberalism and progressivism, but the Court is not in progressive control.

Before 1991, conservatives often argued that the Court should exercise judicial restraint and defer to the democratic process. If the Court were reviewing the constitutionality of a congressional action, to take one example, the justices should refrain from substituting their own values for those of Congress. After Thomas replaced Marshall in 1991 and solidified conservative control of the Court, conservatives lost interest in judicial restraint; they began encouraging the Court to articulate and implement conservative values.[27] What specific values were the justices to articulate and implement? More important, fast forwarding to today, what conservative values animate the later Roberts Court? Numerous recent decisions suggest a disturbing answer. The conservative justices are implementing aspects of a white, Christian, nationalist agenda, favoring the interests and values of white, Christian, heterosexual men.[28]

* * *

This book breaks into three parts. The first focuses on American history, particularly as it relates to democratic government, constitutional jurisprudence, and politics. To start, chapter 2 defines republican democracy and explains how American government was republican democratic from the constitutional framing through the early twentieth century. Particular attention is paid to an ongoing tension between two opposed conceptions of republican democracy: One viewed democracy as exclusive, inegalitarian, and hierarchical, while the second viewed democracy as inclusive, egalitarian, and participatory. The former viewpoint generally predominated during this time period. For instance, during the framing era, the nation was de facto Protestant; non-Christian practices or declarations could provoke official and unofficial retribution. Moreover, racism was sealed into the constitutional framework as five constitutional provisions "directly" protected the institution of chattel slavery.[29]

Chapter 3 defines pluralist democracy and explains how, in the 1930s, the nation shifted from a republican to a pluralist democratic form of government because of a variety of forces, including changing demographics and the economic earthquake of the Great Depression. During this time, the forces favoring an inclusive, egalitarian, and participatory democracy gained the upper hand. The Supreme Court initially resisted this transition, but around 1937, the Court accepted pluralist democracy and began to explore its parameters and implications—emphasizing the processes of fair and open democratic government. As part of this transition, the Court invigorated the individual rights of religious freedom, free expression, and equal protection, rights crucial to recognizing the diversity of interests and values in American society. Chapter 3 concludes with a discussion of the Warren Court and its deepening of the transition to pluralist democracy. For example, the Warren Court held that, in public schools, the Equal Protection Clause prohibited de jure racial segregation and the Establishment Clause precluded religious prayers, even if ostensibly non-sectarian and non-denominational.

Chapter 4 describes conservative reactions to pluralist democracy and the Warren Court, with a focus on judicial conservatism running from the 1970s to the early 1990s. The chapter begins with a discussion of judicial restraint, particularly as it was manifested in the Court's religious freedom decisions. Next, the chapter focuses on the conservative notion that the post-1937 and Warren Courts had exiled the true Constitution: Conservative scholars were exploring a possible return to the republican democratic principles that had predominated in pre-1937 constitutional jurisprudence. The chapter concludes with a discussion of neoliberalism.

Chapter 5 completes the historical discussion by focusing on the emergence of white Christian nationalism and its movement into the conservative mainstream during the late twentieth and early twenty-first centuries. The discussion ranges from the Vietnam War era to the presidential elections of Barack Obama and Donald Trump (in 2016), and then Trump's 2024 campaign. If the 1930s marked the outset of the first sustained period in American history where the forces favoring an inclusive, egalitarian, and participatory democracy held sway, the election of Obama marked a second such period, as it manifested the potential political implications of the nation's changing demographics. Yet, Obama's presidency triggered a white Christian backlash that contributed to Trump's candidacy and election in 2016. The discussion culminates with a focus on white Christian nationalism and Republican conservatism today. While much of the historical discussion in the first part of the book is from 30,000 feet—with occasional zoom-ins for illustrative details—this chapter is more granular, citing and quoting multiple sources written by prominent Christian conservatives, including a Baptist megachurch pastor who has been called Trump's "apostle."[30] While the religious and political views of white, Christian Americans of course vary, the crux of white Christian nationalism, as it is currently manifested in the conservative mainstream, is that white, Christian, heterosexual men are the truest Americans. Finally, while Trump is the current leader of the Republican party and the face of Christian conservatism, white Christian nationalism is likely to remain central to conservative politics for the foreseeable future even if Trump were to exit the political scene.

The second part of the book focuses on the Roberts Court: Following the political agenda of white Christian nationalism, the conservative justices seem intent on returning the nation to an exclusive, inegalitarian, and hierarchical form of democracy. Chapter 6 discusses the early Roberts Court and its demonstrated disdain for pluralist democratic institutions. Several key cases are covered: *National Federation of Independent Business v. Sebelius*, which invalidated part of the Affordable Care Act (ACA), the flagship enactment of President Obama's administration;[31] *Shelby County v. Holder*, which invalidated a crucial provision in the Voting Rights Act and opened the door to a slew of state laws restricting suffrage;[32] and *Citizens United v. Federal Election Commission*, the landmark decision that invalidated congressionally imposed limits on corporate campaign spending.[33]

Chapter 7 switches to a focus on individual rights cases. The chapter focuses on the early Roberts Court and its religious freedom cases under both the Establishment and Free Exercise Clauses. In Establishment Clause cases, the conservative justices rejected the doctrinal tests that the Warren, Burger, and Rehnquist Courts had used. Instead, the Roberts Court conservatives emphasized tradition as determining the scope of the Establishment Clause. And since they understood tradition consistently with the nation's history of de facto Christianity, they readily upheld blatant Christian government actions, such as the public display of a 32-foot Christian cross. In free exercise cases, the conservative justices were quick to find that the government had purposively discriminated against Christianity and that any such discrimination necessarily violated the First Amendment. Hence, the Court held that the government had discriminated against a Christian baker and violated his free exercise rights when it prohibited him from discriminating against a same-sex couple. All in all, the conservative justices of the early Roberts Court manifested Christian grievance, indignant that the nation's religiously diverse population did not welcome manifestations of de facto Christianity. While the justices brooded about discrimination against Christianity, they insisted that Christians themselves must be allowed to discriminate against others with impunity.

Chapter 8 focuses on religious freedom cases decided by the later Roberts Court—that is, after Barrett replaced Ginsburg. The conservative justices, purportedly following originalism, have frozen the meaning of religious freedom to accord with the understandings of the de facto Protestant (Christian) framing generation—though the religious makeup of the American people has become far more diverse (and less Christian) over the centuries. The Court therefore has upheld extravagant displays of Christian symbols and overt Christian prayers, even in the public schools. The government, according to the Court, must treat Christian practices and institutions at least as well as (if not better than) secular practices and institutions. To be sure, the conservative justices sometimes use ecumenical language in their religious freedom opinions, suggesting that the First Amendment protects non-Christians as much as Christians, but the case results do not match the language. Consistent with white Christian nationalism, the later Roberts Court decisions suggest that non-Christians do not fully belong to the People.

Chapter 9 focuses on how the later Roberts Court has interpreted other individual rights to protect the bona fides of a white, Christian nation. In the area of equal protection, the conservative justices have invalidated all race-based affirmative action, including in higher education, while adopting the ostensible principle of colorblindness, a formal conception of equality that ignores context and history. Indeed, the Court's interpretation of the Reconstruction-era Equal Protection Clause produces shockingly perverse results: Rather than promoting racial justice and equality, the Court's equal protection doctrine protects white privilege at the expense of people of color. When it comes to women, *Dobbs* is key. Rather than treating women as active, choosing, autonomous beings, the *Dobbs* Court claimed to follow an originalist interpretation of the Fourteenth Amendment Due Process Clause. Thus, the Court focused on the status of abortion in 1868, the year the Fourteenth Amendment was ratified, and a time when women were openly excluded from the polity, lacking the right to vote and other political and civil rights. By narrowing the meaning of due process, the *Dobbs* Court also implicitly threatened the precedents protecting LGBTQ+ rights, including same-sex marriage. Unsurprisingly, then, the Court subsequently interpreted the First Amendment to allow a business owner to discriminate against same-sex couples based on free speech (rather than free exercise). In sum, the Court has diminished the rights of people of color, women, and LGBTQ+ individuals so that they do not fully belong to the People.[34]

To clarify the organizational structure of the book, chapters 2 and 3, at 30,000 feet, briefly cover approximately 200 years of constitutional history. Rather than being comprehensive, those chapters provide a framework for understanding the following: first, initial conservative reactions to pluralist democracy and the Warren Court (chapter 4); second, the entry of white Christian nationalism into the political mainstream (chapter 5); and third, the resonance between that political movement and the Roberts Court (chapters 6 through 9). The third part of the book consists of a single chapter. As the conclusion, chapter 10 emphasizes that the conservative justices are marching on a crusade to return the United States to an exclusive, inegalitarian, and hierarchical form of democracy. In accordance with white Christian nationalism, they interpret the Constitution to protect a quasi-caste system with white, Christian, heterosexual men at the top. Whether this form of government should still even be called a democracy is questionable, but rather than debating what counts as a (minimal) democracy, this chapter goes in the opposite direction. It focuses on a theoretical issue: What would a robust, uncompromised pluralist democracy look like? The chapter argues that whenever we raise the issue of democratic or constitutional rights, we implicitly ask the question: Rights for whom? Who belongs to the political community, to We the People? The answer is that in a robust pluralist democracy, full and equal citizenship for all individuals must be a premise of the system. If all members of the political community are not afforded rights to full and equal political participation, then pluralist democracy will not be completely realized. Consequently, contrary to the Roberts Court's individual rights decisions, discrimination against non-

Christians, people of color, women, and LGBTQ+ individuals cannot be constitutionally valued or protected, whether under the First Amendment or otherwise.

* * *

A caveat about originalism should be emphasized at the outset. The Roberts Court conservatives often invoke originalism to legitimate their decisions, and conservative scholars and judges typically insist that originalism is the only legitimate interpretive method—while they denigrate or disregard other interpretive approaches.[35] In this book, to be certain, I criticize originalism at different points, yet I do not present a generalized critique of originalism. Regardless, criticisms of originalism abound.[36] For instance, while originalists claim that we must focus on history, originalism itself is not historically grounded in the framing, ratification, and early national years. The earliest American judges and legal scholars approached constitutional interpretation pluralistically, drawing on multiple sources of meaning such as the Constitution's underlying purposes, natural law, original (textual) meaning, framers' intentions, practical consequences, and judicial precedents.[37] In fact, conservative scholars, politicians, and judges first advocated for originalism (or at least one form of originalism) in the 1970s and early 1980s precisely because they could use it to criticize liberal Warren and Burger Court decisions. Originalists claim that the methodology reveals fixed, determinate, and apolitical constitutional meaning, yet they conveniently ignore that different (and competing) versions of originalism can lead to different conclusions.[38] So-called "old originalism," for instance, focuses on the framers' intentions, while "new originalism" focuses on the original public meaning of the text. The two approaches might, in some instances, reach harmonious conclusions, but they might not. Moreover, when professional historians do research, they typically uncover complexity; they find multiple constitutional meanings rather than a single, fixed (objective and apolitical) meaning.[39]

Nowadays, originalism appears to be no more than an interpretive ploy the conservative justices invoke to ostensibly legitimate conservative case outcomes. It is a tool of convenience.[40] When the conservative justices assert that the Constitution must be understood pursuant to the original public meaning, as of the time of ratification—1788 for the original document, 1791 for the Bill of Rights, and 1868 for the Fourteenth Amendment—the justices facilitate interpreting constitutional provisions in accordance with the interests and values of white, Christian (heterosexual) men, who were the only Americans fully invested with political rights at those times (wealth mattered too, especially in 1788 and 1791). States could expressly ban suffrage on the basis of race until 1870, when the Fifteenth Amendment was ratified, and on the basis of sex until 1920, when the Nineteenth Amendment was ratified (states could grant voting rights before those years, and some did so).[41] After the Revolution, state constitutions allowed Jews to vote, but restrictions on office holding continued in some states well into the nineteenth century.[42] Thus, in chapters 6–9, we will see the conservative justices repeatedly invoke originalism (or history and tradition) to protect white, Christian, heterosexual men at the expense of people of color, non-Christians, women, and LGBTQ+ individuals. That is, the conservative justices invoke originalism to provide a façade of political neutrality, even as it supports their march toward an exclusive, inegalitarian, and hierarchical form of democracy.[43]

One simple example of the Roberts Court's (mis)use of originalism will suffice (subsequent chapters will discuss additional examples). As will be discussed in chapter 6, *Citizens United* held that congressionally imposed limits on corporate campaign spending violated the free speech guarantee of the First Amendment. In the majority opinion, Justice Kennedy supported this conclusion with an originalist flourish, quoting from James Madison and reasoning that "[t]here is simply no support for the view that the First Amendment, as originally understood, would permit the suppression of political speech by media corporations."[44] This historical conclusion neatly fit contemporary conservative ideology—protecting wealth and the economic marketplace while undermining an egalitarian democracy—and Justice Antonin Scalia wrote a concurrence elaborating the originalist argument.[45] Regardless, the originalist reasoning was so ahistorical as to be patently false. The framers' generation did not conceptualize corporations in a way that would even resemble the profit-driven multinational behemoths that dominate the twenty-first-century marketplace. During the early decades of nationhood, corporations could be formed only when legislatures specially chartered them—general incorporation laws did not exist—and legislatures infrequently granted the needed special state charters. Moreover, legislatures almost never granted corporate charters to businesses that focused solely on profit-making. Instead, consistent with a premodern mercantilist outlook, states would charter corporations that promoted the common good by performing a function useful to the public, such as the building of infrastructure, including roads, bridges, and canals.[46]

* * *

As the following pages show, the Roberts Court's invocations of originalism typically mask judicial impositions of power that favor white, Christian, heterosexual men at the expense of non-Christians, people of color, women, and LGBTQ+ individuals. Likewise, the ostensible conservative principles that characterized constitutional jurisprudence in the 1970s and 1980s—judicial restraint and deference to democratic decision-making—now look like way stations on the road to power. Ultimately, with a conservative bloc firmly controlling the later Roberts Court, we can see that there are no conservative principles—or at least none that consistently matter in Supreme Court decision-making. There is only conservative power in the judicial propagation of minority rule.[47]

PART I

History and Politics

2

Republican Democracy

Inclusive or Exclusive?

The Constitution was born in a political crucible roiling with tensions over the nature of republican democratic government.[1] With roots reaching back to Aristotelian political philosophy, civic republican government was grounded on two principles: virtue and the common good. In theory, virtuous citizens and officials pursued the common good rather than their own "partial or private interests."[2] Moreover, in the United States, the people were sovereign. The Declaration of Independence unequivocally pronounced that government must rest on "the consent of the governed."[3] In doing so, the Declaration implicitly repudiated aristocratic and monarchic forms of government. Distanced from the British mix of monarchy, aristocracy, and democracy, the Americans were left with some form of democracy—a republican democracy, we might say. Yet, at that time, many feared that a republican democratic government of the people, without the tempering balance provided by the aristocracy and monarchy, would produce chaos and tyranny.[4]

If anything, the Declaration itself exemplified this uncertain endorsement of government by the people. "We hold these truths to be self-evident, that all men are created equal, that they are endowed by their Creator with certain unalienable Rights, that among these are Life, Liberty and the pursuit of Happiness." While the ringing endorsement of equality and liberty for "all men" likely referred, in the contemporary vernacular, to humanity in general—women as well as men—the reality was that the states (nee the North American colonies) were riddled with political inequalities.[5] In fact, state constitutions adopted in 1776 or soon afterward precluded women from voting, with New Jersey being a brief exception. Some states denied suffrage to free Black American men, though many states allowed Black voting—even in most of those latter states, however, the years from 1790 to 1850 would see free Black Americans lose voting rights. No state allowed Black slaves to vote. Non-Christians fared better when it came to suffrage, though many early state constitutions banned non-Protestants from holding public office. Revolutionary-era America thus motioned toward an inclusive democracy while simultaneously acquiescing to exclusion—indeed, the Articles of Confederation and then the Constitution left the state governments in control of voting rights.[6] Not even all white, Christian men enjoyed equal participatory rights, as states limited voting to those who owned property or other indicia of wealth. The Maryland Constitution of 1776, for example, extended suffrage only to those "freemen . . . having a freehold of fifty acres of land [or] having property in this State above the value of thirty pounds current money."[7] Unquestionably, though, the Declaration's most egregious manifestation of exclusion and inequality related to slavery. Thomas Jefferson, in his first draft of the Declaration, included a paragraph condemning the slave trade as "an execrable commerce." But in deference to South Carolina and Georgia as well as northerners who profited from the slave trade, the Continental Congress deleted the paragraph.[8]

The Framing of the Constitution

After the Revolutionary War, as the nation struggled through the 1780s, this ambivalent stance on republican democracy contributed to political tension. Freed of feudal aristocratic and monarchic restraints, property ownership in America was far more widespread than in Europe, at least for white Protestant men. Many of these men farmed their own land, as the economy was thoroughly agrarian. This widespread property ownership, this relative material equality, engendered a growing sense of political equality, as reflected in many of the early state constitutions. For instance, the Massachusetts Constitution of 1780 declared that "[a]ll men are born free and equal, and have certain natural, essential, and unalienable rights."[9] The Revolutionary War further inspired this sense of equality as many small farmers gained confidence and self-esteem by fighting in the military and helping to defeat the powerful British forces. The framers themselves recognized the importance of widespread land ownership. Gouverneur Morris estimated that "nine-tenths of the people are at present freeholders," while Charles Pinckney proclaimed that, because of widespread property ownership, "equality is . . . the leading feature of the U.S."[10] Of course, the framers did not lament what facilitated the availability of so much land—European settlers and their descendants forcibly taking it from Native American tribes.[11]

Through the 1780s, these small farmers—white, Christian men who owned property—saw their state taxes increase as the state governments struggled to pay off Revolutionary War debts. The nation, during this time, plunged into perhaps its deepest economic depression until the 1930s. Speculators in government bonds held much of the war debt, so the farmers believed they were paying taxes to support profiteers, many of whom had not fought in the war. Facing heavy tax burdens, court actions for failure to pay, and even possible foreclosure on their land, the farmers demanded that their respective state legislatures provide tax and debt relief. In fact, state legislatures responded to these democratic pressures by granting some degree of relief, even occasionally closing the courts to creditors. From the perspective of many political leaders and other wealthy men, though, these state legislative actions demonstrated the dangers of excessive democracy: that common men, imbued with political liberty, would form political factions, seize control of government institutions, and then exercise government power to threaten the legitimate (property and contract) rights of the wealthy.[12]

Delegates to the constitutional convention repeatedly expressed their concerns about democracy along these lines. Elbridge Gerry declared that "[t]he evils we experience flow from the excess of democracy. The people do not want virtue, but are the dupes of pretended patriots." Alexander Hamilton saw "evils operating in the States which must soon cure the people of their fondness for democracies." And Edmund Randolph wanted the delegates "to provide a cure for the evils under which the U.S. had laboured; that in tracing these evils to their origin every man had found it in the turbulence and follies of democracy."[13] Subsequently, in the *Federalist Essays*, advocating for ratification of the proposed Constitution, James Madison lamented the likelihood the people would form factions (or political interest groups) bent on corrupting republican government in pursuit of their passions or interests, "adverse to the rights of other citizens, or to the permanent and aggregate interests of the community." Significantly, for Madison, a majority of the people could constitute a faction—the majoritarian will should not necessarily control the levers of government power.[14]

Many of the small farmers saw the political world differently. From their standpoint, the state legislative actions providing tax and debt relief were too small and too slow. State governments were not suffering from an excess of democracy. Rather, the legislatures were insufficiently responsive to the desires and needs of the people—meaning the small farmers. The farmers wanted more democracy, not less—at least for white, Christian men. Indeed, some farmers became so frustrated with the minimal relief coming from the legislatures that they resorted to violence, starting armed insurrections, with Shays' Rebellion in Massachusetts being the most famous.[15]

These small farmers, needless to say, were not chosen as delegates to the constitutional convention. The delegates were relatively homogeneous: Except for two Roman Catholics, all were white Protestant men that were reasonably wealthy. Given their views about the dangers of democracy, they attempted to remedy the excesses of the state legislatures. First, they designed a constitutional system that shifted government power away from the states and to a centralized national government. Second, they designed a national government that would control for the potential effects of democratic factionalism.[16] The framers hoped that a virtuous elite, drawn from wealthy and "speculative men,"[17] would be elected to national offices and serve as "guardians"[18] for "the mass of the citizens."[19] The framers consequently created a system with multiple structural constraints on the majoritarian will. For instance, the people would be able to vote directly for their representatives in only one-half of the legislative branch of the new tripartite government. They could vote directly for members of the House of Representatives, but the state legislatures would choose the Senators—and even in the House, the blatantly antidemocratic three-fifths rule bloated white, male representation from the southern states with large slave populations. The people could choose a president but only indirectly; electors from each state would ultimately vote in an Electoral College, and the states themselves could decide how to choose electors. Meanwhile, Supreme Court justices would be chosen through a more convoluted scheme, nominated by the president and confirmed by the Senate.[20]

Still, the framers knew they could not propose a constitutional government bereft of democracy. A sense of democratic equality had already gained too fierce of a foothold among many Americans, including

some of the framers, many of whom believed strongly in republican democracy. The framers realized, moreover, that the people would never
accept and ratify a proposed Constitution unless it maintained some
degree of democracy. For this reason, George Mason "admitted [at the
convention] that we [Americans] had been too democratic," but he also
worried that they should not "incautiously run into the opposite extreme."[21] In a nod toward democracy, the framers persistently emphasized the sovereignty of the people. Benjamin Franklin declared that
"[in] free Governments the rulers are servants, and the people their su-
periors and sovereigns." In *Federalist, Number 22*, Hamilton emphasized
that "[t]he fabric of American empire ought to rest on the solid basis
of THE CONSENT OF THE PEOPLE." And in *Federalist, Number 37*,
Madison maintained that "all power should be derived from the people."
So long as these homages to the sovereign people sufficed, the framers could create a government system that would control the effects of
democratic factionalism, of "partial interests" or "private passions." The
result would be, in theory, a government pursuing the common or public good. Unsurprisingly, then, in *Federalist, Number 45*, Madison linked
the common good back to the sovereign people, defining the "public
good [as] the real welfare of the great body of the people, [and] the supreme object to be pursued."[22]

Even so, the two central principles of republican democracy, virtue
and the common good, could be and were used to legitimate (supposedly) the exclusion of large swaths of Americans from participating in
the polity. While white, Christian men proclaimed the equality of all
men, they simultaneously denigrated others as lacking the virtue necessary to forego private interests and pursue the common good. In other
words, virtue (or a lack of virtue) was an idea—an ostensible principle—
that white, Christian men could invoke to justify the denial of political
and other legal rights. For instance, with regard to property requirements for voting, the ownership of land or similar wealth purportedly
established a man's independence and gave him a sufficient "stake in
society" or concern for the public good so as to justify the power to vote
and to hold office; the poor were therefore denied suffrage. Moreover,
many white, Christian (wealthy) men were imbued with illicit prejudices
that readily intertwined with concerns about virtue. Denials of rights
often resonated with those prejudices, rooted in racism, sexism, and

antisemitism. Laws of coverture limited the rights of married women, including property rights. Political leaders, such as John Adams, might acknowledge that women possessed virtuous capabilities conducive to work in the home or private sphere, but they denied that women had the type of civic or political virtue necessary for government and the public sphere.[23] Non-Christians were subjected to blasphemy and Sunday law prosecutions and also, pursuant to some state constitutions, precluded from holding (state and local) public offices—though article VI, clause 3, of the national Constitution banned any religious test or oath for federal offices.[24] Racism against people of color, especially Black Americans, was deeply ingrained in white, Christian culture. James Wilson, a delegate renowned for his faith in the virtue of the common (white) man, agreed that "the tendency of the blending of the blacks with the whites [would] give disgust to the people of Pennsylvania," though the state had already passed, in 1780, the first gradual emancipation law in the nation.[25] With so many Americans precluded from full democratic participation, only approximately four percent of the population voted in the crucial state elections to ratify the proposed Constitution.[26]

* * *

Two aspects of this inegalitarian, exclusive, and hierarchical republican democratic world should be elaborated. With regard to religion, the nation was de facto Protestant (Christian) partly because of demographics. The American population was overwhelmingly Protestant, though Protestants themselves were divided among numerous sects. The "vast majority of Americans assumed" the nation was Protestant and the "government would uphold the commonly agreed on Protestant ethos and morality."[27] When Antifederalist opponents of constitutional ratification complained that the new Constitution would open the door "for the Jews, Turks, and Heathen to enter into publick office, and be seated at the head of the government of the United States," the North Carolinian Federalist James Iredell, who would sit on the first U.S. Supreme Court, responded: "[It] is never to be supposed that the people of America will trust their dearest rights to persons who have no religion at all, or a religion materially different from their own." In other words, Iredell summarily dismissed the Constitution's prohibition on religious tests or oaths for federal offices. His message was straightforward: We all know the United States is a Protestant nation, so stop worrying—non-Christians will never be elected. Then, if anything, the nation's de facto Protestantism intensified during the first decades of the nineteenth century. By 1835, 75 percent of the population was regularly attending church, with official church memberships nearly doubling since 1800.[28]

Non-Christian religious practices or declarations could precipitate sudden and fierce (official and unofficial) reactions, long-term legal disabilities, or both. Blasphemy prosecutions, for instance, were not merely theoretical. In upholding a conviction, a Delaware court explained that it had "been long perfectly settled by the common law, that blasphemy against the Deity in general, or a malicious and wanton attack against the christian religion individually, for the purpose of exposing its doctrines to contempt and ridicule, is indictable and punishable."[29] Legal scholars did not view the First Amendment religion clauses as hindering de facto Protestantism. James Kent, a prominent judge and scholar of the early nineteenth century, wrote in 1811: "[W]e are a christian people, and the morality of the country is deeply ingrafted upon christianity and not upon the doctrines or worship of [non-Christian] imposters."[30] Supreme Court Justice Joseph Story, the leading antebellum legal scholar, emphasized religious freedom, yet simultaneously stressed that "it is impossible for those, who believe in the truth of Christianity, as a divine revelation, to doubt, that it is the especial duty of government to foster, and encourage it among all the citizens and subjects." The First Amendment, according to Story, did not require equal treatment for Christian and non-Christian religions: "The real object of the amendment was, not to countenance, much less to advance Mahometanism, or Judaism, or infidelity, by prostrating Christianity; but to exclude all rivalry among Christian sects, and to prevent any national ecclesiastical establishment."[31]

With judges such as Story frequently proclaiming that Christianity was part of the common law, politicians followed suit (though the judges too were following public opinion). Governor James H. Hammond of South Carolina issued a Thanksgiving proclamation that called the United States a Christian nation and invited "our Citizens of all denominations to Assemble at their respective places of worship to offer up their devotions to God the Creator, and his Son Jesus Christ, the redeemer of the world." When Jewish citizens of Charleston, South Carolina, protested, Hammond responded: "The simple truth is, that at the time of writing my Proclamation it did not occur to me, that there might be Israelites, Deists, Atheists, or any other class of persons in the State who denied the divinity of Jesus Christ. [But] as you force me to speak, it is due to candour to say, that had I been fully on my guard, I do not think I should have changed the language of my Proclamation! and that I have no apology to make for it now." As if he had not yet been clear enough, Hammond added: "I must say that up to this time, I have always thought it a settled matter that I lived in a Christian land!"[32] In the 1830s, Alexis de Tocqueville observed that "there is no country in the world where the Christian religion retains a greater influence over the souls of men than in America." Government and Protestantism, he explained, flowed together "in one undivided current." Put in different words, "[i]n the United States, Christianity itself is an established and irresistible fact."[33] Nineteenth-century clergyman and professor Bela Bates Edwards encapsulated the traditional American view of religious freedom: "Perfect religious liberty does not imply that government of the country is not a Christian government."[34]

With regard to race, the institution of slavery unquestionably subjected Black slaves—one-fifth of the population in 1787—to the most complete denial of rights as well as physical and emotional brutalities.[35] At the constitutional convention, the framers not only failed to condemn slavery (or the slave trade) but also included five provisions "directly" protecting slavery as a legal institution—though the framers avoided using the words "slave" and "slavery" in the constitutional text.[36] To be sure, a few delegates to the convention condemned slavery as immoral. When discussing whether Congress should have power to regulate or prohibit the slave trade, Roger Sherman of Connecticut denounced it as "iniquitous." Luther Martin of Maryland described the slave trade as "inconsistent with the principles of the revolution and dishonorable to the American character." Gouverneur Morris, from Pennsylvania, uttered perhaps the strongest condemnation of slavery. "It was a nefarious institution. It was the curse of heaven on the States where it prevailed. [If the northern states accepted it, they would be making the] sacrifice of every principle of right, of every impulse of humanity." George Mason of Virginia owned 300 slaves but combined racism, pragmatism, and moral judgment when he said, "[The presence of slaves] prevent[s] the immigration of Whites, who really enrich and strengthen a Country. They produce the most pernicious effect on manners. Every master of slaves is born a petty tyrant. They bring the judgment of heaven on a Country." Such statements demonstrate that at least some of the delegates understood the moral ramifications of their ultimate acceptance of slavery, but most of the framers disregarded these condemnations. The delegates never engaged in any extended debate on the morality of slavery. John Rutledge of South Carolina spoke for many delegates when he declared: "Religion and humanity had nothing to do with this question. Interest alone is the governing principle with nations."[37]

True, some of the framers hoped or presumed that slavery would eventually wither away, but they did not universally hope or believe as much. To the contrary, many of the delegates were firmly committed to slavery. Of the 55 delegates who participated in the convention, 25 owned slaves. Delegates from South Carolina, North Carolina, and Georgia threatened to leave the convention and abandon the proposed constitution if it did not protect slavery. And in the end, the southern delegates rejoiced. Charles Cotesworth Pinckney reported back to the South Carolina legislature: "In short, considering all circumstances, we have made the best terms for the security of this species of property it was in our power to make. We would have made better if we could; but on the whole, I do not think them bad." Unquestionably, northern delegates at the convention repeatedly accepted constitutional provisions protecting slavery without securing any southern concessions.[38]

In the end, slavery and racism were sealed into the constitutional framework. The seals were strengthened when Eli Whitney invented the cotton gin in 1793. Cotton production, highly reliant on slave labor, soon became an incredibly profitable crop. King Cotton would dominate the southern economy while bolstering the northern textile industry. Slavery was perhaps not emblematic per se of the development of capitalism—slavery, after all, is the antithesis of a capitalist free market in labor—yet slave labor fueled the accumulation of capital that spurred nineteenth-century American economic development. Slavery intertwined crucially and integrally with the geographical expansion of the nation and its evolution into a modern industrialized economy. Meanwhile, slave states enjoyed outsized power in the Electoral College due to the three-fifths counting of slaves. Of the first seven presidents, from

George Washington to Andrew Jackson, from 1789 to 1836, five were slave owners. Equally telling, the two non-slave owning presidents, John Adams and John Quincy Adams, were the only single-term presidents during that time.[39]

* * *

Despite the constitutional and legal significance of the framers' racism—as well as their sexism, antisemitism, and other cultural prejudices—the framers conceived of the common good as objective, as a thing "out there."[40] From their perspective, the framers (who counted themselves among the virtuous elite) could claim to discern the people's "true interests"—that is, the common good—even if the people (or a majority of the people) failed to recognize or have a say in articulating those interests.[41] Going forward, the same would hold true for the virtuous elite (white, Christian men) elected to government offices—they would supposedly discern the common good.[42] Consequently, the interests and values of white, Christian men were effectively validated as the objective common good. Of course, not all white, Christian men shared the same interests and values. After all, the democratic tensions of the 1780s largely pitted different sets of white, Christian men against each other: the small farmers battling wealthy speculators, plantation owners, merchants, and others of their ilk. Regardless, deliberations about the common good were largely debates among white, Christian men, with the interests and values of other Americans being dismissed or ignored (or represented only indirectly by white, Christian men). Consequently, from the framing until the early twentieth century, white, Christian men—especially the wealthy—predominated in American society. With their values and interests enshrined in government goals as the common good, they wielded the controlling power in the public and private (civil) spheres.[43]

Republican Democracy After the Framing

Although the framers sought to limit democracy and readily accepted widespread restrictions on democratic participation and legal rights, they were unable to halt the forces pressing for a more inclusive and egalitarian republican democracy. In the 1790s, under the new

Constitution, as the people—or at least white, Christian men—enjoyed their liberties in both the private (or civil) and the public (or political) spheres, a more individualist, egalitarian, and anti-elitist sentiment took hold of the nation. Freedom in the economic marketplace generated a hunger for more freedom in the democratic arena, and vice versa.[44] As early as 1800, Tunis Wortman accentuated this sentiment in his *Treatise Concerning Political Enquiry, and the Liberty of the Press.* He emphasized that truth and knowledge are accessible by "all men" rather than being "a rare and uncommon gem which [only] a few are destined to monopolize." "Judgment," he wrote, "is a faculty possessed in common by mankind." As to an individualist ethos, he explained: "All our prospects of improvement . . . depend upon the industry and exertion of individuals. It is almost impossible to conceive the extensive effects which may be produced by the agency of a single person." In fact, Tocqueville coined the term "individualism" when discussing American government in the 1830s.[45]

While the republican democratic principles of virtue and the common good remained significant, the meanings of those concepts changed over time (despite the framers' belief in an objective common good). In accordance with the spreading individualist, egalitarian, and anti-elitist attitudes, an increasing number of Americans believed that all common (white, Christian) men were virtuous—few men, it should be emphasized, were then worried about the rights of slaves, women, or others. Amidst these changing attitudes, many states rewrote their constitutions and extended suffrage to all white men. By 1825, all but three states had eliminated property and wealth requirements for voting, though a few states limited voting to taxpayers until the 1850s. In President Andrew Jackson's message vetoing the recharter of the national bank in 1832, he emphasized the equality of all white men: "In the full enjoyment of the gifts of Heaven and the fruits of superior industry, economy, and virtue, every man is equally entitled to protection by law."[46]

Not only did suffrage expand to all white men, but the percentage of eligible voters who participated in elections also increased. During the early national years, the framers' generation viewed political parties as factions intent on pursuing partial or private interests contrary to the common good. Partisanship was inconsistent with virtue. During the 1820s and 1830s, however, political leaders such as Jackson and Martin

Van Buren realized that organized parties, using improved communication and transportation technologies, could generate wider participation among eligible voters. Political parties encouraged the common (white, Christian) man to express his partisan support by attending rallies and voting. And as political parties became an accepted component of virtuous republican democratic government, participation in fact skyrocketed. The percentage of eligible voters who cast their ballots in the presidential election of 1824 was only 16.2 percent, but in 1828, with the election of Jackson, the percentage increased to 51.7 percent. The percentage of voter turnout continued to increase until 1840, when 77.5 percent of eligible voters cast ballots.[47]

To be clear, the extension of suffrage to all white men and the increased voter turnout did not mark linear progress toward ever-growing democratic participation. Throughout American history, voting rights have ebbed and flowed. During the early nineteenth century, as already mentioned, many states withdrew voting rights from free Black men. White, Christian men could talk of citizenship in broad, egalitarian terms, but the reality was otherwise. Congress, in 1790, had limited naturalization to "free white persons [of] good moral character," a racial limitation that would remain in effect into the twentieth century. Women's rights remained minimal, and in *Dred Scott v. Sandford*, the Supreme Court decided in 1857 that Black Americans could never be citizens. The tension between democratic inclusion and exclusion remained persistent as the nation, in the first half of the nineteenth century, became more resolutely a white man's republican democracy.[48]

The tense duality of American democracy was evident even in the constitutional amendments that seemingly expanded equality and suffrage in the late nineteenth and early twentieth centuries. Start with the first of the Reconstruction amendments, the Thirteenth Amendment, which declared that slavery shall no longer "exist within the United States." Despite this strike against institutionalized inequality, the proponents (in Abraham Lincoln's Republican party) of this egalitarian provision did not delineate its precise implications. Would former slaves become the *social equals* of whites? Would Black Americans have the same *political rights* as whites enjoyed? While such questions were obviously important, they went unanswered. The Republican framers of the Reconstruction amendments, in fact, purposefully left many issues unsettled for political reasons. They aimed to generate political consensus in support of the amendments by avoiding clear stances on controversial issues of racial equality and inequality. Widespread agreement on an ambiguous general principle of equality was far easier to achieve than agreement on whether government-sanctioned racial segregation should be allowed in streetcars, public schools, or other specific places or realms of activity.[49]

Regardless of Republican equivocations, former Confederate (slave) states enacted statutes, referred to as Black Codes, which imposed legal disabilities on Black American citizens—the freed slaves—effectively reducing them to peonage.[50] Republicans responded with the 1866 Civil Rights Act, which aimed to protect economic liberties for Black Americans. It would prevent states from enacting "laws which declare, for example, that [freedmen] shall not have the privilege of purchasing a home for themselves and their families," explained Representative Martin Thayer. It would also prohibit "laws which impair their ability to make contracts for labor in such manner as virtually to deprive them of the power of making such contracts, and which then declare them vagrants because they have no homes and because they have no employment." When the constitutionality of this civil rights statute was questioned, the Reconstruction Congress responded by advocating for the adoption of the Fourteenth Amendment. In fact, during debates over the Civil Rights Act and the Fourteenth Amendment, many Republicans emphasized distinctions among various types of rights, including civil and political rights. Moderate Republican Senator Lyman Trumbull explained that "the granting of civil rights does not, and never did in this country, carry with it rights, or, more properly speaking, political privileges. A man may be a citizen in this country without a right to vote or without a right to hold office." From a political standpoint, why did Republicans articulate or accept such distinctions? Some Republicans unquestionably sought to preserve the power of northern states to continue denying suffrage to Black Americans.[51] As ratified in 1868, the Fourteenth Amendment overrode *Dred Scott*—stating that "[a]ll persons born or naturalized in the United States . . . are citizens"—and imposed guarantees to equal protection, due process, and privileges and immunities, theoretically enforceable against state governments. Yet from the perspective of many Republicans, those substantive guarantees protected only economic rather than social and political equality for Black Americans.[52]

Even so, the Fourteenth Amendment failed to generate substantial economic change for Black Americans. Near the end of the Civil War, General William Tecumseh Sherman had unilaterally implemented a program providing freedmen with 40 acres and a mule, albeit in one small segment of the South. Some Radical Republicans, led by Thaddeus Stevens, eventually seized on this idea and suggested that southern plantations be divided into homesteads for freedmen, but few others supported the proposal. Although Black property ownership would have facilitated the transition from slavery to freedom, many Republicans resisted the taking of private property even from southern plantation owners. Without such a transfer of property, however, the economic class structure of the South remained largely intact. By the 1870s, many freedmen had become sharecroppers. When combined with an insidious credit system, sharecropping quickly produced economic oppression and often debt peonage. Ultimately, Stevens and other Radical Republicans reasonably viewed the Fourteenth Amendment to be a failure because it did not engender true substantive equality.[53]

Not all Republicans were willing to leave the political rights of Black Americans to the whims of state governments. Some Radicals had long viewed "black suffrage as the sine qua non of Reconstruction." In any event, the wider Republican view of political rights transformed in the late 1860s in response to Democratic President Andrew Johnson's forgiving attitude toward former Confederates and opposition to Republican Reconstruction. Johnson and the congressional Republicans had become outright antagonists by the time Congress enacted the first Reconstruction Act in March 1867, setting conditions for the readmission of southern states. The 1867 Act required southern states not only to approve the proposed Fourteenth Amendment but also to adopt new constitutions providing for universal manhood suffrage, except for those "disfranchised for participation in the rebellion." Then, in February 1869, mere months after the Fourteenth Amendment had been ratified, Congress approved the Fifteenth Amendment: "The right of citizens of the United States to vote shall not be denied or abridged by the United States or by any State on account of race, color, or previous condition of servitude."[54]

For many Republicans, the Fifteenth Amendment culminated the struggle for Black liberation and equality, but the amendment's guarantees were narrow. On its face, the Fifteenth Amendment ensured only that *suffrage* not be denied due to *race* (or color or previous condition of servitude). The amendment did not expressly protect any other aspects or elements of democratic participation. To the contrary, Congress pared down the amendment's protection of political rights to the bare minimum. Congress rejected language that would have prohibited state-imposed property and literacy requirements for voting. The House and Senate included a provision that would have protected office holding, but the ensuing Conference Committee deleted it. Senator George F. Edmunds protested this substantive change as unnecessary to reconcile differences between the House and Senate versions, none of which related to office holding. The Committee, from his perspective, had instead altered a point of "a real republicanism and a real democracy."[55]

Senator Henry Wilson, a Radical Republican leader, condemned the proposed Fifteenth Amendment as a "half-way proposition" that he would support only because it was likely "the best I can get." The amendment did not even guarantee a right to vote. States retained enormous power to regulate suffrage, as Republican Senator Frederick Frelinghuysen lamented: "[The Fifteenth Amendment] leaves the States to declare in favor of or against female suffrage; to declare that a man shall vote when he is eighteen or when he is thirty-five; to declare that he shall not vote unless possessed of a freehold, or that he shall not vote unless he has an education and can read the Constitution. The whole question of suffrage, subject to the restriction that there shall be no discrimination on account of race, is left as it now is."[56]

As history unfolded, the Fifteenth Amendment protection of suffrage became a hollow shell. Several northern states continued antebellum restrictions on voting based on literacy requirements and the payment of taxes,[57] while southern states developed numerous legal and illegal techniques that de facto disfranchised Black Americans. Even while Reconstruction continued, southern whites unleashed a relentless campaign of vigilante violence to discourage and prevent Black political participation. Hundreds of Blacks were brutalized or murdered every year; this was the era when the Ku Klux Klan developed. The Republican-led national government initially resisted these assaults on Black Americans, but by the early to mid-1870s, Republicans were more concerned with economic issues. They focused on nurturing an "economic nationalism" while sacrificing the protection of Black rights.[58] A typical state Republican platform, for instance, called for the "promotion of national industry" and the "development of national power, wealth, and independence."[59]

With Republican resistance evaporating, white southern vigilantism escalated. As early as 1875, a Republican newspaper called the Fourteenth and Fifteenth Amendments "dead letters."[60] A year later, President Ulysses S. Grant rued the adoption of the Fifteenth Amendment: "It had done the Negro no good, and had been a hindrance to the South, and by no means a political advantage to the North."[61] Southern Democrats used literacy tests, poll taxes, and gerrymandering, as well as fraud and violence, to minimize Black political power. In South Carolina in 1876, to take one example, the Democrats developed a "Plan of Campaign": Each Democrat was to "control the vote of at least one negro by intimidation, purchase, keeping him away or as each individual may determine."[62] One Black southerner explained that "we are in a majority here [in Georgia], but you may vote till your eyes drop out or your tongue drops out, and you can't count your colored man in out of them boxes; there's a hole gets in the bottom of the boxes some way and lets out our votes."[63] In 1882, the *Philadelphia Evening Bulletin* admitted that Black Americans were ill-treated yet nonetheless stated that the "time has passed when the federal government can interfere for the protection of these people."[64]

For decades, then, white southerners openly celebrated the exclusion of Black Americans from democratic participation. At the Virginia constitutional convention of 1901–1902, one delegate declared: "I told the people of my county before they sent me here that I intended . . . to disfranchise every negro that I could disfranchise under the Constitution of the United States, and as few white people as possible."[65] Another delegate exclaimed: "Discrimination! Why, that is precisely what we propose."[66] Throughout the South, Black voting became negligible. Only 1,342 Black Americans were registered to vote in 1904 Louisiana, while only four percent of eligible Black males were registered to vote in 1910 Georgia. From 1888 to 1902, Black voting turnout in Alabama, Louisiana, North Carolina, and Virginia fell by over 90 percent.[67] Consequently, white southerners enjoyed even more bloated electoral power than during the antebellum period because of "an unwritten 'five-fifths' clause." Black citizens were disfranchised, but they now fully counted toward determining congressional representation and state-Electoral-College votes, to the benefit of white voters.[68]

White attacks on Black Americans' rights of course did not stop with suffrage. In 1883, the Supreme Court struck down the Civil Rights Act of 1875, reasoning that Congress could not prohibit private, racial discrimination in places of public accommodation, such as inns and theaters. Although the Civil War had ended less than twenty years earlier, the Court explained: "When a man has emerged from slavery, and by the aid of beneficent legislation has shaken off the inseparable concomitants of that state, there must be some stage in the progress of his elevation when he takes the rank of a mere citizen, and ceases to be the special favorite of the laws, and when his rights as a citizen, or a man, are to be protected in the ordinary modes by which other men's rights are protected."[69] The Court's acquiescence did not stop with private discrimination, as it soon explicitly accepted government or public discrimination as well. In 1896, *Plessy v. Ferguson* upheld the constitutionality of "separate but equal" public facilities, reaffirming already-widespread southern practices.[70] Legally sanctioned racial segregation would be the norm for decades.

The Nineteenth Amendment, which prohibited states from denying voting rights "on account of sex" was far more successful than the Fifteenth Amendment in expanding suffrage. While many women did not take advantage of their new right, the subsequent presidential elections did see "a sizable number of women's votes."[71] Nevertheless, the ratification of the amendment in 1920 had an exclusionary, anti-democratic subtext centered on intense anti-immigrant attitudes prevalent during the early twentieth century. The women's suffrage movement had been unsuccessful for decades, at least at the national level, but massive immigration from 1880 to 1920 changed the calculus. Some years saw over one million immigrants, many of whom were eastern European Jews or Italian Catholics. Many white, American Protestants viewed these immigrants as racially inferior and as threats to American values and democratic government. While many of these Protestants had long resisted women's suffrage as contravening the traditional Protestant role of women in the family, they recognized in the early twentieth century that women's enfranchisement would add millions of white Protestant voters to the rolls, countering non-Protestant voting strength. As one suffragist emphasized: "There are in the United States three times as many American-born women as the whole foreign population, men and women together, so that the votes of women will eventually be the only means of overcoming this foreign influence and maintaining our free institutions." In short, one reason the women's suffrage movement finally achieved success was the xenophobic desire to diminish the democratic potential of immigrant communities.[72]

During the early twentieth century, white, Protestant Americans worked to constrain immigrant communities and their voting power in other ways. Many states introduced additional voting requirements, such as literacy tests and longer residency periods, typically justified as creating "a more competent electorate," but the effect was to prevent immigrants, their offspring, and the poor from voting.[73] One such state was New York: In 1923, it imposed a "scientifically devised" examination that purportedly screened new voters for intelligence and literacy but in practice blocked thousands of would-be voters.[74] A former president of the American Political Science Association, William B. Munro, supported such restrictions to limit suffrage: "About twenty percent of those who get on the voters' list have no business to be there. Taking the country as a whole, the total number of these interlopers must run into the millions." Consistent with these xenophobic and nativist attitudes, Congress in the early 1920s severely restricted immigration from eastern and southern Europe.[75]

* * *

Tensions over inclusive and exclusive democracy also surfaced in court exercises of judicial review. From the framing through the early twentieth century, courts typically reviewed government actions in accordance with the republican democratic principles of virtue and the common good. Courts, including state and federal courts, upheld government actions that ostensibly promoted virtue and the common good while invalidating "class legislation" or other government actions that furthered partial or private (or factional) interests.[76] During the early decades of nationhood, courts often emphasized that government could not indiscriminately take property from one citizen and give it to another. For instance, Chief Justice Stephen Hosmer of Connecticut stated: "If the legislature should enact a law, without any assignable reason, taking from A. his estate, and giving it to B., the injustice would be flagrant, and the act would produce a sensation of universal insecurity."[77] In this way, individual rights and liberties were protected from undue government interference, yet they always remained subordinate to the government's power to act for the common good. As James Kent phrased it, "private interest must be made subservient to the general interest of the community."[78]

Courts generally interpreted virtue and the common good in accordance with the interests and values of white, Christian men, but given the widespread property ownership among such individuals, courts readily approved numerous economic regulations—laws that inevitably favored some white, Christian men over others. Indeed, in the antebellum years, law was understood to be a tool for "the release of [creative and economic] energy."[79] As a renowned Massachusetts judge, Lemuel Shaw, explained in 1851, "the nature of well ordered civil society" demanded that the common good take priority over individual rights, including property ownership. "All property in this commonwealth [is] held subject to those general regulations, which are necessary to the common good and general welfare." Shaw elaborated with a partial list of legitimate government exercises of the state (police) power: "Such are the laws to prohibit the use of warehouses for the storage of gunpowder near habitations or highways; to restrain the height to which wooden buildings may be erected in populous neighborhoods, and require them to be covered with slate or other incombustible material; to prohibit buildings from being used for hospitals for contagious diseases, or for the carrying on of noxious or offensive trades; to prohibit the raising of a dam, and causing stagnant water to spread over meadows, near inhabited villages, thereby raising noxious exhalations, injurious to health and dangerous to life."[80]

Courts would also uphold regulations that harmonized with the moral values of white, Christian men, whether the regulations dealt with gambling, theaters, taverns, brothels, or otherwise. The judicial perception of virtue and the common good from the white, Christian, male perspective could have detrimental consequences for women, people of color, and non-Christians. As already discussed, courts consistently upheld convictions of non-Christians for blasphemy (against Christianity) and Sunday law violations, and judges viewed Christianity to be part of the common law. Meanwhile, prosecutions for morals infractions—often in the form of disorderly conduct prosecutions—could turn on the race of the defendant, so a Black American man would be convicted for conduct permissible for a white man.[81]

Republican Democracy Strained

Republican democratic government had developed in a United States that was rural, agrarian, and relatively homogenous (since women and people of color were mostly excluded from participating in democratic processes, while non-Christians were precluded from holding some state offices). After the Civil War, though, multiple forces, including industrialization, urbanization, and immigration, strained the republican democratic regime. In 1859, the value added from manufacturing (equaling the value of shipments minus the cost of materials and the like) for the entire nation totaled less than 8.6 million dollars, but by 1899, that total had reached approximately 4.6 billion. It nearly doubled over the next decade and continued growing exponentially. From 1870 to 1900, the number of factories in leading industrial states such as New York and Pennsylvania also nearly doubled. Consequently, while in 1870 agricultural workers far outnumbered industrial workers (in manufacturing, construction, transportation, and related jobs), by 1900 the opposite was true. Industrialization contributed to immigration and urbanization. Industrialists, wanting surplus workers for their factories, encouraged immigration, and since many of these immigrants came from southern and eastern Europe, the nation grew more diverse. Plus, the immigrants, laboring in the factories, gravitated toward the cities. In 1870, the rural population approximately tripled the number of urban dwellers, but by 1910, the rural and urban populations were nearly equal.[82]

Industrialization also contributed to the growth of large corporations, including the railroads, and increasing wealth disparities—this was the Gilded Age. Factory employees, faced with grim working conditions and low pay, tried to organize into labor unions, but were met with legal and sometimes violent resistance. As the railroads spread across the country after the Civil War, creating more of a national marketplace, calls for economic regulations increased at not only the local but also the national level. Whereas economic regulations had been widespread during the antebellum era—and as discussed, the courts often upheld such regulations as promoting the common good—postbellum corporate attorneys began to argue that economic regulations unconstitutionally interfered with the marketplace.[83]

Before the Civil War, Lincoln and the Republicans had advocated for free labor and free soil. The crux of this political ideology was the opposition between slave and free labor. The nation, at the time, remained predominantly rural and agrarian, and the Republicans celebrated the labor and soil of the free, small farmer (as well as the independence of the artisan in his shop). According to Lincoln, "Men, with their families . . . work for themselves on their farms, in their houses, and in their shops, taking the whole product to themselves, and asking no favors of capital on the one hand nor of hired laborers or slaves on the other." But in the postbellum, industrialized America, corporations and their attorneys, seeking greater profits, twisted the free-labor ideology into freedom of contract and laissez-faire ideology. Laissez-faire, intertwining with Social Darwinism, engendered encomiums to great fortunes and wealth disparities—ostensibly demonstrating the survival of the fittest (the rich)—while denigrating calls for social welfare legislation. "Society needs first of all to be freed from these meddlers—that is, to be let alone," wrote Yale professor William Graham Sumner. "Here we are, then, once more back at the old doctrine—laissez-faire. Let us translate it into blunt English, and it will read, Mind your own business. It is nothing but the doctrine of liberty."[84]

Laissez-faire ideology transformed conceptions of the common good. Economic regulations—other than those that would aid the railroads or other corporations—were deemed suspicious, likely to be furthering partial or private interests rather than the common good. Government power to regulate the economy diminished at a time when progressives, the ranks of whom included Republicans and Democrats, began to press for legislation protecting workers in factories and, more generally, correcting for marketplace inequities (such as the development of trusts and monopolies). The U.S. Supreme Court, with multiple justices drawn from the ranks of corporate law firms, proved receptive to laissez-faire inflected arguments. In *Allgeyer v. Louisiana*, decided in 1897, the Court invalidated a state law restricting the issuance of illegal insurance contracts. After acknowledging that the government could pass laws in pursuit of the common good, the Court emphasized that due process limited the government's power, precluding laws infringing on "liberty to contract." The Court explained that due process liberty entailed a citizen's right "to live and work where he will; to earn his livelihood by any lawful calling; to pursue any livelihood or avocation; and for that purpose to enter into all contracts which may be proper, necessary, and essential to his carrying out to a successful conclusion the purposes above mentioned." Francis Wharton's *Commentaries on Law*, written in the late nineteenth century, observed that the Fourteenth Amendment appeared to have positive and "permanent" ramifications for "the whole business system" but only "comparatively ephemeral" implications for Black Americans.[85]

In *Lochner v. New York*, decided in 1905, the Court invalidated a progressive state law that restricted the number of hours employees could work in bakeries (ten per day and sixty per week). After acknowledging the state could pass laws in pursuit of the common good, the Court categorized this statute as impermissible class legislation favoring the partial interests of employees (over the interests of employers): "It seems to us that the real object and purpose were simply to regulate the hours of labor between the master and his employees . . . in a private business, not dangerous in any degree to morals, or in any real and substantial degree to the health of the employees." As was typical during this era of Supreme Court decision-making—the so-called *Lochner* era lasted 50 years, from 1887 to 1937—the Court used formalist reasoning. Rather than inquiring into the statute's context or effects, the Court found that the job of a baker was not "unhealthy" to "the common understanding," despite empirical evidence showing otherwise.[86]

In *Allgeyer*, *Lochner*, and similar (*Lochner*-era) cases, the Court perversely transformed Fourteenth Amendment concerns for inclusive, democratic equality into a constitutional doctrine blocking government regulations that could diminish (economic) inequities for workers and the poor. The *Allgeyer* Court expressly linked republican democratic equality with liberty to contract: The individual should enjoy "'upon terms of equality with all others in similar circumstances . . . the privilege of pursuing an ordinary calling or trade, and of acquiring, holding, and selling property.'" Thus, for instance, any statute that attempted to equalize the bargaining power between workers and employers was likely to be invalidated as class legislation: A court would reason that the statute did not treat the workers and employers equally and therefore was not in pursuit of the common good. In accordance with formalist reasoning, courts refused to recognize that workers and employers, the poor and the wealthy, did not enjoy equal resources and power when coming to the bargaining table. In another case, the Court stated: "In all such particulars the employer and the employee have equality of right, and any legislation that disturbs that equality is an arbitrary interference with the liberty of contract which no government can legally justify in a free land." To be sure, the *Lochner*-era Court did not strike down every economic regulation, yet it invalidated nearly 200 state as well as many federal laws.[87]

While the *Lochner*-era Court aggressively reviewed economic statutes, it did not similarly review government actions that potentially violated individual rights to free expression, religious freedom, or equal protection. When it came to racial discrimination and segregation, *Plessy v. Ferguson*, already mentioned, eviscerated equal protection, as it upheld the constitutionality of separate-but-equal public facilities.[88] When it came to the Free Exercise and Establishment Clauses, the Court decided few cases in the nineteenth and early twentieth centuries. In those cases, the Court gave little bite to the religion clauses, especially as protections for non-Christian religions. The Court tended to emphasize that the United States was a Christian nation and that Christianity was embedded in the legal system. The decisions unsurprisingly and consistently reaffirmed the societal and cultural acceptance of Protestant domination—or in other words, the nation's de facto Protestantism.[89] In *Reynolds v. United States*, the defendant, a member of the Church of Latter-Day Saints, challenged a federal, criminal-law conviction for polygamy. The defendant claimed the conviction violated his free exercise rights because he was religiously obligated to follow polygamy. In rejecting the claim, the Court reasoned that Congress must have the power to proscribe "actions which were in violation of social duties or subversive of good order"—or in other words, Congress was empowered to restrict religious practices that contravened virtue and the common good (as understood from the mainstream white, Protestant perspective).[90]

Similarly, the Supreme Court, like the lower courts, gave little bite to the constitutional protection of free expression. The bad tendency test, the predominant doctrine for analyzing free expression claims, followed the usual republican democratic principles for judicial review. While the government could not impose prior restraints, it could punish speech or writing that had bad tendencies or likely harmful consequences. According to Justice Story's *Commentaries on the Constitution*, the government could punish speakers and writers for "what is improper, mischievous, or illegal." Expression with bad tendencies, after all, would likely undermine virtue and contravene the common good. Courts did not generally interpret free expression to protect democratic participation or equality for historically marginalized individuals or groups. For example, workers rarely found refuge in claims of free expression when they sought to organize into labor unions, whether they were marching, holding signs, or otherwise attempting to communicate with fellow workers; courts consistently protected employers rather than workers. Tellingly, the Supreme Court, applying the bad tendency standard, rejected every free speech claim raised before the 1930s.[91]

In short, in cases involving the individual rights to free expression, religious freedom, and equal protection, the Court largely gave free rein to the prejudices and values of the wealthy and the culturally dominant. This judicial attitude was nowhere clearer than in *Plessy*. The dissenting Justice John Marshall Harlan worried that the decision to allow ostensibly separate-but-equal facilities would "stimulate aggressions, more or less brutal and irritating, upon the admitted rights of colored citizens." The Court majority disagreed. It sharply separated the public and private spheres: The government could not affect or alter private racial prejudices and discrimination. "[I]n the nature of things," the Court wrote, "[the Fourteenth Amendment] could not have been intended to abolish distinctions based upon color, or to enforce social . . . equality." In other words, the law segregating Black and white Americans merely reflected preexisting prejudices immune to government influence. According to the Court, the law therefore promoted "the public good" and did not subjugate Black Americans. Indeed, Harlan himself, in his dissent, expressly revealed his own racial prejudices by approving of discrimination against people of Chinese descent.[92]

Regardless, Harlan's dissent was correct insofar as the Court and the government further entrenched racial bias and discrimination against Black Americans as the norm throughout American society. The

separate-but-equal doctrine allowed and implicitly encouraged southern states to mandate separate public facilities in numerous contexts,
from water fountains to swimming pools to public schools. While these
facilities were separate, they were almost never equal. For instance, with
regard to education, Alabama in the early 1900s paid its white public
school teachers at least twice as much its Black teachers. In 1915, South
Carolina spent over ten times more on white school children than on
Black children. In 1935, Mississippi spent more than four times the
amount on white as Black children. And in the 1950s, no southern or
border states spent equal amounts on white and Black children.[93] Ultimately, from a historical perspective, private-sphere discrimination
often went hand in hand with public-sphere discrimination, which in
turn went hand in hand with diminished political rights to democratic
participation. When the forces of exclusionary democracy predominate,
discrimination runs rampant—and vice versa.

* * *

During the post-Civil War era, industrialization, urbanization, and
immigration strained the republican democratic regime, but the principles of republican democracy—virtue and the common good—retained
their significance, though their meanings shifted. Eventually, however,
in the twentieth century, the pressures would increase until the regime
collapsed and a new form of democracy supplanted republican democracy. That is the subject of the next chapter.

3

Pluralist Democracy

Emergence and Development

By the 1920s, industrialization, urbanization, and immigration had been tearing at the republican democratic regime for decades. Even the xenophobic and nativist curtailment of immigration during that decade could not undo the changes in the nation. While old-stock Americans brooded less about the immigrant invasion—since it had been stopped—the agrarian, rural, and relatively homogeneous American society of the nineteenth century was long gone: Americans constituted a racially, ethnically, and religiously diverse population, with a majority of them living in cities and working as wage-laborers in factories or other urban jobs. Then in late October of 1929, the stock market crashed, and the Great Depression hit the United States (and other nations as well). With the Depression compounding the already-extant forces of change, the practices of democratic government radically transformed.[1]

The New Deal and Pluralist Democracy

Franklin Delano Roosevelt (FDR) was the right person to lead Americans into and through this democratic transformation. Many Americans in the early 1930s questioned whether democracy was the best form of government; they doubted whether it could respond adequately to the widespread economic deprivations, not to mention the mounting international crises. From 1929 to 1931, unemployment jumped from 3.2 percent to a monstrous 15.9 percent of the labor force, and then it continued to grow, reaching nearly 25 percent in 1933. The gross national product (GNP) plunged 29 percent. In fact, in the early and mid-1930s, the worldwide economic calamity weakened numerous European democracies to the point of collapse. In the United States, however, with FDR's leadership, the economic disaster helped bond diverse Americans.

FDR and the New Dealers did not dismiss the interests and values of immigrants, indigents, religious minorities, and other peripheral groups as being non-virtuous. Instead, FDR worked to incorporate these groups into the polity and to satisfy their interests. Rather than preaching morality to immigrants and their children and trying to convert them to Protestant values—as the progressives had tried to do earlier in the twentieth century (Prohibition was one such example)—FDR focused on economic issues. One of FDR's close advisors, Rex Tugwell, said, "the New Deal is attempting to do nothing to people, and does not seek at all to alter their way of life, their wants and desires."[2] FDR would tell Frances Perkins, his secretary of labor and the first female cabinet member, that "[w]e are going to make a country in which no one is left out."[3] In short, at the outset of his first term, Roosevelt attempted "to hold together a coalition of all interests," including bankers and corporate business leaders as well as farmers, factory workers, and others.[4]

As the nation opened toward this more inclusive form of democratic government, no single set of cultural values was authoritative. Rather than focusing on mainstream white, Christian values and interests as embodying virtue and the common good, FDR and the New Dealers balanced those values and interests with those of other Americans who constituted the demographically diverse population. In the famed first "100 days" of the New Deal, FDR signed 15 bills into law, creating programs that provided jobs and other economic assistance to millions of Americans. To be sure, at different times in American history, participatory democracy had expanded as voting rights were extended to all white men, regardless of property ownership; to Black American men, though those rights were soon undermined; and to white women. The 1930s differed from those prior times because the Depression spurred Americans to recognize "collective economic rights"; people did not exist as economic islands. Whereas the traditional, American, individualist ethos had obscured a sense of shared interest across economic classes, the Depression—followed soon by World War II—generated a strong sense of "economic solidarity" among many Americans. Thus, the early New Deal statutes extended assistance to a diverse array of Americans: The Civilian Conservation Corps and the Federal Emergency Relief Administration provided jobs and relief for the unemployed; the Emergency Banking Act assisted failing banks; the Agricultural Adjustment Act aided farmers; and the Tennessee Valley Authority controlled flooding, generated hydroelectric power, and boosted the economy of the rural, upper South. Later in the 1930s, this continuing sense of economic intertwinement, shared widely among Americans, enabled the passage of statutes like the Social Security Act, which provided aid to the elderly and incapacitated. The National Industrial Recovery Act, enacted the same year as Social Security, helped industrial manufacturers but also created a right for industrial workers "to organize and bargain collectively." New Dealers recognized how economic interests intertwined across a wide swath of the population.[5]

The 1930s, in other words, produced a revolutionary transformation in democratic government that was simultaneously cultural *and* economic. While forces for both exclusion and inclusion had been present since the nation's founding, exclusion had mostly predominated—with the republican democratic principles of virtue and the common good ostensibly legitimating exclusion of various diverse groups. In the 1930s, though, the forces for inclusion gained the upper hand, and republican democracy was swept away. Americans were inspired to participate in democratic politics: In urban areas, for instance, one might see a Lithuanian Democratic League or Polish Democratic Club. Meanwhile, with the enactment of so many statutes, many of which created new administrative agencies, the government needed to hire numerous lawyers. At a time when most private law firms would hire only white, Protestant men, the Roosevelt administration focused on merit rather than pedigree and hired from a pool of highly qualified but often underemployed Catholic and Jewish attorneys. Similarly, when appointing federal judges, FDR refused to follow traditional nativist attitudes: The three previous presidents had nominated Catholics only four percent of the time, while FDR named Catholics to more than one-fourth of the openings. Likewise, only four Catholics had served in Cabinet positions before 1932, but FDR named two to his first Cabinet.[6]

The enactment of the National Labor Relations Act (NLRA) in 1935 was especially significant. It empowered workers to organize and negotiate as a whole, offsetting the power of corporate-organized employers, at least to a degree. Lobbying became open and aggressive, with organizations representing competing sides joining the fray. A senator could meet in the morning with the National Electrical Manufacturers'

Association and in the afternoon with the International Brotherhood of Boiler Makers, Iron Ship Builders, and Helpers of America. In 1937, the legal scholar Louis L. Jaffe declared that "all legislation . . . is an immediate response, in a greater or less degree, to some group pressure [so that] Congress and the state legislatures pass laws for the farmer, laws for labor, laws for business."[7]

Despite FDR's efforts to consider all interests and values, his policies alienated big business, which had little desire to balance interests with workers and unions. Roosevelt did not waver: "Government by the necessity of things must be . . . the judge of the conflicting interests of all groups in the community, including bankers." Business leaders, he explained, were apt to ignore "the human side, the old-age side, the unemployment side." If anything, then, FDR embraced his break with business. According to Raymond Moley, a member of Roosevelt's renowned Brain Trust, FDR aggressively sought "to gather into the Democratic Party many minorities, including the labor unions." Many Americans responded by expressing their support for the New Deal: Voter turnout, even in off-presidential years, increased steadily during the decade.[8]

By the end of the 1930s, constitutional scholars and political scientists were developing a theory of pluralist democracy to explain the new government practices.[9] Unlike republican democratic theory, which had emphasized an ostensibly objective goal—the common good—pluralist democratic theory emphasized process: All citizens should be able to express and advocate for their particular values and interests within a free and open democratic realm. Government decisions and actions should arise through negotiation, persuasion, and the exertion of pressure through the legitimate channels of the democratic process, including voting and lobbying. Supposedly, all citizens were equal, as no interests and values were either favored or excluded at the outset. By the end of the 1940s, political theorists viewed pluralist democracy as the best means for accommodating "our multigroup society." Meanwhile, the republican democratic claim that citizens and officials virtuously pursued the common good was dismissed as mythical or duplicitous.[10]

During the 1930s, conservative opponents of the New Deal did not readily accept pluralist democratic practices or theory. Most important, conservative justices on the Court continued deciding cases in accordance with republican democratic principles. Moreover, like in *Allgeyer* and *Lochner*, the justices continued interpreting the common good, due process, and the Constitution in general from a formalist perspective emphasizing laissez-faire. The Court consequently invalidated numerous New Deal statutes that extended government regulation into the economic marketplace. The Court's formalism purportedly legitimated disregard for social context, history, and the practical consequences of judicial decisions. Thus, the Court largely ignored the Depression and its effects on the American people. For example, in *Carter v. Carter Coal Company*, decided in 1936, the Court held that Congress had unconstitutionally exceeded its commerce power when it enacted the Bituminous Coal Conservation Act, which regulated coal mining. While ignoring the broader effects of mining on commercial intercourse, the Court formally defined mining to be production, "a purely local activity," separate from interstate commerce.[11]

When FDR was reelected in a landslide at the end of 1936, he saw an opportunity to change the Court and its treatment of the New Deal (and pluralist democracy). Even before the election, Roosevelt and his advisors had begun discussing possible ways to deal with the Court. FDR could not force the conservative justices to retire—he had no appointments to the Court during his first term—so in early 1937, he proposed that Congress pass a statute expanding the size of the Court, adding one position for each justice who was age 70 or older, with a maximum of 15 justices. This court-packing plan sparked political controversy; even some New Dealers opposed it. Yet, with the Senate majority leader's support, it had a reasonable chance of passage.[12]

On March 29, 1937, less than one month after FDR had publicly proposed Court expansion, the Court decided *West Coast Hotel Company v. Parrish*. The moderately conservative Justice Owen Roberts sided with the more progressive justices in a five-to-four decision that upheld a state law setting minimum wages for women. In reaching that conclusion, the Court overruled a 1923 decision that had invalidated a similar minimum wage statute as impermissible class legislation favoring partial or private interests. Near the end of the *West Coast Hotel* opinion, the Court questioned the formalism and laissez-faire-tinged interpretation of the common good characteristic of the *Lochner* era. Instead, the Court emphasized the economic context of the Depression and the government need to bolster workers in their dealings with employers.

The exploitation of a class of workers who are in an unequal position with respect to bargaining power and are thus relatively defenseless against the denial of a living wage is not only detrimental to their health and well being, but casts a direct burden for their support upon the community. What these workers lose in wages the taxpayers are called upon to pay. The bare cost of living must be met. We may take judicial notice of the unparalleled demands for relief which arose during the recent period of depression and still continue to an alarming extent despite the degree of economic recovery which has been achieved. . . . The community is not bound to provide what is in effect a subsidy for unconscionable employers.[13]

Only two weeks later, the Court decided *NLRB v. Jones & Laughlin Steel Corporation*, which upheld the crucial NLRA as a constitutional exercise of Congress's commerce power. *Jones & Laughlin* unequivocally repudiated *Lochner*-era formalism: "We are asked to shut our eyes to the plainest facts of our national life and to deal with the question of . . . effects [on interstate commerce] in an intellectual vacuum." Refusing to follow such a formalist approach, the Court instead understood interstate commerce as a "practical conception." Then, in a point that went hand in hand with the rejection of (judicial) formalism, the Court deferred to Congress's determination of whether the regulated activities bore a sufficiently "close and substantial relation to interstate commerce" as to justify legislative intervention.[14]

Equally important, the Court rejected a distinction between the common good, on the one side, and partial or private interests, on the other. In doing so, the Court implicitly approved the emergent multicultural and egalitarian pluralist democracy and its economic intertwining of diverse Americans. After the Civil War and particularly during the *Lochner* era, the Court had usually deemed statutes benefiting workers and unions to be impermissible class legislation furthering a partial or private interest, while laws promoting business or commerce were found to be for the common good. Labor relations (employer-employee interactions) were generally governed by the common law, which courts typically interpreted favorably to employers. In *Jones & Laughlin*, though, the Court refused to continue favoring employers over employees; both sides had their respective interests and values. "Employees have as clear a right to organize and select their representatives for lawful purposes as the [manufacturer-employer] has to organize its business and select its own officers and agents." If a manufacturer has a "right to conduct its business in an orderly manner," then employees should also have a "correlative right to organize for the purpose of securing the redress of grievances and to promote agreements with employers relating to rates of pay and conditions of work," as recognized in the NLRA. Again, the Court deferred to Congress, letting the legislative branch decide which "evils" it would seek to remedy and in what manner it would do so. Even if the statute were "one-sided"—subjecting "the employer to supervision and restraint" while leaving "untouched the abuses for which employees may be responsible"—it would be constitutional.[15]

While these two cases, *West Coast Hotel* and *Jones & Laughlin*, did not alone cement the Court's repudiation of republican democracy and acceptance of pluralist democracy, they are the primary reason that contemporaries, like Yale law professor Eugene V. Rostow, believed the Court "died and was reborn in 1937." Regardless, whatever jurisprudential flexibility might have remained after the two cases, subsequent changes in the Court's personnel would solidify the transition. In May 1937, one of the conservative justices, Willis Van Devanter, resigned, giving FDR his first opportunity to nominate a Supreme Court justice; he would name the staunch New Deal Senator, Hugo Black. Over the next years, FDR would nominate so many new justices that political scientist C. Herman Pritchett would soon aptly be referring to the "Roosevelt Court."[16]

Pluralist Democratic Judicial Review

With the Court's acceptance of pluralist democracy, its approach to judicial review changed dramatically. Most important, whereas the Court had rarely even mentioned democracy before the 1930s, the justices after 1937 regularly discussed democratic processes and participation.[17] *United States v. Carolene Products Company*, decided in 1938, upheld an economic regulation limiting the interstate shipment of filled milk. In discussing the scope of congressional power over interstate commerce, Justice Harlan F. Stone's majority opinion deferred to Congress, typical for post-1937 pluralist democratic judicial review of (New Deal-type) economic and social welfare laws. He added a footnote, however, explaining when deference might be inappropriate. Footnote four suggested that the Court should reject a "presumption of constitutionality" if legislation either would likely cause or had resulted from a defective democratic process. If legislation would, for instance, prevent some groups from voting or organizing politically in the future, then Stone suggested it should "be subjected to more exacting judicial scrutiny." If allowed to stand, the legislation would interfere with "those political processes which can ordinarily be expected to bring about repeal of undesirable legislation." Similarly, if the legislative or democratic processes had been closed to certain groups or had been otherwise defective, then the legitimacy of any resultant legislation would be questionable. For that reason, if the government had intentionally discriminated against a "discrete and insular" minority, like Black Americans, then judicial deference would be inappropriate, as "the operation of those political processes ordinarily to be relied upon to protect minorities" would be undermined. In a pluralist democratic regime, all societal groups should supposedly be able to press their interests and values in a fair competition with other groups.[18]

The Court became preoccupied with the contours of pluralist democracy—an inclusive, egalitarian, and participatory democracy. To be sure, the justices did not always agree about how to protect and nurture democratic processes. *Colegrove v. Green*, decided in 1946, underscored the potential for such disagreement. Justice Felix Frankfurter wrote for a plurality that held the drawing of congressional district lines in Illinois presented a nonjusticiable political question. Frankfurter believed the point of pluralist democracy, including congressional districting, was to assure widespread participation in political processes. Defects in the process, though, should be allowed to self-correct, whenever possible. If a state legislature drew unfair district lines, the Court should not intervene but rather should allow the people to work through the partisan democratic process until the people themselves had worked the process clean.[19]

Justice Black, joined by Justices William O. Douglas and Frank Murphy, dissented. Black agreed that a pluralist democratic system should promote widespread participation, but he disagreed that the best way to correct for defective congressional districting was to allow the people themselves to work through the democratic process. Black emphasized that the current district lines in Illinois engendered grossly disparate representation: One district had more than 900,000 people, while other districts had fewer than 200,000. Yet, each district could elect one representative. Each vote, therefore, was not accorded "equal weight." The Court could not trust the pluralist democratic process to self-correct because the challenged legislation prevented certain groups from fully participating.[20]

Despite such disagreement among the justices, the Court was committed to hashing out pluralist democracy as a fair, open, and egalitarian process.[21] Even cases that did not directly focus on democracy could be understood as revolving around implications of pluralist democratic government. For instance, during the post-1937 years, the Court began resolving numerous constitutional disputes pursuant to balancing tests, weighing the multiple and diverse competing interests against each other. The balancing tests implicitly recognized that all interests and values should be judicially considered, not merely the interests and values that were culturally or societally designated as virtuous or in pursuit of the common good.[22]

Simultaneously, in this era, the Court invigorated its protection of individual rights, including free speech, religious freedom, and equal protection. In Justice Stone's *Carolene Products* footnote four, he had alluded to this possibility. Recall, he had emphasized that the Court would generally defer to the democratic process but that this "presumption of constitutionality" would be inappropriate if the process was defective or skewed. The Court, in effect, should protect or police democracy. Stone, though, added: "There may [also] be narrower scope for operation of the presumption of constitutionality when legislation appears on its face to be within a specific prohibition of the Constitution, such as those of the first ten Amendments." In other words, even if the Court were generally deferring to the democratic process—that is, deferring to legislative actions—the Court would not necessarily allow democratic majorities to trample on constitutional rights. "The very purpose of a Bill of Rights was to withdraw certain subjects from the vicissitudes of political controversy, to place them beyond the reach of majorities and officials and to establish them as legal principles to be applied by the courts," Justice Jackson wrote during World War II. "One's right to life, liberty, and property, to free speech, a free press, freedom of worship and assembly, and other fundamental rights may not be submitted to vote; they depend on the outcome of no elections."[23]

Consequently, whereas the Court during the republican democratic era had given little bite to free speech, religious freedom, and equal protection, the Court after 1937 handed down numerous individual-rights victories. To be sure, the Court sometimes deviated from this path. Most notoriously, *Korematsu v. United States* upheld during World War II the relocation and incarceration of people of Japanese descent, including Japanese-American citizens.[24] Even so, cases such as *Korematsu* were clearly the exception rather than the rule.[25] For instance, after rejecting every free speech claim raised before the 1930s,[26] the Court upheld one free expression claim after another from 1937 to 1940. These decisions protected the free expression rights of a Black American Communist party organizer,[27] workers seeking to form a union,[28] and a member of a religious minority (Jehovah's Witnesses).[29] In late 1937, Justice Benjamin Cardozo declared that "freedom of thought and speech . . . is the matrix, the indispensable condition, of nearly every other form of freedom,"[30] and in 1943, Jackson would write that free expression was a "fixed star in our constitutional constellation."[31]

The Court similarly invigorated the First Amendment protection of religious freedom, under both the Free Exercise and Establishment Clauses. In 1940, the Court found for the first time that the Free Exercise Clause applied to state and local governments,[32] and in 1947, the Court did the same for the Establishment Clause. In the Establishment Clause case, the Court articulated the metaphor of a "wall of separation" between religion and government.

Neither a state nor the Federal Government can set up a church. Neither can pass laws which aid one religion, aid all religions, or prefer one religion over another. Neither can force nor influence a person to go to or to remain away from church against his will or force him to profess a belief or disbelief in any religion. No person can be punished for entertaining or professing religious beliefs or disbeliefs, for church attendance or non-attendance. No tax in any amount, large or small, can be levied to support any religious activities or institutions, whatever they may be called, or whatever form they may adopt to teach or practice religion. Neither a state nor the Federal Government can, openly or secretly, participate in the affairs of any religious organizations or groups and vice versa. In the words of Jefferson, the clause against establishment of religion by law was intended to erect "a wall of separation between Church and State."

The Court added that the wall between church and state "must be kept high and impregnable."[33]

Indeed, during the 1940s, the justices referred to free expression and religious freedom as the "preferred freedoms." Yet, even in those individual rights cases, which appeared to place certain realms beyond the reach of majorities, the Court seemed concerned with the operation of pluralist democracy. If pluralist democracy prohibited the government from pre-designating certain interests and values as virtuous or the common good, these judicial decisions protected individuals in believing and expressing their diverse interests and values. These cases, in other words, fit with the justices' goal of nurturing an inclusive, egalitarian, and participatory democracy.[34]

Despite the onset and development of pluralist democratic practices and theory, Black Americans had largely been excluded from the benefits of the New Deal. While Roosevelt's Democratic administration supported Black Americans more than any since Reconstruction, FDR accepted the demands of white southern (Democratic) members of Congress, who insisted that New Deal programs not disrupt their racist practices and institutions. Consequently, various programs excluded groups of beneficiaries who were disproportionately Black American while allowing (white racist) state and local officials to administer the programs despite federal funding. The Social Security Act and the NLRA, for example, excluded agricultural and domestic service workers, who constituted more than half of Black workers. Charles Hamilton Houston, the renowned NAACP (National Association for the Advancement of Colored People) lawyer and Dean of Howard University's law school, explained to the Senate Finance Committee: "[The Social Security bill] looks like a sieve with the holes just big enough for the majority of Negroes to fall through."[35]

Even so, in 1938, Black Americans for the first time dented the Court's hard shell shielding racial discrimination: the separate-but-equal doctrine of *Plessy*. An NAACP litigation strategy, attacking the equality component of separate-but-equal, achieved success. In *Missouri ex rel. Gaines v. Canada*, Lloyd Gaines, a Black American, claimed the state violated equal protection by refusing to admit him to the state law school because of his race. Because of the separate-but-equal doctrine, the state offered to pay his tuition at an out-of-state law school. The Court held, though, this offer did not equal the opportunity to attend an in-state school, afforded to white students, and therefore did not satisfy the separate-but-equal doctrine.[36]

Buoyed by this victory, the NAACP continued to urge the Court to expand the reach of equal protection. *Sweatt v. Painter*, decided in 1950, arose when the University of Texas School of Law refused to admit Herman Marion Sweatt because he was Black American. Given the result in *Gaines*, the state realized it should have a law school for Black students, so it created one after the litigation had commenced. The Court rejected this purported remedy, concluding that the new Black law school did not equal the University of Texas School of Law. The Court reached that conclusion by considering tangible factors, such as the number of volumes in the respective libraries, and also intangible qualities, such as the reputation of the University of Texas.[37]

The Court thus invigorated individual rights while simultaneously allowing the government to expand its reach in the economic sphere. The result was a burgeoning participatory, inclusive, and egalitarian pluralist democracy that recognized an economic web weaving throughout American society. True, one could still distinguish public and private (or civil) spheres, but pluralist democracy and the Court now accepted the integral intertwining of the two. Two cases from the 1940s epitomize the degree to which the Court perceived connections between democratic government and the economic marketplace, between the public and private spheres. In *Wickard v. Filburn*, decided in 1942, the Court upheld the constitutionality of the Agricultural Adjustment Act, which regulated the production of wheat even if raised "wholly for consumption on [the grower's] farm." The Court showed great respect for the democratic process and congressional decision-making. The possibility that Congress economically favored one interest group over another when enacting the statute was irrelevant because such legislative decisions typified (pluralist) democracy. "The conflicts of economic interest between the regulated and those who advantage by it are wisely left under our system to resolution by the Congress under its more flexible and responsible legislative process." Congress itself should be limited through the political process of democracy rather than pursuant to formal judicial categories. Congress could therefore consider the empirical or actual effects of a regulated activity, and the people could vote for different legislators if they did not approve of the congressional actions.[38]

In *Shelley v. Kraemer*, decided in 1948, the Court held that a state court's enforcement of a racially restrictive covenant in a private house sale violated equal protection. Since 1883, the Court had reasoned that Fourteenth Amendment equal protection guarantees extended only to state (or government) actions, not to private activities. Hence, if the (private) parties to the contract had voluntarily adhered to the restrictive covenant, the Court reasoned there would have been no state action and no equal protection violation. Nevertheless, in this instance, the state-court enforcement of the contract triggered the Equal Protection Clause, though the case involved contract and property rights—rights traditionally understood to be central to private-sphere activities (and typically enforced in state-court civil actions). The Court would not allow state courts to pretend that discrimination in the private sphere did not have public-sphere ramifications (or vice versa): Restrictive covenants undermined the targeted racial group's "equal footing" in "the community."[39]

The Warren Court

If the Court's 1937 transition solidified the emergence of pluralist democracy—the advance of inclusive democratic forces over exclusion—then in the 1950s and 1960s, the Warren Court continued in this direction, strengthening and developing pluralist democracy. Most famously, in 1954, *Brown v. Board of Education* unanimously held that de jure racial segregation of public school children violated equal protection. While the Court explicitly focused on segregated public schools, it implicitly undermined all Jim Crow laws. Warren's brief opinion emphasized the importance of public education to democratic participation and citizenship. "Compulsory school attendance laws and the great expenditures for education both demonstrate our recognition of the importance of education to our democratic society. It is required in the performance of our most basic public responsibilities, even service in the armed forces. It is the very foundation of good citizenship." Hence, the Court's reasoning at least called into question the long-standing denials of Black political participation.[40]

To be sure, *Brown* did not defeat the forces of exclusion. To achieve unanimity among the justices, Warren strategically agreed to split the case into two parts, treating the merits of the constitutional claim separately from its remedy. The Court resolved the substantive constitutional claim in *Brown*—holding that separate-but-equal public schools violated equal protection—but the Court postponed consideration of the appropriate remedy for the constitutional transgression. In *Brown II*, decided one year later, the Court did not mandate immediate desegregation. Instead, it ordered de jure segregated school districts to desegregate "with all deliberate speed." This weak mandate accomplished little; southern school districts responded by furiously resisting desegregation. Some school districts, for instance, closed all their public schools rather than desegregate, while in other districts, white citizens terrorized Black school children who attempted to attend previously all-white schools. Many white parents, in both the South and the North, sent their children to private schools rather than participate in desegregation (more on this in chapter 5). Consequently, five years after *Brown*, racial segregation of schools had barely changed. Five years after that, in 1964, the Court finally mandated that racial segregation in the schools must end: "There has been entirely too much deliberation and not enough speed." Even so, one year later, "fewer than 1 in 100 black students in the South attended schools formerly white by law, and the number of whites in predominantly black schools was infinitesimally small."[41]

Regardless of the slow progress in public-school desegregation, the Warren Court continued to press for a more inclusive and egalitarian democracy in multiple other ways. For instance, the Court invigorated individual rights in a variety of realms. When it came to religious freedom, the Court pressed for a strong wall of separation between religion and government. In 1962, *Engel v. Vitale* held that the daily recitation of a supposedly nondenominational prayer in the public schools violated the Establishment Clause.[42] In free exercise cases, the Court applied a rigorous strict scrutiny test, requiring the government to show that the application of a law of general applicability (a law applying similarly to all persons) which burdened religion was necessary to achieve a compelling purpose.[43] The protection of religious freedom was far more robust than before 1937, though the Court, particularly the post-Warren Court, sometimes wavered. In Establishment Clause cases, the Court sometimes did not maintain the strong wall of separation—thus allowing, for example, public displays of Christian symbols[44]—while in several subsequent free exercise cases, the Court concluded the government had not violated free exercise (because either strict scrutiny was inappropriate under the facts or the government had satisfied strict scrutiny).[45]

Meanwhile, the Warren Court strongly protected free expression, deciding multiple landmark cases in the 1960s. In 1964, *New York Times v. Sullivan*, interpreted the First Amendment to require an actual malice standard to help protect the press from civil libel actions brought by government officials.[46] In 1969, *Tinker v. Des Moines Independent Community School District*, emphasized that students enjoy strong free speech rights, even when engaging in controversial political protests (against the Vietnam War).[47] In that same final year of the Warren Court, *Brandenburg v. Ohio* dramatically expanded the constitutional protection of expression inciting unlawful conduct.[48] Many of these decisions stressed the importance of free expression to pluralist democracy. In *Sullivan*, to take one example, the Court wrote: "[W]e consider this case against the background of a profound national commitment to the principle that debate on public issues should be uninhibited, robust, and wide-open, and that it may well include vehement, caustic, and sometimes unpleasantly sharp attacks on government and public officials."[49]

The Warren Court also decided many cases that explicitly focused on the pluralist democratic process itself, rendering it more inclusive and fair (or egalitarian). In *Baker v. Carr*, the Court overruled *Colegrove* and held that an allegation of vote dilution based on disproportional representation, whether in a state legislature or the House of Representatives, constituted a justiciable claim.[50] *Baker* opened the door to *Wesberry v. Sanders*, focusing on congressional districts,[51] and *Reynolds v. Sims*, focusing on state legislative districts, which together established the maxim of one person, one vote—that is, each person's vote should have roughly the same weight or importance as any other person's vote.[52] Many of the cases revolving around pluralist democratic processes also involved racial discrimination. *Gomillion v. Lightfoot* arose when the state of Alabama passed a law transforming the city of Tuskegee, Alabama, "from a square

PLURALIST DEMOCRACY: EMERGENCE AND DEVELOPMENT | 57

to an uncouth twenty-eight-sided figure." Given that the effect of the law was to remove "from the city all save four or five of its 400 Negro voters while not removing a single white voter or resident," the Court held the statute to be an unconstitutional gerrymander denying Black Americans "the municipal franchise and consequent rights."[53]

To be clear, even in the cases involving individual rights, the Warren Court rarely decided contrary to the majoritarian will. The Court tended to decide cases in accordance with the contemporary national political regime. Many of the Court's decisions bolstering democracy, particularly cases involving the participatory rights of Black Americans, came only after white Americans demonstrated wide support for the Civil Rights Movement, as illustrated by President Lyndon B. Johnson's ability to push to passage components of his Great Society program, such as the Civil Rights Act of 1964 and the Voting Rights Act of 1965 (VRA), which focused on racial discrimination in suffrage. Given the Court's responsiveness to the national political sentiments, predictable limits tempered the Court's reach toward inclusive egalitarianism. For instance, the Court never recognized a right to protest per se, even in the civil rights context. And before public opinion turned decidedly against the Vietnam War, the Court upheld a conviction for burning a draft card in protest against the war.[54]

The Warren Court not only followed the majoritarian will in general but also continued to show great respect and deference for majoritarian democratic processes. For example, *Heart of Atlanta Motel, Inc. v. United States*, decided in 1964, arose from a challenge to Congress's power to enact Title II of the Civil Rights Act, which prohibited racial discrimination in places of public accommodation, such as hotels, restaurants, and theaters. A unanimous Court upheld the statute as within the scope of Congress's commerce power. Although Congress had passed the law without making any explicit factual findings, the Court found the record was "replete with evidence of the burdens that discrimination by race or color places upon interstate commerce." The Court rejected formalist limits on Congress and quoted Chief Justice John Marshall in reasoning that the commerce power extends to any activities that "affect" commerce in more than one state. The possibility that the regulated activities in this case might have been characterized as local in character or that the question of racial discrimination might be deemed moral in nature did not diminish congressional power. The reach of Congress's power was determined through the democratic process rather than being judicially imposed.[55]

Two points from *Heart of Atlanta* are worth highlighting. First, the division between the public and private spheres was permeable: Congress therefore could regulate economic activities that attacked the "dignity" of individuals.[56] Interpersonal actions, including discriminatory conduct, in civil society deeply affected individual capacities in the public and private realms. As the Senate Commerce Committee explained:

> The primary purpose of [the Civil Rights Act is to account for] the deprivation of personal dignity that surely accompanies denials of equal access to public establishments. Discrimination is not simply dollars and cents, hamburgers and movies; it is the humiliation, frustration, and embarrassment that a person must surely feel when he is told that he is unacceptable as a member of the public because of his race or color. It is equally the inability to explain to a child that regardless of education, civility, courtesy, and morality he will be denied the right to enjoy equal treatment, even though he be a citizen of the United States and may well be called upon to lay down his life to assure this Nation continues.[57]

Second, the Court's respect for the democratic process and deference to Congress was tangible. The justices acknowledged that Congress could have chosen other means to eliminate racial discrimination in interstate commerce but that the choice was "a matter of policy that rests entirely with the Congress [and] not with the courts." The crafting of a legislative solution, that is, lay "within the sound and exclusive discretion of the Congress."[58]

Other Warren Court decisions from the 1960s echoed these crucial points. Indeed, the Warren Court in conjunction with Great Society programs helped move the nation closer to fulfilling the promise of an inclusive and egalitarian democracy suggested by pluralist democratic theory. The VRA, in particular, produced significant substantive changes. To take one southern state as an example: The percentage of Black Americans registered to vote in Mississippi jumped from 6.7 in 1964 to 66.5 percent in 1969. More broadly, from 1966 to 1973, the number of Black Americans elected to state legislatures more than doubled, as did the number elected to Congress. In 1966, no American city had a Black mayor, but by the end of the 1970s many cities, large and small, had elected Black mayors.[59]

The Warren Court contributed by upholding the constitutionality of the VRA. In doing so, the Court broadly construed Congress's power under the Fifteenth Amendment, section two, and the Fourteenth Amendment, section five, while emphasizing that Congress could act in an "inventive manner," if it wished. In *Katzenbach v. Morgan*, the Court underscored Congress's independent power to interpret the Constitution: Congress could invoke its Fourteenth Amendment, section five, power to expand equal protection and due process rights beyond those recognized by the Court—even when the Court had explicitly considered and rejected the possible expansion. In *Katzenbach*, the Court accentuated that democratic participation, the right to vote, was crucial to a person in multiple ways, including "the provision or administration of governmental services, such as public schools, public housing and law enforcement." The VRA was needed "to obtain 'perfect equality of civil rights and the equal protection of the laws.'" The Court would not second-guess Congress: "It was for Congress . . . to assess and weigh the various conflicting considerations [that went into the enactment of the VRA.] It is not for us [the Court] to review the congressional resolution of these factors."[60] Unsurprisingly, then, the Court in a subsequent case interpreted the VRA broadly to give full effect to Congress's purposes.[61]

* * *

Conservatives did not like the New Deal, the Supreme Court's acceptance of pluralist democracy in 1937, or the Warren Court's strengthening and developing of that inclusive, egalitarian, and participatory form of democracy. Conservative reactions would vary over time, though, depending on political possibilities. The next chapter will begin to explore a variety of those reactions.

4

Conservative Reactions to Pluralist Democracy and the Warren Court

How did conservatives react to the New Deal, the advent and development of an inclusive and egalitarian pluralist democracy, and the Warren Court's interrelated invigorations of pluralist democracy and individual rights? Reactions varied over time, based partly on political possibilities. After 1937, with pluralist democracy entrenched and accepted by the Supreme Court, conservative lawyers urged the "wealthy and privileged" to assert their individual rights in court; rights could shield them, after all, from the vagaries of the pluralist democratic process, now open to previously marginalized groups and individuals.[1] In the 1950s, conservative Republican President Dwight D. Eisenhower acquiesced to high income tax rates, expanded Social Security, and encouraged New Deal-like public investment in infrastructure, creating the interstate highway system. Regardless, by the 1970s and 1980s, the widespread public sense of economic solidarity, which had helped fuel the New Deal and the onset of pluralist democracy, had dissipated, replaced by a reinvigorated economic individualism.[2]

Judicial Restraint

Conservative reactions to the Supreme Court, in particular, arose from a combination of the wider conservative trends and the specific makeup of the Court itself. Once Earl Warren retired, the Court began to move gradually rightward. The recently elected Republican president, Richard Nixon, started the shift in 1969, appointing Warren Burger as Chief Justice and Harry Blackmun (who was initially viewed as a conservative) as an Associate Justice. Even so, the Court remained liberal to moderate in its politics for several years; in 1973, the Court decided *Roe v. Wade*, protecting a right to choose whether to have an abortion. Thus, during the sixties, seventies, and eighties, conservative politicians and constitutional scholars attacked the Warren and early Burger Courts for being (liberal) judicial activists. Conservatives argued that the Court should exercise judicial restraint, particularly in individual rights cases—where judicial restraint equated with deference to democratic decisions.[3] Often, the conservative judicial restraint position included a federalism component: The Court should show special respect and deference for the sovereign power of state governments. The first scholars to argue for an originalist approach to constitutional interpretation were, to a great extent, seeking historical pillars to support judicial restraint.[4]

First Amendment religious freedom cases illustrate the implications of judicial restraint for a conservative Court. In 1971, the early Burger Court decided *Lemon v. Kurtzman*, which synthesized Warren Court Establishment Clause cases into a three-part test examining the government's purposes, effects, and entanglements with religion.[5] Manifesting the wall of separation between religion and government that the post-1937 Court had articulated (see chapter 3), the *Lemon* test became the standard doctrinal approach for resolving Establishment Clause issues. Conservative justices, though, grew disgruntled with *Lemon*; they viewed it and the concomitant wall metaphor as mistakenly legitimating an activist Court's hostility toward religion (Christianity). Rejecting the wall of separation, the conservatives favored an alternative theory, nonpreferentialism: The government cannot prefer one religion over another, but it can favor religion over irreligion.[6] If applied, nonpreferentialism would allow more government displays and actions that recognized or bolstered religion—particularly Christianity. Indeed, during the 1980s, conservative justices introduced doctrinal approaches—alternatives to *Lemon* that moved closer to nonpreferentialism—which they occasionally invoked in subsequent years (though some justices continued to invoke *Lemon* too). In 1984, Justice O'Connor articulated a two-pronged endorsement test, which focused on whether the government had endorsed or disapproved of religion.[7] And in 1989, Justice Kennedy articulated a two-pronged coercion test, focusing on whether the government had coerced "anyone to support or participate in any religion or its exercise."[8] Finally, the conservative justices used one additional approach, though it was less a doctrine (for instance, a multi-pronged test) than an invocation of tradition. In 1983, *Marsh v. Chambers* upheld the constitutionality of opening (Nebraska) state legislative sessions with a prayer, offered by a publicly paid chaplain. The Court did not mention *Lemon* or any other Establishment Clause doctrinal test. Instead, the Court reasoned that the opening of legislative sessions "with prayer is deeply embedded in the history and tradition of this country."[9]

Free exercise cases show the conservative justices turning even more strongly toward judicial restraint. Recall, the Warren Court had typically applied strict scrutiny in free exercise cases, requiring the government to show that the enforcement of a law of general applicability, which burdened religion, was necessary to achieve a compelling purpose.[10] In 1990, however, *Employment Division, Department of Human Resources v. Smith* repudiated the application of strict scrutiny for most free exercise cases. The claimant, a member of the Native American Church, sought a free exercise exemption from a criminal law prohibiting the use of peyote. The Court denied the claim, reasoning that the "political process" should, to a great degree, determine the scope of free exercise. In most free exercise cases brought after *Smith*, the government would need to satisfy only a rational basis test, showing that the government action was rationally related to a legitimate interest.[11]

The conservative icon, Justice Antonin Scalia, wrote the *Smith* majority opinion. Whereas the post-Warren Supreme Court had rarely validated free exercise claims, strict scrutiny at least appeared to favor claimants, and they fared well in the lower courts.[12] Scalia and the *Smith* majority, though, seemed wary of non-Christian, religious minorities who might use the courts to limit the (Christian) majoritarian will. "[We] cannot afford the luxury of deeming presumptively invalid, as applied to the religious objector, every regulation of conduct that does not protect an interest of the highest order." Continued judicial application of the strict scrutiny test "would be courting anarchy, [a] danger [that] increases in direct proportion to the society's diversity of religious beliefs." Scalia acknowledged that the Court's new rational basis test and deference to democracy favored the Christian mainstream while potentially harming non-Christians: "It may fairly be said that leaving accommodation to the political process will place at a relative disadvantage those religious practices that are not widely engaged in; but that [is an] unavoidable consequence of democratic government. . . ."[13] *Smith*, it should be added, not only deferred to democracy, but also, at least in that decision itself, deferred to state sovereignty (as the challenged law was from the state of Oregon).

The *Smith* Court did not completely foreclose the judicial application of strict scrutiny in free exercise cases. The Court identified three exceptional circumstances in which strict scrutiny (rather than rational basis) would still be appropriate: first, if the government purposefully discriminated against religion; second, if the claimant challenged the denial of unemployment compensation; and third, if the free exercise claim was combined with another constitutional claim—typically, free expression—to form a type of "hybrid" case.[14] At that time, the most important of the Court's three exceptions appeared to be the hybrid case situation.[15] The first exception, for cases of purposeful government discrimination against religion, seemed unlikely to arise with any frequency. In fact, during the subsequent Rehnquist Court years, the Court found purposeful discrimination in only one case, *Church of the Lukumi Babalu Aye, Inc. v. City of Hialeah*, decided in 1993. Members of the Church of the Lukumi Babalu Aye practiced the Santeria religion, combining elements of the African Yoruba religion with Catholicism and including animal sacrifices. The *Lukumi* case arose when the city of Hialeah enacted ordinances prohibiting religious sacrifices of animals but not otherwise restricting animal slaughter (for instance, for food). After reviewing the record, the Court concluded that the city had not been religiously neutral but rather had purposefully discriminated against the Santeria religion. Emphasizing that "the First Amendment forbids an official purpose to disapprove of a particular religion or of religion in general," the Court applied strict scrutiny and held that the city had violated the Free Exercise Clause.[16] While *Lukumi* was unusual, it illustrated an important aspect of the *Smith* approach. If the government purposefully discriminated against (or targeted) religion, either explicitly or implicitly, then the government law or action was not neutral and generally applicable in the first place. Strict scrutiny was therefore appropriate because the government had not satisfied the prerequisite for applying the deferential *Smith* rational basis test—that the government action be a neutral implementation of a generally applicable law.[17]

The Constitution in Exile

In 1991, the year after the Court decided *Smith*, the ultraconservative Clarence Thomas replaced the liberal Thurgood Marshall and solidified conservative control of the Court. At that point, conservative scholars and jurists became less interested in restraint and more committed to "judicial engagement."[18] Originalists began asserting that the Court should assertively articulate and implement conservative principles and doctrines rather than exercising judicial restraint. Following in this vein, conservative scholars and jurists more aggressively denigrated the Court's 1937 transformation. One-time Supreme Court nominee Douglas Ginsburg maintained that the Court should restore the "Constitution in exile." The conservative scholar Randy Barnett titled a book *Restoring the Lost Constitution*, while Richard Epstein argued the Court should reverse "the mistakes of 1937." Justice Thomas himself declared that the Court took a "wrong turn" in 1937.[19]

When conservatives in that pre-millennium era repudiated 1937, as well as the Warren Court's invigoration of it, what were they aiming to accomplish? In theory, a principled repudiation of 1937 would reject pluralist democracy and all its ramifications. The Court would return to republican democracy and its emphasis on the virtuous pursuit of the common good. Such a transition would have enormous consequences for not only democratic practices but also the judicial protection of individual rights, particularly free speech, religious freedom, and equal protection. Judicial enforcement of these rights would be toned down; the rights would no longer have as much bite (notwithstanding *Smith*). As during the republican democratic era—before the 1930s—the government could restrict rights if in pursuit of the common good (as discussed in chapter 2).

In fact, some conservative scholars had already suggested that a rejection of 1937 might demand a return to principles resonating with republican democracy. The political scientist Walter Berns, for one, wrote extensively about the First Amendment and democracy. "[T]he constitutional law of the First Amendment [after 1937] has not been built on the precedents and principles of the past," Berns wrote, criticizing the Court. "One looks almost in vain for references in the Court's opinions to what the great [nineteenth-century] commentators—Story, Kent, and

Cooley, for example—have written on freedom of speech and religion, or to what the Founders intended with the First Amendment."[20] Focusing on the "problem of free speech," Berns explained it as a "problem of virtue." The Court, when resolving free expression cases, should seek to "promote the virtue of citizens" and to pursue the "general welfare" (or the common good). Berns consequently recommended that the Court return to a doctrinal approach like the bad tendency test: The government should be allowed to punish expression likely to have harmful consequences or bad tendencies but should not be able to punish "good speech"—expression that would likely promote virtue and the common good. In short, Berns advocated for a return to a republican democratic approach to free expression. The Court would necessarily distinguish between "good and evil" as the government shaped citizens of "good character" and censored the licentious.[21]

Conservative legal scholars, such as Alexander Bickel and Robert Bork, followed a similar path. After Bickel explained that democracy could not survive without "a foundation of moral values,"[22] his Yale colleague, Bork, emphasized the importance of such values to free expression cases. The Court, he argued, should follow originalism, staying "close to the text and the history, and their fair implications." The post-1937 Court had wandered from that interpretive approach to the Constitution and, in doing so, had illegitimately expanded First Amendment guarantees of free expression to encompass immorality.[23] Bork argued similarly regarding religious freedom, castigating the post-1937 Court for creating a strict wall of separation between church and state contrary to the original meaning of the First Amendment. He therefore criticized the Warren Court's decision in *Engel v. Vitale*, in which the justices had enforced the wall of separation by holding that prayers in public schools were unconstitutional—a religious practice that, Bork emphasized, "the states had employed for many years."[24]

Regardless, whatever conservatives might have previously meant when they called for the rejection of 1937, their intent today must be understood through the lens of contemporary conservatism—at a time when a six-justice bloc has the Court locked in a conservative vise. In short, what does political conservatism mean for the Roberts Court today? To understand the Roberts Court, we need to explore how political conservatism developed during the late twentieth and early twenty-first centuries. This chapter and the next do not attempt to comprehensively explain the complex and multi-faceted history of conservatism from this era. Rather, these chapters draw on historical threads that intertwine in ways that are especially important for understanding the Court. The remainder of this chapter therefore discusses an intellectual movement, neoliberalism, while the next chapter discusses a grass-roots movement, white Christian nationalism. Aspects of the latter appeared initially on the conservative fringes, but the movement would move eventually into the mainstream, where it would intersect with neoliberalism in recent Republican politics.

* * *

Two main theories of political conservatism emerged after the New Deal and World War II. Libertarians, influenced by Friedrich Hayek's *Road to Serfdom*, published in 1944, emphasized the protection of individual liberties, especially economic liberties. Above all else, they wanted minimal government. Traditionalists, led by Russell Kirk, expressed a Burkean reverence for tradition and religion as sources of values. They, too, preferred minimal or restrained government, particularly in foreign affairs, but unlike libertarians, they worried that individuals would abuse liberty and become licentious. Moral clarity was crucial.[25]

These two forms of conservatism, one emphasizing liberty and the other emphasizing moral clarity, sometimes clashed, but they would both remain prominent through the late twentieth and early twenty-first centuries. Some theorists, such as the neoconservatives, and some politicians, notably Ronald Reagan, tried to harmonize libertarianism and traditionalism, or at least bring them together under a big tent. Yet, distinct variations of each form would develop and eventually gain a stranglehold on the Republican party.[26] Specifically, neoliberalism became a dominant form of libertarianism, while white Christian nationalism, as it began to emerge in the 1960s and 1970s, was a virulent manifestation (or perversion) of traditionalism. For many years, commentators have discussed the influence of neoliberalism on Republican politics—and on the Democrats as well, particularly in the 1990s—but recognition of the influence of white Christian nationalism on mainstream conservatism is relatively recent.[27]

Neoliberalism

Neoliberalism is best understood in relation to laissez-faire ideology.[28] Laissez-faire, which first became prominent in the United States after the Civil War, celebrates the wonders of the economic marketplace. Neoliberalism, taking its name from the classical liberalism of Adam Smith, is laissez-faire on steroids. It celebrates the wonders of the marketplace while simultaneously denigrating democratic government.[29]

Neoliberalism initially developed as an intellectual movement after World War II but gained political clout in the 1970s and 1980s. It promotes a deeply individualist ethos and questions the group decision-making entailed by democratic government, though the earliest postwar neoliberal writings tended to be less hostile to democracy. In a 1951 essay, for example, Milton Friedman contrasted collectivism against individualism. The problem with collectivists, he argued, was not with their goals. "[C]ollectivists have wanted to do good," he acknowledged, "to maintain and extend freedom and democracy, and at the same time to improve the material welfare of the great masses of the people." Problems, however, arose from "the means." Collectivists failed to recognize how difficult it was to efficiently coordinate "the activities of millions of people," a coordination that could naturally occur in the economic marketplace of an individualist system. At this time, shortly after World War II, Friedman believed that maintaining democracy was a worthy goal. A democratic state could contribute in important ways within an individualist system—for instance, by promoting competition and preventing monopolies.[30]

Before long, though, neoliberals were expressing greater hostility to all forms of government, including democracy. Hayek explained in 1960 that government attempts at rational planning for society inevitably undermined individual liberty. The world was too complex to be mastered by human reason, despite humanity's hubristic belief otherwise. "Human reason can neither predict nor deliberately shape its own future. . . . Progress by its very nature cannot be planned."[31] Friedman described an invisible hand that generated rational and efficient outcomes in the economic marketplace while simultaneously producing irrationality in democratic government. To be clear, for Friedman, the invisible hand in the marketplace generated the best results not only for individuals but also for society as a whole. "The market, with each individual going his own way, with no central authority setting social priorities, avoiding duplication, and coordinating activities, looks like chaos to the naked eye," Friedman wrote in 1976. "Yet through [Adam] Smith's eyes we see that it is a finely ordered and delicately tuned system, one which arises out of man's actions, yet is not deliberately created by man. It is a system which enables the dispersed knowledge and skill of millions of people to be coordinated for a common purpose." Friedman's praise of the marketplace starkly contrasted with his description of the invisible hand in government. In fact, he wrote that "an invisible hand in politics . . . is the precise reverse of the invisible hand in the market." Even government officials who have the best of intentions inevitably pursue harmful goals. "The invisible hand in politics is as potent a force for harm as the invisible hand in economics is for good." The government cannot consistently or systematically pursue rational and efficient goals; it necessarily falls prey to the desires of "special interests."[32]

Public choice theorists, following fundamental economic principles, elaborated this neoliberal attack on democratic government. Just as economists assume that individuals in the economic marketplace pursue their own self-interest, public choice theorists assume that government officials do the same. For example, members of Congress vote for or against a legislative bill based on whatever they believe will maximize their chances of reelection; they do not act in pursuit of a common good or public interest. Given this, legislative decisions do not arise from a rational calculation of social utility—the costs and benefits for the group (or society). Rather, they arise from legislators' self-interested calculations and the attempts of interest groups to manipulate the legislators (as they seek reelection). Consequently, from the public choice perspective, majority voting, the crux of democratic government, frequently leads to irrational group (legislative) decisions. When Congress or another legislature enacts a statute, we should not even assume a coherent and rational goal or purpose exists behind the action. Public choice theory underscores how neoliberalism pushes beyond laissez-faire. Laissez-faire celebrates the free economic marketplace, so laissez-faire theorists criticize government regulations that interfere with the market. In theory, though, other government regulations can be rational and worthwhile. But public choice and neoliberal theorists demonize democracy: For them, government regulations are inherently irrational and harmful.[33]

Oddly, neoliberalism and its celebration of the economic marketplace gained prominence in the 1970s when the actual marketplace was in crisis. High inflation and high unemployment plagued the United States and other western industrialized nations. But neoliberals had a ready response for these difficulties: The market was failing precisely because of government regulations that interfered with free market operations. Friedman, for example, said, "Inflation is entirely made in Washington— and nowhere else." And when Friedman's own theories seemingly failed to pan out in application, he claimed that they were not properly executed. The government could always be blamed for market failures.[34]

In any event, neoliberal theory has been extensively incorporated into government policies starting with President Ronald Reagan's administration in the 1980s (1981–1989). He famously proclaimed in his first inaugural address that "government is not the solution to our problem; government is the problem." Reagan attacked labor unions, started deregulation, and relaxed antitrust policies, which facilitated corporate mergers. Cutting the top marginal tax rate from 70 to 28 percent, Reagan insisted that "trickle-down" (supply-side) economics would generate more revenue for the government and greater prosperity for all—the rich and poor alike. Nevertheless, the Reagan tax cuts, when combined with those of the next president, another Republican, George H. W. Bush, more than quadrupled the national debt over a 12-year period while contributing to growing income and wealth disparities. Such empirical realities did not slow the neoliberal freight train. Citibank's Walter Wriston explained in 1992 how markets are better than democracy: "Markets are voting machines; they function by taking referenda. . . . [They give] power to the people."[35]

* * *

While neoliberalism was central to conservative politics for decades, through the late twentieth and early twenty-first centuries, white Christian nationalism would eventually move from the fringes of American politics to the mainstream. As will be discussed in the next chapter, a broad white, Christian, nationalist movement emerged in the twentieth century, but it entered the conservative mainstream only in the new millennium. While neoliberalism and white Christian nationalism overlap, the latter became more important in recent years.

5

White Christian Nationalism Enters the Political Mainstream

Neoliberalism developed initially as an intellectual movement, but white Christian nationalism emerged as a grassroots movement in the 1960s and 1970s.[1] In analyzing this latter movement, some historians and commentators emphasize race—white supremacy and privilege[2]—while others emphasize religion—Christian privilege and power.[3] Yet, as many recognize, whiteness and Christianity are integrally intertwined in American history and society. One cannot fully comprehend white supremacy and privilege without accounting for the role of Christianity, and vice versa, one cannot comprehend the role of Christian privilege and power without accounting for the role of race in America.[4] Of course, white, Christian Americans express varied religious and political views, yet that variability does not preclude us (including white Christians) from recognizing and criticizing white Christian nationalism as a conservative political movement.[5]

Origins of a Broader White Christian Nationalism

White Christian movements and organizations, such as the Ku Klux Klan (KKK), had of course existed before the 1960s, but the movement that emerged in the latter twentieth century eventually moved from the margins to the mainstream and became broader than prior movements and organizations. This broader white Christian nationalism had its origins in the Vietnam War and its aftermath. Numerous American soldiers returned home after the war feeling alienated from fellow citizens and betrayed by the government. They believed the war had been winnable, but the American people and government had failed to provide the necessary support for the soldiers' efforts (other soldiers, to be sure, had themselves turned against the war effort).[6]

This sense of government betrayal combined with a conservative cultural backlash against the 1960s social movements. While many viewed the 1950s as an age of consensus, multiple social and protest movements marked the 1960s: The Civil Rights Movement morphed into the Black power movement; an environmental movement started; and a new women's movement emerged. And, of course, a peace movement opposed the Vietnam War. New civil rights statutes enacted in the 1960s, such as the Civil Rights Act of 1964, rendered it more difficult to discriminate against and to deny benefits and opportunities to people of color—practices that had been consistently and legally done in prior decades (thus preserving white privilege). For some of the angry white soldiers returning from Vietnam, their sense of alienation and resentment—toward other Americans and especially toward the government—only increased. The introduction of race-based affirmative action programs in the 1960s and 1970s intensified this white resentment. From the perspective of these alienated white Christian men, the government had become "a menace to morality and prosperity."[7]

Christianity played a central role in this conservative cultural backlash. After the Supreme Court decided *Brown v. Board of Education* in 1954 and then ordered desegregation "with all deliberate speed" in 1955, many southern school districts began implementing schemes to resist racial desegregation. These schemes were generally successful, as desegregation barely advanced for years (discussed in chapter 3), yet many white families nonetheless sought to exit the public schools. These families moved their children into racially segregated private schools, many of which were religiously affiliated—in fact, "hundreds of private Protestant segregationist academies opened in the South."[8] Initially, these schools enjoyed tax exempt status because they were nonprofit, but in 1970, the IRS began denying that exemption. Largely in reaction to this government action, Christian conservatives started to mobilize politically after several decades of quietude. Eventually, the constitutionality of denying tax exemptions made it to the Supreme Court. Bob Jones University discriminated against Black Americans ostensibly in accord with the school's fundamentalist Christian tenets. When the IRS in 1976 refused to continue granting the University tax advantages, the University sued, claiming that the denial violated its free exercise rights under the First Amendment. The Court held that the IRS had acted constitutionally: The denial of a tax exemption was narrowly tailored to achieve a compelling purpose, "eradicating racial discrimination in education."[9]

By the time the Court decided *Bob Jones University*, in 1983, Christian conservative leaders had already realized they needed a political issue more palatable than racial discrimination (and school segregation) to rally around. They seized on abortion. Many conservative leaders—including Ronald Reagan, Barry Goldwater, Billy Graham, and Betty Ford—had initially supported a right to choose, so when the Court decided *Roe v. Wade* in 1973, it did not immediately provoke a widespread conservative reaction. Nevertheless, by the end of the decade, white Christian leaders were emphasizing opposition to abortion, and they successfully used that political wedge to deepen and widen the Christian conservative (political) movement.[10]

Two Threads Develop

While the white, Christian, conservative movement grew in the 1980s, it split into two threads during that decade. From one perspective, Reagan's presidency not only demonstrated the burgeoning political power of Christian conservatives but also provided a boon for conservatism in general. The grievances of white Vietnam veterans were popularized through movies and music—albeit in a diluted form. For instance, the first two Rambo movies—*First Blood* and *First Blood Part II*—were released in 1982 and 1985, respectively. They starred Sylvester Stallone as a brooding and vengeful Vietnam vet, John Rambo, who became an icon for many white Christian men even if they had never been anywhere near southeast Asia or the war. Like Rambo and actual veterans, these men saw themselves as justifiably aggrieved. They had given their all, sacrificing for the nation, but now they were being blamed for the nation's shortcomings, especially for the failures and weaknesses of people of color and non-Christians—hence, for example, the need for affirmative action. White Christian men believed they were entitled to fight back. Meanwhile, Bruce Springsteen's hit song *Born in the U.S.A.*, about a Vietnam veteran, served as a patriotic anthem for these embittered white Christian men, even if Springsteen had not written it for that reason. White Christian men could now readily see themselves as innocent victims.[11]

Indeed, one might have expected Reagan's presidency to have mostly ameliorated the grievances of white Christian conservatives in general, including actual Vietnam veterans. After all, Reagan himself came to office spouting neoliberal anti-government rhetoric and then implemented multiple anti-government policies (discussed in chapter 4). Yet, many conservatives, including alienated white Christian veterans, quickly grew disenchanted with Reagan. To them, his actions did not fulfill his promises on multiple issues—for instance, he did not fight vigorously enough against abortion. Because of this disappointment with Reagan, his presidency not only failed to dissipate conservative resentment but also provoked some white Christians, in effect, to declare "war against the federal government." To be certain, before that point, alienated Vietnam War veterans were angry with the government, but many other white Christian activists, including Klansmen and neo-Nazis, "had justified their violent actions by claiming to serve state and country." During Reagan's presidency, however, some white Christian nationalists transformed and solidified their movement: "Rather than fighting on behalf of the state, white power activists now fought for a white homeland, attempted to destabilize the federal government, and waged revolutionary race war."[12]

Hence, if Reagan represented mainstream conservatism, this second thread of white Christian nationalism trafficked (and traffics) in extremes, endorsing separatism and violence. Not content merely listening to Springsteen or watching Rambo (and voting for Reagan and other Republicans), participants in this second thread would undertake bombings, assassinations, robberies, and of course stealing and trafficking in weapons. While many of these white Christian nationalists would have undoubtedly welcomed a legally enforced caste system reminiscent of the Jim Crow era—with white, Christian men at the top; white, Christian women in the next tier; and then all people of color and non-Christians at the bottom—the movement ultimately sought a racially and religiously purified nation. They were willing to "burn the entire house down in order to rebuild it from the basement up." Fusing together multiple white supremacist, xenophobic, racist, antisemitic, and sexist organizations, this thread of white Christian nationalism targeted people of color, especially Black Americans; non-Christians, especially Jews; and other outsiders. The movement's sexism was perhaps less virulent than its other xenophobic isms, because white, Christian women were welcomed into the movement but primarily to fill traditional gender roles as wives and mothers—white, Christian men were to protect the bodies of white, Christian women. White, Christian women, in other words, were to be subservient, but they were not considered inherently sub-human and subject to expulsion or death.[13]

Just as neoliberalism can be understood as laissez-faire on steroids, white Christian nationalism can be understood as traditionalism on steroids. The movement's demands for moral clarity centered, of course, around Christianity. And just as some Vietnam veterans adopted extreme positions, some Christian leaders did the same. Rousas John (RJ) Rushdoony was a key early figure in what would later become known as Dominion theology. Rushdoony articulated a program called Christian Reconstruction, which demanded that the United States follow biblical law. Indeed, Rushdoony believed the nation was founded for that purpose: In his words, the First Amendment established freedom "not from religion but for religion."[14] In his multi-volume treatise, *The Institutes of Biblical Law*, he argued that the "heresy of democracy has . . . worked havoc in church and state. . . . Christianity and democracy are inevitably enemies."[15] Christians, therefore, should not seek to bolster democratic government; rather they should "exercise absolute dominion over the earth and all of its inhabitants."[16] Unsurprisingly, then, Rushdoony's writings retroactively supported the Confederacy's defense of slavery— similar to John C. Calhoun, Rushdoony maintained that slavery was in effect a positive good for Black Americans—and absolved Christians of responsibility for the persecution of Jews, even going so far as to deny the Holocaust.[17]

Among alienated Vietnam War veterans, Louis Beam was an early leader who emphasized the importance of a fundamentalist Christianity (belief in a plain and literal interpretation of the Protestant Bible generally opposed to a modern, scientific worldview). More specifically, Beam was a proponent of Christian Identity ideology, which originated in the United States during the mid-1940s and grew increasingly significant later in the twentieth century.[18] According to Christian Identity, Jews misinterpret the Bible when they claim to be the people of ancient Israel. Instead, only white Europeans and their descendants are the true children of Israel. The *Kingdom Identity Ministries Doctrinal Statement of*

Beliefs states as follows: "We believe the White, Anglo-Saxon, Germanic and kindred people to be God's true, literal Children of Israel. Only this race fulfills every detail of Biblical Prophecy and World History concerning Israel and continues in these latter days to be heirs and possessors of the Covenants, Prophecies, Promises and Blessings of YHVH God made to Israel. This chosen seedline making up the 'Christian Nations' of the earth stands far superior to all other peoples in their call as God's servant race."[19] Furthermore, only white people are made in God's image and are descended from Adam and Eve. People of color are "considered less-than-human, 'mud people.'"[20] Jews themselves are, according to the *Doctrinal Statement of Beliefs*, the "children of Satan."[21] From the Christian Identity viewpoint, then, Jews and people of color can and should be exterminated. Killing them is no different from killing animals "because only Whites are human."[22] Indeed, Christian Identity is a post-millennial movement: Adherents believe that, to usher in Christ's return, they must "fight Christ's enemies during a period of 'tribulation.'"[23]

Christianity provided the white nationalist movement with a religious zeal as it aimed for an apocalyptic transformation of the United States—the elimination of all people of color, Jewish Americans, and other outsiders. Most Christian fundamentalists, though, do not explicitly subscribe to Christian Identity ideology; the same is true of evangelicals, who emphasize salvation by Christian faith alone and the preaching and spreading of that faith (most fundamentalists are evangelical, and vice versa).[24] Even so, fundamentalism is theologically close to Christian Identity, and those attracted to fundamentalism can easily slide into a derivative of Christian Identity. In fact, during the 1980s, some leaders of the Christian right accepted post-millennialism and became associated with Christian Identity. Moreover, many Protestant fundamentalists who do not fully subscribe to Christian Identity ideology still display explicit and implicit racist and antisemitic attitudes. Given that nowadays more than 25 percent of the country identifies as evangelical Protestant—near another 15 percent identify as mainline Protestant—such attitudes are alarming. As many commentators have observed, Christian fundamentalists and evangelicals have become deeply conservative, often aligning themselves with "nationalistic, and racist politics."[25]

In fact, hostility against Jews and other non-Christians, particularly Muslims, is not only widespread among Protestant fundamentalists but also definitive to the white, Christian, nationalist movement. One manifestation of antisemitism lies in the proliferation of conspiracy theories, many of which claim that Jews orchestrate the oppression and killing of white Christians. Such conspiracy theories are standard antisemitic fare and have been spread in various narratives for centuries. For instance, Christians have long condemned Jews for the notorious blood libel, which accuses Jews of killing Christian children and using their blood for Passover rituals. Another standard antisemitic trope is that Jews control the world's banking and money supply. Such antisemitic conspiracy theories provide narratives that help bind together the multiple strands of the white, Christian, nationalist movement. In the words of the historian Kathleen Belew: "[W]hite power activists believed that the Jewish-led ZOG [the Zionist Occupational Government—later referred to as the New World Order] controlled the United Nations, the U.S. federal government, and the banks, and that ZOG used people of color, communists, liberals, journalists, [and] academics . . . as puppets in a conspiracy to eradicate the white race and its economic, social, and cultural accomplishments."[26]

As these conspiracy theories spotlight, the white, Christian, nationalist movement is not closely tied to empirical reality. Indeed, a primary inspirational source for the movement was and is a novel, *The Turner Diaries*, first printed in serial form from 1974 to 1976 and then published as a book in 1978. The novel sold approximately 500,000 copies in the first 20 years after its publication. It describes a white-supremacist-militia uprising against the United States government—a government supposedly controlled by Jews who are assisted by Black Americans in a systematic effort to oppress the white race. The book ends with the creation of a white Christian utopia where all Jews and Black Americans have been either killed or banished. Inspired partly by *The Turner Diaries*, Louis Beam conceived of a guerrilla war against the federal government that would be carried on by "leaderless resistance factions" organized into largely independent cell structures.[27] Beam believed this strategy would preserve and sustain the white power movement even if individual participants were arrested or killed. "Any one cell can be infiltrated, exposed and destroyed," he wrote, "but this will have no effect on the others; in fact, the members of the other cells will be supporting that cell which is under attack."[28]

Relationship with Democracy

A conundrum at the heart of white Christian nationalism, particularly in its more extreme manifestations, was its violent targeting of democratic government in the name of democracy. In rhetoric and in action, white activists targeted the officials, institutions, and buildings of duly elected democratic governments. Yet, they were not anarchists. After cleansing the nation of all unacceptable people—non-whites and non-Christians—white Christian activists dreamed of "the founding of a racial utopian nation," of planting "the flag of an Aryans-only republic." The end goal, that is, was less the eradication of the United States than the creation of "a white America."[29]

The white power movement's paradoxical stance toward democracy was unsurprising. In fact, it harmonized with the history of vigilantism in America. Vigilantes have often viewed themselves as instruments of justice representing the true people. From this perspective, when the government falls into corruption, failing to fulfill the demands of justice and democracy, then the people themselves must respond with direct action. Vigilantes therefore typically claim that their use of violence is legitimate and even necessary to correct the government's perpetration of an injustice. They can even point to the Declaration of Independence and the American Revolution as setting a precedent for violent opposition to the government. After all, the Declaration began by briefly proclaiming certain "truths to be self-evident, that all men are created equal, that they are endowed by their Creator with certain unalienable Rights, that among these are Life, Liberty and the pursuit of Happiness." But after that introduction, the Declaration delineated an exhaustive list of corrupt actions perpetrated by the British government that justified an armed insurrection.[30]

With the Declaration of Independence and Revolution as founding events for the nation, violent resistance to supposedly unjust or illegitimate government became part of the American persona and traditions. In fact, many towns and cities celebrate and glorify prior vigilante actions by holding parades and reenactments. In the state of Wyoming, Charles Coutant was the state librarian and custodian of the historical society from 1901 to 1905. He extolled numerous vigilante actions, particularly in the city of Cheyenne. He wrote: "[Where] the authorities are powerless to act—[or] if they do so act with public enemies openly or covertly—then it sometimes happens that lynch law is the only apparently practicable way by which life and property can be protected."[31] Despite such tributes, we should not forget that vigilante actions were frequently violent assertions of power over socially and culturally marginalized individuals and groups. In the American South, where white lynchings of Black Americans were common occurrences for many decades after the Civil War, the threat and execution of lynchings were means for enforcing a racist and hierarchical social ordering. From 1889 to the end of the 1920s, at least one Black American was lynched every four days, on average. For the white mobs, these lynchings were often carnival-like gatherings worthy of memorialization: White participants and observers frequently collected souvenirs, such as body parts or pieces of rope. These "ritualistic slaughters [were often justified] on a false rumor that the victim had raped a White woman."[32] In other words, southern white men frequently inflicted violence on Black men supposedly to protect the bodies of white, Christian women—actions that resonate, not incidentally, with the current beliefs of the white Christian nationalists.

In sum, white Christian nationalism, in its extreme manifestations, has always stood against democratic government as it was and is currently constituted in the United States. White Christian activists would accept democracy, but only if the proper individuals and groups participate. In other words, "We the People" should rule, but only white Christians can belong to the people. From the white, Christian, nationalist perspective, the people cannot be expanded to include Jews, other non-Christians, or people of color. Therefore, a non-Christian, a person of color, or even a white Christian who politically sympathizes and aligns with outsiders cannot legitimately win a democratic election. Even if that person seemingly garners more votes, those votes are illegitimate— fraudulent, we might say—because the true people cannot possibly choose an outsider for a leadership position. If only white, Christian men can stand for and uphold the proper values, then only white, Christian men can legitimately vote and be elected to office. Or, to put this in the converse, the inclusion of non-Christian or non-white people within the polity threatens the integrity of a white, Christian nation. From this perspective, white, Christian men justifiably resent the intrusion of outsiders. White, Christian men believe they are legitimately aggrieved by the participation and even mere presence of people of color, Jews, and other non-Christians.[33]

Deeper into the Political Mainstream

As neoliberalism and white Christian nationalism initially developed in the latter half of the twentieth century, they appeared to be starkly separate and distinct. Neoliberalism was an intellectual movement supposedly developed from a commitment to economic principles. White Christian nationalism was a grassroots movement born of resentment and ostensible betrayals that, in its extreme forms, endorsed violence. Nevertheless, neoliberalism and white Christian nationalism shared a key component: a distrust of democratic government.

Even so, this overlap—the distrust of democratic government—might have been no more than happenstance, with little importance. After all, with its apparent grounding on economic principles, neoliberalism claimed to have universal appeal for all reasonable people. White Christian nationalism was and is inherently exclusionary, purposively separating white Christians from all other people. Indeed, many observers have characterized white power activities, such as shootings and bombings, as actions of isolated individuals. For example, the 1995 bombing of the Alfred P. Murrah Federal Building in Oklahoma City, which killed 168 people, was often described as the work of one emotionally disturbed individual, Timothy McVeigh—or at most the action of two men, McVeigh and Terry Nichols.[34] But to attribute the Oklahoma City bombing and other similar violent actions to so-called lone wolves is a mistake. These actions have arisen from a social movement—the white, Christian, nationalist movement—that has intentionally attempted to disguise its more violent activities as those of a few solitary men. That was the point of Beam's leaderless resistance strategy: It disguised the interconnected movements of independent cells as the products of isolated individuals. In fact, white power activists had targeted the Alfred P. Murrah Federal Building as a potential target as early as 1983, and McVeigh carried a copy of *The Turner Diaries* in his car. The public failure to recognize and understand such violent actions as the work of a white, Christian, nationalist movement has had significant consequences: facilitating the continuing advancement of the movement, even in its extreme manifestations, and allowing it to move from the margins of society deeper into the mainstream.[35]

Given the advancing of white Christian nationalism, the overlap between it and neoliberalism—the distrust of democratic government—fostered an intertwining of the two under the umbrella of the Republican party. Four major events helped bring the movements together: the end of the Cold War; the September 11, 2001, terrorist attacks on the Twin Towers; the election of Barack Obama as president; and the subsequent (first) election of Donald Trump as president.

The End of the Cold War

The first key event was the end of the Cold War in late 1991 and early 1992. In one way, the Cold War had been a unifying force within the United States. It had provided a common enemy—communism as manifested in the Soviet Union—for diverse Americans across the political spectrum. Neoliberals, for example, celebrated the free economic marketplace of capitalism—they therefore could not accept a government-controlled communist economy. The white, Christian, nationalist movement had its roots in the anti-communist war in Vietnam. And, of course, Christian fundamentalists and evangelicals could not abide the godless communists.[36]

Consequently, for the vast majority of Americans, the end of the Cold War was a great victory. Democracy and capitalism had defeated communism and the Soviet Union. In the words of an influential neoconservative, Francis Fukuyama, the collapse of the Soviet Union marked the "end of history."[37] Most observers at the time assumed that "capitalism and democracy would evolve along compatible lines and mutually reinforce each other."[38] But without communism to brood about, neoliberals increasingly focused on democratic government as an enemy, even as their influence continued to grow through Bill Clinton's and George W. Bush's presidential administrations. Neoliberals pushed for the privatization of numerous government institutions, such as prisons, schools, policing, and the military. From the neoliberal perspective, "[e]fficiency can only be achieved through the incentives that are built into markets. . . . Incentive structures, profit and loss, and customer satisfaction are the values that should drive public service, just as they drive private enterprise."[39] Corporations merged and went multinational, reaching into former communist countries that had been behind the Iron Curtain. During the first decade after the end of the Cold War, the number of multinational corporations catapulted from approximately 37 thousand to 63 thousand.[40] And corporations were not merely doing business; they were becoming increasingly involved in American democratic processes. Corporations (and wealthy individuals) became so effective at manipulating elections and government for their own advantages that one can reasonably label this era "Democracy, Inc."[41] With ever-increasing proficiency, corporations used government power to benefit the respective corporations as well as corporate business in toto. In 2012, the president of the conservative American Enterprise Institute, Arthur Brooks, echoed Ronald Reagan: "The best government philosophy is one that starts every day with the question, 'What can we do today to get out of Americans' way?'"[42]

Meanwhile, the extremist thread of white Christian nationalism also transformed with the end of the Cold War. Given that Soviet communism no longer hovered portentously in the distance, white Christian nationalists intensified their targeting of the government, people of color, Jews, and other non-Christians. The government's violent siege of a white separatist compound at Ruby Ridge, Idaho, in 1992 only reinforced the white Christian demonization of the federal government. Fears of a coming apocalypse heightened even further when, in 1993, the government, suspecting the presence of illegal weapons and sexual abuse, attacked a fundamentalist sect's (the Branch Davidians) compound at Waco, Texas. Afterward, white Christian nationalists prepared for a government- and Jewish-led attack on white Christendom likely ending with a violent transformation of the nation. Indeed, the Oklahoma City bombing can be understood, in part, as ostensible retribution for the Waco violence.[43]

In 1992, the fiery Pat Buchanan campaigned for the Republican presidential nomination and began gradually interweaving the two threads of white Christian nationalism. He would eventually drop out of the campaign—the mainstream Republican, President George H. W. Bush, was renominated—but Buchanan gave a prime-time speech at the Republican National Convention. In words that even extremist white

Christian activists would have approved, he declared: "[T]his election is about more than who gets what. It is about who we are. It is about what we believe, and what we stand for as Americans. There is a religious war going on in this country. It is a cultural war, as critical to the kind of nation we shall be as was the Cold War itself, for this war is for the soul of America." He attacked the Democratic nominee, Bill Clinton, and his wife, Hillary Rodham Clinton, for their stances on "abortion . . . the Supreme Court . . . homosexual rights, discrimination against religious schools, women in combat units." If Clinton were elected, Buchanan warned, the United States would no longer be "God's country."[44]

Buchanan was a key figure in bringing the values of white Christian nationalism more deeply into the political mainstream. Given that Buchanan was a traditionalist Catholic, his prominence demonstrated a perhaps surprising aspect of the white, Christian, nationalist movement. Although Protestants and Catholics have often been at odds through American (and world) history, white Christian nationalism has not been virulently anti-Catholic, despite the movement's close ties to Protestant fundamentalism. Thus, Buchanan, in his run for the presidency, drew strong support from the likes of David Duke, a national leader of the Ku Klux Klan (the KKK had traditionally been anti-Catholic). Buchanan thundered about "moral absolutes" in opposition to "shared citizenship." From his perspective, compromise with opponents equated with betrayal; victory was an imperative, by any means necessary.[45]

Buchanan's strong showing in 1992 had significant ramifications for the Republican party. In the short term, Buchanan's candidacy pushed Bush's campaign to adopt increasingly conservative positions. In the long term, Buchanan presaged the presidential candidacy of Donald Trump. Buchanan had been a TV talk-show host, proudly styled himself a "right-wing populist,"[46] and was an "uninhibited practitioner of the politics of resentment."[47] He did not shy from uttering racist and antisemitic statements. In 1992, he declared that "[t]he United States is now undergoing the greatest invasion in history, a mass immigration of millions of illegal aliens yearly from Mexico."[48] He added that "[a] nation that cannot control its own borders can scarcely call itself a state any longer."[49] He told his followers that "we must take back our cities, and take back our culture, and take back our country."[50] His presidential campaign slogan was "America First," as he sought to diminish the nation's intervention abroad and involvement in international institutions, such as the United Nations.[51]

In the years after Buchanan's candidacy, conservatives more frequently interweaved anti-government rhetoric with invocations of traditional Christian values. Rather than arguing that government must enforce traditional values, conservatives began to suggest that government was causing a degradation of American values. If the government stopped interfering in the private sphere, then real Americans would be free to uphold their true moral values. From this perspective, it was government that promoted abortion, encouraged homosexuality, and broke apart families. Thus, in Oregon and Colorado, referenda on the respective state ballots, if approved, would have prohibited the governments from granting privileges or anti-discrimination protections to LGBTQ+ individuals. The Oregon measure failed, but Colorado voters approved their referendum—though the Supreme Court would invalidate the Colorado law in 1996.[52]

September 11 Terrorist Attacks on the Twin Towers

The next major event interweaving neoliberalism and white Christian nationalism was the terrorist destruction of the Twin Towers in New York City on September 11, 2001. This event spurred increased nativism and xenophobia, consonant with white Christian nationalism. Neoliberalism, though, was already so deeply entrenched in Republican politics that conservatives readily incorporated a newfound fear of outsiders with an ongoing neoliberal pro-marketplace, anti-government rhetoric. To be sure, within days after 9/11, Republican President George W. Bush made a speech emphasizing that Islam should not be equated with terrorism. "The face of terror is not the true faith of Islam. That's not what Islam is all about. Islam is peace. These terrorists don't represent peace. They represent evil and war." Yet, many Americans dismissed that message once Bush declared a "war on terror" and launched military attacks on Afghanistan and Iraq, largely Muslim countries.[53] Bush himself emphasized the need for "moral clarity," "firm moral purpose," and aggressive "preemptive action": "We must take the battle to the enemy, disrupt his plans, and confront the worst threats before they emerge."[54] With the Bush administration claiming that even torture of enemies was justified in a war on terror, many white Christian Americans readily blamed not only Muslims but also all people of color and Jews—who were accused of bearing responsibility for the 9/11 attacks.[55]

The Election of Barack Obama

The next key event was the presidency of Barack Obama—including his election in 2008 and reelection in 2012—or more precisely, the reaction to Obama's presidency. If the 1930s and the New Deal marked an unusual period in American history when the forces for an inclusive and egalitarian democracy gained the upper hand, the presidency of Obama marked a second such period. As in the 1930s, demographic changes spurred the democratic forces of the early twenty-first century. As of 2020, "African Americans, Hispanic Americans, Asian Americans, and Native Americans . . . constituted 40 percent of the country. Among Americans under the age of eighteen, they were a majority." The nation had also become less Christian and more religiously diverse: "Whereas more than 80 percent of Americans identified as white and Christian (Protestant or Catholic) in 1976, only 43 percent did so in 2016."[56]

The election and reelection of Obama, a Black American, demonstrated the tangible democratic power of this increasingly diverse America. And the white, Christian backlash was just as tangible. When Obama emerged as a serious candidate for the Democratic nomination in 2008, some white conservatives began to question whether he was truly born in the United States. If he had been born in a different country, he would have been ineligible to be president. The so-called birthers demanded that Obama show his birth certificate to prove his legitimacy. But even after he showed it, birthers continued to doubt him. Then, during the campaign leading to Obama's 2012 reelection, none other than Donald Trump emerged to resurrect the birther movement, demanding that Obama produce a "long-form" birth certificate. Moreover, soon after Obama was first elected, the so-called Tea Party emerged on the far right of the Republican party. Tea Partiers focused on economic and fiscal rather than social issues—so they were more in the neoliberal than white, Christian, nationalist camp—but they nonetheless infused their demands with a strong dose of populist anti-establishment and anti-government rage, which translated into strong resistance to Obama.

They were adamant opponents, for instance, of Obama's signature Affordable Care Act (Obamacare).[57]

Lest anyone be mistaken, Obama's election did not usher in an era of post-racial harmony. To the contrary, opposition to Obama was often explicitly or implicitly racist. The birthers' racist motivations were undeniable: Obama, the first Black American to be a major-party presidential nominee, was also the first candidate to be placed under "a searing nativity microscope."[58] He was denounced as the "food stamp" president, and he and Michelle Obama were portrayed as simians. During his presidency, "anti-black attitudes and racial stereotyping rose, rather than fell," and unsurprisingly, the number of hate groups increased.[59] Rightwing radio host Rush Limbaugh lamented that "we've lost the country. I don't know how else you look at this [Obama's reelection]." To rephrase Limbaugh, Obama could not be a real American because he was not white. In fact, could someone named Barack Hussein Obama really be Christian? Or was he a clandestine Muslim, as many Republican opponents seemed to believe?[60]

The (First) Election of Donald Trump

Obama's presidency triggered the final event in the mainstreaming of white Christian nationalism: the presidential candidacy and election of Donald Trump, who rode to victory in 2016 atop a white Christian backlash against Obama. While some commentators claimed that working class whites supported Trump primarily because of economic displacement and stress, one political science study after another concluded otherwise. White Christians perceived a loss of status, and their resulting resentment and anxiety fueled Trump's election.[61] Empirical studies generally show that "voters primarily look for politicians who match their identities," and "[in] contemporary American politics, perhaps the most powerful social identity is race." While racial identity is always significant in the United States, Obama's presidency evoked "psychological forces" that rendered white racial anxiety even more salient than usual.[62] To be forced to submit to the governing rule of Obama, a Black American with a Muslim-like name, was too much for many white Christian Americans to abide. This reaction against Obama and endorsement of Trump proved especially true for white evangelicals, despite Trump's seeming character flaws—being a serial adulterer, assaulting women, bragging about sexual assaults, lying and cheating repeatedly, and displaying monumental narcissism. Enfolding themselves deeply within their racial and religious identities, white evangelicals closely identified with Trump's message of white, Christian grievance.[63]

Without doubt, not all white evangelicals supported and approved of Trump, but surveys demonstrate that they strongly identified with him because of race and religion. A Pew Research Center poll revealed that 81 percent of white, born-again/evangelical Christians voted for Trump in 2016. What were the next most Trump-supportive religious groups? Sixty-one percent of Mormons and 60 percent of white Catholics voted for him. And to avoid any confusion, Trump's support among white evangelicals was stronger than that received by the Republican candidates in the prior four elections.[64] This white Christian support for Trump continued after he became president. A subsequent Pew Research Center poll showed that 78 percent of white evangelical Protestants approved of his job performance, with the support being strongest among those who attended church regularly.[65] Significantly, race as well as religion played a key role in prompting support for Trump. White evangelicals are far more conservative than Black American, Latinx, and Asian American evangelicals. White evangelical conservatism arises partly from a sense of resentment and anxiety: White evangelicals feel "a kind of nostalgia for a period in American history when Black and non-White immigrants were considered outside the bounds or peripheral to the American national community." A majority of white evangelicals believe that, as white Christians, they face greater discrimination than do people of color and non-Christians, including Muslims.[66] As Seth Dowland concluded in *The Christian Century*, white evangelicals "rallied around Trump to defend a white Protestant nation. They have proven to be loyal foot soldiers in the battle against undocumented immigrants and Muslims. [Along with other factors] the election of Barack Obama signaled to them a need to fight for the America they once knew."[67] In fact, the number of evangelicals increased during the years of Trump's presidency.[68]

Trump himself personified a politics of white Christian resentment and grievance. He and his administration constantly cast non-white and non-Christian Americans as if they were outsiders who threatened the integrity of the nation. Consequently, Trump regularly "primed" the resentment of already aggrieved white Christians.[69] When he first launched his 2016 campaign, Trump notoriously denounced undocumented immigrants from Mexico: "They're not sending [people like] you," Trump said to his followers. "They're bringing drugs. They're bringing crime. They're rapists."[70] These types of statements were not mistakes uttered in the heat of the moment—later apologized for and withdrawn. Rather, such statements were central to Trump's campaign and subsequent presidency. In another infamous example, a "Unite the Right" rally in Charlottesville, Virginia, drew white Christian nationalists who chanted, "Jews will not replace us."[71] Violent outbursts left numerous counterprotesters injured and one dead, when a white supremacist drove his car into a crowd. Afterward, Trump declared that there had been "very fine people, on both sides."[72] Trump's statements, whether calculated or not, had consequences. "The Trump administration's rhetoric and policies targeting non-white immigrants, Muslims, Arabs, Latinos, and others has cast marginalized minorities as un-American, un-assimilable, and threats to the public order," explained Dana M. Moss, a sociologist. "By declaring them as fifth columns and as threats for anti-Americanism, our leaders suggest that minority immigrants and American citizens alike warrant persecution as if they were foreign combatants in our numerous wars overseas." For much of Trump's presidency, his only consistent policy position appeared to be racism and xenophobia.[73]

Trump's reaction to his election loss in 2020 underscored not only his accentuation of white Christian resentment and grievance but also the great degree to which Trump, his supporters, and many elected Republican officials have accepted tenets characteristic of white Christian nationalism. Trump's attitude appeared to be that he could not have legitimately lost the election to Joe Biden precisely because Biden was sympathetic to and supported by people of color, Jews, and other non-Christians. Even after Trump's many legal challenges to Biden's election were repudiated, he continued to maintain he had won. The election, he insisted, had been corrupt or fraudulent. Biden and his supporters had stolen the election. This nation was no longer the United States—the true United States, a white Christian nation—if non-whites and non-Christians had installed their preferred candidate in the presidency.[74]

To be clear, the integration of white Christian nationalism into the Republican party had been advancing for years. Trump, though, accelerated this intertwinement by amplifying and seemingly legitimating white Christian supremacist tenets, including racism, antisemitism, and white grievance. A 2023 poll reported that 55 percent of Trump supporters either adhere to or sympathize with Christian nationalist views.[75] Predictably, starting with Trump's election in 2016, the threat of white Christian domestic terrorism increased dramatically: From 2016 to 2018, the percentage of terrorism-related deaths attributable to white supremacists jumped from 20 to 98 percent. The Department of Homeland Security (DHS) identified Domestic Violent Extremists (DVEs) and particularly white supremacist extremists (WSEs)—who target people of color, non-Christians, and LGBTQ+ individuals, and are often anti-government—as "the most persistent and lethal threat" to the United States. In October 2020, DHS reported: "Some DVEs and other violent actors might target events related to the 2020 Presidential campaigns, the election itself, election results, or the post-election period."[76] Yet, Trump and his administration continually suppressed concerns about white Christian nationalism and the potential for a violent insurrection—even after armed protesters stormed the Michigan State Capitol in April 2020 demanding an end to coronavirus lockdown orders, and the F.B.I. foiled a subsequent plot to kidnap Michigan Governor Gretchen Whitmer and bomb the state Capitol.[77]

Thus, before election day on November 3, 2020, Trump was inspiring and nurturing right-wing extremists who were reasonably likely to engage in electoral violence. Then, after Trump lost the election, he continued his instigation, ranting about the stolen election, despite a lack of substantiating evidence. Trump, with the support of legal scholar John Eastman, a former Supreme Court clerk for Clarence Thomas, urged Vice President Mike Pence, in his role as President of the Senate, to declare (falsely) that because seven states had contested slates of electors, Trump had actually won the election. Pence resisted, questioning Eastman's factual and constitutional assertions. The unsurprising result was the siege on the Capitol on January 6, 2021, which temporarily prevented Congress from formally certifying the electoral votes and declaring Biden the next president. And just as white Christian nationalism encompassed diverse smaller movements and organizations, the Capitol riot brought together numerous white supremacist, antisemitic, and anti-government groups. Many of them marked themselves by wearing or carrying symbols of their beliefs. There were the obvious symbols, such as the Confederate battle flag, Nazi swastikas, and a gallows and noose (partly indicating the lynching and terrorization of Black Americans). But there were also more obscure symbols, such as 'Appeal to Heaven' flags, T-shirts with Qs (for conspiracy theorists believing in QAnon), the Roman numeral III (for the anti-government Three Percenters), and even Hawaiian shirts (for the anti-government and radical libertarian Boogaloo Bois).[78]

The Capitol insurrection ultimately resulted in the deaths of five individuals and injuries to dozens of others, including many police officers; after the riot, four more police officers died by suicide. Even in the midst of the chaotic violence, Trump continued to insist the election had been stolen. In a tweeted message, apparently to the rioters themselves, he said: "I know your pain. I know you're hurt. We had an election that was stolen from us. . . . This was a fraudulent election, but we can't play into the hands of these people. We have to have peace. So go home, we love you, you're very special."[79] Then, after Vice President Pence had been escorted from the Senate chamber for his safety—and Trump reportedly knew of Pence's continuing endangerment—Trump nonetheless tweeted a denigration of the Vice President: "Mike Pence didn't have the courage to do what should have been done to protect our Country and our Constitution, giving States a chance to certify a corrected set of facts, not the fraudulent or inaccurate ones which they were asked to previously certify. USA demands the truth!" In short, while Trump occasionally appeared to call for peace during the insurrection, he refused to call off the rioters and even seemed to revel in their violent support.[80]

Trump, it should be emphasized, did not become a pariah in the Republican party because of his denial of the election results or seeming support for the insurrectionists. True, after the riot, some Republicans left the party, and there was talk of the creation of a new moderate-right conservative party. Plus, ten Republicans in the House of Representatives voted to impeach Trump for his role in the riot, and seven Republican Senators voted to convict him after a Senate trial. Regardless, the overwhelming majority of Republicans remained loyal to Trump. Republican Senate Minority Leader Mitch McConnell condemned Trump for being "practically and morally responsible" for the Capitol insurrection yet nonetheless voted to acquit him. Immediately after the riot, 147 Republican Senators and Representatives refused to certify Biden's electoral votes. Then, when the House sought to impeach Trump for "incitement of insurrection," 197 House Republicans voted against impeachment, and 43 Senate Republicans voted against Trump's conviction (despite the Republican opposition, the House impeached Trump, but the Senate failed to reach the two-thirds supermajority required to convict him). Moreover, the few Republicans in the House and Senate who voted either to impeach or convict Trump were met with a swift Republican backlash. State Republican parties issued censures of these members, and several were almost immediately threatened with being challenged in the next primaries.[81]

In sum, the Republican party largely remains loyal to Trump; the party nominated him again in 2024 to run for the presidency—and he would win the election. Most Republicans apparently either affirmatively believe or at least acquiesce in conspiracy theories, which range from Trump's unsupported claim that the Democrats stole the 2020 election to such bizarre views as those of QAnon, which asserts that the Clintons and other Democrats worship Satan, run a child sex-trafficking ring, and eat children. One can no longer reasonably describe these beliefs as limited to the fringe of the Republican party. Rather, to a great degree, this is the Republican party today. Many if not most Republicans now either believe in white Christian supremacy or are "comfortable playing footsie with white [Christian] supremacists."[82] In a recent survey conducted by two political scientists, Rachel M. Blum and Christopher Sebastian Parker, 88 percent of Trump supporters believed that "real Americans are losing [their] freedoms," while more than 90 percent believe that "our lives are controlled by secret plots [and] the American way of life is disappearing." At least 60 percent of the Trump supporters are white, Christian men.[83] Meanwhile, Michael Humphrey, a professor of journalism and media communication, analyzed the corpus of Trump's tweets over several years. Humphrey concluded that Trump had five main, regular themes. "1. The true version of the United States is beset with invaders; 2. Real Americans can see this; 3. I (Trump) am uniquely qualified to stop this invasion; 4. The establishment and its agents are hindering me; 5. The U.S. is in mortal danger because of this." To underscore a crucial point, these themes resonate strongly with white Christian nationalism.[84]

White Christian Nationalism and Republican Conservatism Today

The current Republican party cannot simply be equated with the most extreme thread of white Christian nationalism. Donald Trump is not identical to Louis Beam or Timothy McVeigh. Two key ways in which current Republican ideology departs from extremist white Christian nationalism relate to, first, neoliberalism, and second, a racial and religious caste system. With regard to neoliberalism, Trump rejected some fundamental neoliberal principles. Most importantly, Trump's advocacy for and implementation of tariffs contravened the neoliberal commitment to a global free market. Yet perhaps the only significant legislative achievement of his presidency was an old neoliberal favorite, massive tax cuts primarily benefiting the wealthy—with benefits supposedly trickling down to others (which empirically has never proven true). Moreover, Trump continued and intensified the crucial neoliberal theme of attacking democratic government. Of course, this anti-government theme has also been central to white Christian nationalism. Indeed, Trump's Republican party not only showed disdain for constitutional and democratic norms but also accepted white Christian nationalism's more violent anti-government stance, at least to a degree, as demonstrated by the siege on the Capitol. Trump, in his demand for fealty, had managed to fuse together former supporters of Buchanan—individuals inclined toward white Christian nationalism—and what had been the more mainstream strand of the Republican party—what might be called the "Court Conservatives"—which had been more committed to neoliberalism.[85]

The historian Lisa McGirr underscores that hallmarks of the first Trump presidency—"nativism, extreme polarization, truth-bashing, white nationalism and anti-democratic policies"—are likely to remain central to Republican ideology in the future precisely because "Republicans have been fueling the conditions that enabled Mr. Trump's rise since the 1980s." McGirr points to an underlying irony in the current support for the Republican party: Namely, Republican-championed neoliberal policies economically harmed the white, Christian working class, but Republicans sidestepped responsibility by scapegoating people of color, immigrants, and non-Christians. For decades, Republicans pushed for and implemented neoliberal policies while exploiting "white cultural resentments for political gain." As McGirr concludes: "Trump championed ideas that had been bubbling up among the Republican grass roots since the late 20th century." Consequently, even if Trump were to exit the political scene, for whatever reason, the centrality of white Christian nationalism to the Republican party is unlikely to dissipate in the near future.[86]

With regard to a racial and religious caste system, the most hard-core white Christian nationalists, as discussed, would not have been satisfied with even a legally enforced caste structure reminiscent of the Jim Crow era. They sought a nation purged of people of color, non-Christians, LGBTQ+ individuals, and other marginalized groups.[87] Yet, most Republicans today do not seemingly want to banish or kill all non-white and non-Christian Americans. Rather, they would likely be satisfied with a partly de jure and partly de facto racial and religious caste system, structured to recognize and support both formally and informally white, Christian supremacy and privilege. From this Republican perspective, the presidency of Obama, the apparent successes (for example, professionally and economically) of some non-whites and non-Christians, the Black Lives Matter movement, and the immigration of people of color all seemingly justify white, Christian resentment and grievance. The American system appears to need a course correction to return white Christians (especially white, Christian, heterosexual men) to their rightful hegemonic position.[88]

I do not mean to suggest that white Christian anxiety is nonsensical. As discussed above (in the section on Barack Obama's election), the demographics of the American population have, in fact, shifted. The U.S. Census Bureau has predicted that, by mid-century, the majority of the American people will no longer be white. Moreover, the percentage of white Christian Americans is already slightly less than a majority, while the number of religiously unaffiliated Americans is growing. These demographic shifts have contributed to concrete changes—breakthroughs—in the makeup of at least some government institutions. For instance, the election of Obama, a Black American, as president would have been unimaginable only a few decades earlier. On the Supreme Court, there are currently six Catholics, one Jew, and two Protestants (including Gorsuch, who was raised Catholic but attends an Episcopalian church). Throughout Supreme Court history, the overwhelming majority of justices have been Protestant; 90 of the first 101 justices were Protestant. The first Catholic to sit on the Court was Roger Taney, nominated as Chief Justice in 1836, but the second, Edward Douglass White, was not nominated until 1894. The first Jewish justice was Louis Brandeis, nominated in 1916. For much of the twentieth century, only a single Catholic and a single Jewish justice would be on the Court at any one time. In short, the religious makeup of the Court today is strikingly unprecedented.[89]

Yet, even with these demographic and institutional changes, a "pervasive Christian privilege prevails in the United States today." The structures of white Christian supremacy and privilege, built and reinforced over the centuries, remain strong. The very definition of religion in America, centered around faith and belief, arose from a Protestant Christian perspective. From a religious and cultural standpoint, Christianity determines what is normal as opposed to what is strange, abnormal, or unacceptable. To take one example, if a grade school has a 'Holiday' party, it will be held in December, near Christmas, rather than in September or October, near the Jewish high holy days (Rosh Hashanah and Yom Kippur). While conservative Christians nowadays might occasionally face criticism (for their religious views), Christianity remains the de facto religion of the United States. As Khyati Y. Joshi emphasizes: "White Christians alone can count on consistently seeing themselves reflected in the nation's structures, and enjoying calendars and expectations that coincide with their beliefs and practices."[90]

Christians who are anxious and resentful, then, are largely reacting to their perceptions of threatened privilege. White Christian supremacy and privilege remain intact, even if white, Christian, cultural hegemony is no longer as thorough and complete as it once was. Putting this in different words, demographic and institutional changes have intensified the salience of white Christian identity and fears of decreasing dominance and privilege. "Nothing feels so imbalanced as a level playing field," writes Joshi, "when for as long as you can remember the field has been tilted in your favor. But of course, the playing field is still far from level."[91] Predictably, then, polling shows that attitudes characteristic of white Christian nationalism "can be found within every Christian denomination." Indeed, examples of white Christian resentment and grievance are plentiful.[92] Leading Christian writers assert that the United States was founded to be an evangelical Christian light for the world, but now, Christians are under siege: "Hostile secular nihilism has won the day in our nation's government, and the culture has turned powerfully against traditional Christians."[93] Robert Jeffress, pastor of a Baptist megachurch in Dallas, Texas, and a regular on Fox News—he has been called Donald Trump's "apostle"[94]—broods that "Christians are being outfought, outargued, and outmarketed when it comes to the issue of salvation through Christ alone."[95] In the words of another prominent Christian conservative writer, Rod Dreher, "We faithful orthodox Christians didn't ask for internal exile from a country we thought was our own, but that's where we find ourselves." Americans today are supposedly "living under barbarism." According to Dreher, Christians in the United States now suffer oppression analogous to that formerly experienced by dissidents in the Soviet Union.[96]

Conservative Christians therefore must fight to impose their views while pushing others to accept Christian redemption and "eternal life." Retired evangelical pastor Erwin W. Lutzer explains that Christians should not hesitate to judge and condemn "ungodly lifestyles." He therefore insists that Christians must "speak against the culture" of the LGBTQ+ community.[97] Dreher specifies: "For a Christian, there is only one right way to use the gift of sex: within marriage between one man and one woman." Jeffress reiterates the same point and condemns the Supreme Court for caving "to political correctness" when it decided *Obergefell v. Hodges*, which held that same-sex couples enjoy a constitutional right to marry.[98] Conservative Christians further emphasize that they must defend traditional family roles and adamantly oppose abortion. Perhaps less predictably, they also maintain that Christianity requires defense of capitalism and opposition to critical race theory. If the government prevents Christians from imposing their views on others, the government is not protecting equality. It is expressing animus against Christians—a "profoundly anti-Christian militancy"—because Christians are seeking merely to enforce the "truth."[99]

From this perspective, religious liberty entails the freedom to live a Christian life rather than equal respect for all religions. Lutzer worries about Islam being taught in American schools because, in his view, "[n]o religion in all the world is as repressive as Islam."[100] Jeffress declares that "Islam is a false religion, built on a false book, written by a false prophet."[101] Jews should be "judged," thunders Lutzer, because they "failed" god when "they had the responsibility to be a light to other nations."[102] Consequently, evangelical Christians are obliged to proselytize non-Christians. "[We] ought to pray for Muslims," Jeffress tells his congregation. "We ought to pray and do everything we can to introduce them to faith in Jesus Christ." Unsurprisingly, then, he unflinchingly "[preaches] that Jews, like everyone else, must trust in Christ for salvation." Jews, Hindus, Buddhists, atheists, and others are all on the "highway to hell," Jeffress presses, because they have embraced "lies." Indeed, "[a]ny religion that denies that salvation is exclusively through the Lord Jesus Christ is a false, demonic religion being used by evil forces to lure people away from the true God." And don't forget, Jeffress adds, Jews killed Jesus [author's note: at least that is the story in the Christian Bible]: "[Jesus's claim to be the one and only God] kept the Jewish leaders in a perpetual state of apoplexy and ultimately placed Him on a cross." To be clear, Jeffress proudly and significantly emphasizes that his beliefs are "'squarely within the mainstream of contemporary right-wing Christian thought.'"[103]

Most portentously, perhaps, Christian conservatism no longer harmonizes with democracy. To the contrary, conservative Christians perceive a conflict between democracy and Christianity. According to Dreher, "liberal democracy" is transforming into a type of "totalitarianism." Consequently, "in the years to come," he explains, "faithful Christians may have to choose between being a good American and being a good Christian."[104] Jeffress maintains that "the real Jesus . . . drives a stake through universalism, pluralism, and inclusivism."[105] In its extreme Dominion theological manifestation, Christian conservatism maintains that only devout white Christians can legitimately participate in democratic processes and lead the polity. "In this [Dominion theocratic] way of thinking," Virginia Garrard explains, "there is no room for dissent or difference in opinion. . . . Others are demonized, literally."[106] Thus, in 2019, Pastor Paula White-Cain, who was chair of Trump's evangelical advisory board (during his first presidential term), delivered an invocation at his 2024 reelection campaign Florida kickoff: "Let every demonic network that is aligned itself against the purpose, against the calling of President Trump, let it be broken, let it be torn down in the name of Jesus."[107] As Jeffress unequivocally declares, "faith in Christ is the only way to heaven," while "Satan's purpose . . . is to thwart God's work and destroy His people." When non-Christians and people of color are demonized, there is "fertile ground for the growth of conspiracy theories and absurd, even obscene accusations against 'enemies,' because Satan, always a trickster, can and does readily colonize the human mind and soul." Ultimately, if necessary to restore Christian values and leadership, Christians can act "by any means necessary, including through violence."[108]

Given these views—and I do not question their sincerity—the widespread white Christian support for the Trump-led Republican party is understandable. Motivated by antagonism toward non-Christians, people of color, and the LGBTQ+ community, as well as an intensified sense of white Christian identity, Trumpian Republicans reject any democratic process that denies Trump's and Christian conservatives' supremacy. From the Trumpian viewpoint, non-Christians, people of color, and LGBTQ+ individuals "dilute and pollute what is genuinely American: Whiteness and Christianity."[109] Predictably, then, we get pronouncements such as that of then South Dakota Republican Governor (and current Secretary of Homeland Security) Kristi Noem: "I look at Joe Biden's America, and I don't recognize the country that I grew up in." Likewise, a blogger for the Claremont Institute, a conservative think tank, wrote: "Most people living in the United States today—certainly more than half—are not Americans in any meaningful sense of the term." A 2024 Pew Research Center study reported that, among Trump supporters, 43 percent believe "government policies should support religious values and beliefs," and 36 percent believe the "Bible should have a great deal of influence on the laws of the U.S."[110]

In a significant way, Trump peddled innocence to white Christian nationalists. Under Trump, white Christians—especially white, Christian, heterosexual men—hoped to return to an era when they were privileged without recognizing that race, religion, or gender mattered. Largely for this reason, many Republicans now oppose any realistic discussions of race or gender in America, including the history of slavery or current concerns about diversity, equity, and inclusion (DEI). Of course, as a matter of policy, during Trump's first presidential term, his administration actively sought to propagate white Christian privilege. And even beyond those policy maneuvers, Trump's overt appeals to white Christian supremacy harkened to a time when open and explicit racism and antisemitism were widespread and socially acceptable.[111] Ultimately, consistent with the American tradition of vigilantism, Trump supported violence if it was necessary to save America for white Christian nationalists. Unsurprisingly, a 2021 poll showed that 55 percent of Republican voters believed that "the traditional American way of life is disappearing so fast we may have to use force to save it,"[112] while another poll showed that more than half of Trump voters characterized the January 6 insurrection as an act of "patriotism."[113]

If there was any remaining doubt about Trump's connection to white Christian nationalism, he erased it during the 2024 presidential campaign when, mere days before Easter, he endorsed the "God Bless the USA Bible." Trump will receive royalties from sales of this version of the King James (Christian) Bible, priced at $59.99. Besides the King James Bible, the volume contains the chorus of a country-western song, as well as "copies of the Constitution, the Bill of Rights, the Declaration of Independence and the Pledge of Allegiance."[114] Trump unequivocally intertwined the nation with Christianity. "'That's why our country is going haywire: We've lost religion in our country,'" he said. "'All Americans need a Bible in their home and I have many. It's my favorite book.'" He then emphasized that Christians are "'under siege'" and that "'we have to protect anything that is pro-God.'"[115]

* * *

While gradations of white Christian nationalism exist, the thrust of the political movement is to affirm that white, Christian, heterosexual men are the only true Americans. They are We the People. From this perspective, non-Christians, people of color, LGBTQ+ individuals, and women are lesser Americans. They do not fully belong to We the People. For what it's worth, members of these particular societal groups— for instance, women, Jewish Americans, or Black Americans—can themselves support the white, Christian, nationalist, political movement so long as they accept the subordinate position of their group members in general. Regardless, the overarching goal of the broad white, Christian, nationalist movement is to return the United States to its ostensible roots as an exclusive, inegalitarian, and hierarchical democracy. The next part of the book focuses on the Roberts Court and its support for the white, Christian, nationalist, political agenda. The next chapter, in particular, explores how the Roberts Court has demonstrated disdain for a more inclusive, egalitarian, and participatory (pluralist) democracy.

PART II

The Roberts Court: Who Belongs?

6

The Roberts Court's Disdain for Pluralist Democracy

The New Deal manifested one of the rare sustained periods in American history when the forces of an inclusive and egalitarian democracy overcame the forces of exclusion and hierarchy, at least in part. Starting in 1937, the Supreme Court began exploring the contours of pluralist democracy, and then the Warren Court further developed and elaborated pluralist democracy. Meanwhile, conservatives pushed back in various ways against pluralist democracy and the changes that followed the 1937 Supreme Court transition. Regardless of those varied conservative reactions, the Roberts Court today—the most conservative Court since World War II—must be understood within the context of current conservative politics. What conservatives might have desired in 1950, 1970, or 1990 is not necessarily the same as that sought in 2024, particularly in relation to Supreme Court decision-making.

Even so, the Roberts Court has directly followed the Rehnquist Court in undoing one aspect of the 1937 transition. The Court during the *Lochner* era, influenced by laissez-faire ideology, had judicially imposed formalist constraints on Congress. With the 1937 transition, the Court rejected judicial formalism and began deferring to Congress. In cases involving the scope of Congress's commerce power—when Congress had enacted economic and social welfare laws—the Court applied a rational basis test that focused on empirical reality rather than a priori (judicial) categories. In practice, then, congressional reach increased or decreased in accordance with the political desires of the people as expressed through the democratic process. From the late 1930s onward, for nearly six decades, congressional power was checked at the ballot box, not at the courthouse.[1]

In the late twentieth and early twenty-first centuries, the Rehnquist and Roberts Courts adopted stances wary of and even hostile to pluralist democratic government (while protecting wealth and the economic marketplace)—stances harmonious with the anti-democracy ideologies of neoliberalism and white Christian nationalism. The conservative justices implemented their anti-democracy views partly by becoming more formalist in congressional power cases (similar to the *Lochner*-era Court's use of formalism to implement laissez-faire ideology). The Rehnquist Court began its formalist turn after Clarence Thomas replaced Thurgood Marshall.[2] In *United States v. Lopez*, decided in 1995, the Court held that Congress had exceeded its commerce power when it enacted the Gun-Free School Zones Act, which proscribed the possession of firearms at school. Chief Justice William Rehnquist wrote the majority opinion for the conservative bloc of five justices (Scalia, Thomas, Kennedy, and O'Connor joined Rehnquist's opinion). He reasoned that Congress can regulate "three broad categories of activity": the channels of interstate commerce, the instrumentalities of interstate commerce, and activities substantially affecting interstate commerce. Up to this point, Rehnquist's doctrinal approach was not novel, but when he focused on the final category, substantial effects, he added a formalist twist. Distinguishing between economic and non-economic activities, Rehnquist maintained that gun possession at schools is a non-economic enterprise that "has nothing to do with 'commerce.'"[3] Next, distinguishing between national and local concerns, Rehnquist reasoned that gun possession at schools is a local matter. His terminology, dividing "what is truly national and what is truly local," resembled *Lochner*-era formalist language separating "a purely federal matter" from "a matter purely local in its character." By parsing congressional power pursuant to these formalist categories, the Court concluded that Congress had exceeded its commerce power.[4]

The Roberts Court followed *Lopez* and extended its formalist reasoning in *National Federation of Independent Business v. Sebelius*, which invalidated part of the Affordable Care Act (ACA), the flagship progressive enactment of President Obama's administration. The ACA's individual mandate required most Americans to maintain "minimum essential" health insurance coverage. Individuals failing to comply with the mandate were required to pay a "penalty" to the Internal Revenue Service.[5] When determining whether Congress had exceeded its commerce power in enacting the individual mandate, Roberts's opinion applied the *Lopez* doctrine while also articulating and applying two new formalist categories. First, distinguishing action from inaction, Roberts reasoned that Congress can regulate activity but not inactivity pursuant to the Commerce Clause. The individual mandate forced individuals to buy health insurance even when they did not want to do so. Congress had therefore overstepped its commerce power, Roberts concluded, because the mandate compelled inactive individuals to enter or become active in the health insurance market. Second, distinguishing regulation from creation, Roberts reasoned that Congress can regulate but not create commerce. With the individual mandate, Roberts maintained, Congress exceeded its power by attempting to create commercial activity where none previously existed. Roberts's use of formalist categories facilitated a conservative disregard for the economic realities of the health insurance marketplace while strengthening the *Lopez* limitations on Congress. The other conservative justices agreed with Roberts's formalist limitations on Congress's commerce power, though they did not join his opinion.[6]

The Roberts Court in *Sebelius* went even further beyond the Rehnquist Court's conservatism by also narrowing Congress's spending power, again with new formalist limits. Congress had invoked its spending power when enacting another ACA provision, the Medicaid expansion, which encouraged states to expand the scope of Medicaid (extending coverage to more individuals) by providing additional funds. After the 1937 transition, the Court had broadly interpreted the Spending Clause (as it had the Commerce Clause) by generally deferring to Congress; limitations on the spending power arose from the democratic process, rather than by judicial imposition. Pursuant to this broad spending power, Congress could attach conditions to grants or subsidies that it offered to state and local governments. For example, Congress could require state governments to set the drinking age at 21 as a condition for receiving federal highway funds.[7]

Under the ACA Medicaid expansion, Congress conditioned a state's continued receipt of Medicaid funding on the respective state's acceptance of the expansion; if a state rejected the expansion, it would lose all of its Medicaid funding. Roberts and the other conservative justices held that this Medicaid expansion exceeded the scope of Congress's spending power. Roberts's opinion acknowledged that, since 1937, the Court had not invalidated exercises of Congress's spending power, but he nonetheless reasoned that the spending power must be subject to judicial limits. What are those limits? Roberts again invoked formalist categories, distinguishing congressional "encouragement" from congressional "coercion." In other words, Congress can provide financial incentives that encourage or pressure states to take certain actions, but Congress cannot coerce or compel state government actions. At some point, according to Roberts, congressional incentives cross the line from encouragement to compulsion.[8]

In considering the ACA Medicaid expansion, Roberts concluded that Congress had crossed that line. He reasoned that a state's potential loss of all federal Medicaid funding was so severe as to preclude any real choice; in Roberts's words, it was like "a gun to the head." States could not truly choose whether to accept the Medicaid expansion because they lacked any reasonable alternatives. And again, the other conservative justices agreed with Roberts's formalist limitation on Congress's spending power, though they did not join his opinion. Consequently, the Roberts Court in *Sebelius* constrained both Congress's commerce and spending powers by imposing formalist limits that harkened back to the *Lochner* era.[9]

* * *

In another case (and in another way), the Roberts Court followed the Rehnquist Court in undermining congressional power and pluralist democratic government, though the Roberts Court again went beyond the Rehnquist Court. In *Lopez*, Rehnquist acknowledged that the Court, after 1937, had not required Congress to deliberate or "to make formal findings" when enacting legislation. "But," Rehnquist wrote, "to the extent that congressional findings would enable us to evaluate the legislative judgment that the activity in question substantially affected interstate commerce, even though no such substantial effect was visible to the naked eye, they are lacking here." In other words, the *Lopez* Court displayed a neoliberal (conservative) skepticism toward legislative and democratic decision-making. If Congress deliberated and made detailed and relevant findings, the Court seemed to suggest, then Congress would be less likely to pass a law that might produce irrational or unforeseen detrimental consequences. Even so, the *Lopez* Court did not ultimately appear to ground its decision on a lack of congressional evidence or findings.[10]

The Roberts Court would take that step, however, in a crucial voting rights case. In *Shelby County v. Holder*, a five-to-four decision, the Court invalidated a provision of the Voting Rights Act (VRA) passed pursuant to Congress's power under the Fifteenth Amendment. The coverage provision of the VRA specified which jurisdictions needed special government approval or preclearance before they could change their voting laws. The Court, in an opinion by Roberts, acknowledged that the coverage provision was sensible in 1965, when Congress first enacted the statute. Congress, though, had reauthorized the VRA several times over the years—the most recent reauthorization came in 2006—and the Court concluded that the coverage provision did not fit the nation's current circumstances. "Coverage today is based on decades-old data and eradicated practices." The Court, in other words, grounded its decision on Congress's purported failure to make adequate findings.[11]

Justice Ruth Bader Ginsburg's *Shelby County* dissent, however, pointed to extensive and detailed congressional findings. "Congress determined, based on a voluminous record, that the scourge of [voting] discrimination was not yet extirpated," Ginsburg explained. "With overwhelming support in both Houses, Congress concluded that, for two prime reasons, [the VRA] should continue in force, unabated. First, continuance would facilitate completion of the impressive gains thus far made; and second, continuance would guard against backsliding. Those assessments were well within Congress's province to make and should elicit this Court's unstinting approbation." If anything, Ginsburg's dissent underscored the conservative majority's disdain for Congress and its democratic processes. The Court did not merely ask Congress to make more specific findings. Rather, the Court demanded that Congress make different findings.[12] To be sure, the conservative justices might not have been satisfied by any congressional findings, given that the justices apparently did not approve of the substance of Congress's action supporting an inclusive and egalitarian democratic process. And in fact, as Ginsburg feared, the Court's invalidation of the preclearance provision prompted an outburst of discriminatory attacks on the democratic process. In recent years, more than 31 states have enacted laws restricting suffrage. For instance, a Texas voter identification law denies suffrage to individuals showing student photo IDs (while allowing individuals with concealed-gun permits to vote). Texas alone has more unregistered voters than the populations of 20 states; the overwhelming majority of the unregistered Texas voters are people of color.[13]

* * *

The Roberts Court has continued in subsequent cases to disdain pluralist democratic institutions while protecting the economic marketplace. Besides invalidating congressional actions under the Commerce Clause, the Spending Clause, and the Reconstruction Amendments,[14] the Court has narrowly interpreted congressional statutes,[15] persistently restricted executive and administrative agency actions,[16] allowed corporations and the wealthy to unduly influence political campaigns,[17] refused to restrict extreme political gerrymandering,[18] and rendered racial gerrymandering practically impossible to prove unconstitutional (in a case to be discussed in chapter 9).[19] Moreover, the Court has invalidated numerous state laws, so the conservative justices' hostility to democratic decision-making is not limited to the federal level.[20] In this context, the Court has perhaps made itself the most powerful government institution, as it has restricted other government actors while aggrandizing its own power.

The Roberts Court's simultaneous disdain for pluralist democracy and solicitude for wealth and the economic marketplace were nowhere clearer than in the landmark campaign finance case, *Citizens United v. Federal Election Commission*, decided in 2010. In a five-to-four decision, the conservative bloc invalidated provisions of the Bipartisan Campaign Reform Act of 2002 (BCRA) that imposed limits on corporate spending for political campaign advertisements.[21] The Court's majority opinion, written by Justice Kennedy, began by articulating two First Amendment premises. First, reiterating a 1976 decision, Kennedy stated that spending on political campaigns constitutes speech.[22] Second, reiterating a 1978 decision, the Court stated that free speech protections extend to corporations.[23] With those premises in hand, Kennedy moved to a pillar of his reasoning, the self-governance rationale, which links the strong constitutional protection of expression to democratic government. According to this theory, free expression is necessary to allow diverse groups and individuals to contribute their views in the pluralist democratic arena. If government officials interfere with the pluralist process, if they dictate or control public debates, then they skew the democratic outcomes and undermine the consent of the governed. As explained by the *Citizens United* Court, "Speech is an essential mechanism of democracy. . . . The right of citizens to inquire, to hear, to speak, and to use information to reach consensus is a precondition to enlightened self-government and a necessary means to protect it." Free expression (especially political speech and writing)—including corporate campaign spending—must be absolutely protected because democracy cannot exist without it.[24]

The Roberts Court, that is, again used a formalist approach to facilitate a conservative conclusion: *Citizens United* maintained that the First Amendment must be enforced as a formal and rigid rule regardless of context or effects. Kennedy thus explained the limitation on corporate campaign expenditures in the most alarming terms: "The censorship we now confront is vast in its reach." Because restrictions on corporate political expression destroy "'liberty,'" the government must satisfy strict scrutiny, proving that the regulation is necessary (or narrowly tailored) to achieve a compelling purpose.[25] Nevertheless, when Congress enacted the BCRA, it compiled and relied on findings showing that corporate campaign spending corrupted democracy. Bolstering the congressional findings, social science research showed that excessive political spending, whether corporate or otherwise, can corrupt or distort democracy. The Court brushed aside this empirical evidence by narrowing the definition of corruption so dramatically that anything short of a bribe or the appearance of a bribe would be permissible.[26] Finally, the Court bolstered its formalist protection of corporate spending, as political expression, by invoking the constitutional framers and original meaning. After quoting from James Madison and *Federalist, Number 10*, Kennedy concluded that "[t]here is simply no support for the view that the First Amendment, as originally understood, would permit the suppression of political speech by media corporations."[27]

The Court's constitutional protection of corporate campaign spending harmonized closely with neoliberalism. While the *Citizens United* opinion emphasized the self-governance rationale and the democratic process, other Roberts Court decisions, including *Lopez* and *Shelby County*, reveal that the conservative justices are wary of and even hostile to democratic government. But the Court is committed to protecting private-sphere economic power and the extension of that power into the public sphere. From that perspective, the *Citizens United* decision seemed totally predictable, as were the political consequences of the decision. The amount of money flowing into political campaigns exploded. In an era of exorbitant income and wealth inequality, the unfettered ability of corporations and wealthy individuals to influence elections and government contributed to citizen doubts about the operation of democracy.[28]

The Roberts Court in subsequent campaign finance cases nonetheless continued using formalist reasoning to protect economic power in the public sphere. *Arizona Free Enterprise Club's Freedom Club PAC v. Bennett* arose when the state of Arizona created a campaign-finance "matching funds scheme": A candidate for state office who accepted public financing would receive additional funds if a privately financed opponent spent more than the publicly financed candidate's initial allocation. Publicly and privately financed candidates therefore could spend roughly the same amounts on their respective campaigns. In a five-to-four decision, the conservative bloc held that this campaign finance scheme violated the First Amendment. The Court reasoned that the flexible public financing system imposed a "penalty" by diminishing the privately financed candidate's expression. In dissent, Justice Kagan argued that the financing scheme was the opposite of a penalty if viewed in context. The public financing, she wrote, "subsidizes and so produces *more* political speech." But the conservative majority applied a formal rule and disregarded context: Any regulation of campaign financing constituted an unconstitutional burden on free speech. "[E]ven if the matching funds provision did result in more speech by publicly financed candidates and more speech in general, it would do so at the expense of impermissibly burdening (and thus reducing) the speech of privately financed candidates and independent expenditure groups." The Court's formalist approach to free speech mandated that an individual be allowed to translate private-sphere wealth into political power. The First Amendment, as interpreted by the Court, prohibited the government from attempting to correct for that economic skewing of political power—for instance, by providing equal funding to the less wealthy.[29]

The following year, 2012, the Roberts Court again protected the prerogatives of wealth at the expense of pluralist democracy. *American Tradition Partnership, Inc. v. Bullock* held unconstitutional a Montana statute providing that a "corporation may not make . . . an expenditure in connection with a candidate or a political committee that supports or opposes a candidate or a political party." The Montana Supreme Court had upheld this statute in the face of a First Amendment challenge because of a specific history of corporate-engineered corruption in the Montana democratic process. Regardless, with another five-to-four vote, the U.S. Supreme Court's conservative bloc found a free speech violation. Reasoning that "[t]here can be no serious doubt" that *Citizens United* controlled, the Court prevented the state from demonstrating that its factual situation uniquely needed regulation.[30] *Citizens United*, it seemed, had created an iron clad rule prohibiting campaign finance restrictions regardless of context or effects.[31]

* * *

The later Roberts Court (after Barrett joined), while showing no signs of deviating from these goals—undermining and denigrating pluralist democracy while favoring wealth and the marketplace—has nonetheless focused more sharply on protecting and empowering white, Christian, heterosexual men.[32] Contrary to the recommendations of conservative scholars such as Robert Bork, Alexander Bickel, and Walter Berns (discussed in chapter 4), the conservative justices apparently do not intend to return to the constitutional principles typically invoked in individual rights cases before the 1937 constitutional transformation. Indeed, the justices often invoke principles and rights recognized and strengthened during the post-1937 era—rights to free speech, religious freedom, and equal protection—but they are reinterpreting those principles and rights largely to protect and empower a narrow segment of the American people, namely white, Christian, heterosexual men. The Court's individual rights cases, then, go hand-in-hand with their decisions more directly undermining pluralist democratic government, such as those narrowly construing congressional power.[33] Ultimately, the Court is acting in service of minority rule, returning the nation to an exclusive, hierarchical, and inegalitarian democracy. The current conservative justices want to return to a pre-1937 version of the Constitution, but to them, that Constitution embodies the political and cultural privileging of white, Christian, heterosexual men. People of color, non-Christians, women, and LGBTQ+ individuals are, in a sense, lesser Americans. The next chapter begins the discussion of individual rights cases by focusing on religious freedom.

7

Religious Freedom at the Early Roberts Court

The Roberts Court's decisions and opinions that most clearly manifest aspects of white Christian nationalism involve religious freedom,
encompassing both the Establishment and Free Exercise Clauses. While
the Rehnquist Court's conservative doctrinal alternatives to the *Lemon*
test in Establishment Clause cases and the *Smith* free exercise decision
seemed harmonious with the judicial conservatism of 1990, conservative politics would change, as discussed in chapter 4. By the time the
Roberts Court was on the scene—given the demographic changes in
the American population and the growing politics of grievance among
white Christians—the idea of judicial restraint struck a bell of alarm.
With conservatives worried that white Christians are being discriminated against and persecuted—and with a conservative bloc of justices
controlling the Supreme Court—conservative Christians wanted stronger judicial protection of religious freedom, particularly for Christians,
whether under the Free Exercise or the Establishment Clause.[1] From
this perspective, if conservative Christians are to fulfill their religious
duty to push others to redemption, then they must be allowed to press
their beliefs and practices on others, especially non-Christians. Courts,
then, must interpret religious freedom in accord with America's roots as
a de facto Christian nation. Non-Christians can be tolerated, but only
insofar as they accept that the nation is de facto Christian—and they
might need frequent reminders on that point.[2]

Establishment Clause

The Roberts Court strongly signaled that it was changing direction in 2014 when it decided *Town of Greece v. Galloway*.[3] The town
in 1999 began inviting clergy to deliver prayers at the start of town
board meetings. In a five-to-four decision, with the then-standard
conservative-progressive divide, the Court upheld this practice under

the Establishment Clause. Justice Kennedy's majority opinion was significant in three ways. First, the opinion did not even mention the *Lemon* test. Given that the conservative justices had long been wary of *Lemon*—and the Court had previously applied *Lemon* (or aspects of it) to prohibit nondenominational prayers in public schools,[4] moments of silence in the public schools,[5] and the posting of the Ten Commandments in county buildings[6]—the failure to mention *Lemon* was portentous. Moreover, the majority opinion did not invoke either of the alternative multi-pronged doctrinal tests: the endorsement and coercion tests.

Second, and related to the first point, the majority opinion relied on tradition to justify the opening of the town board meetings with prayers. Citing *Marsh v. Chambers* as precedent (discussed in chapter 4), the Court emphasized that tradition does not create an exception to the usual coverage of the Establishment Clause. Rather, tradition determines the scope of the anti-establishment principle. The majority opinion's reliance on tradition is underscored when one realizes that Kennedy, in fact, also discussed the coercion test—yet two of the conservative justices, Scalia and Thomas, refused to join that portion of Kennedy's opinion, though conservatives had previously favored that doctrinal test. In other words, when Kennedy relied on tradition, his opinion was majority, but when he applied the coercion test, he wrote for a plurality of only three, including himself. Scalia and Thomas appeared to be expressing a strong preference for determining the scope of the Establishment Clause in accord with tradition.[7]

Third, in relying on tradition, the majority opinion did not temper its invocation of an American religious history defined by de facto Christianity. The Court emphasized that the prayers did not need to be nonsectarian (or nondenominational). Indeed, in the town of Greece, clergy had sometimes opened the town board meetings with overtly Christian prayers, referring to the "death, resurrection, and ascension of the Savior Jesus Christ," the "saving sacrifice of Jesus Christ on the cross," and "the plan of redemption that is fulfilled in Jesus Christ."[8] The Court added that the demographic religious transformation of the nation—as it went from being overwhelmingly Protestant at the time of the constitutional framing to being religiously diverse—neither changed American tradition nor the meaning of the Establishment Clause. "The decidedly

Christian nature of these prayers must not be dismissed as the relic of a time when our Nation was less pluralistic than it is today." Alito wrote a concurrence underscoring this point. The fact that overtly Christian prayers might offend some non-Christians was irrelevant: "Not only is there no historical support for the proposition that only generic prayer is allowed, but as our country has become more diverse, composing a prayer that is acceptable to all members of the community who hold religious beliefs has become harder and harder."[9] Given the Court's invocation of the nation's de facto Christian history, the actual tradition in the town of Greece—before 1999, prayers were not offered at town board meetings—was rendered irrelevant.

American Legion v. American Humanist Association, decided in 2019, solidified the Court's conservative turn to tradition and repudiation of Lemon. American Legion involved a challenge to the constitutionality of a 32-foot Christian cross displayed on a traffic island (public land) in a busy intersection of Bladensburg, Maryland. The cross purportedly honored the community's fallen soldiers from World War I. Tellingly, the Fourth Circuit Court of Appeals had applied the Lemon test and held the Bladensburg Cross to be unconstitutional. The Supreme Court reversed, with Justice Alito writing the opinion for the Court, though parts of his opinion were plurality. Alito explicitly criticized the Lemon test, running through a litany of its "shortcomings." He wrote: "[The Lemon test] could not 'explain the Establishment Clause's tolerance, for example, of the prayers that open legislative meetings, . . . certain references to, and invocations of, the Deity in the public words of public officials; the public references to God on coins, decrees, and buildings; or the attention paid to the religious objectives of certain holidays, including Thanksgiving.' The test has been harshly criticized by Members of this Court, lamented by lower court judges, and questioned by a diverse roster of scholars."[10]

After rejecting Lemon, Alito's opinion emphasized the importance of tradition, reasoning that the Court should view the Bladensburg Cross in its "historical context." Considering the cross and its meaning in that context, Alito concluded that its public display did not violate the Establishment Clause. In a striking statement of that conclusion, Alito wrote: "The Religion Clauses of the Constitution aim to foster a society in which people of all beliefs can live together harmoniously, and the presence of the Bladensburg Cross on the land where it has stood for so many years is fully consistent with that aim." The implication appears to be that all individuals are welcome to live "together harmoniously," so long they accept de facto Christianity, symbolized in this instance by the government display of a 32-foot Christian cross.[11] Justice Ginsburg's dissent put the lie to Alito's conclusion—that members of all religions should genially live together while gazing at a giant Christian cross. Ginsburg made a simple point: A public display of a cross does not honor those fallen soldiers who observed non-Christian religions or no religion at all. Without suggesting that all non-Christians or all Christians shared identical views, Ginsburg wrote: "Just as a Star of David is not suitable to honor Christians who died serving their country," Ginsburg explained, "so a cross is not suitable to honor those of other faiths who died defending their nation. Soldiers of all faiths 'are united by their love of country, but they are not united by the cross.'"[12] To Alito, however, love of country apparently equated with love of the Christian cross, and vice versa.

The significance of the *American Legion* decision is clarified when Alito's opinion is viewed in conjunction with the concurrences. Two progressive justices, Breyer and Kagan, joined Alito's opinion in full and part, respectively. They both wrote concurrences, however, which accentuated their concerns that history and tradition should not become the touchstone for an Establishment Clause analysis. Breyer explicitly wrote: "Nor do I understand the Court's opinion today to adopt a 'history and tradition test.'"[13] But the conservative justices' concurrences expressed the exact opposite sentiment. In fact, two of the conservatives, Thomas and Gorsuch, concurred in the judgment only, refusing to join Alito's opinion because they viewed it as insufficiently clear in its repudiation of *Lemon* and turn to tradition. After Thomas reiterated his previously articulated argument that the Establishment Clause should not apply at all against state and local governments, he explained that, even if the Establishment Clause applied, the Bladensburg Cross should be constitutional based on history and tradition: "'[An] insistence on nonsectarian' religious speech is inconsistent with our Nation's history and traditions." And of course, Thomas repudiated *Lemon* as a "long-discredited test."[14] Gorsuch, also repudiating *Lemon*, explained that lower courts had mistakenly granted standing to offended observers bringing Establishment Clause claims because of the *Lemon* "misadventure." He then emphasized that the Bladensburg Cross was undoubtedly constitutional "in light of the nation's traditions." The correct judicial approach was to "apply *Town of Greece*, not *Lemon*." Likewise, Kavanaugh, who joined Alito's opinion in full, wrote a concurrence that repudiated *Lemon* and emphasized history and tradition.[15]

The conservative bloc's turn to tradition in Establishment Clause cases marks the justices' acceptance of the nonpreferentialist position (discussed in chapter 4) within a de facto Christian society. In other words, based on American history and tradition, the government can recognize and favor religion over nonreligion. And even beyond that—again, because of the nation's history of de facto Christianity—the government's recognition and favoring of religion can be manifested in explicitly Christian terms, including Christian prayers to open legislative sessions (and town board meetings) and public displays of giant Christian crosses. Given the conservative bloc's approach, the Court's decisions in other cases that resonate with Establishment Clause issues have been unsurprising.[16] For example, in two taxpayer standing cases, the Roberts Court found that the taxpayers lacked standing to challenge government practices favoring Christianity. The Court has long used the standing doctrine to preclude taxpayers from suing the government because they did not like government policies or expenditures.[17] In *Flast v. Cohen*, however, the Warren Court in 1968 created an exception to this taxpayer-standing barrier for cases raising Establishment Clause issues, such as a challenge to government subsidies for religious schools.[18] The Roberts Court confronted the *Flast* exception first in 2007 and then in 2011.

Hein v. Freedom From Religion Foundation, Inc., arose as an Establishment Clause challenge to President George W. Bush's "Faith-Based and Community Initiatives program," created pursuant to executive order. The program was supposed to provide government funds to faith-based institutions, including churches, synagogues, and mosques, to help provide for social services. The lower court granted taxpayer standing under *Flast*, but the Supreme Court reversed in a five-to-four decision, with the typical conservative-progressive split. Alito, writing another plurality opinion, distinguished *Flast* from *Hein*. *Flast* involved expenditures made pursuant to a congressionally enacted statute, while *Hein* involved general executive expenditures. Scalia, joined by Thomas, concurred in the judgment, arguing that Alito did not go far enough: *Flast*, Scalia maintained, should be overruled. The dissenters argued that Alito's distinction between funding under a statute and funding pursuant to executive action was nonsensical under Establishment Clause principles.[19] Regardless, the Court reasoned similarly in *Arizona Christian School Tuition Organization v. Winn*, another five-to-four decision rejecting taxpayer standing under the Establishment Clause. State law granted a tax credit to taxpayers who contributed money to school tuition organizations (STOs), which then provided scholarships to students attending private schools, most of which were religious. The Court denied standing, again (tenuously) distinguishing *Flast*: *Flast* involved government expenditures, while *Winn* involved tax credits, which individual taxpayers triggered by choosing to contribute to STOs.[20]

The consequences of these two taxpayer standing cases, *Hein* and *Winn*, were clear: Government funding of Christianity will be insulated from judicial scrutiny.[21] After all, in the United States, any government program or policy that provides subsidies, funding, tax credits, or other financial support for either specifically religious institutions or private schools in general will inevitably channel most of the money to Christians.[22] As Kagan's *Winn* dissent put it, these cases will "result [in] the effective demise of taxpayer standing [which] will diminish the Establishment Clause's force and meaning."[23] In fact, even if the Roberts Court had granted standing in *Winn*, the Court's Establishment Clause jurisprudence would have undoubtedly led to a decision upholding Arizona's tax credit program. In *Espinoza v. Montana Department of Revenue*, which also involved tax credits, the Court focused on the Free Exercise Clause while brushing past an Establishment Clause claim (the free exercise claim will be discussed in the next section). Roberts's majority opinion reasoned "that the Establishment Clause is not offended when religious observers and organizations benefit from neutral government programs." According to Roberts, the First Amendment allows government funding to be channeled to religious institutions, including schools, so long as individuals are "independently choosing" to give their patronage (and hence, the government funding) to the religious institutions.[24]

* * *

Scalia once lamented the persistent vitality of *Lemon*: "Like some ghoul in a late-night horror movie that repeatedly sits up in its grave and shuffles abroad, after being repeatedly killed and buried, *Lemon* stalks our Establishment Clause jurisprudence. . . ."[25] Well, Scalia can now rest assured: The conservative justices have killed *Lemon*, once and for all. In its stead, the Court has adopted an approach protecting an American tradition of de facto Christianity. Opposition to manifestations of that tradition will be met with ominous expressions of Christian resentment. In *American Legion*, the Bladensburg Cross case, Alito warned: "[T]earing down monuments with religious symbolism and scrubbing away any reference to the divine will strike many as aggressively hostile to religion."[26] So far, such expressions of Christian grievance have been rare in Establishment Clause cases, but they have been made frequently in recent free exercise cases.

Free Exercise Clause

The Roberts Court has not explicitly overruled *Employment Division, Department of Human Resources v. Smith*, which emphasized judicial restraint, deferred to democracy, and led to the application of a rational basis test in most free exercise cases. The Court nonetheless has effectively undermined *Smith*, repudiating most of its doctrinal significance. First, the Court has held that the Free Exercise Clause requires a ministerial exception to laws of general applicability. *Hosanna-Tabor Evangelical Lutheran Church & School v. Equal Employment Opportunity Commission*, decided in 2012, arose when an evangelical church and school fired Cheryl Perich, a teacher who was also commissioned as a minister. Perich had been unable to perform her duties because she had been suffering from narcolepsy. She claimed that her termination violated the Americans with Disabilities Act (ADA), which prohibits employment discrimination based on a disability. As the Court acknowledged, the ADA "is a valid and neutral law of general applicability," so *Smith* would seem, in effect, to preclude the judicial granting of a free exercise exemption. But the *Hosanna-Tabor* Court distinguished *Smith*: *Smith* involved government regulation of conduct—"outward physical acts"—while *Hosanna-Tabor* involved "an internal church decision that affects the faith and mission of the church itself." The Free Exercise Clause, the

Court reasoned, prohibits the government from interfering with "the internal governance of [a] church." If the government tries to dictate to a church who will be hired (or fired) as a minister, then the government violates the First Amendment, "which protects a religious group's right to shape its own faith and mission through its appointments." In short, the First Amendment mandates the judicial recognition of a ministerial exception from laws of general applicability.[27]

The Court expanded this ministerial exception in *Our Lady of Guadalupe School v. Morrissey-Berru*, decided in 2020. In that case, the Court considered two instances in which private Catholic schools fired elementary school "lay teachers" in violation of anti-discrimination statutes.[28] One teacher had breast cancer and was protected under the ADA. The other teacher, fired because of her age, was protected under the Age Discrimination in Employment Act (ADEA). Although the *Hosanna-Tabor* Court had emphasized that Perich, the fired teacher, had also been a minister, Alito's majority opinion in *Morrissey-Berru* expanded the ministerial exception to include all teachers at private religious schools—which, as mentioned earlier, are predominantly Christian. Alito emphasized that the purpose of religious schools was to educate students consistently with the particular religion and that, therefore, government interference with employment decisions would contravene religious freedom.[29] Yet, as Sotomayor pointed out in dissent, these "teachers taught primarily secular subjects, lacked substantial religious titles and training, and were not even required to be Catholic." Thus, *Morrissey-Berru* has enormous consequences: Teachers (and presumably other employees) at religious schools can "be fired for any reason, whether religious or nonreligious, benign or bigoted, without legal recourse."[30]

While *Hosanna-Tabor* and *Morrissey-Berru* allow "religious entities to discriminate widely and with impunity for reasons wholly divorced from religious beliefs,"[31] a second line of Roberts Court cases now protects Christians and Christian institutions from even a whiff of discrimination. These cases focused mostly on the first *Smith* exception, cases where the government purposefully discriminates against religion (the *Smith* exceptions are discussed in chapter 4). Although the Rehnquist Court had relied on this exception only once, in *Lukumi* (also discussed in chapter 4), the Roberts Court has found the government discriminating against religion so frequently that the exception has, in effect, swallowed the *Smith* rational basis test (at least for Christians). The first such case was *Trinity Lutheran Church of Columbia, Inc. v. Comer*, decided in 2017. Pursuant to a Missouri state program, Trinity Lutheran Church applied for funding to resurface a preschool and daycare playground. The state policy was to deny all applications from religious entities because of an anti-establishment provision in the Missouri constitution, and consequently, the state denied the Trinity Lutheran application. The Court, with an opinion by Roberts, held that the state's policy and denial of funding to Trinity Lutheran violated the Free Exercise Clause. Roberts acknowledged *Smith*, but immediately emphasized the purposeful-discrimination exception and *Lukumi*. Roberts then determined that the state was purposefully penalizing religion, which triggered the Court's application of strict scrutiny. Finding that the state's anti-establishment principle did not amount to a compelling purpose—an "interest 'of the highest order'"—the Court concluded that the state failed the strict scrutiny test and therefore violated free exercise.[32]

In *Trinity Lutheran*, the state policy explicitly discriminated against religious entities—albeit in an effort to remain consistent with anti-establishment principles under the state constitution. One year later, however, the Court confronted a state anti-discrimination law of general applicability. The Colorado Civil Rights Commission had concluded that a baker, Jack Phillips, violated the Colorado Anti-Discrimination Act (CADA), a statute prohibiting discrimination based on sexual orientation. Phillips, "a devout Christian"—his religious beliefs were seemingly sincere—had refused to bake a cake for a same-sex couple's wedding reception because he opposed such marriages on religious grounds. Consequently, he argued that the Commission had violated his right to the free exercise of religion. The Court, in *Masterpiece Cakeshop, Ltd. v. Colorado Civil Rights Commission*, agreed with Phillips and held that the Commission had violated the First Amendment.[33]

From one angle, *Masterpiece Cakeshop* appeared to be a standard free exercise exemption case. Since CADA was a law of general applicability, Phillips would be entitled to an exemption—allowing him to discriminate in contravention of CADA—only if the state could not satisfy the deferential rational basis test, as mandated by *Smith*. Yet, the *Masterpiece Cakeshop* Court dug down into the Commission's proceedings and uncovered ostensible hostility toward Phillips's religion. According to Justice Kennedy, who wrote the majority opinion, the most important evidence of hostility was a statement by one commissioner made during a Commission meeting. The commissioner said: "I would also like to reiterate what we said in the hearing or the last meeting. Freedom of religion and religion has been used to justify all kinds of discrimination throughout history, whether it be slavery, whether it be the holocaust, whether it be—I mean, we—we can list hundreds of situations where freedom of religion has been used to justify discrimination. And to me it is one of the most despicable pieces of rhetoric that people can use to—to use their religion to hurt others."[34]

According to the Court, this statement demonstrated "religious hostility" and "animosity." And once the Court found that the Commission had been hostile to Phillips's religion, the Commission's conclusion—that Phillips had violated CADA—was no longer subject to mere rational basis review. Now the case fell into the purposeful discrimination exception from *Smith*. From this perspective, the most important precedent became *Lukumi*, not *Smith*. The Commission's failure to maintain "religious neutrality" violated free exercise, which led the Court to invalidate the Commission's decision.[35]

To be clear, the *Masterpiece Cakeshop* Court did not hold that either Christian beliefs, specifically, or religious beliefs, in general, must always justify an exemption from anti-discrimination statutes, such as CADA. The Court even suggested that its decision might have little precedential value: "The outcome of cases like this in other circumstances must await further elaboration in the courts."[36] Yet, the Court's worried search for anti-Christian animus in this case seemed significant. Moreover, the *Masterpiece Cakeshop* Court's emphasis on the one commissioner's statement was problematic in at least two ways. First, the commissioner was factually correct: Many times throughout history, people have justified discrimination and persecution based on their religious convictions. For instance, numerous European rulers, acting on their Christian beliefs, forced Jews to live in isolated ghettos or exiled them completely.[37] In the United States, Christians invoked the Bible as justifying slavery,[38] and then, in the twentieth century, as legitimating Jim Crow segregation and anti-miscegenation laws.[39] Second, as Justice Ginsburg emphasized in her *Masterpiece Cakeshop* dissent, the state of Colorado had concluded that Phillips had violated CADA only after a multilayered series of proceedings, including a decision by the Colorado Court of Appeals. The commissioner's statement constituted a minor element in those proceedings and did not undermine the unequivocal fact that Phillips had indeed discriminated by refusing to bake a cake for a couple because they were LGBTQ+.[40] Nevertheless, Gorsuch's concurrence, joined by Alito, highlighted the justices' sensitivity toward government slights of religion: "[I]t is our job [to] afford legal protection to any sincere act of faith."[41]

The Court's next free exercise case was part of the Court's so-called "shadow docket," cases where the petitioners seek emergency or temporary relief. The Court typically decides such cases without full argument and without issuing a full opinion. In theory, the Court should grant such petitions in only extraordinary circumstances, but the Trump administration began requesting relief frequently—and the Roberts Court responded favorably in nearly two-thirds of the cases.[42] *South Bay United Pentecostal Church v. Newsom*, decided on May 29, 2020, was the first of a series of cases arising during the Covid-19 (coronavirus) pandemic. In *South Bay*, the governor of California, trying to stem the spread of the disease, issued an executive order that restricted the number of people allowed in public gatherings. South Bay United Pentecostal Church and others sought an injunction preventing enforcement of the executive order. The Court, in one sentence, refused to grant the injunction. Roberts wrote a concurrence emphasizing that the requested relief was extraordinary and that the Court should defer to local officials during an emergency. Significantly, though, four of the conservative justices dissented—all but Roberts—and Kavanaugh wrote a dissenting opinion joined by Thomas and Gorsuch. Kavanaugh worried that California was discriminating against religion in violation of the First Amendment. Quoting *Lukumi*, he emphasized that the government could justify such discrimination only if it could satisfy strict scrutiny.[43]

Approximately one month later, on June 30, 2020, the Court decided another free exercise case, though this time with full argument and a signed opinion. *Espinoza v. Montana Department of Revenue* arose after the Montana state legislature created a scholarship program for students attending private schools in the state. Under the program, anyone donating money to student scholarship organizations received a tax credit, and the scholarship money could be used at any private school, which would include religious schools. Yet, because the state constitution precluded public funding of religious schools, the Montana Department of Revenue promulgated a rule prohibiting families from using the scholarship money at such schools. Parents of children attending the Stillwater Christian School challenged the Department of Revenue rule. In response to this challenge, the Montana Supreme Court eliminated the entire tax credit program in an attempt to attain neutrality: Going forward, no private schools, religious or otherwise, would receive scholarship money.[44]

The U.S. Supreme Court reversed—Roberts voted with his conservative cohort and wrote the opinion for the five-justice majority. The *Espinoza* Court did not even cite *Smith*. Instead, citing and quoting *Lukumi* and *Trinity Lutheran*, the Court reasoned that the Free Exercise Clause "'protects religious observers against unequal treatment' and against 'laws that impose special disabilities on the basis of religious status.'" If the government penalizes religion, then the government must justify its action by satisfying strict scrutiny. And of course, the Court held that the state could not do so: The Department of Revenue rule and the state court decision violated free exercise.[45] Ginsburg's dissent, joined by Kagan, found the Court's decision puzzling: The parent-petitioners argued "that the Free Exercise Clause requires a State to treat institutions and people neutrally when doling out a benefit—and neutrally is how Montana treats them in the wake of the state court's decision."[46] In other words, the Court's decision would in effect force the state to provide financial support to religious schools.[47] And as even Roberts admitted, "most of the private schools that would benefit from the [scholarship] program were 'religiously affiliated' and 'controlled by churches.'"[48] In fact, "94 percent of the scholarships [in 2018] went to students attending religious schools," with religious schools constituting 70 percent of the private schools in the state—and the vast majority of the religious schools being associated with some form of Christianity.[49]

The Court decided one more free exercise case on its shadow docket during the summer of 2020—and it would be Ginsburg's final free exercise case before her death on September 18, 2020. Like *South Bay United Pentecostal Church*, the dispute in *Calvary Chapel Dayton Valley v. Sisolak* arose after a governor—this time, the governor of Nevada—

issued an order limiting attendance at religious services because of the Covid-19 pandemic. And again, as in *South Bay*, Roberts joined the progressive justices in a five-to-four decision, with another one-sentence order denying the request for an injunction. Alito, joined by Thomas and Kavanaugh, wrote a lengthy dissent. Citing and quoting *Lukumi* and *Masterpiece Cakeshop*, Alito emphasized that the government must remain neutral in relation to religion: "[R]estrictions on religious exercise that are not 'neutral and of general applicability' must survive strict scrutiny." Alito seemed particularly aggrieved because, from his perspective, Nevada favored casinos over houses of worship. "The Constitution guarantees the free exercise of religion. It says nothing about the freedom to play craps or blackjack, to feed tokens into a slot machine, or to engage in any other game of chance. But the Governor of Nevada apparently has different priorities." Not only did the state fail to satisfy strict scrutiny, according to Alito, but also "the State's efforts to justify the [religious] discrimination [were] feeble."[50]

Religious Freedom Transformed

The Rehnquist Court conservatives, in Establishment Clause cases, retreated from the wall of separation (manifested by the *Lemon* test) and, in free exercise cases, rejected strict scrutiny in favor of *Smith* and its rational basis doctrine. In that era, political conservatism was manifested in a constitutional jurisprudence of judicial restraint, which demanded that courts defer to democracy. The early Roberts Court, though, inhabited a different world of conservative politics, and the conservative justices began to turn religious freedom in a direction commensurate with their (political) worldview. More particularly, the justices seemed worried that Christianity and its dominant position in the United States were under threat. The perceived threat came in two forms. First, growing secularism threatened all religion, but especially Christianity. Second, religious pluralism threatened to undermine Christianity's hegemonic place in American society. The early Roberts Court's religious freedom decisions and opinions responded to these concerns, at least in part.

In Establishment Clause cases, the Roberts Court in effect rejected not only the *Lemon* test but also the alternative multi-pronged (Rehnquist

Court) doctrines, the endorsement and coercion tests. Instead, the conservative justices turned to tradition to determine the parameters of the Establishment Clause, and they interpreted tradition in accordance with the nation's long history of de facto Christianity. Pursuant to this new approach, the government can recognize and favor religion over non-religion. Moreover, this government recognition and favoring of religion can be in explicitly Christian terms—publicly displaying Christian crosses, uttering Christian prayers, and so on. The conservative justices have taken a sledgehammer to Jefferson's wall of separation.

In free exercise cases, the conservative justices effectively rejected the *Smith* rational basis test, with its deference to the political process. Instead, the Court has created and expansively interpreted a ministerial exception that allows religious institutions to discriminate despite generally applicable anti-discrimination laws. Furthermore, the conservative justices worry exceedingly about government slights of religion, particularly Christianity, and readily find that the government has purposefully discriminated against Christianity or religion in general. If any such discrimination is found, then the Court requires the government to satisfy strict scrutiny. Moreover, it should be underscored, the Roberts Court's free exercise decisions have invalidated numerous state government actions; respect for state sovereignty and federalism principles, a former (ostensible) hallmark of judicial conservatism, is apparently now irrelevant.[51]

In short, the conservative justices of the early Roberts Court manifested Christian grievance, indignant that the nation's religiously diverse population did not welcome manifestations of de facto Christianity.[52] The justices allowed Christian organizations and institutions to discriminate, yet zealously protected Christians from discrimination. Regardless, after Justice Ginsburg died and the conservative Justice Amy Coney Barrett filled her seat, the Roberts Court solidified and deepened the changes to religious freedom, as will be discussed in the next chapter. One might wonder, though, whether the conservative justices truly manifested *Christian* grievance and resentment. To be sure, they accepted the nonpreferentialist position, allowing government to favor religion over nonreligion, but were they equally protective of all religions rather than only Christianity? That crucial question will also be addressed in the next chapter.

8

Non-Christians Do Not Fully Belong

The Later Roberts Court Solidifies the
Transformation of Religious Freedom

Justice Ruth Bader Ginsburg's death and the rushed nomination and confirmation of Justice Amy Coney Barrett ushered in dramatic transformative Supreme Court decisions in multiple realms of constitutional law. Barrett's effect on the Court and its decision-making was immediately manifested in the context of religious freedom. During Ginsburg's final term on the Court, free exercise cases involving government Covid-19 restrictions on public gatherings began appearing on the Court's shadow docket (discussed in chapter 7). Ginsburg participated in deciding the first two of those cases, *South Bay* and *Calvary Chapel*. In both, the Court denied requests for injunctions, with Chief Justice Roberts joining Ginsburg and the other progressive justices to form narrow five-to-four majorities. Also in both cases, a conservative justice wrote a dissent (first Kavanaugh and then Alito) arguing that the Court was being insufficiently sensitive to denials of religious freedom.[1]

Covid-19 and Free Exercise

With Barrett on the Court, the result flipped in the next Covid-19, free exercise case, also on the shadow docket. In *Roman Catholic Diocese of Brooklyn v. Cuomo*, decided on November 25, 2020, the Court granted the requested injunction. The Roman Catholic Diocese of Brooklyn and Agudath Israel of America (representing Orthodox Jews) challenged an executive order from the governor of New York that restricted attendance at religious services. A five-justice majority consisting of Thomas, Alito, Gorsuch, Kavanaugh, and Barrett issued a per curiam opinion. Citing *Lukumi*, the Court emphasized that government actions violating "'the minimum requirement of neutrality' to religion" can be justified only pursuant to strict scrutiny. As in *Masterpiece Cakebox*, the Court here dug into a government official's comments (it was the governor) to demonstrate hostility against religion (specifically targeting the Orthodox Jewish community). The Court added, though, that "even if we put those comments aside, the regulations cannot be viewed as neutral because they single out houses of worship for especially harsh treatment." In applying strict scrutiny, the Court acknowledged that preventing the spread of Covid-19 amounted to a compelling interest, but the restrictions on religious services were not narrowly tailored to achieving that result. Therefore, the Court enjoined enforcement of the governor's order and concluded: "[Even] in a pandemic, the Constitution cannot be put away and forgotten."[2]

Concurrences written by Gorsuch and Kavanaugh demonstrated again a sharp sensitivity toward government slights of religion. Gorsuch, for example, worried that the executive order revealed the governor believed that "what happens [in religious places] just isn't as 'essential' as what happens in secular spaces." Gorsuch therefore emphasized that the First Amendment prohibits the government "from treating religious exercises worse than comparable secular activities," unless the government can satisfy strict scrutiny.[3] But Kavanaugh went even further in articulating free exercise doctrine to thwart purported government discrimination against religion (or the religious). Citing *Lukumi* and *Smith*, Kavanaugh explained that "once a State creates a favored class of businesses, as New York has done in this case, the State must justify why houses of worship are excluded from that favored class."[4] In other words, if a government creates a policy or rule and, in doing so, simultaneously carves out exceptions to that policy or rule, then the government must justify, pursuant to strict scrutiny, its decision not to include religion (houses of worship) within the exceptions. But as Sotomayor emphasized in dissent, *Lukumi* and *Smith* did not stand for "the proposition that states must justify treating even *noncomparable* secular institutions more favorably than houses of worship." In fact, contrary to the Court's conservative majority, Sotomayor maintained that in this case New York had treated "houses of worship far more favorably than their secular comparators."[5]

After *Roman Catholic Diocese of Brooklyn v. Cuomo*, the Court disposed of three more shadow docket cases in short order, two on December 15 and one on December 17, 2020. *High Plains Harvest Church v. Polis* challenged the Colorado governor's Covid-19 order limiting worship services.[6] The Court granted the injunction and remanded the case with instructions to follow *Roman Catholic Diocese of Brooklyn*. The Court similarly resolved *Robinson v. Murphy*, out of New Jersey.[7] In *Danville Christian Academy, Inc. v. Beshear*, the challenge was to the Kentucky governor's order closing the schools, including religious schools. The Court denied the application for an injunction solely because of timing: The governor's order was expiring soon. Regardless, Gorsuch wrote a dissenting opinion, joined by Alito, which explicitly questioned the logic and vitality of *Smith* as a precedent for free exercise cases.[8]

Eventually, the case from California, *South Bay United Pentecostal Church v. Newsom*, returned to the Court's shadow docket. In the first *South Bay* decision, Ginsburg was still on the Court, and Roberts joined the progressive justices in denying injunctive relief.[9] The second time around, the Court, in a six-to-three decision issued on February 5, 2021, granted the requested injunction in part, with the six conservatives aligned against the remaining three progressives.[10] In the first *South Bay* decision, Roberts had voted to deny the injunction while emphasizing the need to defer to local officials during an emergency, but in this second decision (*South Bay II*), he flipped his vote while writing: "Deference, though broad, has its limits."[11] Gorsuch wrote an opinion, joined by Thomas and Alito, that maintained California was "obviously" targeting religion. "California has openly imposed more stringent regulations on religious institutions than on many businesses."[12] Consequently, he argued that the Court must apply strict scrutiny, and in apparent response to Roberts, emphasized that strict scrutiny is a rigorous judicial test, citing *Lukumi*, which does not allow for deference to the government or political process. In applying strict scrutiny, Gorsuch acknowledged, as the Court had done in *Roman Catholic Diocese of Brooklyn*, that reducing the risk of spreading Covid-19 amounted to a compelling state interest. Nevertheless, California failed strict scrutiny because the state's restrictions, according to Gorsuch, were not narrowly tailored to achieve that goal.[13]

In a dissenting opinion joined by Breyer and Sotomayor, Kagan accentuated the emerging doctrinal disagreement between the conservative and progressive justices—a disagreement that first clearly surfaced in *Roman Catholic Diocese of Brooklyn.* Namely, at least some of the conservative justices, being hypersensitive about possible government slights of religion, demand the government treat religious activities more favorably than similar secular activities—a demand that contravenes the *Smith* rational basis test with its deference to the political process. From this conservative standpoint, the government must treat religious activities at least as well as the most favored secular activities, even if the religious and secular activities differ significantly.[14]

Meanwhile, the progressive justices argue that the Court should require the government to treat like cases alike. Thus, Kagan began her *South Bay* dissent as follows: "Justices of this Court are not scientists. Nor do we know much about public health policy. Yet today the Court displaces the judgments of experts about how to respond to a raging pandemic. The Court orders California to weaken its restrictions on public gatherings by making a special exception for worship services. The majority does so even though the State's policies treat worship just as favorably as secular activities (including political assemblies) that, according to medical evidence, pose the same risk of COVID transmission. Under the Court's injunction, the State must instead treat worship services like secular activities that pose a much lesser danger." Kagan then detailed the expert evidence that California had relied upon in developing its Covid-19 restrictions, including those applied to religious gatherings. Significantly, the evidence showed that the virus spread more readily in indoor rather than outdoor gatherings. Given that information, California had tailored and applied its "rules equivalently to religious activities and to secular activities." In other words, the state had treated like cases alike while treating unlike cases differently. The problem for Kagan, then, was that the Court, not California, "insists on treating unlike cases, not like ones, equivalently."[15]

California's Covid-19 restrictions returned yet again to the Court in another shadow docket decision, *Tandon v. Newsom*, issued on April 9, 2021. In this instance, the state applied its restrictions on private gatherings to limit at-home religious exercises. All too predictably, the Court concluded that the state's action violated the First Amendment, with the per curiam opinion clarifying its new approach to free exercise. In particular, the Court elaborated the judicial comparison of religious and secular activities. "[W]hether two activities are comparable for purposes of the Free Exercise Clause must be judged against the asserted government interest that justifies the regulation at issue. . . . Comparability is concerned with the risks various activities pose, not the reasons why people gather." If the government treats "any comparable secular activity more favorably than religious exercise," as the Court found in this case, then the government must satisfy strict scrutiny.[16] Kagan's dissent, joined again by Breyer and Sotomayor, accentuated the same problems the dissenters had articulated in *Roman Catholic Diocese of Brooklyn* and *South Bay II.* Namely, the conservative justices were comparing dissimilar religious and secular activities and ignoring expert public-health evidence.[17]

Fulton and the Future of Free Exercise

By the time the Court decided *Roman Catholic Diocese of Brooklyn* on its shadow docket, the Court had already heard oral argument in yet another free exercise case, *Fulton v. City of Philadelphia, Pennsylvania.*[18] Given that the petition for certiorari had asked the Court to revisit *Smith* and that the case received full argument—including more than 80 amicus briefs—Court observers anticipated that the conservative justices would seize on *Fulton* as the perfect vehicle for explicitly overruling *Smith.*[19] In *Fulton*, Catholic Social Services (CSS) had contracted with the city of Philadelphia to provide foster care services for the city. According to its religious tenets, however, CSS asserted "that 'marriage is a sacred bond between a man and a woman.'" CSS therefore refused to consider same-sex couples for foster care placements, which prompted the city to object on two related grounds: Discrimination against same-sex couples violated, first, a provision of a municipal Fair Practices Ordinance, and second, a provision in the contract. Based on those objections, the city stopped referring children to CSS for foster care placements. In response, CSS sued the city for violating the First Amendment, particularly the Free Exercise Clause.[20]

Given the Court's recent decisions, its conclusion was unsurprising: The Court held that the city had violated CSS's free exercise rights. More surprising, though, was the alignment of justices. The decision was unanimous. Roberts's majority opinion was joined by the progressives, Kagan, Sotomayor, and Breyer, and the most recent conservative appointees, Kavanaugh and Barrett. Unhappy that Roberts avoided over-ruling *Smith*, Thomas, Alito, and Gorsuch refused to join his opinion. Alito and Gorsuch both wrote opinions concurring in the judgment and recommending that *Smith* be expressly overruled (they joined each other's opinions, with Thomas also joining both opinions). Barrett, besides joining Roberts's opinion, also wrote a concurrence agreeing with Roberts's conclusion that the Court, at this time, did not need to explicitly reexamine *Smith*.[21]

Although Roberts's opinion did not explicitly overrule *Smith*, it continued hollowing out its precedential importance. Roberts briefly disposed of the claim related to the Fair Practices Ordinance by interpreting the ordinance to not apply "to CSS in the first place."[22] The bulk of his opinion concentrated on whether the contractual provisions violated free exercise. In resolving that issue, Roberts pushed beyond prior decisions by invoking two rather than one of the *Smith* exceptions—recall that *Smith* had identified three exceptions in which rational basis review would be insufficiently rigorous. Based on the two exceptions, Roberts reasoned that the city's contract was not generally applicable, and the *Smith* rational basis test was inappropriate—*Smith* had applied the deferential rational basis test only to neutral laws of general applicability.[23]

With regard to the two exceptions, Roberts unsurprisingly invoked the prohibition against purposeful discrimination (of religion), the exception that the conservative justices had already expanded and applied repeatedly. As Roberts interpreted this *Smith* exception, if the government has discretion to grant individual exemptions to its law (or contract, as in this case), then the government is discriminating against religion if it can grant exemptions to secular activities without granting exemptions to religious activities that similarly threaten the government's interests. "A law . . . lacks general applicability," Roberts wrote, "if it prohibits religious conduct while permitting secular conduct that undermines the government's asserted interests in a similar way."[24]

Going further, Roberts also drew upon the *Smith* exception for government denials of unemployment compensation. While this *Smith* exception could have been understood as little more than an attempt to harmonize *Smith* with prior free exercise decisions involving unemployment compensation, Roberts articulated a deeper justification for it. A problem arose with an unemployment compensation law, Roberts explained, if the law allowed the government to grant exemptions to otherwise mandated denials of unemployment compensation. For instance, in *Sherbert v. Verner*, the government had denied benefits to the claimant pursuant to a law prohibiting compensation to those "who had 'failed without good cause . . . to accept available suitable work.'" This statutory exception might allow the government to find good cause for an unemployment-compensation claimant who relied on a secular justification (for refusing a job offer) while denying compensation for a claimant who relied on a religious justification (for similarly refusing a job offer). In short, an unemployment compensation law that allowed the government to grant individual exemptions was not a law of general applicability.[25]

In *Fulton*, Roberts reasoned that the city's contract with CSS allowed the government to grant "an exception" from its non-discrimination requirement.[26] Thus, under the two *Smith* exceptions, as interpreted by Roberts, the city's contract with CSS was not generally applicable, and the city consequently needed to satisfy strict scrutiny rather than rational basis. To be clear, the city had never actually granted any exemptions, whether for secular or religious reasons. Since Roberts viewed that fact to be irrelevant, the Court did not need to overrule *Smith*: The Court was already applying the most rigorous level of judicial scrutiny—the likely judicial standard if the Court were to explicitly overrule *Smith*. Citing *Lukumi* while echoing *Tandon* and Gorsuch in *South Bay II*, Roberts also emphasized that strict scrutiny would not be diluted: "[S]o long as the government can achieve its interests in a manner that does not burden religion, it must do so."[27] Then, when applying strict scrutiny, Roberts found that none of the city's asserted interests could be deemed compelling. Most important, even the city's desire to prevent CSS from discriminating against same-sex couples did not amount to a compelling interest. Ultimately, Roberts concluded, the city failed to satisfy strict scrutiny.[28]

Alito's opinion, concurring in the judgment, argued at length for expressly overruling *Smith*.[29] I will emphasize two of his arguments. First, he argued that many of the Court's recent decisions are difficult to harmonize with *Smith*. On this point, Alito was correct. Roberts himself, in his *Fulton* majority opinion, continued the steady trend of recent free exercise cases, interpreting the *Smith* exceptions so broadly that the *Smith* rational basis approach seems effectively repudiated.[30] Partly for that reason, Roberts repeatedly cited *Lukumi*—now, the key free exercise precedent.[31] In short, the *Smith* exceptions have swallowed the rule: In most cases, strict scrutiny will be applied. From Alito's standpoint, the Court might as well have acknowledged explicitly what it had already done implicitly, replacing the *Smith* rational basis test with strict scrutiny.[32]

Second, Alito exemplified the dramatic transformation of political (and hence judicial) conservatism by expressly and strongly criticizing none other than Justice Scalia and his *Smith* opinion. More than any other justice or scholar, Scalia was responsible for the prominent position of originalism in constitutional jurisprudence generally and within the conservative domain particularly. In fact, Alito fully acknowledged Scalia's importance in articulating originalist methodology. Alito quoted Scalia: "'What I look for in the Constitution is precisely what I look for in a statute: the original meaning of the text.'"[33] Alito elaborated by drawing on Scalia's "judicial magnum opus,"[34] the Second Amendment case of *District of Columbia v. Heller*, in which Scalia maintained that "words and phrases" of the constitutional text should presumptively "carry 'their normal and ordinary . . . meaning.'"[35] Yet, Alito nonetheless launched into a searing critique of Scalia's *Smith* opinion. *Smith*, Alito wrote, "paid shockingly little attention to the text of the Free Exercise Clause. Instead of examining what readers would have understood its words to mean when adopted, the opinion merely asked whether it was 'permissible' to read the text to have the meaning that the majority favored."[36]

Whereas Scalia's *Smith* opinion appeared, at the time, to be harmonious with conservative politics, Alito's *Fulton* opinion better manifests current conservative (Christian) politics and hence delineates the near future of free exercise jurisprudence. According to Alito's (supposedly) originalist interpretation of the Free Exercise Clause, "the ordinary meaning of 'prohibiting the free exercise of religion' was (and still is) forbidding or hindering unrestrained religious practices or worship." Contrary to *Smith*, it "does not suggest a distinction between laws that are generally applicable and laws that are targeted [at religion]." From Alito's perspective, then, any government action that burdens religion should trigger strict scrutiny, whether the government targets religion or otherwise—even if the government has merely enacted a neutral law of general applicability. The right to free exercise should be judicially protected, with vigor, rather than being left to the democratic process, as *Smith* had suggested. "The key point for present purposes is that the text of the Free Exercise Clause gives a specific group of people (those who wish to engage in the 'exercise of religion') the right to do so without hindrance."[37]

Alito therefore recommended a specific doctrinal approach for free exercise issues: "A law that imposes a substantial burden on religious exercise can be sustained only if it is narrowly tailored to serve a compelling government interest."[38] In other words, if a law imposes a substantial burden on religion, then strict scrutiny is triggered. If the Court were to apply this test, crucial initial and overlapping questions would arise: What beliefs and conduct would be deemed *religious*? And what burdens (on religious exercise) would be deemed *substantial*? Drawing on his originalist reading of the First Amendment, Alito suggested answers to these questions. He emphasized that the originalist meaning of free exercise would need to account for the "defined dimensions" of free exercise at the time of the First Amendment's adoption.[39] Alito added that "[n]o one has ever seriously argued that the Free Exercise Clause protects every conceivable religious practice or even every conceivable form of worship, including such things as human sacrifice."[40] So what would count as being within the defined dimensions of protected religious practices? Apparently, Alito would have no trouble recognizing mainstream Christian (Protestant and Catholic) practices as being constitutionally protected. He described "the religious demographics" of the late eighteenth and early nineteenth centuries: "The population was overwhelmingly Christian and Protestant, the major Protestant denominations made up the great bulk of the religious adherents." Minority religious groups at the time were, as Alito put it, "tiny." In other words, during the early national years, the United States was de facto Protestant Christian, and most Americans would have understood free exercise to protect Protestant Christian practices and beliefs.[41] Consequently, then, Alito noted that, in *Fulton*, "[w]hatever the outer boundaries of the term 'religion' as used in the First Amendment, there can be no doubt that CSS's contested [Christian] policy represents an exercise of 'religion.'"[42]

To be sure, as professional historians have emphasized, Supreme Court justices typically do a poor job when analyzing historical sources.

Even so, Alito's religious history of the early republic was largely correct. Moreover, as Alito's *Fulton* opinion illustrated, he and the other conservative justices often claim to follow originalist methodology, which would ostensibly fix the meaning of the religion clauses as they were predominantly understood at the time of ratification.[43] In theory, then, following originalism would facilitate an interpretation of the Free Exercise Clause that harmonizes with white Christian nationalism, protecting and bolstering the United States as a (de facto) Christian nation.[44] Indeed, two overlapping points of agreement between Alito's and Roberts's respective *Fulton* opinions illuminated the extent to which the conservative justices will push free exercise jurisprudence to protect Christianity. First, consistent with conservative Christian politics, both Roberts and Alito suggested that the strict scrutiny applied in free exercise cases should be the most rigorous level of judicial scrutiny possible. Free exercise judicial review should never be strict scrutiny lite, where the Court dilutes aspects of the inquiry. Rather, strict scrutiny under free exercise should be strict in theory, but fatal in fact: a level of judicial scrutiny that, in reality, the government can never satisfy.[45] Throughout the recent spate of free exercise decisions, the conservative justices have persistently stressed that strict scrutiny will not be "watered down." "[S]trict scrutiny requires the State to further 'interests of the highest order' by means 'narrowly tailored in pursuit of those interests.' . . . That standard . . . 'really means what it says.'"[46] Therefore, when reviewing any law that burdens religion (read: Christianity), the justices will either invalidate it or require the government to grant a free exercise exemption. Christians must be protected from any burden on or hint of discrimination against their practices or beliefs.

Second, and again consistent with conservative Christian politics, both Roberts and Alito suggested that Christians must be allowed to push their own beliefs and practices, even if doing so entails insulting, denouncing, and discriminating against others (those whose beliefs and practices might contravene Christianity). Specifically, in *Fulton*, CSS discriminated against same-sex couples by refusing to consider them for foster care placements. The city responded by asserting that it had a compelling interest in protecting same-sex couples from discrimination and that, therefore, the city was justified when it stopped referring children to CSS for foster care placements. After all, as the Court held in *Obergefell v. Hodges*, same-sex couples have a protected constitutional right to choose whether to marry. Both Roberts and Alito, however, found that the city's interest was not compelling (and consequently, the interest was insufficient to satisfy strict scrutiny). In other words, CSS had a protected free exercise right to discriminate against same-sex couples. This conclusion harmonized with Roberts's and Alito's suggestion that, for free exercise, strict scrutiny should be strict in theory but fatal in fact.[47]

Roberts reasoned that the city's non-discrimination policy (against same-sex couples) could not be compelling because the city could grant exceptions from that policy. Citing *Lukumi* once again, Roberts explained: "The creation of a system of exceptions under the contract undermines the city's contention that its non-discrimination policies can brook no departures."[48] Alito went further, extensively elaborating why the city's anti-discrimination policy did not amount to a compelling interest. He began by suggesting that CSS's opposition to same-sex marriage had minimal effect: "CSS's policy has only one effect: It expresses the idea that same-sex couples should not be foster parents because only a man and a woman should marry." He admitted, though, that "[m]any people today find this idea not only objectionable but hurtful." Even so, he concluded, "protecting against this form of harm is not an interest that can justify the abridgment of First Amendment rights." Alito did not leave it there, though. In a passage bristling with indignation, he reminded the justices that the *Obergefell* majority opinion had "made a commitment" to religious believers (read: Christians).

> While CSS's ideas about marriage are likely to be objectionable to same-sex couples, lumping those who hold traditional beliefs about marriage together with racial bigots is insulting to those who retain such beliefs. In *Obergefell v. Hodges*, the majority made a commitment. It refused to equate traditional [religious] beliefs about marriage, which it termed "decent and honorable," with racism, which is neither. And it promised that "religions, and those who adhere to religious doctrines, may continue to advocate with utmost, sincere conviction that, by divine precepts, same-sex marriage should not be condoned." An open society can keep that promise while still respecting the "dignity," "worth," and fundamental equality of all members of the community.[49]

What is most noteworthy about this passage, besides Alito's lingering resentment of the *Obergefell* decision, is his hypersensitivity toward insults directed at Christians combined with his disregard for LGBTQ+ individuals. He insisted that CSS and presumably other Christians should not be subjected to insults as if they were "racial bigots." Yet, CSS must be allowed to express its "ideas about marriage"—that "'marriage is a sacred bond between a man and a woman'"—regardless of whether CSS insulted same-sex couples.[50] In fact, Alito never seemed to acknowledge that CSS was doing any more than expressing its religious beliefs or ideas. In actuality, CSS discriminated against same-sex couples: CSS's conduct was injurious. Alito brushed aside any potential injury, attributable to CSS's conduct, because same-sex couples could feasibly go to other foster care agencies (that did not discriminate against same-sex couples).[51] The logic of this argument is disturbing, to say the least: Would Alito similarly reason that racially restrictive covenants did not injure Black American home buyers because, after all, they could buy and live elsewhere?[52] Alito's final line (in the above passage), emphasizing respect for the dignity, worth, and equality of everyone, was dripping with unintended irony. Apparently, from Alito's perspective, we are all equal, so long as Christians are more equal—which of course makes sense if the First Amendment is interpreted to ensure that the United States is de facto Christian.

* * *

Alito's *Fulton* concurrence laid out the argument for overruling *Smith*,[53] yet the failure of the Court to do so explicitly is unlikely to have any long-term significance. Petitioners will occasionally ask the Court again to revisit *Smith*, but the Court already has effectively overruled it to a large degree. Supreme Court history is littered with examples of the Court effectively repudiating the doctrinal rule of a precedent without explicitly overruling the precedent itself. Most famously, *Brown v. Board of Education* is celebrated for holding unconstitutional the separate-but-equal doctrine of *Plessy v. Ferguson*, yet *Brown* did not explicitly overrule *Plessy*.[54] More recently, *City of Boerne v. Flores* severely limited Congress's power under section five of the Fourteenth Amendment, thus contravening the rule articulated in *Katzenbach v. Morgan*, which had recognized a broad congressional power. Rather than admitting it was overruling *Katzenbach*, though, the *Boerne* Court claimed to merely clarify its meaning.[55] Now, the conservative Roberts Court justices have rejected the *Smith* doctrinal approach to free exercise. Given this, the path forward in free exercise cases is unlikely to change regardless of whether the Court explicitly overrules *Smith*.

The Roberts Court and Non-Christians

Let's pause here and consider a crucial question. Dissenting in an Establishment Clause case, Justice Sotomayor quoted a 1982 decision and wrote, "The 'clearest command' of the Establishment Clause is that the Government cannot favor or disfavor one religion over another." In the same case, Chief Justice Roberts's majority opinion largely echoed this same point.[56] Is this fundamental proposition true, whether we focus on the Establishment or Free Exercise Clause? In other words, in religious freedom cases, are the conservative justices equally protective of all religions, or do they favor Christianity?

Significantly, perhaps, the conservative justices used ecumenical language in several of the Covid-19 cases, suggesting that First Amendment protections extend as much to non-Christians as to Christians.[57] In *Calvary Chapel*, decided before Ginsburg's death, Alito's, Gorsuch's, and Kavanaugh's respective dissents repeatedly mentioned how the Nevada executive order restricting religious services applied to "churches, synagogues, and mosques."[58] In *South Bay II*, decided after Barrett joined the Court, Gorsuch issued a statement, joined by Thomas and Alito, which fretted about the effects of the California executive order on not only "California's churches," but also "synagogues, and mosques." The executive order, Gorsuch pointed out, would interfere with attendance at services for Passover and Ramadan as well as Lent.[59] Likewise, in *Roman Catholic Diocese of Brooklyn*, the conservative justices' per curiam opinion worried about how the New York governor had targeted both the Roman Catholic Diocese and an Orthodox Jewish community.[60]

Yet, one should not read too much into these ecumenical statements from the conservative justices. To be sure, they willingly protect non-Christians when their interests and values converge with Christian interests and values.[61] In other words, the justices will protect the religious freedom of non-Christians so long as it harmonizes with de facto

Christianity. Thus, in the free exercise, Covid-19 cases, the conservative justices talked of an expansive religious freedom that protected non-Christians *and Christians*. Yet, those same justices have not extended constitutional protections to non-Christians when a convergence of interests was not apparent. For example, in *Dunn v. Ray*, a prisoner, Domineque Ray, invoked his Muslim religion when requesting a stay of execution for his death sentence. The Alabama prison that housed Ray regularly allowed a Christian chaplain to accompany prisoners into the execution chamber, but when Ray requested the presence of an imam, the prison refused. The Eleventh Circuit granted the requested stay, reasoning that the prison was likely violating the Establishment Clause. In a five-to-four Supreme Court decision, the conservative justices reversed, reasoning that the stay application was untimely; the execution could proceed.[62]

In multiple cases, the conservative justices have interpreted religious freedom in ways that resurrect and bolster de facto Christianity. An Establishment Clause case, *Trump v. Hawaii*, decided in 2018, tellingly suggests the conservative justices' wariness of non-Christian religions. The case challenged a presidentially imposed travel ban that restricted entry into the United States. The Trump administration had adopted the ban supposedly to protect national security, though in response to various legal challenges, the administration had revised the ban several times. When it reached the Supreme Court for final adjudication, the ban (as modified) applied to nationals from eight nations—"Chad, Iran, Iraq, Libya, North Korea, Syria, Venezuela, and Yemen"—six of which were predominantly Muslim. The Court upheld the ban five-to-four, with the then standard conservative-progressive split and Chief Justice Roberts writing the majority opinion.[63]

Justice Sotomayor, dissenting, emphasized that President Trump had fervently denounced Islam throughout the various stages of litigation and revision.

> Taking all the relevant evidence together, a reasonable observer would conclude that the Proclamation was driven primarily by anti-Muslim animus, rather than by the Government's asserted national-security justifications. Even before being sworn into office, then-candidate Trump stated that "Islam hates us," warned that "[w]e're having problems with

the Muslims, and we're having problems with Muslims coming into the country," promised to enact a "total and complete shutdown of Muslims entering the United States," and instructed one of his advisers to find a "lega[l]" way to enact a Muslim ban. The President continued to make similar statements well after his inauguration. . . . Moreover, despite several opportunities to do so, President Trump has never disavowed any of his prior statements about Islam. Instead, he has continued to make remarks that a reasonable observer would view as an unrelenting attack on the Muslim religion and its followers.[64]

Since the ban specifically aimed at Islam, Sotomayor argued that it violated the Establishment Clause. The Trump administration appeared, in fact, to include the non-Muslim countries of North Korea and Venezuela on the final list of eight nations merely to disguise the travel ban's "otherwise clear targeting of Muslims."[65]

In response, Roberts and the conservative bloc diluted the Establishment Clause protections to the point of evasion. Roberts emphasized that the travel ban was a presidentially issued "national security directive regulating the entry of aliens abroad." Because the ban related to immigration and national security, Roberts reasoned the Court should defer to the administration's judgments, at least to a degree. "[The Court] may consider plaintiffs' extrinsic evidence [of anti-Muslim animus]," Roberts explained, "but will uphold the policy so long as it can reasonably be understood to result from a justification independent of unconstitutional grounds."[66] Applying this deferential standard, the Court concluded that the ban did not violate the Establishment Clause. From Sotomayor's perspective, though, the Court failed "to safeguard [the] fundamental principle [of religious liberty]. [The Court's decision] leaves undisturbed a policy first advertised openly and unequivocally as a 'total and complete shutdown of Muslims entering the United States' because the policy now masquerades behind a facade of national-security concerns."[67]

The Court's decision in *Trump v. Hawaii* sharply contrasted with *Masterpiece Cakeshop* (discussed in chapter 6), where the conservative justices anxiously dug through the record to find evidence of animus against Christianity. In *Trump*, the justices did not even need to dig to find anti-Muslim animus—if they had cared to look—since it was splattered all over the surface. In fact, as in *Trump*, the conservative justices have consistently evaded constitutional principles that might have otherwise protected non-Christians when the non-Christian interests did not converge with Christian interests. Two government speech cases involving religious expression strongly suggest the conservative justices do not view or treat non-Christians the same as Christians, though these cases were not expressly decided under the religion clauses. *Pleasant Grove City v. Summum*, decided in 2009, involved the display of a religious monument.[68] The city already displayed several monuments in a public park, including one showing the Ten Commandments, contributed years earlier by the Fraternal Order of Eagles. The city nonetheless rebuffed Summum, a non-Christian religion, when it offered to donate a Seven-Aphorisms monument for inclusion with the other monuments. Previously, Rehnquist Court decisions involving religious speech had designated certain public school properties to be public forums and therefore held those properties open to Christian organizations pursuant to free speech principles.[69] Those precedents appeared to require Pleasant Grove to display the Summum monument because a public park is a traditional public forum.[70] But the Roberts Court allowed the city to skirt the First Amendment: "[T]he placement of a permanent monument in a public park is best viewed as a form of government speech and is therefore not subject to scrutiny under the Free Speech Clause." That is, pursuant to the Court's "recently minted" government speech doctrine, the Summum monument was "not a form of expression to which [public] forum analysis applies."[71]

Summum contrasts sharply with a more recent government speech decision, *Shurtleff v. City of Boston, Massachusetts*, decided in 2022. Boston allowed private groups to fly flags from a pole in its City Hall Plaza. When Harold Shurtleff, however, requested permission to fly a "Christian flag," commemorating "contributions of the Christian community," the city refused. The Court's majority opinion began by distinguishing two types of cases. First, when the government creates a public forum, "the First Amendment prevents it from discriminating against speakers based on their viewpoint." The Court cited the Rehnquist Court religious speech precedents, including *Summum*, to support this proposition. Second, "when the government speaks for itself," then First Amendment free speech restrictions do not apply. The Court cited Roberts Court government speech precedents to support this proposition.

The issue in *Shurtleff* was whether Boston had either opened the flagpole as a forum for private, citizen speech or reserved it for government-approved speech. After articulating a standard for determining when expression constitutes government speech—and thus is outside First Amendment parameters—the Court held that the flagpole had been opened for private expression. The government speech doctrine did not apply, so the First Amendment mandated that Shurtleff be allowed to fly the Christian flag. By denying Shurtleff access, Boston had engaged in unconstitutional viewpoint discrimination.[72]

Interestingly, the decision was unanimous, with Breyer writing the Court's opinion. Only five other justices, though, joined Breyer's opinion; the three most conservative justices concurred in the judgment only. To a degree, the content of the concurring opinions illuminated the justices' views about religious freedom and religion (Christianity). Kavanaugh joined Breyer's opinion but wrote a concurrence to underscore that "a government may not treat religious persons, religious organizations, or religious speech as second-class."[73] Gorsuch, joined by Thomas, wrote an opinion concurring in the judgment to emphasize that the *Lemon* test was really and truly dead. Alito, concurring in the judgment and joined by Thomas and Gorsuch, penned what might become the most important opinion in the case. Alito disagreed with Breyer about the doctrine for identifying expression as government speech. Breyer articulated an ad hoc multifactor standard, while Alito articulated a more formal rule, as the conservative justices generally prefer—formalism facilitates (without mandating) judicial decisions that allow those with private-sphere power, such as the wealthy (or mainstream white, Christian denominations, for that matter), to dominate American society.[74] Either way, the ultimate conclusion diverged from *Summum*. In *Shurtleff*, the Court forced the government to allow a Christian display or expression (flying a flag), while in *Summum*, the Court allowed the government to suppress (or deny) a non-Christian display (a monument).

In light of cases such as *Trump v. Hawaii*, *Summum*, and *Shurtleff*, the ecumenical language the conservative justices have inserted in some opinions seems less significant. Rather than showing that First Amendment protections extend as much to non-Christians as to Christians, the language demonstrates instances of interest convergence. That is, the conservative justices invoke an expansive religious freedom that encompasses non-Christians when doing so also protects Christians and converges or harmonizes with de facto Christianity. But those same justices interpret religious freedom (and related constitutional rights) far more narrowly when only non-Christian interests and values are at stake, particularly when those non-Christian interests and values either diverge from or are not obviously commensurate with Christian interests and values. In fact, one should not expect anything else from a conservative Court committed to de facto Christianity denoting a white, Christian nation.[75]

The Intersection of the Free Exercise and Establishment Clauses in a de Facto Christian Nation

The most recent Roberts Court religious freedom decisions underscore the conservative justices' pro-Christian interpretation of the religion clauses. *Kennedy v. Bremerton School District*, decided in 2022, involved both the Free Exercise and Establishment Clauses. A high school assistant football coach, Joseph Kennedy, repeatedly prayed at midfield after games and eventually lost his job (because of tensions with the school district over the Christian prayers).[76] The Court majority and dissenters disagreed about the factual details of the praying. The majority opinion, written by Gorsuch and joined by the rest of the conservative bloc (Roberts, Thomas, Alito, Kavanaugh, and Barrett) described Kennedy as saying "a short, private, personal prayer"—"for engaging in a brief, quiet, personal religious observance."[77] Sotomayor's dissent described Kennedy's prayers differently: They were not private and quiet. To the contrary, Kennedy insisted on praying at the 50-yard line, many students participated with Kennedy (as illustrated in photographs), and some of those students felt coerced into praying because they feared retribution if they failed to join. When the school district urged Kennedy to stop praying at midfield—the district never discouraged Kennedy's truly private prayers—Kennedy responded with media appearances. Eventually, the head coach of 11 years resigned because he feared violence might arise from the public controversy surrounding Kennedy's prayers.[78]

The school district had urged Kennedy to halt his public prayers because of the First Amendment: The district reasonably believed, based on the Court's precedents, that the practice violated the Establishment Clause. Prior cases had invalidated the recitation of prayers in the public schools, whether in the classroom, during graduation ceremonies, or at high school football games.[79] Regardless, the Court held not only that Kennedy's prayers had not violated the Establishment Clause but also that the school district had violated Kennedy's free exercise rights by restricting his prayers.[80] Concerning free exercise, Gorsuch's majority opinion unequivocally articulated the Court's new doctrinal approach, replacing the *Smith* rational basis test (though the Court still has not expressly overruled *Smith*). Rather than applying strict scrutiny in only unusual (or exceptional) cases, the Court will now apply it as a matter of course. A free exercise claimant no longer needs to prove overt discrimination to trigger strict scrutiny. Now, any government treatment of religious (read: Christian) practices, institutions, or beliefs that differs from government treatment of secular practices, institutions, or beliefs will suffice. In effect, from the conservative justices' perspective, any such differential treatment amounts to purposeful discrimination. Gorsuch wrote: "[A] plaintiff may carry the burden of proving a free-exercise violation in various ways, including by showing that a government entity has burdened his sincere religious practice pursuant to a policy that is not 'neutral' or 'generally applicable.'" Gorsuch elaborated: "A government policy will not qualify as neutral if it is 'specifically directed at . . . religious practice.' A policy can fail this test if it 'discriminate[s] on its face,' or if a religious exercise is otherwise its 'object.' A government policy will fail the general applicability requirement if it 'prohibits religious conduct while permitting secular conduct that undermines the government's asserted interests in a similar way,' or if it provides 'a mechanism for individualized exemptions.'"[81]

To be clear, any generally applicable law that allows the government to recognize individual exemptions for cause must allow exemptions for religious practices and beliefs.[82] Otherwise, the government will need to satisfy strict scrutiny. As Justices Sotomayor and Kagan have suggested in dissents, the Court's new free exercise doctrine effectively entrenches religion (Christianity) with a "most-favored nation status."[83] The government, that is, must treat religious activities at least as well as the most favored secular activities, even if the religious and secular activities differ.[84]

Based on this free exercise doctrine, the Bremerton School District needed to satisfy strict scrutiny, showing that its action—prohibiting

Kennedy from praying at midfield—was narrowly tailored to achieve a compelling state purpose. And since the district had prohibited the prayers to avoid violating the Establishment Clause—in other words, the district's claimed compelling purpose was to remain consistent with the First Amendment—the Court segued into a discussion of establishment principles. Gorsuch's majority opinion clarified the new Establishment Clause doctrine that the conservative justices had been articulating in prior cases. First, he stated that the Court had "long ago abandoned" the *Lemon* test.[85] While this statement was factually questionable, it made the point: The Roberts Court had buried the *Lemon* test, even if it was not yet officially dead (overruled). Second, Gorsuch reasoned that the proper interpretation of the Establishment Clause was in accordance with history and tradition. Third, Gorsuch added that this judicial focus on history and tradition corresponds with a focus on the original public meaning of the First Amendment: "'[T]he line' that courts and governments 'must draw between the permissible and the impermissible' has to 'accor[d] with history and faithfully reflec[t] the understanding of the Founding Fathers.'"[86]

Finally, Gorsuch emphasized that the Free Exercise and Establishment Clauses have "'complementary' purposes, not warring ones."[87] As Sotomayor noted in dissent, this interpretation of the First Amendment departed from the typical view recognizing a tension between the two religion clauses: According to this widely accepted view, the Establishment Clause prevents government from becoming too supportive of religion, while the Free Exercise Clause prevents government from becoming too hostile toward religion.[88] Gorsuch and the *Kennedy* Court rejected that position: They insisted the two clauses are consistent.[89] But how did they attain such consistency? Without admitting as much, the conservative justices have strengthened the free exercise guarantee, to afford greater protection to Christian practices and beliefs, while simultaneously weakening the antiestablishment guarantee, to facilitate public support for and bolstering of Christianity.

In short, pursuant to originalist claims, the Roberts Court has apparently frozen the meaning of religious freedom to accord with the understandings of a de facto Protestant (Christian) framing generation. In a society that was overwhelmingly Protestant, few would have been brave enough to question the predominant religious practices and beliefs. In fact, as discussed in chapter 2, non-Christians (as well as Catholics and, subsequently, Mormons) who openly doubted mainstream Protestantism might find themselves prosecuted for blasphemy. Moreover, through the nineteenth and into the twentieth century, many states continued to enforce the Christian Sabbath of Sunday as either common-law doctrine or by statute (called Blue Laws). One 1912 account reported that police had arrested tens of thousands of Jews for violating Sunday laws, which courts repeatedly upheld as constitutional.[90]

Under the Roberts Court, then, as borne out in one religious freedom case after another, the conservative justices will readily recognize and constitutionally protect Protestant, Catholic, and most other Christian practices and beliefs. Yet those same justices will likely fail to recognize and protect the practices and beliefs of non-Christians, including Jews, Muslims, and others (except for cases of interest convergence). The conservative justices will insist that Christian individuals and entities must be allowed to discriminate as a matter of religious freedom, yet those same justices will rigorously shield Christianity itself from discrimination. The United States, from their perspective, is and should be de facto Christian, or in other words, it is a white, Christian nation. Consequently, in *Kennedy v. Bremerton School District*, with the conservative justices following their de facto Christian interpretation of the religion clauses, the Court of course concluded that Kennedy's Christian prayers at midfield did not violate the Establishment Clause. And since the school district could not invoke antiestablishment concerns to justify prohibiting Kennedy's prayers, then of course the district could not articulate a compelling purpose to satisfy strict scrutiny under the Free Exercise Clause.[91]

In *Carson v. Makin*, another case decided in 2022, the Court predictably reached a result that resonated with *Kennedy*. In the state of Maine, some rural school districts did not operate a secondary school. To compensate, the state created a tuition assistance program to aid parents sending their children to private schools, but Maine prohibited assistance payments from going to religious schools. The issue was whether the state restriction on the payments violated free exercise. The Court, with the same conservative-progressive split as in *Kennedy*, reasoned that Maine, to remain within free exercise requirements, must satisfy strict scrutiny. The state argued that it restricted payments for a compelling purpose: to avoid violating state antiestablishment principles.

Rejecting that argument, the Court reasoned that the state restriction obviously violated the Free Exercise Clause. Furthermore, the state's "interest in separating church and state 'more fiercely' than the Federal Constitution . . . 'cannot qualify as compelling' in the face of the infringement of free exercise."[92]

Justice Breyer, dissenting, worried about the extreme consequences flowing from the Court's de facto Christian interpretation of the religion clauses. "We have never previously held what the Court holds today, namely, that a State must (not may) use state funds to pay for religious education as part of a tuition program designed to ensure the provision of free statewide public school education." For a society as religiously diverse as that of the United States, the implications were frightening: The Court's approach to the religion clauses was likely to generate "religious strife." "We are today a Nation with well over 100 different religious groups, from Free Will Baptist to African Methodist, Buddhist to Humanist," Breyer explained. "People in our country adhere to a vast array of beliefs, ideals, and philosophies. And with greater religious diversity comes greater risk of religiously based strife, conflict, and social division."[93] In *Kennedy*, the conservative justices answered this concern about religious strife. Non-Christians need to develop a tougher skin. "Of course, some will take offense to certain forms of speech or prayer," the Court reasoned. But such occasional offense is the cost of living in a religiously diverse America. "[L]earning how to tolerate speech or prayer of all kinds is 'part of learning how to live in a pluralistic society.'"[94]

* * *

The Roberts Court's conservatives have thoroughly transformed the constitutional jurisprudence of religious freedom. In Establishment Clause cases, the Court now defines the parameters of government-religion relations in accordance with history and tradition, a doctrinal approach that supposedly harmonizes with originalism. The justices equate American history and tradition with de facto Christianity. Although the religious makeup of the American people has changed dramatically since the framing and ratification of the First Amendment, becoming far more diverse (and less Christian), the meaning of the Establishment Clause is static, at least from the conservatives' perspective. Hence, ostentatious displays of Christian symbols and overt

Christian prayers, even in the public schools, do not trouble the conservative justices.

In Free Exercise Clause cases, a Christian claimant challenging government restrictions on religious beliefs, practices, or symbols can readily get to strict scrutiny. Even a neutral and generally applicable law must allow exemptions for (Christian) religious practices and beliefs if it allows the government to recognize any individual exemptions for (secular) cause.[95] If the law does not provide for religious exemptions, the government will need to satisfy strict scrutiny.[96] Furthermore, unlike in years past, the government is unlikely to be able to satisfy this free exercise strict scrutiny: It is strict in theory but fatal in fact. Christian practices and institutions must be treated at least as well as secular practices and institutions. Free exercise, according to the Court, can now require the government to support Christian institutions and practices.

To be clear, then, the conservative justices have not returned the jurisprudence of religious freedom to pre-1937 judicial principles consistent with republican democracy. Following that route, which some scholars had recommended, would have led the Roberts Court to render both religion clauses relatively toothless. To be sure, the conservative justices have weakened the antiestablishment guarantee, but they have invigorated the Free Exercise Clause with a vengeance, at least for Christians. While the conservative justices occasionally use ecumenical language, suggesting that the First Amendment protects non-Christians as much as Christians, the case results do not match the language. Yes, the conservative justices extend constitutional protections to non-Christians when doing so converges with Christian interests and values. But if non-Christian practices and beliefs depart from Christian interests and values, then the justices refuse to recognize non-Christian constitutional claims. Non-Christians do not fully belong to We the People.

In short, the conservative justices interpret religious freedom under the First Amendment in harmony with the politics of white Christian nationalism. While the justices are unlikely to riot at the Capitol, they are apt to understand and sympathize with the grievance of a white Christian man who is asked to bake a cake for a gay couple.[97] Likewise, the conservative justices are unlikely to support the murder or banishment of non-Christians and people of color, but the justices will find that white Christians have a constitutional right to discriminate against same-sex couples and numerous others.[98] The justices will be hypersensitive about any perceived slights of or discrimination against Christianity, while ensuring that white Christians remain free to impose their beliefs and practices on non-Christians. In sum, the justices will interpret the First Amendment to bolster and propagate the structures of white Christian privilege in American society.

Significantly, though, to protect the bona fides of a white, Christian nation, the Court's conservatives are going beyond their transformation of the religion clauses. The white Christian nationalism that currently occupies the mainstream of American political conservatism aims to enforce a quasi-caste system with white, Christian, heterosexual men at the top. Unsurprisingly, then, the Roberts Court has interpreted other constitutional provisions in ways that diminish the rights of women, the rights of LGBTQ+ individuals, and the rights of people of color. The following chapter examines the key cases in these areas.

9

Who Fully Belongs? Not People of Color,
Women, or LGBTQ+ Individuals

The later Roberts Court has decided religious freedom cases in accordance with the political agenda of white Christian nationalism, enhancing the rights of Christians while diminishing the rights of non-Christians. The political agenda extends well beyond religion, however. This chapter will explore the ways the Court has also diminished the rights of people of color, women, and LGBTQ+ individuals. In the exclusionary, inegalitarian, and hierarchical democracy that the Court is constructing, these societal groups and their members do not fully belong to We the People.

People of Color Do Not Fully Belong

In 1954, as discussed in chapter 3, the Warren Court decided *Brown v. Board of Education*, repudiating the separate-but-equal doctrine from *Plessy v. Ferguson* and holding that "[s]eparate educational facilities are inherently unequal," in violation of the Fourteenth Amendment.[1] While the Warren Court's *Brown II* decision wavered significantly in its support for equality—the remedy of desegregation with all deliberate speed often translated into slow or no desegregation—the Warren Court supported the Civil Rights Movement in a variety of other cases (though not always). For example, during the 1960s, the Court decided several cases in which civil rights protesters encountered hostile white crowds or audiences. After the protesters or their leaders were convicted in the local courts for breach of the peace, the Warren Court tended to reverse the convictions and protect the free speech rights of the protesters.[2] *New York Times v. Sullivan*, decided in 1964, is renowned for imposing an actual malice standard to help protect the press from civil libel actions brought by government officials. Yet *Sullivan* also concerned the Civil Rights Movement. The focus of the underlying defamation action was a full-page advertisement in the *Times* that solicited support for Dr. Martin Luther King, Jr., and voting rights. The Court's decision in effect protected the expression of civil rights leaders while also assuring that newspapers, like the *Times*, could continue to report the atrocities visited on civil rights protesters in the South.[3] In a similar vein, *Heart of Atlanta Motel, Inc. v. United States*, also decided in 1964, saw the Court upholding a federal statute while focusing on an expansive interpretation of Congress's commerce power. More to the point, the disputed statute prohibited racial discrimination in places of public accommodation, such as hotels, restaurants, and theaters.[4]

Regardless, as the Burger and Rehnquist Courts moved rightward, the justices became increasingly hostile to people of color. For example, if a school district desegregated, some white families resisted by exiting the public schools, sending their children to either private (usually Christian) schools or public schools in different (whiter) school districts. *Milliken v. Bradley*, decided in 1974, involved the latter situation— the phenomenon of so-called "white flight."[5] A district court had found that the Detroit school system was unconstitutionally segregated. The issue was whether the court could fashion a desegregation remedy that included not only the Detroit schools but also public schools in the surrounding, suburban (and whiter) areas. The Supreme Court held that such interdistrict remedies were, in most instances, impermissible—a holding that rendered school desegregation practically impossible.[6]

Meanwhile, as Jim Crow laws expressly segregating schools and other public places (very) slowly faded from the American legal landscape, the Court confronted laws that appeared facially neutral but that nonetheless had racially disparate or discriminatory effects. In *Washington v. Davis*, decided in 1976, the Court reviewed a government policy requiring applicants for the Washington, D.C., police force to take a written test. While this policy was facially neutral, it eliminated a disproportionate number of Black applicants. The Court held that such facially neutral laws should be subject to rational basis review, the lowest level of judicial scrutiny (requiring the government to show that its action was rationally related to a legitimate government purpose). The Court would apply the more rigorous strict scrutiny (requiring the government to show that its action was narrowly tailored to achieve a compelling government purpose) only if the challenger proved the government had *intentionally* discriminated against a suspect class, such as Black Americans. Proving intentional discrimination and triggering strict scrutiny was difficult. Most important, evidence of even grossly disparate or discriminatory effects was insufficient to prove intentional discrimination.[7]

Before long, the Court confronted race-based affirmative action programs, where government institutions adopted policies favoring Black Americans and other people of color in order to help remedy the harms of past societal discrimination. What level of judicial scrutiny should apply if a white person challenged such a program? In a couple of cases, the Rehnquist Court held that any such affirmative action program should be subject to strict scrutiny. Since strict scrutiny under equal protection was generally strict in theory but fatal in fact, these decisions largely doomed race-based affirmative action. One exception emerged, however: university admissions. The Court had already decided a case in 1978, *University of California Regents v. Bakke*, that involved a quota-like affirmative action program; a medical school was allocating a minimum number of entry-class positions for people of color. Without a majority opinion, the Court invalidated that program, but in doing so, a majority of justices constitutionally approved an alternative form of affirmative action, used by Harvard College, which gave people of color a "plus" in the admissions process (without creating a quota). Moreover, in an opinion joined by no other justices, Justice Lewis Powell applied strict scrutiny but found that attaining a diverse student body constituted a compelling government purpose.[8]

The Rehnquist Court reaffirmed the *Bakke* approach to race-plus affirmative action programs in higher education in *Grutter v. Bollinger*, decided in 2003. The moderately conservative Justice Sandra Day O'Connor provided the crucial vote and wrote the Court's opinion. Applying strict scrutiny but denying that it is fatal in fact, she too found that student-body diversity constituted a compelling government purpose. Partly on that ground, she concluded that a race-based affirmative action program that granted people of color a plus in the admissions process passed constitutional muster—that the government, in other words, satisfied strict scrutiny—though a program that quantified the plus would be too much like a quota and would fail strict scrutiny. Furthermore, O'Connor suggested that race-based affirmative action should have a sunset: "We expect that 25 years from now, the use of racial preferences will no longer be necessary to further the interest approved today."[9]

Finally, in *Fisher v. University of Texas at Austin (Fisher II)*, decided in 2016, the early Roberts Court reaffirmed *Bakke* and *Grutter* by allowing race to be considered in university admissions. The Court emphasized that, in the University of Texas admissions process, "race is but a 'factor of a factor of a factor' in [a] holistic-review calculus"; the university did not use race as a "mechanical plus." Given this, the Court concluded the university had satisfied strict scrutiny.[10] Regardless, the precedential weight of *Fisher II* was feathery light. Most important, the Court decided the case shorthanded, with a four-to-three vote, because Justice Antonin Scalia had died after oral argument and Justice Elena Kagan recused herself. Moreover, it was the first (and only) case where Justice Kennedy voted to uphold an affirmative action program.[11]

In fact, the more conservative justices have consistently objected to the opinions and results in *Bakke*, *Grutter*, and *Fisher II*. They asserted that the majorities in *Grutter* and *Fisher II* had inappropriately diluted strict scrutiny: Once the Court required the government to justify affirmative action programs in accordance with strict scrutiny, the conservatives insisted that the government should always lose, that strict scrutiny (under equal protection) must be strict in theory but fatal in fact.[12] Affirmative action programs should always violate equal protection. To be clear, the conservative justices did not admit or believe that they were rejecting equality. Rather, they conceived of equality in formal terms: Equality was an abstract concept that was the same for everyone, regardless of context or circumstances. For many years, conservatives had been connoting this formal concept of equality with the idea of colorblindness. In the 1970s, for example, Nathan Glazer's neoconservative arguments against affirmative action maintained that the government, in the fields of employment, education, and housing, should guarantee equal opportunity (and remedy personal discrimination) but should not enforce rigid statistical distributions based on group memberships. From Glazer's perspective, affirmative action programs that smacked of quotas contravened a need for government neutrality, or, as other neocons would proclaim, government actions and policies had to be colorblind.[13]

In *Adarand Constructors, Inc. v. Pena*, decided in 1995, the Rehnquist Court held all race-based affirmative action programs are subject to strict scrutiny. Justice O'Connor's majority opinion therefore emphasized that the government could justify an affirmative action program only if it could prove the program was narrowly tailored to achieve a compelling government purpose. Nevertheless, O'Connor reasoned that the government might be able, in some circumstances, to adopt an affirmative action program that would pass constitutional muster (for instance, in university admissions).[14] Justices Scalia and Thomas strongly disagreed: Both wrote concurrences arguing for a more formal concept of equal protection that would preclude the government from ever justifying affirmative action. Scalia insisted the government could never justify treating one race different from another: "[U]nder our Constitution there can be no such thing as either a creditor or a debtor race."[15] Justice Clarence Thomas argued even more fervently for a colorblind Constitution.

> [T]here can be no doubt that racial paternalism and its unintended consequences can be as poisonous and pernicious as any other form of discrimination. So-called "benign" discrimination teaches many that because of chronic and apparently immutable handicaps, minorities cannot compete with them without their patronizing indulgence. Inevitably, such programs engender attitudes of superiority or, alternatively, provoke resentment among those who believe that they have been wronged by the government's use of race. These programs stamp minorities with a badge of inferiority and may cause them to develop dependencies or to adopt an attitude that they are "entitled" to preferences. . . . In my mind, government-sponsored racial discrimination based on benign prejudice is just as noxious as discrimination inspired by malicious prejudice. In each instance, it is racial discrimination, plain and simple.[16]

The early Roberts Court clarified and furthered the judicial commitment to a formal concept of equal protection. Chief Justice John Roberts's majority opinion in *Parents Involved in Community Schools v. Seattle School District No. 1*, decided in 2007, applied strict scrutiny and invalidated affirmative action programs allowing school officials to consider race when assigning students to elementary and high schools. In a plurality section of his opinion, Roberts insisted that affirmative action programs and Jim Crow laws are constitutionally indistinguishable. A rule is a rule. The rule of equality embodied in *Brown v. Board of*

Education, Roberts explained, mandated the invalidation of the *Parents Involved* affirmative action programs. "The way to stop discrimination on the basis of race is to stop discriminating on the basis of race."[17]

Thomas wrote another concurrence in *Parents Involved* that emphasized colorblindness. "Disfavoring a color-blind interpretation of the Constitution," Thomas wrote, "[the dissenters] would give school boards a free hand to make decisions on the basis of race—an approach reminiscent of that advocated by the segregationists in *Brown v. Board of Education*. This approach is just as wrong today as it was a half-century ago."[18] Indeed, conservative and progressive disagreements over affirmative action can be translated into a dispute about the meaning of *Brown* and its rejection of separate-but-equal. Conservative justices insist that *Brown* manifested an anticlassification principle: That *Brown* held the government can never classify on the basis of race, regardless of the government's claimed purposes. Progressive justices maintain that *Brown* manifested an antisubordination principle: That *Brown* held that government classifications, such as Jim Crow laws, are unconstitutional when they contribute to the subordination of a marginalized societal group, including Black Americans. From the progressive position, *Brown's* antisubordination principle prohibits the government from creating or bolstering a caste-like social system.[19]

As this debate over *Brown* suggests, the conservative enforcement of the anticlassification principle—or in other words, colorblindness—either ignores or erases the existence of structural or systemic racial inequalities in American society. Conservatives can proclaim that the nation is committed to the righteous path of equality while many Americans nonetheless trudge through a quagmire of inequality (or subordination). When conservatives acknowledge the existence of racial inequality, they categorize it as anomalous in American society, as violating basic norms of (formal) equality. They dismiss the nation's history of slavery and Jim Crow as irrelevant to today's world and deny that certain privileges have historically accrued to whites and continue to this day.[20] A June 2020 Senate Judiciary Hearing on police reform illustrates the rhetorical power of colorblindness. Senator John Cornyn, a Republican from Texas, asked witnesses about the prevalence of racism in America. He became particularly provoked when Vanita Gupta, president and CEO of the Leadership Conference on Civil and Human

Rights, stated: "I don't think there's an institution in this country that isn't suffering from structural racism, given our history." Gupta proceeded to explain structural racism and how it imbues individuals with implicit racial biases. An intrigued Cornyn then asked: "Do you agree basically that all Americans are racists?" Gupta replied: "I think we all have implicitly bias and racial biases. Yes, I do." Cornyn responded with alarm: "Wow. . . . You lost me when you want to take the acts of a few misguided, perhaps malicious individuals and subscribe that to all Americans."[21] Cornyn, in short, articulated a corollary of colorblindness: The United States is fully committed to equality, though a few bad apples are still not on board.[22]

Colorblindness pretends that the recognition or acknowledgment of race itself is problematic, that the recognition of race undermines equality. If one views the June 2020 Senate Judiciary through the lens of (ostensible) colorblindness, then it is Gupta who is the racist. Cornyn describes a world where race and racism no longer exist, except for the words and actions of a few bad apples. And apparently, Gupta is one of those bad apples: By discussing structural racism and implicit or unconscious bias, she is guilty of propagating racism. If she (and others like her) would just stop talking about race and racism, then all Americans would be equal, would be the same (color—white), and would join together and sing Kumbaya.[23]

But the very opposite is true: "Colorblindness ignores the lived reality of people of color."[24] Social science research demonstrates that the best way to start attacking racism and its correlative inequality is to talk openly about race. Silence about race, which follows from the rhetoric of colorblindness, "is a socialization strategy that perpetuates a racist status quo" of inequality and white privilege, where "being white means never having to say you're white."[25] Colorblindness insidiously reinforces and propagates inequality while claiming to pursue equality. Therefore, the rhetoric of colorblindness allows conservatives to ostensibly justify policies and practices that contravene the experiences and interests of most Black Americans, the existence of a few Black conservatives notwithstanding. To be sure, not all Black Americans share the same values and political views (the same, of course, can be said about women, Jews and other non-Christians, and LGBTQ+ individuals), yet colorblindness amounts to "an epistemology of ignorance."[26]

Statistics demonstrate stark material disparities between white and Black Americans. For instance, the median income of white households is approximately 173 percent of the median for Black households. The median net worth (in wealth) of white households is ten times that of Black households. Black unemployment is consistently higher than white unemployment. Black Americans lack health insurance at approximately twice the rate of white Americans. Black-owned housing is valued 35 percent lower than white-owned housing. Black men amount to 36 percent of the imprisoned population though Black Americans constitute only 14 percent of the national population. It goes on and on.[27] Yet, if the nation is truly colorblind, if racism is behind us, if most Americans do not even see race, then who or what is responsible for these material disparities? Colorblindness leaves only one answer: Black Americans. If racism is behind us, then Black Americans must be primarily responsible for their relatively low income levels; they must be primarily responsible for their lack of wealth; they must be primarily responsible for their high prison population; and so forth. This emphasis on Black responsibility—and concomitant white innocence—is not new in American history. At different points in time, whites have blamed Black biology, Black culture, or Black behavior for the nation's racial inequalities or disparities. In effect, a colorblind nation has persistently denied the existence of white privilege sustained by structural and systemic racism. Yet, throughout American history, "Whites have remained on the living and winning end, while Blacks remained on the losing and dying end."[28]

When conservatives combine colorblindness with dog whistle politics, it transforms into a type of invidious discrimination. Dog whistles tacitly appeal to racist attitudes without expressly invoking race—think of President Ronald Reagan repeatedly telling the "story of the Cadillac-driving welfare queen."[29] Evidence suggests that, nowadays, dog whistling is more effective than overt racist appeals in provoking racist sentiments and conduct. Dog whistles prompt many middle-class and poor whites to contravene not only Black interests but also their own interests. As Ian Haney Lopez writes about dog whistling, "race constitutes the dark magic by which middle-class voters have been convinced to turn government over to the wildly affluent, notwithstanding the harm this does to themselves."[30] In a similar vein, the progressive dissenters in

Parents Involved denounced the perverse logic that allowed Roberts and Thomas to equate Jim Crow and affirmative action through the prism of colorblindness.

> There is a cruel irony in the Chief Justice's reliance on our decision in *Brown v. Board of Education.* The first sentence in the concluding paragraph of his opinion states: "Before *Brown,* schoolchildren were told where they could and could not go to school based on the color of their skin." This sentence reminds me of Anatole France's observation: "[T]he majestic equality of the la[w], forbid[s] rich and poor alike to sleep under bridges, to beg in the streets, and to steal their bread." The Chief Justice fails to note that it was only black schoolchildren who were so ordered; indeed, the history books do not tell stories of white children struggling to attend black schools. In this and other ways, the Chief Justice rewrites the history of one of this Court's most important decisions.[31]

The abstract logic of colorblindness might be perverse, but the narrative logic is compelling: Colorblindness is the perfect trope to burnish the nation's commitment to equality while simultaneously obliterating an overwhelming history and continuing presence of racial inequality.[32]

Colorblindness elucidates the early Roberts Court's decision in *Shelby County v. Holder* (discussed in chapter 6)—a case that significantly moved the nation toward inegalitarian, hierarchical, and exclusionary democracy. Recall that *Shelby County* held that Congress's reenactment of the VRA's crucial preclearance provision was beyond the scope of congressional power. Roberts's majority opinion reasoned that the nation no longer needed the VRA preclearance protections because racial discrimination in voting had been eradicated. From his perspective, the evidence suggested that Congress might have correctly enacted the law in 1965, but times had changed: The nation had reached a point where colorblindness fulfilled the constitutional mandate of equality.

Yet, as soon as the Court announced its *Shelby County* decision, Americans learned how much times had not changed, as more than half the states imposed new restrictions on voting that disproportionately disfranchised Black American voters. In the three years after the Court decided *Shelby County,* (red) states purged 33 percent more voters than between 2006 and 2008. In fact, disfranchisement laws tend to discriminate most severely against people of color, the poor, and the uneducated.[33] And if there was any doubt, disfranchised voters can change election results: A study of the 2014 midterm elections concluded that disfranchisement laws potentially swung several gubernatorial and senate races.[34]

Despite the landslide of disfranchisement laws passed in red states, the Roberts Court conservatives refused to change direction. In *Abbott v. Perez*, a three-judge federal district court held that the Texas legislature violated equal protection and the VRA by intentionally discriminating on the basis of race when it adopted a districting plan for Congress and the Texas (legislative) House. In a five-to-four decision, with a conservative-progressive split typical of the early Roberts Court, the Court reversed the lower court and upheld the districting plan, except for one Texas House district.[35] Justice Alito's majority opinion emphasized that, in an equal protection case, the challenger bears the burden of proving the government intentionally discriminated on the basis of race (echoing the *Washington v. Davis* holding). Alito concluded that the lower court "committed a fundamental legal error" by shifting the burden of proof onto the government. Moreover, from Alito's standpoint, evidence of the Texas legislature's history of racial discrimination in congressional districting was insufficient to prove that the legislature had intentionally discriminated in adopting its new districting plan.[36]

Justice Sonia Sotomayor dissented, emphasizing that the lower court had not shifted the burden of proof. To the contrary, the lower court had applied a multi-factor test, spelled out in *Arlington Heights v. Metropolitan Housing Development Corporation*, in determining that the legislature had intentionally discriminated on the basis of race. A "substantial amount of evidence," including the legislature's history of discrimination, supported this conclusion.[37] Sotomayor underscored the degree to which the Court majority was shielding inequality in the democratic process. The Court's decision "comes at serious costs to our democracy. It means that . . . minority voters in Texas—despite constituting a majority of the population within the State—will continue to be underrepresented in the political process." Whereas "all voters in our country, regardless of race, [should securely enjoy] the right to equal participation in our political processes," Sotomayor wrote, the Court was facilitating "States' efforts to undermine" the meaningful exercise of suffrage.[38]

* * *

With decisions such as *Shelby County* and *Abbott v. Perez*, the Roberts Court conservatives marched the nation steadily toward an exclusive, inegalitarian, and hierarchical democracy. Even so, the Court had never mustered a majority opinion that endorsed colorblindness: The dispute over the meaning of *Brown* and the anticlassification and antisubordination principles had not been definitively resolved. That changed when Amy Coney Barrett took Ginsburg's seat, and the Court decided a monumental affirmative action case focused on university admissions. In *Students for Fair Admissions, Inc. (or SFFA) v. President & Fellows of Harvard College*, decided in 2023, the later Roberts Court held unconstitutional the Harvard and University of North Carolina race-plus affirmative action programs and effectively overruled *Bakke*, *Grutter*, and *Fisher II*, to the degree they allowed any race-based affirmative action. With an opinion written by Roberts, the Court unequivocally adopted the anticlassification principle and constitutional colorblindness: "Eliminating racial discrimination means eliminating all of it."[39] Roberts insisted this principle followed from *Brown*: "Separate but equal is 'inherently unequal,' said *Brown*." And of course, Roberts quoted from the first Justice Harlan's renowned dissent in *Plessy v. Ferguson*: "[I]n view of the Constitution, in the eye of the law, there is in this country no superior, dominant, ruling class of citizens. There is no caste here. Our Constitution is color-blind."[40]

Because the Court held that all race-based affirmative action programs offend equal protection, the Court required the universities to satisfy strict scrutiny. Most important, then, the Court repudiated the claim that student-body diversity constituted a compelling purpose. Even if student-body diversity could have once justified affirmative action, that time had ended. A full 25 years had not passed since the Court decided *Grutter*—recall that O'Connor's *Grutter* opinion had asserted that affirmative action would be unnecessary in 25 years—but the *SFFA* Court reasoned that enough was enough. The Court rejected all of the universities' asserted compelling purposes and also concluded that they had failed to prove that their affirmative action programs were narrowly tailored to achieve their claimed purposes.[41]

The implications of *SFFA* for racial justice and equality in American society are large and pernicious—though the conservative justices seemingly welcome them. First, by adopting the anticlassification principle and the formal rule of colorblindness, the decision implicitly rejected the antisubordination principle. The government can never act "to remedy the effects of societal discrimination through explicitly race-based measures."[42] The history and current structures of racial subordination are simply of no constitutional significance. As Justice Sotomayor explained in dissent, "equating state-sponsored [Jim Crow] segregation with race-conscious admissions policies that promote racial integration trivializes the harms of segregation and offends *Brown's* transformative legacy"[43]—that is, a transformative legacy animated by the antisubordination principle.

Second (and related to the first point), the Court's formal rule of colorblindness will help maintain the current structures of power in the United States, therefore reinforcing the racial status quo. Again, Sotomayor's dissent made the point: "Entrenched racial inequality remains a reality today. . . . Ignoring race will not equalize a society that is racially unequal. What was true in the 1860s, and again in 1954, is true today: Equality requires acknowledgment of inequality."[44] Both Sotomayor and Justice Ketanji Brown Jackson, in her dissent, eloquently articulated the evidence that American society persists in its structural or systemic racism. "Gulf-sized race-based gaps exist with respect to the health, wealth, and well-being of American citizens," Justice Jackson explained. "They were created in the distant past, but have indisputably been passed down to the present day through the generations."[45] Here is just a taste of the evidence Sotomayor and Jackson marshaled: "Students of color, particularly Black students, are disproportionately disciplined or suspended, interrupting their academic progress and increasing their risk of involvement with the criminal justice system. Underrepresented minorities are less likely to have parents with a postsecondary education who may be familiar with the college application process. Further, low-income children of color are less likely to attend preschool and other early childhood education programs that increase educational attainment. All of these interlocked factors place underrepresented minorities multiple steps behind the starting line in the race for college admissions." In short, the enforcement of colorblind formal equality will in actuality propagate inequality.[46]

Third, the Court denied that racial subordination in American society has personal significance that might partly shape an individual's experiences and views. "By singling out race, the Court imposes a special burden on racial minorities for whom race is a crucial component of their identity," Sotomayor explained. "'[By] foreclosing racial considerations, colorblindness denies those who racially self-identify the full expression of their identity' and treats 'racial identity as inferior' among all 'other forms of social identity.'" For a Court that accentuates and robustly protects (under the First Amendment) religious identity—so long as it is Christian—the Court's diminishment of racial identity is especially striking. The Court drains the Equal Protection Clause of its power, turning it "on its head."[47] From the Court's perspective, any acknowledgment or recognition of racial identity, of its potential importance to individual experiences and viewpoints, is no more than invidious racial stereotyping.[48]

Finally, Jackson emphasized that the *SFFA* decision is literally about who belongs: It goes "to the very concept of who 'merits' admission." And equality in education is crucial for "equal citizenship" in our democracy.[49] Invoking *Brown*, Sotomayor underscored the bankruptcy of the Court's colorblind approach: Education is crucial for full and equal participation in American democracy, she explained, and overcoming the harms imposed by historical segregation is crucial for just and equal educational opportunities.[50]

* * *

The Roberts Court's equal protection doctrine and endorsement of colorblindness manifest a shockingly iniquitous implementation of the Reconstruction-era Equal Protection Clause. On the one hand, if a white plaintiff challenges under equal protection a race-based affirmative action program involving university admissions or otherwise, then *SFFA* and *Parents Involved* mandate the application of strict scrutiny, the most rigorous level of judicial scrutiny. With strict scrutiny being strict in theory but fatal in fact, the government would unquestionably lose, even if it adopted the affirmative action program to correct for racial inequality and injustice—that is, to benefit historically subordinated people of color, including Black Americans. On the other hand, if a Black American plaintiff challenges a facially neutral law that has disparate or discriminatory racial effects—think of the legislative districting law in *Abbott v. Perez* or the police test in *Washington v. Davis*—then the Court would likely apply rational basis review, the lowest level of judicial scrutiny. The Court would not apply strict scrutiny unless the plaintiff proves the government intentionally discriminated on the basis of race. Proving intentional discrimination is typically problematic, as *Abbott* demonstrated. Under the Court's doctrinal framework, then, the Black American challenger will almost always lose, while the white challenger to affirmative action will almost always win.[51]

The Court's equal protection doctrine, in other words, seems designed to protect white privilege at the expense of people of color—not to produce equality under the Fourteenth Amendment. Imagine a city with a diverse population, half white and half people of color. Now imagine that for the past 70 years, this city has awarded 99 percent of its construction contracts to white contractors. If a Black contractor sues the city for violating equal protection, the contractor will need to prove the city intentionally discriminated against nonwhite contractors. The statistical evidence showing the grossly disparate or discriminatory 99 percent will not, standing alone, be sufficient to prove intent. The Black contractor will almost certainly lose this case. Imagine, though, the city realizes it has a problem with racial inequality (or discrimination) in construction contracts, so it voluntarily adopts a race-based affirmative action program to guarantee that, going forward, a reasonable number of contracts will go to nonwhite contractors. If a white contractor sues the city and challenges the affirmative action program, a court will automatically apply strict scrutiny. The white contractor will likely win the case, and the affirmative action program will be scrapped. No matter how one looks at it, the equal protection doctrine practically assures that the status quo of racial inequality and injustice remains intact.[52]

* * *

The later Roberts Court continued pushing down this road of colorblindness and racial inequality in an equal protection case directly involving democratic participation. In *Alexander v. South Carolina State Conference of the NAACP*, Black voters and the NAACP challenged a state's congressional districting scheme as being an unconstitutional racial gerrymander. Prior cases held that, to prove a racial gerrymander violates equal protection, a challenger must "show that race was the 'predominant factor motivating the legislature's decision to place a significant number of voters within or without a particular district.'" To be sure, this predominant-factor standard (like the *Washington v. Davis* intent requirement) was always difficult to satisfy, but *Alexander* made it near impossible. In 2019, the early Roberts Court, with a standard five-to-four conservative-progressive split, held in *Rucho v. Common Cause* that partisan gerrymandering (no matter how extreme) was a nonjusticiable political question. In *Alexander*, then, the Republican-controlled state legislature claimed that it had drawn district lines based on partisan rather than racial gerrymandering (because the legality of a partisan gerrymander would be nonjusticiable). Justice Alito, writing for the six-justice conservative bloc, therefore insisted that the Black voters and NAACP (as the challenger) "must disentangle race and politics if it wishes to prove that the legislature was motivated by race as opposed to partisanship."[53]

Significantly, a three-judge district court, after "overseeing broad discovery" and holding "a 9-day trial," concluded that the NAACP had carried its burden of proof, showing that race had been the predominant factor in the drawing of the congressional district lines. As Justice Kagan stated in her dissent: "The [district] court, to put the matter bluntly, did not believe the state officials."[54] Ordinarily, on appeal, the Supreme Court should have deferred to the district court findings of fact, reversing the lower court only for "clear error," as Alito acknowledged. Yet Alito and the conservative majority turned this deference on its head by introducing two legal twists. First, "in assessing a legislature's work," Alito explained, "we start with a presumption that the legislature acted in good faith." Why start with a presumption of good faith when it clearly runs counter to the clear error standard? According to Alito, the Court must show "due respect" for the state legislature rather than accusing it of "'offensive and demeaning' conduct."[55]

The conservative justices' respect for state officials and consequent presumption of good faith was egregious in two ways. First, the justices' forgiving attitude contravened their approach in religious freedom cases, where they had readily found purposeful government discrimination against Christians—even when the justices first needed to dig vigorously through a lower court record for some hint of anti-Christian animus (see chapters 7–8). Of course, in *Alexander*, the justices were evaluating the claims of Black voters and the NAACP rather than (white) Christians. Second, recall that Congress had, in its VRA preclearance provisions, effectively created a presumption against (certain) state changes to voting laws that might have racially disparate or discriminatory impacts; states needed federal approval before being allowed to change their laws. The early Roberts Court, however, emasculated the preclearance mechanism in *Shelby County v. Holder*, as discussed in chapter 6. Now, in *Alexander*, having previously swept away the congressional presumption, the conservative justices presumed the opposite, that the state officials acted in good faith vis-à-vis Black voters. In fact, under *Alexander*, state officials are constitutionally permitted to impose an ostensibly partisan gerrymander even if they are fully aware or "conscious" that it will have racially disparate or discriminatory effects.[56]

The Court's second legal twist, countering the clear error standard, supposedly followed from the presumption of good faith. Alito and the majority asserted that a challenger cannot overcome the presumption unless they present an "alternative map" that would have similarly achieved the legislature's partisan goals.[57] In this case, then, the Black voters and NAACP would have needed to hand the Republican-controlled legislature an alternative map that would have effectively preserved the same (extreme) degree of Republican control (or, in other words, white privilege) in the state. As Kagan noted in dissent, the Court introduced the alternative map as a prerequisite to a successful equal protection claim regardless of the challenger's other evidence; "[such] micro-management of a plaintiff's case is elsewhere unheard of in constitutional litigation."[58]

In short, Alito and the conservative majority went to extraordinary ends to undermine all racial gerrymandering cases brought under the Equal Protection Clause. "The [majority's] suspicion, and indeed derision, of suits brought to stop racial gerrymanders are self-evident," wrote Kagan; "the intent to insulate States from those suits no less so." Moreover, as Kagan emphasized, the case entailed the potential sorting of "citizens by their race with respect to the most fundamental of all their political rights."[59] Alito and the majority ultimately acknowledged that

WHO FULLY BELONGS? | 165

if the challenger could somehow prove that race was the predominant factor in the drawing of the congressional district lines, then the burden would shift to the state to satisfy strict scrutiny. Alito explained: "This standard [of strict scrutiny] is extraordinarily onerous because the Fourteenth Amendment was designed to eradicate race-based state action." He then pinpoint cited *SFFA*, the affirmative action decision, at a page where it endorsed colorblindness. Was Alito being subtly ironic or merely smug (more likely) by invoking colorblindness in a decision, *Alexander*, which interpreted the Reconstruction-era Fourteenth Amendment to deal a crushing blow against racial equality in the democratic process?[60] Either way, the conservative justices appear determined to mangle equal protection to ensure that Black Americans (and people of color, more generally) do not fully belong to the People. In a portentous sign that no precedent is safe from these justices, Justice Thomas, concurring in part in *Alexander*, argued that the Constitution's original meaning together with the reasoning in *Alexander* and *Rucho* suggest that *Brown v. Board of Education*—both *Brown I* and *Brown II* (discussed in chapter 3)—were incorrectly decided.[61]

Women Do Not Fully Belong

For five decades since 1973, when the Court decided *Roe v. Wade*, holding that women have a constitutionally protected right to choose whether to have an abortion, conservative justices on the Rehnquist and Roberts Courts worked to hollow out the right, diminishing women's reproductive autonomy.[62] Through those decades, the Court nonetheless continued to protect at least some minimal right for women to choose to have pre-viability abortions. As the Court stated in *Planned Parenthood v. Casey*, decided in 1992, it was "reaffirming the central holding of *Roe*."[63] But with Barrett on the Court and a solid six-justice conservative bloc in control, that minimal constitutional protection evaporated in 2022.

The *Roe* Court located a woman's right to choose in the Due Process Clause of the Fourteenth Amendment—that is, *Roe* was a substantive due process decision.[64] Post-1937 substantive (as opposed to procedural) due process decisions, like *Roe*, had generally divided into two lines. One line, based primarily on opinions written by progressive or liberal justices, reasoned that substantive due process rights encompassed two protected and often overlapping interests: an interest in intimate associations,[65] and an interest in making important personal decisions.[66] The interest in intimate associations could safeguard various relationships, including marriage and other sexual relationships.[67] The interest in making important personal decisions could safeguard decisions related to sex, procreation, child-rearing, and the like. This line of cases, emphasizing the two protected interests, viewed due process as flexible and evolving over time.[68] The second line, based primarily on opinions written by conservative justices, viewed substantive due process more narrowly and rigidly. It reasoned that substantive due process protected only those rights deeply rooted in American tradition and history.[69] Most often, when the Court followed this thread, the conclusion would be that due process did not protect the disputed interest.[70] *Roe* was a prototypical case in the first line: It protected a woman's right to make important personal decisions regarding her body, reproduction, and abortion.[71]

In *Dobbs v. Jackson Women's Health Organization*, the Court unequivocally followed the second line of cases. Alito's majority opinion stated: "We have held that the 'established method of substantive-due-process analysis' requires that an unenumerated right be 'deeply rooted in this Nation's history and tradition' before it can be recognized as a component of the 'liberty' protected in the Due Process Clause."[72] While this categorical assertion about substantive due process would appear to repudiate the entire first line of cases, the Court suggested that, in *Dobbs*, it was concerned solely with abortion.[73] As Alito repeatedly stated, abortion is "unique" because it involves "potential life." In any event, the Court emphasized that *Roe* had not fallen into the second (and acceptable) line of cases. Being in the first line, the Court deemed the "constitutional analysis [in *Roe* to be] far outside the bounds of any reasonable interpretation of the various constitutional provisions." *Roe*, the Court concluded, must therefore be overruled: "*Roe* was egregiously wrong from the start. Its reasoning was exceptionally weak, and the decision has had damaging consequences."[74]

As in *Kennedy v. Bremerton School District*, the praying-coach, religious-freedom case, the *Dobbs* Court tied its focus on history and tradition to originalism. Thus, Alito's opinion emphasized the status of abortion in 1868, the year the Fourteenth Amendment was ratified.[75] Just as the Court ostensibly froze the meaning of religious freedom, tying it to a time when the nation was de facto Protestant, the *Dobbs* Court froze the meaning of substantive due process, tying it to a time when women were openly excluded from the polity, lacking the right to vote and other political and civil rights.[76] Given the focus on 1868, the conservative justices could readily disregard women's interests in bodily and reproductive autonomy while shriveling the scope of women's constitutional rights. All too predictably, then, the Court concluded that a "right to abortion" was not deeply rooted in American tradition and history.[77]

Indeed, Alito's majority opinion is remarkable for eliding any concern for women's interests and rights—even though the case involves women's bodies and reproductive autonomy. Contrary to the joint dissent of Justices Breyer, Sotomayor, and Kagan, Alito's opinion did not even acknowledge that women's interests and rights might be at stake.[78] The Court repeatedly described the issue as being about the "right to abortion" rather than a right to choose whether to have an abortion.[79] Discussing a right to choose would necessarily recognize that *women are choosing*—that women are autonomous beings with their own interests, values, and constitutional rights.[80] And while the *Dobbs* majority opinion disregarded women's interests, it listed multiple "legitimate" state legislative interests (in prohibiting abortion). Among other interests, Alito mentioned "respect for and preservation of prenatal life at all stages of development; . . . the elimination of particularly gruesome or barbaric medical procedures; the preservation of the integrity of the medical profession; [and] the mitigation of fetal pain." These interests, Alito reasoned, justified the challenged state statute intended to protect "the unborn human being."[81]

Rather than viewing women as active, choosing, autonomous beings, Alito claimed the Court must follow the original public meaning of the Fourteenth Amendment. Originalist methodology, he insisted, is the only way to discern the objective meaning of the Constitution and to avoid politicizing constitutional decision-making.[82] Yet, as mentioned in chapter 8, Supreme Court justices are generally poor historians, and Alito did not prove otherwise in this case. While his majority opinion accurately maintained that, by 1868, multiple states had adopted laws restricting abortion, Alito failed to consider seriously the historical reasons for those laws. Even after suggesting the Court should not question legislative motives, Alito asserted that state legislatures enacted anti-abortion laws in the nineteenth century to protect fetal life: "There is ample evidence that the passage of these laws was . . . spurred by a sincere belief that abortion kills a human being."[83] But historical evidence casts doubt on Alito's assertion and reveals far greater complexity: Nineteenth-century anti-abortionists were strongly concerned with maintaining women's traditional roles in American society. Alito's tenuous historical reasoning suggests the Court's invocation of originalism was a means to disguise a politically driven decision, overruling five decades of precedents, including *Roe* and *Casey*, rather than a method for discerning objective constitutional meaning.[84]

The Court shamelessly reasoned that its decision, eliminating the constitutional right to choose, would bolster democracy. The *Dobbs* decision, Alito wrote, would "return the issue of abortion to the people's elected representatives." The citizens in the respective states would be able to negotiate, lobby, and vote as they debated the status of abortion under state laws.[85] The problem is that, time and again, the conservative justices have revealed disdain for democratic government and for fair and equal democratic participation, as discussed in chapter 6. The Roberts Court has repeatedly invalidated congressional actions,[86] narrowly interpreted congressional statutes,[87] restricted executive and administrative agency actions,[88] undermined the Voting Rights Act,[89] allowed corporations and the wealthy to unduly influence political campaigns,[90] refused to restrict extreme political gerrymandering,[91] and rendered racial gerrymandering practically impossible to prove unconstitutional.[92] Moreover, the Court has invalidated numerous state laws, so the conservative justices' hostility to democratic decision-making is not limited to the federal level.[93]

Rather than bolstering pluralist democracy, the Roberts Court has persistently undermined the full and equal participation of various marginalized groups in the American polity. No case underscores this point more clearly than *Dobbs*. When women cannot control their own bodies and reproductive capabilities, wide repercussions follow. Women's freedom, independence, and equality are diminished in the democratic sphere as well as in the civil and private spheres. The joint dissent explained this reliance interest:

> [P]eople today rely on their ability to control and time pregnancies when making countless life decisions: where to live, whether and how to invest in education or careers, how to allocate financial resources, and how to approach intimate and family relationships. Women may count on abortion access for when contraception fails. They may count on abortion access for when contraception cannot be used, for example, if they were raped. They may count on abortion for when something changes in the midst of a pregnancy, whether it involves family or financial circumstances, unanticipated medical complications, or heartbreaking fetal diagnoses. Taking away the right to abortion, as the majority does today, destroys all those individual plans and expectations. In so doing, it diminishes women's opportunities to participate fully and equally in the Nation's political, social, and economic life.[94]

How did Alito's majority opinion respond to these important reliance concerns? It didn't. After acknowledging the argument, Alito dismissed it, reasoning that the Court was "ill-equipped to assess" such assertions.[95] Of course, such an easy dismissal of these concerns flowed smoothly when women's interests and values were obscured and ignored.[96]

LGBTQ+ Individuals Do Not Fully Belong

Through the twentieth century, many state laws treated LGBTQ+ individuals as deviant sexual criminals.[97] As public opinion shifted, though, two Supreme Court decisions contributed to the recognition and protection of LGBTQ+ rights in American society. In *Lawrence v. Texas*, decided in 2003, the Rehnquist Court held that substantive due process protects a right to engage in homosexual conduct.[98] Then in *Obergefell v. Hodges*, decided in 2015, the Roberts Court extended *Lawrence* by holding that same-sex couples had a protected substantive due process right to marry.[99] In both cases, the moderately conservative Justice Kennedy provided crucial votes on closely divided Courts and wrote the majority opinions.[100]

In more recent years, the Roberts Court, especially after Justice Barrett joined, has chipped away at LGBTQ+ rights. As discussed in chapters 7 and 8, focused on religious freedom and non-Christians, the Court has already decided two cases that explicitly allow Christians to discriminate against LGBTQ+ individuals (or same-sex couples). In *Masterpiece Cakeshop*, the Court held that the state could not enforce its antidiscrimination statute against a baker who refused, on religious grounds, to bake a cake for a same-sex couple. The state had violated the baker's free exercise rights, according to the Court, because the Civil Rights Commission had expressed animus against Christians.[101] Similarly, in *Fulton v. City of Philadelphia*, another free exercise decision, the Court held that the city could not prevent Catholic Social Services from discriminating against same-sex couples when placing children in foster care homes. To be clear, when the *Fulton* Court required the city to satisfy strict scrutiny, the city argued it had a compelling interest—namely, protecting same-sex couples from discrimination.[102] After all, *Obergefell* had held that same-sex couples have a constitutional right to marry.[103] Regardless, the Court rejected the city's argument: The city's interest, preventing discrimination against same-sex couples, was not compelling.[104]

More recently, *303 Creative LLC v. Elenis*, decided in 2023, held that a wedding website designer had a free speech right to discriminate against same-sex couples despite a state statute prohibiting discrimination based on sexual orientation.[105] The Court reasoned that the website designer had a constitutional right to "acts of 'expressive association.'"[106] On that ground, the First Amendment insulated the website designer from the mandate of the antidiscrimination statute: She could, in other words, choose not to associate with a same-sex couple and their wedding—a discriminatory action (refusing service) that would have otherwise violated the statute. If the state could enforce its antidiscrimination statute, the Court concluded, then the state would have, in effect, compelled the website designer to express support for same-sex weddings, contrary to her beliefs.[107]

The *303 Creative* Court, in a sense, pushed the envelope by allowing a business owner to discriminate against same-sex couples based on free speech rather than free exercise rights. Although Christian religious beliefs motivated the business owner, the Court did not explicitly rely on those religious beliefs in justifying its decision.[108] Going forward, then, an individual who wants to discriminate against LGBTQ+ individuals does not need to assert a specific religious claim or belief, but can instead proceed successfully with a more generalized free speech claim. Presumably, more people would be able to claim, "I don't want to express my support for same-sex marriage," than would be able to claim, "I don't want to express my support for same-sex marriage *because* my specific religious beliefs preclude doing so." Moreover, the limits of the *303 Creative* decision are unclear. If, as suggested by the Court, discrimination against LGBTQ+ individuals can be construed to be political or personal expression rather than conduct, then when could such discrimination be prohibited? Put in other words, when would an individual who wants to discriminate be unable to claim that their discrimination was expressive?[109]

These various First Amendment decisions, whether under the Free Exercise or Free Speech Clause, diminish the status of LGBTQ+ individuals in American society.[110] As Sotomayor emphasized in her *303 Creative* dissent, the purpose behind antidiscrimination statutes is "to include more persons as full and equal members of 'the public.'" She explained that full and equal citizenship in the democratic sphere intertwines with full and equal status in the civil and private spheres, including in the economic marketplace: "[I]n a free and democratic society, there can be no social castes. And for that to be true, it must be true in the public market."[111]

Even with the damage already done—with the Court, in effect, constitutionalizing discrimination against LGBTQ+ individuals—the perhaps greater threat to LGBTQ+ rights lies in Alito's majority opinion in *Dobbs*. Although Alito claimed to question the precedential value of only cases focused on abortion, his reasoning seemed to undermine *Obergefell* and *Lawrence*, the key decisions recognizing LGBTQ+ constitutional rights. Both fell into the line of substantive due process cases emphasizing the overlapping interests in intimate associations and making important personal decisions.[112] With *Dobbs* stressing that only those rights deeply rooted in American tradition and history were within the compass of substantive due process,[113] where will that leave LGBTQ+ rights? As Justice Thomas wrote in his *Dobbs* concurrence, the logic of the decision should lead the justices to "reconsider all of [the] Court's substantive due process precedents, including . . . *Lawrence*, and *Obergefell*." From his perspective, all substantive due process decisions are "demonstrably erroneous."[114] At this stage, LGBTQ+ rights are tenuous.

* * *

Conservatives have talked of undoing the mistakes of 1937, yet the Roberts Court seems uninterested in any wholesale return to the principles of republican democracy, which animated pre-1937 Supreme Court decision-making. While individual rights such as religious freedom, free expression, and equal protection remained relatively toothless before 1937, the Roberts Court has selectively invigorated those rights— selectively in support of white, Christian, heterosexual men. Ironically, the one individual right the pre-1937 Court had vigorously enforced, substantive due process—think of the liberty of contract cases discussed in chapter 2—is the one the Roberts Court has undermined. By doing so, in *Dobbs*, the Court not only undermined women's reproductive rights but also weakened the constitutional supports for LGBTQ+ rights. If anything, then, the Roberts Court's vision of a pre-1937 constitutional world is one of minority rule. The Roberts Court seems determined to return the United States to an exclusive, inegalitarian, and hierarchical form of democracy.

Indeed, the later Roberts Court, in its effort to protect the prerogatives of white, Christian, heterosexual men, has moved disturbingly close to the reasoning of *Plessy v. Ferguson*, discussed in chapter 2. In other words, the Court is interpreting individual rights to protect white, Christian, heterosexual men, even as they express their prejudices and discriminate against others. The Constitution, from this perspective, cannot protect or encourage social equality.[115] It is worth recalling, then, Justice Harlan's dissent in *Plessy* and his warning that the Court's decision would likely "stimulate aggressions, more or less brutal and irritating."[116] The later Roberts Court, no less so than the *Plessy* Court, is not an innocent bystander merely applying a neutral rule of law. The later Roberts Court manifests a tangible threat to non-Christians, people of color, women, and LGBTQ+ individuals.

PART III

Conclusion

10

Toward a Fully Realized Democracy

Many conservative scholars and jurists insist that the Supreme Court took a "wrong turn" in 1937, as Justice Thomas has written.[1] To a great degree, then, the Roberts Court seems intent on undoing that ostensible mistake. Regardless, returning to a pre-1937 Constitution does not, for the current conservative justices, require the resurrection of the republican democratic principles of virtue and the common good, often invoked before 1937. In fact, the Court continues to invoke individual rights to free speech, religious freedom, and equal protection that remained relatively toothless until after the 1937 transition. Yet, rather than invoking those rights in the service of an inclusive, egalitarian, and participatory pluralist democracy, as the post-1937 and Warren Courts often did, the Roberts Court interprets those rights (and substantive due process) to protect and empower white, Christian, heterosexual men— usually at the expense of people of color, non-Christians, women, and LGBTQ+ individuals. The crux of the pre-1937 constitutional order, for the Roberts Court conservatives, appears to be an exclusive, inegalitarian, and hierarchical democracy—a constitutional order enforcing minority rule.

In retrospect, the hallmarks of the judicial conservatism that characterized the 1970s and 1980s, judicial restraint and deference to democratic decision-making, no longer look like rock-solid principles: They were talking points that conveniently fit the contemporary political circumstances. Nowadays, the protection and bolstering of white, Christian political and cultural prerogatives seem to animate the Roberts Court's decisions. The two elections of President Barack Obama, a Black American, are crucial to understanding this judicial dynamic. If the 1930s and the New Deal marked an unusual period in American history when the forces for an inclusive and egalitarian democracy gained the upper hand, the presidency of Obama marked a second such period.[2] As in the 1930s, demographic changes spurred the democratic forces of the early twenty-first century. The nation had become significantly more diverse both racially and religiously, and the election (and reelection) of Obama demonstrated the tangible democratic power of this increasingly diverse America.[3]

But the white, Christian backlash, manifested in Donald Trump's 2016 election, was just as tangible. Numerous political science studies showed that white Christians perceived a loss of status, resented it, and consequently voted for Trump.[4] Even so, Trump won the 2016 election despite losing the popular vote, and he proceeded to nominate three of the justices on the later Roberts Court. With those justices in place, ultraconservative Republicans have captured the Court: It has become one institution in a network of institutions, which includes the Senate and the Electoral College, that enforces minority rule while undermining democratic equality.[5]

With regard to the politics of the current justices, numerous Roberts Court decisions harmonize with a white Christian nationalism that has entered the conservative, political mainstream.[6] Mainstream white Christian nationalists believe the United States was founded to be a Christian light for the world; the nation is "becoming less and less Christian"; and it is therefore "being overrun by moral chaos."[7] In response, white Christian nationalists not only celebrate Christianity but also often denigrate non-Christian religions. The Christian roots and nature of the nation must be aggressively reestablished, nurtured, and protected through a muscular political agenda. Consequently, white Christian nationalists adamantly defend traditional gendered family roles, oppose abortion, and denounce LGBTQ+ rights.[8] Americans who oppose these political goals, whether government actors or otherwise, are not preserving equality or democracy, regardless of what they might claim. Rather, they are attacking Christianity: Since Christians are merely seeking to enforce the "truth," these opponents must be expressing animus against Christianity.[9] Ultimately, white Christian nationalists want to enforce a quasi-caste system with white, Christian, heterosexual men at the top. Others may be tolerated, permitted to live in this country, but they are not fully American.[10]

To be sure, the conservative justices do not openly voice or manifest the most extreme forms of the white, Christian, nationalist movement. They do not seek, for example, to banish non-Christians, people of color, and LGBTQ+ individuals from the United States. True, Justice Alito and his wife (he blamed her) flew flags on their homes that symbolized, first, the ostensible illegitimacy of Joe Biden's presidential election (an upside-down American flag) and, second, "a push to remake American government in Christian terms" (an 'Appeal to Heaven' flag, which insurrectionists carried on January 6, 2021).[11] In fact, an undercover political activist (posing as a Catholic conservative) recorded Alito at a Supreme Court gala arguably articulating mainstream white, Christian, nationalist tenets. "One side or the other is going to win," Alito said, "because there are differences on fundamental things that really can't be compromised." The activist then asserted that "people in this country who believe in God have got to keep fighting for that, to return our country to a place of godliness." Alito answered ominously, given his position of power on the Supreme Court: "I agree with you, I agree with you."[12] Regardless of the degree to which Alito was voicing explicit white, Christian, nationalist views, the key point is that he and the other conservative justices consistently issue judicial decisions and opinions resonating with mainstream white Christian nationalism.[13]

To make an obvious but important point, white, Christian, nationalist beliefs and goals are widespread throughout American conservatism and are not dependent on Donald Trump's leadership. A recent Public Religion Research Institute (PRRI) poll shows 55 percent of Republicans holding Christian nationalist views.[14] Unsurprisingly, then, the conservative Heritage Foundation's *Project 2025, Mandate for Leadership* underscores the likely ongoing prominence of a white, Christian, nationalist agenda. Think of the *Mandate* as a roadmap for the government, particularly the executive branch, to implement (or impose) conservative values on American society. As stated in a prefatory section, "The task at hand [is to] restore our Republic to its original moorings." What does this mean? The *Mandate* worries about the status of Christian schools and clubs, about the CDC (Centers for Disease Control and Prevention) and other government agencies that might interfere with Christian holy days and saving souls during health emergencies, and about the Department of Justice interfering with the religious freedom and free expression of Christians. The *Mandate* wants the government to prohibit the mailing of abortion-inducing medications and to enforce colorblindness, stopping "affirmative discrimination"—that is, affirmative action. And related to the proscription of abortion, the *Mandate* emphasizes that the traditional role of motherhood is religiously grounded.[15] In early July 2024, the Heritage Foundation president declared that "we are in the process of the second American Revolution, which will remain bloodless if the left allows it to be."[16]

From this Christian conservative standpoint, in a nation marked by religious pluralism and growing secularism, democracy is fraught with danger. Or to be more precise, an inclusive, egalitarian, and participatory pluralist democracy portends danger for Christian conservatives and must be resisted. An exclusive, inegalitarian, and hierarchical democracy is acceptable so long as white, Christian, heterosexual men control the levers of power. Minority rule must be enforced. Unsurprisingly, then, the Roberts Court's individual rights decisions go hand-in-hand with their anti-democracy rulings. The Court denigrates democratic government and disempowers democratic majorities—for instance, by constraining congressional power—while also protecting and bolstering the privileges and predominance of white, Christian, heterosexual men, though they represent only a fraction of the American population.[17]

So, who belongs to "We the People"?[18] If one follows the Roberts Court, then white, Christian, heterosexual men fully belong. For years, the Court has been on a crusade against people of color, non-Christians, women, and LGBTQ+ individuals. Once Justice Barrett joined the Court, the conservative justices were able to intensify the fight, claiming victories where their crusade had been previously slowed or thwarted— think of *Dobbs* overruling *Roe v. Wade* and eliminating women's right to choose. While vigorously protecting the rights of white, Christian, heterosexual men, the Roberts Court has been narrowing and diminishing the rights of others—of historically marginalized groups.[19]

Of course, the conservative justices do not openly declare that any individuals or groups should be lesser Americans—that their rights should be narrowed. Justice Alito has even emphasized "respecting the 'dignity,' 'worth,' and fundamental equality of all members of the community." That declaration, though, came in Alito's concurrence (in the judgment) in *Fulton v. City of Philadelphia*, which held that the Free Exercise Clause protected a right for Catholic Social Services to discriminate against same-sex couples in foster care placements.[20] *Fulton* and other recent decisions constitutionally protecting white Christian discrimination in the private sphere (or civil society) intertwine with the conservative assault on democracy. When historically marginalized groups are disparaged and discriminated against in civil society, then their ability to participate fully in democratic government is diminished.[21]

The post-1937 and Warren Courts recognized this crucial connection between the private and public spheres, as do the progressive justices on the Roberts Court. In the *SFFA* affirmative action case, Jackson's dissent emphasized that equality and fairness in university admissions are crucial for "equal citizenship" in our democracy.[22] Likewise, in Sotomayor's *303 Creative* dissent, she stressed that antidiscrimination statutes protect "persons as full and equal members of 'the public.'"[23] The progressive justices underscored this point in their joint dissent in *Dobbs*. When women cannot control their bodies and reproductive capabilities, their freedom, independence, and equality are diminished in the democratic sphere as well as in the civil and private spheres. If women can choose whether to have an abortion, then they can "control and time pregnancies when making countless life decisions." By deciding *Dobbs* and eliminating the right to choose, the conservative justices undermined "women's opportunities to participate fully and equally in the Nation's political, social, and economic life."[24]

Ultimately, then, Alito and the other conservative justices appear to believe, "We're all equal, but white, Christian, heterosexual men are more equal." It is their nation. Others will be tolerated—but they must accept that the United States is a white, Christian nation (with all that white, Christian nationhood entails).[25] We might question whether this form of government should still be called a democracy, but rather than exploring the minimal requisites for democracy, I will go in the opposite direction and ask: What would a robust, uncompromised pluralist democracy look like?

* * *

Even during the heyday of the Warren Court, with its bolstering of an inclusive, egalitarian, and participatory democracy, the nation never became a fully realized democracy. To be certain, under the current Roberts Court, any discussion of such a democracy must be at the level of pure theory, or perhaps more precisely, pure fantasy. Regardless, suppose that, at some future time, a progressive majority controls the Court, and it seeks to interpret the Constitution to nurture and protect a fully inclusive, egalitarian, and participatory pluralist democracy.[26] What would a robust, uncompromised pluralist democracy look like? While a comprehensive description of such a democracy would require a separate book, we can focus on one key element that contrasts with the Roberts Court's bankrupt vision of democracy. The Constitution must be interpreted to allow the enactment and enforcement of comprehensive antidiscrimination laws. More precisely, the government must be able to prohibit discrimination against historically marginalized societal groups—non-Christians, people of color, women, and LGBTQ+ individuals—even if the would-be discriminator claims that proscribing discrimination would violate their religious freedom or free expression.

Numerous constitutional and political theorists center process as the cornerstone of pluralist democracy.[27] A pluralist democratic government is one that follows certain processes (or procedures) rather than pursuing some specific substantive goal, such as the common good or general welfare. Robert A. Dahl, perhaps the preeminent theorist of pluralist democracy, specified the processes required for the operation of a democratic government. For instance, each individual must be allocated a vote of identical weight with all other voters, and the option receiving the greatest number of votes wins. Dahl emphasized, though, that "effective participation" is the most important component of democracy. Citizens and interest groups must be able to participate fully and effectively by expressing their respective values and interests in the democratic arena.[28] The government cannot dictate any particular goals or visions for a good and proper life. Rather, from this perspective, the government must remain neutral, providing a framework of processes (and rights) that allows individuals and interest groups to assert a plurality of visions.[29]

Even so, while theorists have emphasized the centrality of process to pluralist democracy, Dahl and others have also maintained that process alone cannot define democracy. Following the proper processes is crucial, but pluralist democracy cannot be maintained without the sustenance of certain substantive norms or conditions.[30] A democratic community, for instance, must maintain its democratic culture. If citizens are not widely committed to the rules of the democratic game—

negotiation, compromise, and coalition-building—then the political community will splinter into sharply polarized interest groups.[31] Moreover, a citizen's right to participate fully and effectively is not merely formal. Rather, citizens must have sufficient resources to participate. Individuals who lack the fundamentals of housing, education, or medical care cannot fully engage in political discussion and participation regardless of their desire to play by the rules of the game.[32]

These substantive conditions or prerequisites limit the reach of pluralist democratic processes. For example, a legislature cannot constitutionally enact a law that would abridge some citizens' abilities and opportunities to participate, even if a supermajority of citizens and legislators followed the proper processes in enacting the law.[33] Certain government actions must be off the table, beyond democratic debate, because they would contravene the substantive conditions necessary for robust pluralist democracy. Most important, all individuals, regardless of sub-culture or societal grouping, must be treated as full and equal citizens in good standing. Even if a supermajority of Americans were to support a law discriminating against LGBTQ+ individuals—or people of color, or non-Christians, or women—such government action must be unconstitutional because it would relegate the targeted group to second-class citizenship.[34]

John Hart Ely's constitutional theory of representation reinforcement, grounded on pluralist democracy—and the criticisms of the theory—underscore that the definition of democracy must include a substantive component; pluralist democracy cannot be reduced solely to formal rules or processes.[35] Ely argued to the contrary, that representation-reinforcement theory was pure process-based: When the Court exercised its power of judicial review, reviewing the constitutionality of a legislative action, the Court should "police" the democratic process but should never enunciate or enforce substantive principles or values.[36] Only the legislature, when following the proper pluralist democratic processes, could determine appropriate communal goals (or values). When reviewing the constitutionality of a legislative action, the Court needed to defer to the legislature so long as the democratic process had been fair and open—regardless of the substantive content of the legislative action. But if the democratic process had been defective, then the Court should deem the legislative action unconstitutional.[37]

The Court, Ely explained, can police the democratic process in two ways. First, the Court can clear the channels of political change.[38] Political "ins" cannot be allowed to protect their power by choking the channels of political change and permanently excluding the political "outs." Denying or diluting the right to vote through legislative malapportionment is a "quintessential stoppage" in the democratic process and therefore unconstitutional.[39] Second, the Court can facilitate the representation of "minorities."[40] Democratic representatives cannot be allowed to systematically disadvantage minorities because of hostility or prejudice. The democratic process malfunctions if everyone is not "actually or virtually represented." Therefore, when a legislature intentionally discriminates against a minority for an improper motive, such as racial hostility, the Court should find the legislative action unconstitutional.[41]

As numerous critics pointed out, however, Ely's representation-reinforcement theory was not pure process-based. Political battles in pluralist democracy always produce winners and losers; some societal groups win while others lose. Yet Ely argued that the Court should police the democratic process by facilitating the representation of minorities. To do so, the Court itself had to differentiate among the numerous societal groups that had lost in the pluralist democratic arena. The Court needed to designate some such groups as discrete and insular minorities deserving special judicial protection while deeming other groups mere losers in the democratic process.[42] But this judicial designation of discrete and insular minorities required the Court to engage in exactly those substantive value choices supposedly forbidden by representation-reinforcement theory; the Court needed to differentiate among the various groups of democratic losers.[43] Rather than remaining neutral among societal groups (and their respective values and interests), the Court necessarily deemed some groups as deserving special judicial protection. One critic, Paul Brest, commented that Ely had articulated a process-based constitutional theory so artfully that his failure unwittingly demonstrated its impossibility: "John Hart Ely has come as close as anyone could to proving that it can't be done."[44] The criticisms of Ely's representation-reinforcement theory underscore that we cannot discuss democracy as solely a matter of process. We must also discuss the status of different societal groups within the democratic community—a substantive issue. Do all groups have full and equal standing?[45]

Dahl underscored that whenever we raise the issue of democratic or constitutional rights, we implicitly ask the question: Rights for whom? *Who belongs?* Who belongs to and can fully and equally participate in the political community?[46] Under republican democracy, this question led to a focus on civic virtue. Supposedly, only those individuals virtuous enough to pursue the common good rather than their own private interests were entitled to full and equal citizenship, to rights to speak and vote. But in a robust pluralist democracy, full "[e]qual citizenship" for all individuals must be a premise of the system.[47] All members of the political community deserve "equal concern and respect"—without full and equal citizenship, allowing for equal political participation for all, then pluralist democracy does not truly exist.[48]

This substantive component of pluralist democracy provides a crucial fulcrum for analyzing the Roberts Court's individual rights decisions. Consider, for instance, discriminatory actions targeting the LGBTQ+ community or individuals. Such discrimination warps the boundaries of the political community. Any individual who is a full and equal citizen in good standing should be "entitled to the same liberties, protections, and powers" that all other citizens enjoy. Each individual, regardless of whether they are LGBTQ+, should be able "to walk down the street without fear of insult or humiliation, to find the shops and exchanges open to him, and to proceed with an implicit assurance of being able to interact with others without being treated as a pariah."[49] If the government allows or facilitates discrimination against LGBTQ+ individuals, if they can be treated as less than full and equal citizens, then democracy is necessarily stunted. Discriminatory conduct might not contravene democracy as overtly as does a denial of suffrage, yet such conduct still undermines the substantive conditions for democracy and should not be constitutionally protected. Discrimination treats individuals differently (or unequally) from other citizens exactly because they belong to the targeted group. Discrimination sends the message that the targeted group and its members should not get too comfortable because other Americans would gladly mistreat them or cast them out altogether. In such a social and political environment, the targeted group and its members cannot possibly participate in democratic negotiations, coalitions, and compromises on an equal basis with other citizens. Their political strength is diminished before the democratic process even gets underway. Discrimination mutes the voices of the targeted group and its members, thus allowing other citizens to readily discredit or ignore their values and interests.[50]

In fact, legally protected discrimination appears to legitimate further political debate about the status of LGBTQ+ individuals while simultaneously diminishing their full and equal ability to participate in the democratic process. Discrimination thrusts LGBTQ+ individuals into a second-class position in our polity. Some individuals, in such circumstances, will react by remaining silent or hiding their differences from the mainstream. Others will attempt to continue participating openly in the democratic arena—perhaps by defending their right to equal concern and respect—yet their words and ideas must overcome the disadvantages of a diminished communal status.[51] "The issue is," according to Jeremy Waldron, "the harm done to individuals and groups through the disfiguring of our social environment . . . to the effect that in the opinion of one group in the community, perhaps the majority, members of another group are not worthy of equal citizenship."[52] A fair and open democratic dialogue or exchange of ideas is impossible if social or political power is skewed before the dialogue even begins. Pluralist democracy fails when some in the political community treat others as less than citizens of full and equal standing.[53]

The crucial point is that in a well-functioning pluralist democracy, some issues must be off the table. All citizens in good standing should be treated as such (with equal concern and respect) and entitled to participate fully and equally in the democratic process. This must be true for not only LGBTQ+ individuals but also non-Christians, people of color, and women—their full and equal citizenship should not be treated as an issue still open for debate. Contrary to the Roberts Court's decisions in *Masterpiece Cakebox* and *Fulton*, for example, religious freedom should not overcome antidiscrimination laws and protect or justify discrimination that diminishes the citizenship and participatory rights of LGBTQ+ individuals. The same must be true for the citizenship and participatory rights of non-Christians, people of color, and women. Likewise, contrary to the decision in *303 Creative*, free expression should not overcome antidiscrimination laws and protect or justify discrimination that diminishes the citizenship and participatory rights of others. Full and equal citizenship for LGBTQ+ individuals, non-Christians, people of color, and women should be among the "settled features of the social environment to which we are visibly and pervasively committed."[54] More broadly, while free expression is generally necessary for full and equal participation in pluralist democracy, free expression must be limited if it undermines the substantive component of pluralist democracy.[55] The fact that critics of LGBTQ+ individuals, non-Christians, people of color, and women might be inspired or motivated by religion or claim a First Amendment (free expression) right to not associate with a targeted group is irrelevant.[56]

The substantive component of pluralist democracy similarly illuminates *Dobbs* and its overruling of *Roe v. Wade*. When the Court decided *Dobbs*, the Court did more than eliminate a woman's right to choose whether to have an abortion. Although the *Dobbs* Court claimed that its decision would bolster democracy, the decision in reality contravened the substantive conditions for full and equal democratic participation.[57] If women cannot control their own bodies and reproductive capabilities, then they do not enjoy "the same liberties, protections, and powers" that men enjoy.[58] After *Dobbs*, women are not being treated as full and equal citizens in good standing. *Dobbs* in effect constitutionalized discriminatory treatment of women. As the joint dissenters emphasized, "[t]aking away the right to abortion . . . diminishes women's opportunities to participate fully and equally in the Nation's political, social, and economic life." Indeed, in not only *Dobbs* but also *SFFA* and *303 Creative*, the progressive justices have hammered home the point that the conservative-controlled Court's individual rights decisions are stunting American democracy.[59]

In short, to attain a fully realized pluralist democracy, discrimination against non-Christians, people of color, women, and LGBTQ+ individuals cannot be constitutionally valued or protected, whether under the First Amendment or otherwise.[60] Yet, what about "equal concern and respect" for white, Christian, heterosexual men?[61] They, too, should be "entitled to the same liberties, protections, and powers" that all other citizens enjoy.[62] After all, the Court must protect their rights to religious freedom, free speech, equal protection, and substantive due process. Ultimately, though, if all Americans are to be full and equal citizens, then *all* must have *diminished* rights and democratic power if and when they discriminate against or advocate for the discriminatory treatment of others, particularly historically marginalized groups. In other words, diminished rights and democratic power can be justified, but only when individuals, organizations, or other groups want to diminish the rights and powers of others. If, for example, one's religious identity is bound up with or demands discrimination against non-Christians, or women, or LGBTQ+ individuals, or people of color, then one's religious freedom must necessarily be narrowed. Such individuals remain free to believe anything—that non-Christians and LGBTQ+ individuals will go to hell and should be barred from public schools, for instance—but they should be barred from acting on or advocating for the implementation of those beliefs. Throughout American history, white, Christian, heterosexual men have invoked their own legal-constitutional rights to justify discrimination and persecution of marginalized groups and their members. Think of slavery, Jim Crow laws, blasphemy laws, Sunday closing laws, coverture laws, anti-abortion laws, and so on. This must end if we are to have a democratic society where all are full and equal citizens.[63]

To be sure, in a fully realized pluralist democracy, the government would not aim for a specious neutrality. Rather, the government would affirmatively nurture democratic culture by ensuring that all citizens can fully and equally participate in the polity—therefore, the government should enact antidiscrimination laws. If the government allows an individual or business to discriminate against non-Christians, people of color, women, or LGBTQ+ individuals, the government is not acting neutrally. Instead, the government is facilitating the continued marginalization of the targeted group within the political community. The citizenship of that group and its members will be diminished as their ability to speak and otherwise participate within the community will be undermined.[64] Ultimately, a pluralist democratic government cannot merely provide an abstract framework of rules or procedures that allows individuals to assert their respective interests and values. Regardless of the content or source of those individual interests and values—even if the content or source is religious—certain substantive questions and matters must be off the table if a pluralist democracy is to exist. All individuals must be treated as full and equal citizens in good standing.[65]

* * *

The conservative justices on the Roberts Court are not interpreting the Constitution in accordance with a fully realized pluralist democracy. To the contrary, the conservative justices are marching on a crusade toward an exclusive, inegalitarian, and hierarchical form of government. My discussion of a fully realized pluralist democracy, as I admitted at the outset, should be understood as theoretical or even fantastical. What would need to happen, though, to transform that fantasy into reality? In brief, if we assume the current conservative justices will remain on the Court for the foreseeable future, then the following four steps must be implemented in the specified order. First, on the electoral front, progressive Democrats must gain simultaneous control of the presidency, the Senate, and the House of Representatives (sometime far in the future, given the results of the November 2024 election). Second, once in control of the Senate, the Democrats must eliminate the filibuster, an institutional barrier to democratic rule that is merely a matter of Senate tradition. Third, the progressive Democrats must pass a statute adding at least four seats to the Supreme Court, the minimum number needed to overcome the Roberts Court's conservative six-to-three majority. The Democratic president would then nominate four progressives, and the Senate would confirm the nominees as the newest justices. Only then would the Court's political views correspond with those of a majority of Americans (as reflected in recent popular votes for the presidency, with the exceptions of the 2004 and 2024 elections—Trump won a plurality but not a majority of the popular vote in 2024).[66] Finally, Congress could then enact a series of statutory provisions to move the nation closer to the reality of an inclusive, egalitarian, and participatory democracy. For instance, Congress could seek to protect voter registration and access while restricting political (and racial) gerrymandering, political (campaign) spending, and voter purges.[67]

Each of these steps toward a fully realized pluralist democracy must be implemented in the proper order. If Congress were to enact democracy-boosting statutes without first changing the makeup of the Court, the conservative justices, bent on minority rule, would almost certainly use their power of judicial review to invalidate the congressional actions. And if Democrats attempted to pass a statute expanding the Court without first eliminating the filibuster, then Republican Senators would almost certainly block the legislation. But of course, none of this can happen without the first step in the program, progressive Democrats winning elections and gaining control of the presidency, the Senate, and the House. Yet, achieving that first step is problematic exactly because the Court and other institutions (such as the Electoral College) impede democratic rule by the majority.

To be fair, the Roberts Court's anti-democratic interpretation of the Constitution is not arbitrary or unreasonable, at least from a historical standpoint. Throughout American history, the forces of exclusion have more often predominated over the forces of inclusion. Regardless, an inclusive and egalitarian reading of the Constitution is also reasonable and historically rooted. The post-1937 and Warren Courts were not arbitrarily interpreting the Constitution. The choice between exclusion and inclusion is political, notwithstanding the Roberts Court's frequent invocations of originalism to support their conclusions as being politically neutral. Originalism is not an apolitical interpretive method; it is a rhetorical tactic that obscures the Court's *choice* to be anti-democratic and to protect minority rule.[68]

The Roberts Court's choice to be anti-democratic—or to cast democracy as exclusionary, inegalitarian, and hierarchical—debases the Constitution and the nation. If white, Christian, heterosexual men are to rule, if they are to be fully invested with rights denied to others—as the conservative justices have been deciding—then the United States does not differ from dozens of other nations. If the Roberts Court has its way, the nation will no longer be a laudable experiment in inclusive, egalitarian, and participatory democracy, despite its many historical failings. Instead, the nation will be just another country based on "Blood and Soil"—one where only white Christians fully belong.[69] Which nation is more compelling? To me, the choice is clear: Rather than focusing on ethnicity and religion, Americans should choose, in the words of Hamilton, "good government from reflection and choice."[70]

ACKNOWLEDGMENTS

I thank Paul Finkelman, Frank Ravitz, and Laura L. Feldman for reading and commenting on the book manuscript. In writing the manuscript, I derived parts from numerous articles, and I thank those who helped along the way with their comments on the various article manuscripts, including Richard Delgado, Howard Gillman, and Sam Kalen. I also thank the panelists and audience members for feedback on my paper presentation at the "We the Peoples" session, 2024 Law and Society Conference. The Housel/Arnold endowment provided financial assistance for the work. The librarians at the University of Wyoming College of Law provided support through all stages of the research and writing process. Also, I thank Deans Klint Alexander and Julie Hill for their support of my work. Finally, I thank Clara Platter of NYU Press for her support of this project.

I used (and modified) parts from the following articles:

Searching for Truth that Speaks to Power: Free Speech and Equality on Campus, 73 Am. U. L. Rev. 807 (2024).

Who Belongs? "We the People" in the Twenty-First Century, 52 Fordham Urban L.J. 1 (2024).

The Roberts Court and the Meaning of 1937: Individual Rights, Democracy, and Minority Rule, 16 Ala. C.R. & C.L. L. Rev. 1 (2024-2025).

Blinded by the White: The Nation's Fatal Flaw, 33 Cornell J. Law & Public Policy 1 (2023).

White Christian Nationalism Enters the Political Mainstream: Implications for the Roberts Court and Religious Freedom, 53 Seton Hall L. Rev. 667 (2023).

The Roberts Court's Transformative Religious Freedom Cases: The Doctrine and the Politics of Grievance, 28 Cardozo J. of Equal Rights & Social Justice 507 (2022).

Free-Speech Formalism Is Not Formal, 12 Drexel L. Rev. 723 (2020).

Free-Speech Formalism and Social Injustice, 26 Wm. & Mary J. Race, Gender & Social Justice 47 (2019).

Hate Speech and Democracy, 32 Criminal Justice Ethics 78 (2013).

NOTES

On the format of the Notes: The source of each quotation is identified in the endnotes below. If a series of quotations is from the same source, then one note is placed at the end of the final quotation (or at the next advantageous position). In many instances, though, I append one note for an entire paragraph—usually at the end of the paragraph—rather than using multiple notes within individual paragraphs. If a paragraph contains multiple quotations (but only one note), I cite the source of the first quotation first, the source of the second quotation next, and so on—plus, I often link each quotation with its respective source by including the first words of the quotation in a parenthetical. If, however, a subsequent quotation in the paragraph is derived from a source previously cited in the same note, I then add the page number to the earlier citation of that source (without repeating the entire citation). After citing the sources for all quotations, I sometimes cite additional materials, whether primary or secondary, that provide supplemental support and information. If I have already cited one of those additional primary or secondary sources in that particular note—because it was the source of a quotation—then I typically include the additional page numbers in the original citation (so I do not need to cite the same source more than once in any note).

1. WE THE PEOPLE
  1 U.S. Const. pmbl.
  2 Stephen M. Feldman, Pack the Court! A Defense of Supreme Court Expansion 136–44 (2021) (discussing Roberts Court cases protecting wealth and the economic marketplace) [hereinafter, Feldman, Pack].
  3 303 Creative LLC v. Elenis, 143 S. Ct. 2298 (2023) (holding that wedding website designer had free-speech right to discriminate against same-sex couples); Students for Fair Admissions, Inc. v. President & Fellows of Harvard Coll., 143 S. Ct. 2141 (2023) (holding that race-based affirmative action in university admis-

sions violates equal protection); Kennedy v. Bremerton Sch. Dist., 142 S. Ct. 2407 (2022) (holding that religious freedom requires high school to allow football coach to pray at midfield); Dobbs v. Jackson Women's Health Org., 142 S. Ct. 2228 (2022) (holding that women do not have a substantive due process right to choose whether to have an abortion).

4 Jonathan Gienapp, The Second Creation 2 (2018). The "people" did not speak once at the framing, only to have "then disappeared." Larry D. Kramer, The People Themselves: Popular Constitutionalism and Judicial Review 253 (2004).

5 Gienapp, *supra* note 4, at 2–3.

6 Kermit Roosevelt, The Nation That Never Was: Reconstructing America's Story 6 (2022); *see* Joseph Fishkin & William E. Forbath, The Anti-Oligarchy Constitution: Reconstructing the Economic Foundations of American Democracy 6–7 (2022) (arguing the Constitution is open to two opposed interpretations, one anti-oligarchic and one emphasizing exclusion and subordination); Steven Hahn, Illiberal America: A History 1–3 (2024) (page citations to Kindle ed.) (the United States is rooted in competing currents of liberalism and illiberalism); Peniel E. Joseph, The Third Reconstruction 10 (2022) (on the nation's "dual identity"); Steven Levitsky & Daniel Ziblatt, Tyranny of the Minority: Why American Democracy Reached the Breaking Point 225 (2023) (discussing the nation's struggle over multiracial democracy); Heather Cox Richardson, Democracy Awakening: Notes on the State of America xiv–xv (2023) (American history shows conflict between egalitarian democracy and authoritarianism).

7 *See* chapter 2; Stephen M. Feldman, Free Expression and Democracy in America: A History 3 (2008) (explaining contrast between republican democracy and pluralist democracy). The Roberts Court justices are also participating in a centuries-long debate over the meaning of freedom. As Jefferson Cowie and Annelien De Dijn have shown, the understanding of freedom is historically contingent. At times, freedom has been invoked to counter democracy and to justify subjugation and discrimination. Jefferson Cowie, Freedom's Dominion: A Saga of White Resistance to Federal Power (2022); Annelien De Dijn, Freedom: An Unruly History (2020). Of course, there have been many individuals who were not white, Christian (heterosexual) men that exercised power and had great influence. For examples of important lawyers and judges: Jane Sherron de Hart, Ruth Bader Ginsburg: A Life (2018); Brad Snyder, Democratic Justice: Felix Frankfurter, the Supreme Court, and the Making of the Liberal Establishment (2022); Juan Williams, Thurgood Marshall: American Revolutionary (2000).

8 *See* chapter 3; Ken I. Kersch, Conservatives and the Constitution vii–viii (2019) (discussing the conservatism preceding the New Deal).

9 *See* chapter 3.

10 *See* chapters 4–5; Kersch, *supra* note 8, at x–xi (emphasizing varied conservative responses to New Deal and Warren Court).

11 United States v. Lopez, 514 U.S. 549, 599 (1995) (Thomas, J., concurring). For recent conservative laments about the lost or exiled Constitution: Mike Sabo, *The*

Constitution is not Holy Writ, American Reformer (May 23, 2024); Helen Andrews, *The Law that Ate the Constitution*, Claremont Rev. of Books (Winter 2020).

12 142 S. Ct. 2228, 2243 (2022), *overruling* Roe v. Wade, 410 U.S. 113 (1973). Although the Burger rather than the Warren Court decided *Roe*, many view *Roe* as the "fruition" of the Warren Court's protection of individual rights. William E. Nelson, *Byron White: A Liberal of 1960, in* The Warren Court in Historical and Political Perspective 139, 154 (Mark Tushnet ed., 1993); *see* Mark Tushnet, *The Warren Court as History: An Interpretation, in* The Warren Court in Historical and Political Perspective 1, 32 (1993) (explaining *Roe* as an extension of Warren Court "activism").

13 *SFFA*, 143 S. Ct. at 2177–85 (Thomas, J., concurring) (claiming that original meaning of the Fourteenth Amendment prohibits race-based affirmative action); *Bremerton*, 142 S. Ct. at 2428 (invoking the original public meaning of the Establishment Clause); *see* Neil Gorsuch, A Republic, If You Can Keep It 10, 107, 110 (2019) (defending originalism).

14 National Federation of Independent Business v. Sebelius, 132 S. Ct. 2566 (2012) (limiting Congress's power under the Commerce and Spending Clauses); *see* Aziz Z. Huq, *The Counterdemocratic Difficulty*, 117 Nw. U. L. Rev. 1099, 1100–07 (2023) (discussing Court's undermining of democracy); Michael J. Klarman, *Foreword: The Degradation of American Democracy – And the Court*, 134 Harv. L. Rev. 1, 4–11 (2020) (same).

15 Ari Berman, Minority Rule: The Right-Wing Attack on the Will of the People 12–14 (2024) (page citations to Kindle ed.); *see* Eric L. Goldstein, The Price of Whiteness: Jews, Race, and American Identity 1–5 (2006) (discussing complex interrelationships or intersectionalities of race and religion in understanding American society); Pamela S. Karlan, *The New Countermajoritarian Difficulty*, 109 Cal. L. Rev. 2323, 2344–54 (2021) (Roberts Court cases on voting and elections were countermajoritarian); Jon D. Michaels & David L. Noll, *Vigilante Federalism*, 108 Cornell L. Rev. 1187, 1189–94 (2023) (Court is part of conservative program enforcing minority rule favoring white Christians); Melissa Murray, *Children of Men: The Roberts Court's Jurisprudence of Masculinity*, 60 Hous. L. Rev. 799, 804 (2023) (Court is following a "jurisprudence of masculinity").

16 Feldman, Pack, *supra* note 2, at 67–93; Michael A. Bailey & Forrest Maltzman, The Constrained Court: Law, Politics, and the Decisions Justices Make 15–16, 65–66 (2011); Charles Gardner Geyh, Courting Peril 8 (2016); Lucas A. Powe, Jr., The Supreme Court and the American Elite, 1789–2008 (2009); Mark Tushnet, Taking Back the Constitution 219 (2020); Lawrence Baum, *Law and Policy: More and Less Than a Dichotomy, in* What's Law Got to Do With It? 71 (Charles Gardner Geyh ed., 2011); Frank B. Cross & Blake J. Nelson, *Strategic Institutional Effects on Supreme Court Decisionmaking*, 95 Nw. U. L. Rev. 1437 (2001); Howard Gillman, *What's Law Got to Do with It? Judicial Behavioralists Test the "Legal Model" of Judicial Decision Making*, 26 L. & Soc. Inquiry 465 (2001).

17 Hans-Georg Gadamer, Truth and Method 282–84, 295, 302, 306, 309, 365 (Joel Weinsheimer & Donald Marshall trans., 2d rev. ed. 1989); Feldman, Pack, *supra* note 2, at 71; Ronald Dworkin, *How Law is Like Literature, in* A Matter of Principle 146, 160 (1985); Stephen M. Feldman, *Supreme Court Alchemy: Turning Law and Politics Into Mayonnaise*, 12 Geo. J. L. & Pub. Pol'y 57, 79–80 (2014) (explaining interpretive horizons); Calvin TerBeek, *Originalism's Obituary*, 2015 Utah L. Rev. OnLaw 29, 47 (2015) (criticizing originalism's quest for objectivity because constitutional interpretation is "inextricably intertwined with politics"); *see* Barry Friedman, *The Politics of Judicial Review*, 84 Tex. L. Rev. 257, 271 (2005) (defining politics capaciously); Gregory C. Sisk et al., *Searching for the Soul of Judicial Decisionmaking: An Empirical Study of Religious Freedom Decisions*, 65 Ohio St. L.J. 491 (2004) (lower court study concluding judge's religion is most salient factor affecting outcome of religious-freedom cases).

18 For rankings of Supreme Court justices based on political ideology, see Lee Epstein et al., The Behavior of Federal Judges 106–16 (2013), which includes comparisons with the Martin-Quinn scores (accounting for changes over time) <http://mqscores.wustl.edu/index.php>, and the Segal-Cover scores (quantifying Court nominees' perceived political ideologies at the time of appointment) <http://www.sunysb.edu/polsci/jsegal/qualtable.pdf> (data drawn from Jeffrey Segal & Albert Cover, *Ideological Values and the Votes of Supreme Court Justices*, 83 Am. Pol. Sci. Rev. 557–565 (1989); updated in Lee Epstein & Jeffrey A. Segal, Advice and Consent: The Politics of Judicial Appointments (2005)). For examples of conservative decisions: Abbott v. Perez, 138 S. Ct. 2305 (2018) (upholding Texas voting restrictions); Sorrell v. IMS Health Inc., 131 S. Ct. 2653 (2011) (invalidating state law restricting corporate sale of medical data); Citizens United v. FEC, 558 U.S. 310 (2010) (invalidating restriction on corporate campaign expenditures).

19 United States v. Morrison, 529 U.S. 598 (2000) (invalidating the Violence Against Women Act); City of Boerne v. Flores, 521 U.S. 527 (1997) (invalidating Religious Freedom Restoration Act of 1993); United States v. Lopez, 514 U.S. 549 (1995) (invalidating the Gun-Free School Zones Act); New York v. United States, 505 U.S. 144 (1992) (focusing on Tenth Amendment).

20 Rucho v. Common Cause, 139 S. Ct. 2484 (2019) (holding that political gerrymandering, no matter how extreme, is a nonjusticiable political question); Shelby County v. Holder, 133 S. Ct. 2612 (2013) (invalidating section of Voting Rights Act).

21 505 U.S. 833 (1992).

22 539 U.S. 558, 578–79 (2003).

23 576 U.S. 644 (2015). For an example of Roberts joining his progressive colleagues: NFIB v. Sebelius, 132 S. Ct. 2566 (2012) (upholding statutory individual mandate under congressional taxing power).

24 Barbara Sprunt, *Amy Coney Barrett Confirmed To Supreme Court, Takes Constitutional Oath*, NPR.org (Oct. 26, 2020); *see* chapter 8.

25 Berman, *supra* note 15, at 14; Ian Millhiser, The Agenda: How a Republican
Supreme Court is Reshaping America 27 (2021). On the popular vote in 2024:
Amy Walter, *2024 National Popular Vote Tracker*, The Cook Political Report
<https://www.cookpolitical.com/vote-tracker/2024/electoral-college>; Domenico
Montanaro, *Trump Falls Just Below 50% in Popular Vote, But Gets More than
in Past Elections*, NPR (December 3, 2024) <https://www.npr.org/2024/12/03/
nx-s1-5213810/2024-presidential-election-popular-vote-trump-kamala-harris>.
On the popular votes and nominations of justices: *Share of Popular Votes for the
Democratic and Republican Parties in Presidential Elections From 1860 to 2020*
<https://www.statista.com/statistics/1035521/popular-votes-republican-demo-
cratic-parties-since-1828/>. I am not double-counting justices nominated and
confirmed twice, first as an associate justice and then as the chief justice. *Supreme
Court of the United States*, Ballotpedia.org <https://ballotpedia.org/Supreme_
Court_of_the_United_States>; United States Senate, *Supreme Court Nominations
(1789–Present)*, Senate.gov <https://www.senate.gov/legislative/nominations/Su-
premeCourtNominations1789present.htm>.
26 *See* chapters 4–6; Donald T. Critchlow, American Political History: A Very Short
Introduction (2015) (a general introduction to major political transitions through
American history).
27 Clark M. Neily III, Terms of Engagement: How Our Courts Should Enforce the
Constitution's Promise of Limited Government 10 (2013); Jack M. Balkin, *Why
Liberals and Conservatives Flipped on Judicial Restraint: Judicial Review in the
Cycles of Constitutional Time*, 98 Tex. L. Rev. 215, 255 (2019); *e.g.*, Fulton v. City
of Philadelphia, Pennsylvania, 141 S. Ct. 1868, 1931 (2021) (suggesting the Court
should overrule decisions inconsistent with original meaning) (Gorsuch, J.,
concurring in the judgment); Douglas H. Ginsburg, *Delegation Running Riot*,
Regulation, No. 1, 1995, at 83, 84 (arguing to restore the "Constitution in Exile").
28 For definitions of white Christian nationalism: John Fanestil, American Heresy:
The Roots and Reach of White Christian Nationalism 2–3 (2023); Philip S. Gorski
& Samuel L. Perry, The Flag and the Cross: White Christian Nationalism and the
Threat to American Democracy 4–5 (2022).
29 Paul Finkelman, Slavery and the Founders 6 (3d ed. 2014); *see id.* at 7–10 (additional provisions indirectly supported slavery).
30 Michael J. Mooney, *Trump's Apostle*, Texas Monthly (Aug. 2019) <https://www.
texasmonthly.com/news-politics/donald-trump-defender-dallas-pastor-robert-
jeffress/>.
31 132 S. Ct. 2566 (2012).
32 133 S. Ct. 2612 (2013).
33 558 U.S. 310 (2010).
34 While I mention Native Americans at several points in the book, I do not focus
on the Court's treatment of them or Native American tribes. To be sure, the
nation's treatment of Native Americans, including their forced removal from
tribal lands, manifested exclusionary, hierarchical, and inegalitarian government

actions and policies. Nevertheless, these actions and policies encompassed unique complexities. See Hahn, supra note 6, at 129-36 (discussing treatment of tribes in the 1830s). For instance, many Native Americans are tribal members, and the Court has characterized tribes as "domestic dependent nations." Cherokee Nation v. Georgia, 30 U.S. (5 Pet.) 1, 17 (1831). In other words, tribes and their members occupy a unique political status within the constitutional system. Federal Indian Law therefore encompasses an enormous set of cases, statutes, and treaties that is distinct from the general corpus of constitutional jurisprudence. Felix Cohen, Handbook of Federal Indian Law (1982 ed., compiled by a board of editors). For a summary of Native American voting rights prior to the Civil War, see Alexander Keyssar, The Right to Vote: The Contested History of Democracy in the United States 349–53 (2000) (Table A.4).

35 Gorsuch, *supra* note 13, at 110–13 (denigrating living constitutionalism); Antonin Scalia, *Originalism: The Lesser Evil*, 57 U. Cin. L. Rev. 849, 855 (1989). On the current Court, Thomas, Gorsuch, and Barrett are avowed originalists, while Alito calls himself a "practical originalist." Roberts and Kavanaugh often invoke originalism and sign on to originalist opinions. Madiba K. Dennie, The Originalism Trap: How Extremists Stole the Constitution and How We the People Can Take It Back 26 n.*9 (2024); Erwin Chemerinsky, Worse Than Nothing: The Dangerous Fallacy of Originalism x (2022).

36 For a defense of originalism, see Lawrence B. Solum, *We Are All Originalists Now*, *in* Constitutional Originalism: A Debate 1 (2011). For criticisms of originalism, see Jonathan Gienapp, Against Constitutional Originalism: A Historical Critique (2024); Eric J. Segall, Originalism as Faith (2018); Saul Cornell, *Reading the Constitution, 1787–91: History, Originalism, and Constitutional Meaning*, 37 Law & Hist. Rev. 821 (2019); Stephen M. Feldman, *Constitutional Interpretation and History: New Originalism or Eclecticism?*, 28 B.Y.U. J. Pub. L. 283 (2014); Richard Posner, *The Spirit Killeth, But the Letter Giveth Life*, New Republic at 19 (Aug. 24, 2012).

37 Feldman, *supra* note 36, at 317–34. Gienapp argues that even the originalist conception of the Constitution is ahistorical. Gienapp, *supra* note 36, at 6–10, 68–78, 205–06.

38 Some originalists claim that the theory is "working itself pure." Vasan Kesavan & Michael Stokes Paulsen, *The Interpretive Force of the Constitution's Secret Drafting History*, 91 Geo. L.J. 1113, 114 (2003).

39 Jack N. Rakove, Original Meanings (1996); Feldman, *supra* note 36, at 284–86 (contrasting old and new originalisms). There are currently a multitude of originalist theories. Gienapp, *supra* note 36, at 19–26.

40 Stephen M. Feldman, *Justice Scalia and the Originalist Fallacy, in* The Conservative Revolution of Antonin Scalia 189 (Howard Schweber & David A. Schultz eds., Lexington Books, 2018); *see* Eric J. Segall, *Will the Real Justice Scalia Please Stand Up?*, 50 Wake Forest L. Rev. Online 101, 101 (2015) (criticizing Scalia and originalism for disguising policy or political choices).

41 Richard L. Hasen, A Real Right to Vote 1 (2024) (blames federal Constitution for not protecting a right to vote and thus allowing many restrictions); Keyssar, *supra* note 34, at 186 (on the few states that granted women's suffrage in late 1800s).

42 On Jewish voting rights: Keyssar, *supra* note 34, at 20. On Jewish office holding: Morton Borden, Jews, Turks, and Infidels 11–15, 23 (1984); Naomi W. Cohen, Jews in Christian America: The Pursuit of Religious Equality 28 (1992); Paul Finkelman & Lance J. Sussman, *The American Revolution and the Emergence of Jewish Legal and Political Equality in the New Nation*, 75 Am. Jewish Archives J. 1, 3 (2023) (emphasizing that most states allowed Jewish office holding).

43 Despite Thomas's efforts, *SFFA*, 143 S. Ct. 2141, 2177–85 (2023) (Thomas, J., concurring), it is difficult to square the Court's decision eliminating race-based affirmative action in university admissions with the originalist sources. *Id.* at 2228–30 (Sotomayor, J., dissenting) (showing that the Reconstruction Congress was persistently race conscious). Despite their frequent invocations of originalism, the conservative justices ignore historical evidence if it is politically inconvenient. *Trump v. Anderson*, 601 U.S. 100 (2024), held that the state of Colorado could not disqualify former President Trump from again running for office under the Fourteenth Amendment, § 3. Numerous historians had filed amicus briefs advocating for a different outcome. *E.g.*, Brief of Amici Curiae American Historians in Support of Respondents, Trump v. Anderson, 601 U.S. 100 (2024) (No. 23–719); Brief of Amici Curiae Professors Orville Vernon Burton et al., in Support of Respondents, Trump v. Anderson, 601 U.S. 100 (2024) (No. 23–719); *see* Brief for Amicus Curiae Constitutional Law Professor Mark A. Graber in Support of Petitioners-Appellants, Anderson v. Griswold, 2023 CO 63, 543 P.3d 283 (2023) (brief to Colorado Supreme Court filed by author of recent peer-reviewed book focusing on adoption of Fourteenth Amendment, including § 3). For another example, see *Janus v. Am. Fed'n of State, Cty., & Mun. Employees, Council 31*, 138 S. Ct. 2448 (2018), holding the free speech clause prohibited the government from requiring public employees to pay union fees. Alito's majority opinion largely dismissed originalist (historical) evidence—he called it "halfway originalism," *id.* at 2470—because, he claimed, it would be inconsistent with precedents. *Id.* at 2469–70.

44 558 U.S. 310, 353 (2010).

45 *Id.* at 385–93 (Scalia, J., concurring).

46 Lawrence M. Friedman, A History of American Law 179–81 (2d ed. 1985) (examples of corporate charters from early-nineteenth century); *see id.* at 194–96 (general incorporation laws); James Willard Hurst, The Legitimacy of the Business Corporation 14–17 (1970) (corporations in early national years); Pauline Maier, *The Revolutionary Origins of the American Corporation*, 50 William & Mary Q. 51, 53–55 (1993) (corporations were to pursue the common good); Jud Campbell, *Natural Rights and the First Amendment*, 127 Yale L.J. 246 (2017) (the Court's free-expression decisions are inconsistent with history). Justice Scalia's originalist opinion in *District of Columbia v. Heller*, 554 U.S. 570 (2008), provides another

example of shoddy historical research and analysis. Saul Cornell, *"Half Cocked"*: *The Persistence of Anachronism and Presentism in the Academic Debate Over the Second Amendment*, 106 J. Criminal L. & Criminology 203 (2016). For instance, in minimizing the prefatory clause of the Second Amendment, Scalia relied partly on an article by Eugene Volokh. 554 U.S. at 577 (citing Eugene Volokh, *The Commonplace Second Amendment*, 73 N.Y.U. L. Rev. 793 (1998)). Volokh's research, however, has been discredited. David Thomas König, *Why the Second Amendment Has a Preamble: Original Public Meaning and the Political Culture of Written Constitutions in Revolutionary America*, 56 UCLA L. Rev. 1295 (2009); Thomas König, *The Second Amendment: A Missing Transatlantic Context for the Historical Meaning of the Right of the People to Keep and Bear Arms*, 22 Law & Hist. Rev. 119 (2004). In fact, Justice Stevens's dissent in *Heller* extensively analyzed the historical evidence and concluded differently from Scalia. 554 U.S. at 636–80.

47 Robert L. Tsai & Mary Ziegler, *Abortion Politics and the Rise of Movement Jurists*, 57 U.C. Davis L. Rev. 2149 (2024) (Roberts Court is controlled by movement jurists).

2. REPUBLICAN DEMOCRACY

1 Helpful sources on the Revolution and the constitutional framing: Willi Paul Adams, The First American Constitutions (2001); Bernard Bailyn, The Ideological Origins of the American Revolution (1967); Richard Beeman, Plain, Honest Men (2009); Annelien De Dijn, Freedom: An Unruly History (2020) (page citations to Kindle ed.); Steven Hahn, Illiberal America: A History (2024) (page citations to Kindle ed.); Woody Holton, Unruly Americans and the Origins of the Constitution (2007); Alexander Keyssar, The Right to Vote: The Contested History of Democracy in the United States (2000); Michael J. Klarman, The Framers' Coup: The Making of the United States Constitution (2016); Gerald Leonard & Saul Cornell, The Partisan Republic: Democracy, Exclusion, and the Fall of the Founders' Constitution, 1780s–1830s (2019); Pauline Maier, Ratification (2010); Forrest McDonald, Novus Ordo Seclorum (1985); Jennifer Nedelsky, Private Property and the Limits of American Constitutionalism (1990); Rogers M. Smith, Civic Ideals (1997); Gordon S. Wood, The Creation of the American Republic, 1776–1787 (1969) [hereinafter Creation]; Gordon S. Wood, The Radicalism of the American Revolution (1991) [hereinafter Radicalism]; The Federal and State Constitutions, Colonial Charters, and other Organic Laws of the United States (Ben Perley Poore ed., 2d ed. 1878) [hereinafter Poore]. For the most complete record of the constitutional convention, see The Records of the Federal Convention of 1787 (Max Farrand ed., 1966 reprint of 1937 rev. ed.) [hereinafter Farrand].

2 Creation, *supra* note 1, at 59; *e.g.*, Virginia Bill of Rights (1776), *reprinted in* 2 Poore, *supra* note 1, at 1908, 1908 (establishing government for "the common benefit"); *see* Stephen M. Feldman, Free Expression and Democracy in America: A History 14–45, 153–208 (2008) [hereinafter Feldman, Free Expression] (discussing republican democracy).

3 Declaration of Independence: A Transcription <https://www.archives.gov/founding-docs/declaration-transcript> [hereinafter Declaration].

4 Klarman, *supra* note 1, at 74–75 (fear of democracy); Leonard & Cornell, *supra* note 1, at 8 (same); Radicalism, *supra* note 1, at 96, 229 (rejection of aristocracies and monarchies).

5 Declaration, *supra* note 3. Jefferson might have been referring to equality for the colonists as a people (rather than as individuals) entitled to self-government. Stanford Report, *When Thomas Jefferson Penned 'all men are created equal,' He Did Not Mean Individual Equality, Says Stanford Scholar* July 1, 2020 (statement of Jack Rakove); Jack Rakove, Revolutionaries 298–301 (2010) (the meanings of certain words in the Declaration of Independence changed over time).

6 Hahn, *supra* note 1, at 101–04 (while Jefferson did not primarily intend to present abstract and universal principles, other Americans immediately recognized the universalist possibilities of the Declaration); Holton, *supra* note 1, at 173 (pressure to expand suffrage); Leonard & Cornell, *supra* note 1, at 4–5 (agitation for rights for women, people of color, and others during the early national years); Creation, *supra* note 1, at 182–83 (Americans arguing for universal suffrage during Revolutionary era); *see* Keyssar, *supra* note 1, at 54–60 (disfranchisement of women, African Americans, and Native Americans). On women's suffrage: Ellen Carol DuBois, Suffrage: Women's Long Battle for the Vote 5–8 (2020) (a women's suffrage movement first emerged in the 1840s); Linda K. Kerber, Women of the Republic: Intellect and Ideology in Revolutionary America 7–12 (1980) (on women's political incapacity during the Revolutionary era); Keyssar, *supra* note 1, at 20, 54, 174–75 (on New Jersey). On Black Americans' suffrage: John Hope Franklin & Alfred A. Moss, Jr., From Slavery to Freedom 153 (7th ed. 1994); Keyssar, *supra* note 1, at 54–55, 349–53 (Table A.4); Paul Finkelman, *The First Civil Rights Movement: Black Rights in the Age of the Revolution and Chief Taney's Originalism in* Dred Scott, 24 U. Pa. J. Const. L. 676, 677–79 (2022). On Jewish voting rights: Keyssar, *supra* note 1, at 20. On non-Protestant office holding: Morton Borden, Jews, Turks, and Infidels 11–15, 23 (1984); Naomi W. Cohen, Jews in Christian America: The Pursuit of Religious Equality 28 (1992); McDonald, *supra* note 1, at 42–43; Paul Finkelman & Lance J. Sussman, *The American Revolution and the Emergence of Jewish Legal and Political Equality in the New Nation*, 75 Am. Jewish Archives J. 1, 3 (2023) (emphasizing that most states allowed Jewish office holding). For examples of religious restrictions: Constitution of Maryland (1776), *reprinted in* 1 Poore, *supra* note 1, at 817, 820; Constitution of North Carolina (1776), *reprinted in* 2 Poore, *supra* note 1, at 1409, 1410, 1413–14.

7 Constitution of Maryland (1776), *reprinted in* 1 Poore, *supra* note 1, at 817, 821; Adams, *supra* note 1, at 315–27; Keyssar, *supra* note 1, at 8–24, 340–41; Smith, *supra* note 1, at 170–73. As of 1787, the one state without a property or wealth requirement in its constitution was Vermont (Vermont, though, was not officially admitted to the Union until 1791). Constitution of Vermont (1777), *reprinted in* 2 Poore, *supra* note 1, at 1857.

8 Thomas Jefferson, *A Declaration by the Representatives of the United States of America, in General Congress Assembled* (1776), *reprinted in* Jefferson: Writings 19, 22 (Library of America 1984); Thomas Jefferson, *Debate on the Declaration* (1776), *reprinted in* Jefferson: Writings 13, 18 (Library of America 1984).

9 Constitution of Massachusetts (1780), *reprinted in* 1 Poore, *supra* note 1, at 956, 957; Klarman, *supra* note 1, at 76–77; Edmund S. Morgan, The Birth of the Republic, 1763–89, at 7, 293 (rev. ed. 1977); Radicalism, *supra* note 1, at 123. "Equality was in fact the most radical and most powerful ideological force let loose in the Revolution." Radicalism, *supra* note 1, at 232.

10 2 Farrand, *supra* note 1, at 203 (Aug. 7, 1787) (Morris); 1 Farrand, *supra* note 1, at 400–01 (June 25, 1787) (Pinckney); Holton, *supra* note 1, at 164–68 (farmers' confidence).

11 Sven Beckert, The Empire of Cotton 105–08 (2014); Patricia Nelson Limerick, The Legacy of Conquest (1987).

12 Holton, *supra* note 1, at 4–5, 7–9, 34–36, 40–44, 55–64, 106–07, 127; Klarman, *supra* note 1, at 76–82, 606–07; Radicalism, *supra* note 1, at 229–31; Woody Holton, *An "Excess of Democracy"—Or a Shortage? The Crisis that Led to the Constitution*, 86 Phi Kappa Phi Forum 39 (2006). On economic depressions: Hahn, *supra* note 1, at 88–89; Ari Berman, Minority Rule: The Right-Wing Attack on the Will of the People 42 (2024) (page citations to Kindle ed.).

13 1 Farrand, *supra* note 1, at 48 (May 31, 1787) (Gerry); at 291 (June 18, 1787) (Hamilton); at 51 (May 31, 1787) (Randolph).

14 Federalist No. 10 (Madison) (note: all citations to the Federalist are to the Project Gutenberg Etext of The Federalist Papers); *see* James Madison, *In Virginia Convention*, June 5, 1788, *reprinted in* The Complete Madison: His Basic Writings 46, 46 (Saul K. Padover ed., 1953) (arguing that majority factions have produced unjust laws).

15 Klarman, *supra* note 1, at 83, 88–92; Holton, *supra* note 1, at 17, 130–31, 176, 275; George R. Minot, The History of the Insurrections, In Massachusetts 83–86 (1788). Adonijah Mathews led an armed rebellion in Virginia. Holton, *supra* note 1, at 10–13.

16 Beeman, *supra* note 1, at 66–67, 180, 359–68; Hahn, *supra* note 1, at 90–94; Holton, *supra* note 1, at 189–91; Klarman, *supra* note 1, at 239.

17 Federalist No. 17 (Hamilton); Beeman, *supra* note 1, at 66–67, 114; Nedelsky, *supra* note 1, at 142–44.

18 Federalist No. 71 (Hamilton).

19 Federalist No. 17 (Hamilton); *see* Morton White, Philosophy, The Federalist, and the Constitution 125–27 (1987) (discussing framers' elitism).

20 U.S. Const. art. I, § 2, cl. 1; § 3, cl. 1; § 3, cl. 3; art. II, § 1, cl. 2; § 2, cl. 2; Holton, *supra* note 1, at 9–10; Klarman, *supra* note 1, at 606–07, 622–23; Robin Einhorn, *Ordinary People: Woody Holton's History of America's Origins Celebrates the Contributions of the Common People*, The Nation (March 20, 2008) <https://www.thenation.com/article/archive/ordinary-people/> (three-fifths rule).

21 1 Farrand, *supra* note 1, at 49 (May 31, 1787); Holton, *supra* note 1, at 191–93; Klarman, *supra* note 1, at 607.

22 2 Farrand, *supra* note 1, at 120 (July 26, 1787); Federalist No. 22 (Hamilton) (emphasis in original); Federalist No. 37 (Madison); Federalist No. 6 (Hamilton); Federalist No. 45 (Madison); Klarman, *supra* note 1, at 608; *see* Suzanne Mettler & Robert C. Lieberman, Four Threats: The Recurring Crises of American Democracy 9–10 (2020) (explaining why the early nation should be deemed democratic despite the many exclusions). A constitution should aim "first to obtain for rulers men who possess most wisdom to discern, and most virtue to pursue, the common good of the society; and in the next place, to take the most effectual precautions for keeping them virtuous whilst they continue to hold their public trust." Federalist No. 57 (Madison).

23 Keyssar, *supra* note 1, at 5, 9; Michael J. Sandel, Democracy's Discontent 318 (1996); Smith, *supra* note 1, at 17, 85; Women and the Law: Coverture in England and the Common Law World (Tim Stretton & Krista Kesselring eds., 2013); Mary Anne Case, *The Ladies? Forget About Them. A Feminist Perspective on the Limits of Originalism*, 29 Const. Comment. 431, 435–36 (2014).

24 U.S. Const. art. VI, cl. 3 ("no religious Test shall ever be required as a Qualification to any [national] Office or public Trust"); City Council of Charleston v. Benjamin, 33 S.C.L. 508 (1848) (convicting Jewish defendant for violating Sunday law); State v. Chandler, 2 Del. 553, 555 (1837); Leonard W. Levy, Blasphemy 400–423 (1993) (state blasphemy cases from pre-Civil War America); Smith, *supra* note 1, at 75–76, 85, 125 (discussing inconsistent views toward non-Protestants); *supra* note 6 (state limits on non-Protestant office holding).

25 1 Farrand, *supra* note 1, at 587 (July 11, 1787); James Wilson, The Works of James Wilson 759–60 (1967 ed.; first published in 3 volumes in 1804) (Wilson's speech at the Pennsylvania ratification convention, Nov. 26, 1787); Morton White, The Philosophy of the American Revolution 97–101, 132–37 (1978) (Wilson's populism); Franklin & Moss, *supra* note 6, at 81; Sean Wilentz, No Property in Man: Slavery and Antislavery at the Nation's Founding 31 (2018).

26 Leslie Paul Thiele, Thinking Politics 87 (1997). The Constitution "was approved by less than one-sixth of the country's adult male population." Berman, *supra* note 12, at 65; Gregory Ablavsky & W. Tanner Allread, *We the (Native) People?: How Indigenous Peoples Debated the U.S. Constitution*, 123 Colum. L. Rev. 243, 244–53 (2023) (exclusion of Indigenous people from official drafting and ratification debates of the Constitution). One might question whether the framing should be viewed as a coup against the people. Klarman, *supra* note 1, at 1–10 (characterizing the framing and ratification as a coup); Paul Finkelman, *The Nefarious Intentions of the Framers?*, 84 U. Chi. L. Rev. 2139, 2145–49 (2017) (arguing that not a coup).

27 Thomas J. Curry, The First Freedoms: Church and State in America to the Passage of the First Amendment 219 (1986); *id.* at 162; McDonald, *supra* note 1, at 42; Hahn, *supra* note 1, at 87–88 (on early state constitutions and de facto Protestant-

ism); Finkelman & Sussman, *supra* note 6, at 2 (during the Founding era, "at least 95 percent of all free people in the nation were Protestants"). Helpful discussions of religion in America, including Protestantism, include: Sydney E. Ahlstrom, A Religious History of the American People (1972); Jon Butler, Awash in a Sea of Faith: Christianizing the American People (1990); Nathan O. Hatch, The Democratization of American Christianity (1989); Winthrop S. Hudson & John Corrigan, Religion in America (5th ed. 1992); Martin E. Marty, Protestantism in the United States: Righteous Empire (2d ed. 1986).

28 A Watchman, *Letter From a Bostonian* (Feb. 4, 1788), *in* 4 The Complete Anti-Federalist 229 (Herbert J. Storing ed., 1981); 4 The Debates in the Several State Conventions on the Adoption of the Federal Constitution 192–94 (Jonathan Elliot ed., 1836) (Iredell at North Carolina ratifying convention); U.S. Const. art. VI, cl. 3; Hudson & Corrigan, *supra* note 27, at 129–30; Marty, *supra* note 27, at 169; *see* Cohen, *supra* note 6, at 31 (fear of a Jewish president); Finkelman & Sussman, *supra* note 6, at 25–47 (discussion of Jewish office holding). On the importance of Protestant anti-Catholicism, see Hahn, *supra* note 1, at 70–73 (going back to colonial era); Philip Hamburger, Separation of Church and State 193–251 (2002) (significance of nineteenth-century anti-Catholicism to developing the separation of church and state).

29 State v. Chandler, 2 Del. 553, 555 (1837); City Council of Charleston v. Benjamin, 33 S.C.L. 508 (1848) (conviction of Jewish defendant for violating Sunday law); Butler, *supra* note 27, at 284–85. For additional blasphemy cases: Commonwealth v. Kneeland, 37 Mass. 206 (1838); Updegraph v. Commonwealth, 11 Serg. & Rawle 394 (Pa. 1824) (approving blasphemy statute but overturning indictment on technical grounds); People v. Ruggles, 8 Johns. R. 290 (N.Y. 1811); *see* Perry v. Perry, 1 Barb. Ch. 516 (1846) (reasoning that the use of blasphemous language was probative of violent action); Levy, *supra* note 24, at 400–23 (state blasphemy cases from pre-Civil War America).

30 People v. Ruggles, 8 Johns. R. 290 (N.Y. 1811), *reprinted in* 5 The Founders' Constitution 101, 101 (Philip B. Kurland & Ralph Lerner eds., 1987).

31 Joseph Story, 3 Commentaries on the Constitution of the United States §§ 1865, 1870–71 (1833).

32 Exchange of Letters on South Carolina Gov. Hammond's Thanksgiving Proclamation of 1844, with a Public Protest, *reprinted in* Religion and State in the American Jewish Experience 112, 113, 116 (Jonathan D. Sarna & David G. Dalin eds., 1997); Vidal v. Girard's Executors, 43 U.S. (2 How.) 127, 198 (1844) (common law); Stuart Banner, *When Christianity was Part of the Common Law*, 16 Law & History Rev. 27, 27 (1998).

33 Alexis de Tocqueville, 1 Democracy in America 302–3 (Henry Reeve text, revised by Francis Bowen, edited by Phillips Bradley; Vintage Books ed. 1990); 2 Tocqueville, *supra*, at 6.

34 Robert T. Handy, A Christian America 49 (2d ed. 1984) (quoting Bela Bates Edwards, 1 Writings of Bela Bates Edwards 490 (Boston 1853)).

35 Ibram X. Kendi, Stamped From the Beginning 49–51 (2016) (absolute dominion of slaveholders); Jacob D. Wheeler, A Practical Treatise on the Law of Slavery 190–200 (1837; 1968 reprint ed.) (legal incapacities of slaves); *see* Beeman, *supra* note 1, at 310; Franklin & Moss, *supra* note 6, at 68–104 (slavery and early nationhood); Dorothy Roberts, Killing the Black Body: Race, Reproduction, and the Meaning of Liberty 22–55 (1997) (on the control of Black women and their reproductive capabilities during slavery); Harry L. Watson, Liberty and Power 22 (1990) (slaves had "no rights of any kind").

36 U.S. Const. art. I, § 2, cl. 3; § 9, cl. 1., cl. 4; art. IV, § 2, cl. 3; art. V; Paul Finkelman, Slavery and the Founders 6 (3d ed. 2014) ("directly") [hereinafter Finkelman, Slavery]; *see* Finkelman, Slavery, *supra*, at 7–10 (additional constitutional provisions indirectly supporting slavery). For discussions of the various constitutional provisions, see Derrick Bell, Race, Racism, and American Law 22–23 (2d ed. 1980); Finkelman, Slavery, *supra*, at 6–10.

37 2 Farrand, *supra* note 1, at 220 (Aug. 8, 1787) (Sherman); *id.* at 364 (Aug. 21, 1787) (Martin); *id.* at 221–22 (Aug. 8, 1787) (Morris); *id.* at 370 (Aug. 22, 1787) (Mason); *id.* at 364 (Aug. 21, 1787) (Rutledge); Beeman, *supra* note 36, at 321–22 (discussing Mason as slave owner).

38 Finkelman, Slavery, *supra* note 36, at 103 (quoting Pinckney); *id.* at 34–35; 2 Farrand, *supra* note 1, at 364 (Aug. 21, 1787) (Charles Pinckney stating "South Carolina can never receive the plan if it prohibits the slave trade"); Beeman, *supra* note 36, at 309–11, 332–33; Donald L. Robinson, Slavery in the Structure of American Politics, 1765–1820 (1971); Gordon S. Wood, Empire of Liberty: A History of the Early Republic, 1789–1815, at 518–24 (2009). Madison might have purposefully centered blame for slavery on Georgia and South Carolina. Mary Sarah Bilder, Madison's Hand: Revising the Constitutional Convention 156, 169–70, 188–89 (2015). During ratification debates in the northern states, the proposed constitutional protections of slavery generated contentious deliberations. Finkelman, Slavery, *supra* note 36, at 35–36; Maier, *supra* note 1, at 175–76, 351–52.

39 Edward E. Baptist, The Half Has Never Been Told xxii–xxv, 312, 412–14 (2014); Beckert, *supra* note 11, at 98–140; Kermit L. Hall, The Magic Mirror 130 (1989); Ronald E. Seavoy, An Economic History of the United States From 1607 to the Present 111 (2006); Sven Beckert & Seth Rockman, *Slavery's Capitalism, in* Slavery's Capitalism: A New History of American Economic Development 1 (2016). On presidents: Erik W. Austin, Political Facts of the United States Since 1789, at 94–95 (1986) (Table 3.1, National Electoral and Popular Vote Cast for President, 1789–1984). Remember, too, slave-owning presidents were empowered to nominate federal judges that supported and protected slavery. For an argument that the omission of the words slave and slavery from the constitutional text was politically significant, see Sean Wilentz, No Property in Man: Slavery and Antislavery at the Nation's Founding (2018). Wilentz's book has been heavily criticized: Nicholas Guyatt, *How Proslavery Was the Constitution?* NY Rev. of Books (June 6, 2019); *see* Juan F. Perea, *Echoes of Slavery II: How Slavery's Legacy Distorts Democracy,*

51 U.C. Davis L. Rev. 1081 (2018) (the historical protection of slavery continues to influence our understanding of the Constitution).

40 Morton White, Philosophy, The Federalist, and the Constitution 120 (1987); Holton, *supra* note 1, at 276.

41 1 Farrand, *supra* note 1, at 422 (June 26, 1787) (Madison).

42 Plus, the framers sought to structure the national government to control for the effects of factionalism even if the elected officials were insufficiently virtuous. Federalist No. 51 (Madison).

43 *See* Sandel, *supra* note 23, at 318 (linking republican notions of citizenship to exclusion); Smith, *supra* note 1, at 470–71 (emphasizing the importance of inegalitarian ascriptive traditions in American history).

44 Radicalism, *supra* note 1, at 230–32, 340; *see* Dijn, *supra* note 1, at 341–43 (a conception of freedom as freedom to participate in self-government was perhaps the more widespread understanding of freedom during the American founding and early national years); Joseph Fishkin & William E. Forbath, The Anti-Oligarchy Constitution: Reconstructing the Economic Foundations of American Democracy 2–6 (2022) (tradition of an anti-oligarchic Constitution); Watson, *supra* note 35, at 27, 50 (communications revolution contributed to a leveling egalitarianism).

45 Tunis Wortman, A Treatise Concerning Political Enquiry, and the Liberty of the Press 48–49, 128 (1800; 1970 reprint ed.); 2 Tocqueville, *supra* note 33, at 98–105; Joyce Appleby, Capitalism and a New Social Order: The Republican Vision of the 1790s, at 15 (1984) (emergence of individualism).

46 Andrew Jackson, *Bank Veto Message* (July 10, 1832) <https://avalon.law.yale.edu/19th_century/ajveto01.asp>; Richard Hofstadter, Anti-Intellectualism in American Life (1962); Keyssar, *supra* note 1, at 26–30; Jill Lepore, These Truths: A History of the United States 182–85 (2018); Smith, *supra* note 1, at 170–73, 201; Radicalism, *supra* note 1, at 294, 332. During the Second Great Awakening, the individualist and egalitarian ethos spread also through American Protestantism. Hatch, *supra* note 27, at 3 (1989).

47 Federalist No. 10 (Madison); Austin, *supra* note 39, at 378 (Table 3.12); Michael E. McGerr, The Decline of Popular Politics: The American North, 1865–1928, at 5, 22–29 (1986); Edward Pessen, Jacksonian America 132 (rev. ed. 1985); Norman L. Rosenberg, Protecting the Best Men 140–42 (1986); Watson, *supra* note 35, at 25–26. A political party became a means for overcoming local interests or factions. Watson, *supra* note 35, at 66–72, 172–73; Richard Hofstadter, The Idea of a Party System 208–13, 251–59 (1969).

48 Naturalization Act of 1790, 1 Stat. 103 (March 26, 1790); 160 U.S. (19 How.) 393, 404–05 (1857); Matthew Frye Jacobson, Whiteness of a Different Color 13–14, 22, 26–27 (1998); Leonard & Cornell, *supra* note 1, at 165–75; Lepore, *supra* note 46, at 313–14; *see* Finkelman & Sussman, *supra* note 6, at 16 (naturalization was not limited to Christians). On Black voting rights: Franklin & Moss, *supra* note 6, at 153; Keyssar, *supra* note 1, at 54–55, 349–53 (Table A.4); Finkelman, *supra* note 6, at 677–79. Throughout American history, certain Americans—often white Christian

men—have invoked their right to freedom as a right to subjugate and discriminate against others. Freedom is a crucial element of democracy that can readily
be turned toward suppression. Jefferson Cowie, Freedom's Dominion: A Saga of
White Resistance to Federal Power 17–18 (2022) (page citations to Kindle ed.).

49 U.S. Const. amend. XIII, § 1; William E. Nelson, The Fourteenth Amendment:
From Political Principle to Judicial Doctrine 123–45 (1988); see Pamela Brandwein,
Reconstructing Reconstruction 23 (1999) (different interpretations of the problem
of slavery).

50 Brandwein, supra note 49, at 39; Eric Foner, Reconstruction, 1863–1877, at 199–
201, 242, 257–58 (1988); Franklin & Moss, supra note 6, at 225.

51 Cong. Globe, 39th Cong., 1st Sess. 1151 (March 2, 1866) (Thayer); id. at 1757 (April
4, 1866) (Trumbull). "[P]olitical rights are regulated, as we all admit, without
regard to citizenship." Id. at 1781 (April 5, 1866) (Trumbull); see id. at 1832–33
(April 7, 1866) (Representative Willliam Lawrence of Ohio distinguishing political
and civil rights); id. at 41–42 (Dec. 13, 1865) (Republican Senator John Sherman of
Ohio explaining that Ohio and New York denied the vote to some Black Americans).

52 U.S. Const. amend. XIV, § 1; Cong. Globe, 39th Cong., 2d Sess. 252 (Jan. 3, 1867)
(Thaddeus Stevens); Charge to Grand Jury—The Civil Rights Act, 30 F. Cas. 999,
1000 (C.C.W.D.N.C. 1875) (No. 18,258) (statement of Republican judge Robert P.
Dick). I do not mean to suggest that the Republicans focused predominantly on
those substantive guarantees. Mark A. Graber, Punish Treason, Reward Loyalty:
The Forgotten Goals of Constitutional Reform After the Civil War (2023).

53 Bruce Ackerman, We the People (vol. 3): The Civil Rights Revolution 339 (2014);
Foner, supra note 50, at 70–71, 235–37, 246, 409; James M. McPherson, Battle Cry
of Freedom: The Civil War Era 841–42 (1988); Smith, supra note 1, at 299–304.
Black southerners understood the importance of land for their freedom. Kendi,
supra note 35, at 230–31.

54 Foner, supra note 50, at 178, 277, 448; The Reconstruction Act (March 2, 1867), § 5,
14 Stat. 428; U.S. Const. amend. XV, § 1; Franklin & Moss, supra note 6, at 224–27.
While some Republicans accepted the narrow definition of civil rights, which dif-
ferentiated such rights from political rights, other Republicans disagreed. See, e.g.,
Cong. Globe, 40th Cong., 2d Sess. app. 352 (June 11, 1868) (Senator Richard Yates
of Illinois; civil rights included political rights). John Bingham, author of the first
House draft of the Fourteenth Amendment, § 1, spoke ambiguously and incon-
sistently about the overlap between civil and political rights. Cong. Globe, 39th
Cong., 1st Sess. 2542 (May 10, 1866); Cong. Globe, 40th Cong., 2d Sess. 2463 (May
14, 1868).

55 Cong. Globe, 40th Cong., 3rd Sess. 1625–26 (Feb. 26, 1869) (Edmunds); id. at 727–
28 (Jan. 29, 1869); id. at 1623–25 (Feb. 26, 1869); Foner, supra note 50, at 448–49.

56 Cong. Globe, 40th Cong., 3rd Sess. 1626 (Feb. 26, 1869) (Wilson); id. at 979 (Feb.
8, 1869) (Frelinghuysen); id. at 1625 (Feb. 26, 1869) (Radical Republican Senator
Jacob Howard wishing Fifteenth Amendment conferred a right to vote).

57 1857 Amendments to Constitution of Massachusetts (1780), *reprinted in* 2 Poore, *supra* note 1, at 979 (imposing literacy requirement); Constitution of Pennsylvania (1873), *reprinted in* 2 Poore, *supra* note 1, at 1583 (imposing taxpaying requirement). Maine, Massachusetts, Connecticut, Delaware, and New Hampshire were among the states with literacy requirements after the Civil War. Keyssar, *supra* note 1, at 363–89; *see* Foner, *supra* note 50, at 447.

58 Howard Gillman, *How Political Parties Can Use the Courts to Advance Their Agendas: Federal Courts in the United States, 1875–1891*, 96 Am. Pol. Sci. Rev. 511, 516 (2002); The Ku Klux Klan Act (April 20, 1871), § 1, 17 Stat. 13 (creating a federal cause-of-action for state violations of federal constitutional and statutory rights); Foner, *supra* note 50, at 426, 486–87, 496–99, 524–29; Keyssar, *supra* note 1, at 106; James M. McPherson, Ordeal By Fire 543–44, 585–86, 593 (1982) [hereinafter McPherson, Ordeal].

59 Morton Keller, Affairs of State: Public Life in Late Nineteenth Century America 181, 559 (1977) (quoting 1881 Maryland Republican platform).

60 Keyssar, *supra* note 1, at 106–07.

61 Foner, *supra* note 50, at 577 (quoting Grant).

62 *Id.* at 570; Keyssar, *supra* note 1, at 107–08; McPherson, Ordeal, *supra* note 58, at 594.

63 Keyssar, *supra* note 1, at 107–08.

64 Foner, *supra* note 50, at 587 (quoting Philadelphia Evening Bulletin (Jan. 11, 1882)).

65 Keyssar, *supra* note 1, at 113 (quoting R. L. Gordon).

66 *Id.* at 112 (quoting Carter Glass, a future Senator).

67 *Id.* at 114–15; Smith, *supra* note 1, at 383, 605 n.110.

68 Alexander Keyssar, Why Do We Still Have the Electoral College? 189–92, 373 (2020).

69 Civil Rights Cases, 109 U.S. 3, 10–12, 25 (1883); Civil Rights Act (March 1, 1875), § 1, 18 Stat. 335.

70 163 U.S. 537 (1896). Harlan's dissenting opinion used the phrase "separate but equal accommodations." 163 U.S. at 552 (Harlan, J., dissenting).

71 U.S. Const. amend. XIX, § 1; Keyssar, *supra* note 1, at 218.

72 Keyssar, *supra* note 1, at 198 (quoting Olympia Brown); Austin, *supra* note 39, at 470 (Table 7.4, Total Number of Immigrants Arriving Annually in the United States, 1820–1980); Lynn Dumenil, The Modern Temper 202 (1995); Smith, *supra* note 1, at 314–16, 339–41; *see* United States Immigration Commission (Chair: Senator William P. Dillingham), Dictionary of Races or Peoples (Dec. 5, 1910; printed 1911) (as part of effort to restrict immigration, describing racial differences of different immigrant groups).

73 Keyssar, *supra* note 1, at 128; Dumenil, *supra* note 72, at 53; Arthur S. Link & Richard L. McCormick, Progressivism 53–55 (1983) (discussing voting in poor and immigrant communities).

74 *New Literacy Test Adopted by State*, New York Times, Aug. 9, 1923, at 30; William J. O'Shea, *Literacy Test of Voters is Pronounced a Success*, New York Times, Jan 4, 1925, at X12; *The Literacy Law*, New York Times, March 28, 1931, at 15.

75 Keyssar, *supra* note 1, at 226 (Munro); E. P. Hutchinson, Legislative History of American Immigration Policy, 1798–1965, at 187–92 (1981).

76 Howard Gillman, The Constitution Besieged: The Rise and Demise of *Lochner* Era Police Powers Jurisprudence 12–13 (1993); *see* Feldman, Free Expression, *supra* note 2, at 155, 199–208 (discussing republican democratic judicial review); William J. Novak, The People's Welfare (1996) (reviewing nineteenth-century judicial actions).

77 Goshen v. Stonington, 4 Conn. 209, 221 (1822). For additional examples, see State Bank v. Cooper, 10 Tenn. 599 (1831) (Green, J.); Eakin v. Raub, 12 Serg. & Rawle 330 (Pa. 1825); Calder v. Bull, 3 U.S. (3 Dall.) 386, 388 (1798) (Chase, J.); Van-Horne's Lessee v. Dorrance, 28 F. Cas. 1012 (C.C. Pa. 1795).

78 James Kent, 2 Commentaries on American Law 276 (1827; Legal Classics Library Reprint).

79 James Willard Hurst, Law and the Conditions of Freedom in the Nineteenth-century United States 21 (1956).

80 Commonwealth v. Alger, 61 Mass. 53, 7 Cush. 53, 84–86 (1851); *see* Thorpe v. Rutland & Burlington Railroad Company, 27 Vt. 140, 156 n.a1 (1855) (listing legitimate police-power actions).

81 Novak, *supra* note 76, at 158–62; *see supra* note 24 (blasphemy and Sunday law prosecutions).

82 The Statistical History of the United States from Colonial Times to the Present 409 (1965) (Table: Manufactures Summary: 1849 to 1954); *id.* at 74 (Table: Industrial Distribution of Gainful Workers: 1820–1940); *id.* at 14 (Table: Population in Urban and Rural Territory); The Statistics of the Wealth and Industry of the United States; Compiled From the Original Returns of the Ninth Census 392 (1872); Austin, *supra* note 39, at 470 (Table 7.4, Total Number of Immigrants Arriving Annually in the United States, 1820–1980); Richard F. Bensel, The Political Economy of American Industrialization, 1877–1900, at 19–100 (2000); Feldman, Free Expression, *supra* note 2, at 166–97 (discussing in greater detail the development and effects of industrialization, urbanization, and immigration).

83 Benjamin R. Twiss, Lawyers and the Constitution: How Laissez Faire Came to the Supreme Court 3–4 (1962); George E. McNeill, *Progress of the Movement From 1861 to 1886, in* The Labor Movement: The Problem of Today 124 (1887; 1971 reprint) (unions); Herbert Hovenkamp, *Regulatory Conflict in the Gilded Age: Federalism and the Railroad Problem*, 97 Yale L.J. 1017, 1019 (1988) (complexity of railroad regulation). Congress eventually acted: The Interstate Commerce Act (Feb. 4, 1887), §§ 1–20, 24 Stat. 379; The Sherman Anti-Trust Act (July 2, 1890), 26 Stat. 209.

84 Foner, *supra* note 50, at 29 (quoting Lincoln); William Graham Sumner, What the Social Classes Owe To Each Other 47, 103–04 (1883; 1966 ed.); Eric Foner, Free Soil, Free Labor, Free Men (1970); Richard Hofstadter, Social Darwinism in American Thought (1992); Twiss, *supra* note 83, at 254–57; *e.g., How Shall We Vote*, N.Y. Daily Times, Oct. 21, 1856, at 2 (celebrating small farmer); Andrew Carnegie,

Wealth, 148 North American Rev. 653 (June 1889) (celebrating business competition); *see* Stephen M. Feldman, The New Roberts Court, Donald Trump, and Our Failing Constitution 89–98 (2017) (transition from free labor, free soil ideology to freedom of contract and laissez-faire).

85 165 U.S. 578, 589, 591 (1897); Francis Wharton, Commentaries on Law, Embracing Chapters on the Nature, the Source, and the History of Law; on International Law, Public and Private; and on Constitutional and Statutory Law 681 (1884; 2001 reprint ed.); Gillman, *supra* note 58, at 517–18; Arthur F. McEvoy, *Freedom of Contract, Labor, and the Administrative State, in* The State and Freedom of Contract 198, 210–11 (Harry N. Scheiber ed., 1998). On land grants to the railroads: John A. Garraty, The New Commonwealth 9 (1968); Joseph E. Stiglitz, The Price of Inequality 45–48 (2013 ed.).

86 198 U.S. 45, 59, 64 (1905); *see id.* at 67–73 (Harlan, J., dissenting) (state legislature relied on empirical evidence).

87 165 U.S. at 589–90 (quoting Powell v. Pennsylvania, 127 U.S. 678, 684 (1888)); Adair v. United States, 208 U.S. 161, 175 (1908) (invalidating federal law proscribing yellow dog contracts—employment contracts prohibiting employees from belonging to labor unions); Millett v. People, 117 Ill. 294, 301 (1886) (invalidating a law preventing coal companies from cheating their miners when weighing the quantity mined); Muller v. Oregon, 208 U.S. 412 (1908) (upholding state law prescribing maximum hours for female employees). On number of invalidated laws: Erwin Chemerinsky, Constitutional Law: Principles and Policies 644 (5th ed. 2011); Karen Orren, Belated Feudalism 111–17 (1991).

88 163 U.S. 537 (1896).

89 Church of the Holy Trinity v. United States, 143 U.S. 457, 471 (1892) ("this is a Christian nation"); Vidal v. Girard's Executors, 43 U.S. (2 How.) 127, 198 (1844) ("Christianity [is] part of the common law"); Stephen M. Feldman, Please Don't Wish Me a Merry Christmas: A Critical History of the Separation of Church and State 188–89, 229–30 (1997); *see* Henry J. Abraham, Freedom and the Court 308–18 (5th ed. 1988) (Table 6.1 & Table 6.2: listing the Supreme Court's free exercise decisions); *Id.* at 364–76 (Table 6.3 & Table 6.4: listing the Supreme Court's Establishment-Clause decisions).

90 98 U.S. 145, 164 (1878).

91 3 Story, *supra* note 31, at §1878; Knowles v. United States, 170 F. 409 (8th Cir. 1909); Castle v. Houston, 19 Kan. 417 (1877); Commonwealth v. Morris, 3 Va. 176 (1811). The bad tendency test developed from the truth-conditional standard that first emerged in seditious libel cases. Feldman, Free Expression, *supra* note 2, at 110–18, 221–34; Genevieve Lakier, *The Invention of Low-Value Speech*, 128 Harv. L. Rev. 2166, 2184–86 (2015) (referring to this standard as the "truth-plus defense"). On Supreme Court: Debs v. United States, 249 U.S. 211 (1919) (upholding Espionage Act conviction); Halter v. Nebraska, 205 U.S. 34 (1907) (upholding conviction under flag desecration statute).

92 163 U.S. 537, 560 (1896) (Harlan, J., dissenting); *id.* at 544, 550–51; *id.* at 561 (discussing discrimination against "the Chinese race"); Gabriel J. Chin, *The Plessy Myth: Justice Harlan and the Chinese Cases*, 82 Iowa L. Rev. 151 (1996) (discussing Harlan's attitude towards Chinese Americans).

93 Bell, *supra* note 36, at 373; Franklin & Moss, *supra* note 6, at 247–63; Robert A. Margo, Race and Schooling in the South, 1880–1950: An Economic History 21–22 (1990) (Table 2.5, Per Pupil Expenditures on Instruction); Gordon Harvey, *Public Education in the Early Twentieth Century*, in Encyclopedia of Alabama, June 8, 2010 <http://www.encyclopediaofalabama.org/article/h-2601>.

3. PLURALIST DEMOCRACY

1 On diversity: Anthony J. Badger, The New Deal: The Depression Years, 1933–1940, at 248–49 (1989); William E. Leuchtenburg, Franklin D. Roosevelt and the New Deal 184 (1963) [hereinafter Leuchtenburg, New Deal]. On Great Depression: David M. Kennedy, Freedom from Fear: The American People in Depression and War, 1929–1945, at 35–38 (1999); William E. Leuchtenburg, The Perils of Prosperity, 1914–1932, at 243–44 (1958) [hereinafter Leuchtenburg, Perils]. Additional sources on the transition in democracy and the New Deal: Lizabeth Cohen, Making a New Deal (1990); Jefferson Cowie, The Great Exception: The New Deal and the Limits of American Politics (2016); Howard Gillman, The Constitution Besieged: The Rise and Demise of *Lochner* Era Police Powers Jurisprudence (1993); Robert S. McElvaine, The Great Depression (1984); Kevin J. McMahon, Reconsidering Roosevelt on Race (2004).

2 Leuchtenburg, New Deal, *supra* note 1, at 339 (quoting Tugwell); The Statistical History of the United States from Colonial Times to the Present 73 (1965) (Table: Unemployment); *id.* at 139 (Table: Gross National Product); Stephen M. Feldman, Free Expression and Democracy in America: A History 194–97 (2008) [hereinafter Feldman, Free Expression] (discussing Progressivism and Prohibition); Jeffry A. Frieden, Global Capitalism 209 (2006) (collapsing democracies); Joseph R. Gusfield, Symbolic Crusade: Status Politics and the American Temperance Movement 122–23 (1963) (anti-immigrant sentiment had led many Progressives to support Prohibition); Robert H. Wiebe, Self-Rule: A Cultural History of American Democracy 209–10 (1995) (New Dealers not only ended Prohibition, but showed less concern about prostitution); Walter J. Shepard, *Democracy in Transition*, 29 Am. Pol. Sci. Rev. 1, 19 (1935) (president of the American Political Science Association recommending fascism).

3 Kennedy, *supra* note 1, at 378 (quoting FDR).

4 Leuchtenburg, New Deal, *supra* note 1, at 146–47.

5 Cowie, *supra* note 1, at 9, 184; National Industrial Recovery Act (July 5, 1935), 49 Stat. 449; The Social Security Act (Aug. 14, 1935), 49 Stat. 620; Kennedy, *supra* note 1, at 131–59, 378–79; Leuchtenburg, New Deal, *supra* note 1, at 41–62.

6 Jerold S. Auerbach, Unequal Justice: Lawyers and Social Change in Modern America (1976); Badger, *supra* note 1, at 249; Cowie, *supra* note 1, at 9–28 (unique-

ness of New Deal); Cohen, *supra* note 1, at 362; Leuchtenburg, New Deal, *supra* note 1, at 184–85, 347; Howard M. Sachar, A History of the Jews in America 446–50 (1992); G. Edward White, *Recapturing New Deal Lawyers*, 102 Harv. L. Rev. 489, 514–15 (1988).

7 Louis L. Jaffe, *Law Making by Private Groups*, 51 Harv. L. Rev. 201, 201–03 (1937); National Labor Relations Act (July 5, 1935), 49 Stat. 449; National Labor Relations Board, Legislative History of the National Labor Relations Act, 1935, at 1620–21 (1985 Commemorative ed.); Jerold S. Auerbach, Labor and Liberty 53–60, 211–13 (1966); Melvyn Dubofsky, The State and Labor in Modern America 129–30 (1994).

8 Leuchtenburg, New Deal, *supra* note 1, at 89–90, 147–48 (quoting FDR); Frances Fox Piven & Richard A. Cloward, Poor People's Movements 130–31 (1977) (quoting Moley); Erik W. Austin, Political Facts of the United States Since 1789, at 378–79 (1986) (Table 3.12, National Voter Turnout, 1824–1984).

9 John G. Gunnell, The Descent of Political Theory 105, 122–23, 127–45 (1993); Edward A. Purcell, Jr., The Crisis of Democratic Theory 112–14, 138 (1973).

10 Wilfred E. Binkley & Malcolm C. Moos, A Grammar of American Politics 8–11 (1949); Robert A. Dahl, A Preface to Democratic Theory 67–71 (1956); V. O. Key, Politics, Parties, and Pressure Groups (1942); Pendleton Herring, The Politics of Democracy 424–25 (1940); *see* Michael J. Sandel, Democracy's Discontent 250 (1996) (transition to procedural democracy). Pluralist democracy accepted a plurality of values (or ethical relativism). Franklin D. Roosevelt, *Commonwealth Club Speech* (Sept. 23, 1932), *reprinted in* III Great Issues in American History 335, 341–42 (Richard Hofstadter ed., 1982); *see* John Dewey, Freedom and Culture 176 (1939) (contrasting authoritarian methods with the "plural, partial, and experimental methods" of democracy).

11 298 U.S. 238, 304 (1936); United States v. Butler, 297 U.S. 1 (1936) (invalidating Agricultural Adjustment Act provisions); A.L.A. Schechter Poultry Corp. v. United States, 295 U.S. 495 (1935) (invalidating National Industrial Recovery Act); Railroad Retirement Board v. Alton Railroad Company, 295 U.S. 330, 374 (1935) (formalism).

12 81 Cong. Rec., Appendix at 469–71, 75th Cong., 1st Sess. (March 10, 1937); 81 Cong. Rec., 75th Cong., 1st Sess. 877–79 (Feb. 5, 1937); *Three Senators Score Court Plan Here as Peril to Nation*, New York Times, March 13, 1937, at 1; Ira Jewell Williams & Ira Jewell Williams Jr., *What Are a Man's Rights?*, Saturday Evening Post, May 29, 1937, at 17; Austin, *supra* note 8, at 94, 97 (Table: National Electoral and Popular Vote Cast for President); William E. Leuchtenburg, The Supreme Court Reborn 112–31, 135 (1995) [hereinafter Leuchtenburg, Reborn]; Tara Leigh Grove, *The Origins (and Fragility) of Judicial Independence*, 71 Vand. L. Rev. 465, 509 (2018).

13 300 U.S. 379, 399–400 (1937), *overruling* Adkins v. Children's Hospital, 261 U.S. 525 (1923); Leuchtenburg, Reborn, *supra* note 12, at 142–44, 177.

14 301 U.S. 1, 37, 41–42 (1937).

15 301 U.S. at 33, 43–44, 46; Feldman, Free Expression, *supra* note 2, at 183–87; Karen Orren, Belated Feudalism (1991) (labor relations moved from common law to legislation).

16 Eugene V. Rostow, *Book Review*, 56 Yale L.J. 1469, 1472 (1947) (punctuation modified); C. Herman Pritchett, The Roosevelt Court: A Study in Judicial Politics and Values, 1937–1947 (1948); Leuchtenburg, Reborn, *supra* note 12, at 180–85. Constitutional historians disagree about whether the 1937 transition was revolutionary. Leuchtenburg, Reborn, *supra* note 12, at 231 (revolutionary); *see* Barry Cushman, Rethinking the New Deal Court: The Structure of a Constitutional Revolution 105 (1998) (not revolutionary).

17 Morton J. Horwitz, *Foreword: The Constitution of Change: Legal Fundamentality Without Fundamentalism*, 107 Harv. L. Rev. 30, 56–57 (1993).

18 304 U.S. 144, 152–53 & n.4 (1938). Filled milk is "skimmed milk compounded with any fat or oil other than milk fat." *Id.* at 146.

19 328 U.S. 549, 552–56 (1946) (Frankfurter, J., plurality).

20 *Id.* at 566–68, 570–71 (Black, J., dissenting).

21 McMahon, *supra* note 1, at 14 (after 1937, the Court became "the defender of a more inclusive democracy").

22 T. Alexander Aleinikoff, *Constitutional Law in the Age of Balancing*, 96 Yale L.J. 943 (1987); *e.g.*, Parker v. Brown, 317 U.S. 341, 362 (1943) (dormant commerce clause case); Schneider v. State, 308 U.S. 147, 161 (1939) (free speech case).

23 *Carolene Products*, 304 U.S. 144, 152–53 n.4 (1938); West Virginia State Board of Ed. v. Barnette, 319 U.S. 624, 638 (1943); John H. Ely, Democracy and Distrust 102 (1980) (policing democracy).

24 323 U.S. 214 (1944).

25 For example, during World War II, the Court first held that compulsory flag salutes did not violate the First Amendment, Minersville School Dis. v. Gobitis, 310 U.S. 586 (1940), but the Court reversed itself and held that such flag salutes were unconstitutional. West Virginia State Board of Ed. v. Barnette, 319 U.S. 624 (1943).

26 *E.g.*, Debs v. United States, 249 U.S. 211 (1919) (upholding Espionage Act conviction); Halter v. Nebraska, 205 U.S. 34 (1907) (upholding conviction under flag desecration statute).

27 Herndon v. Lowry, 301 U.S. 242 (1937).

28 Hague v. C.I.O., 307 U.S. 496 (1939).

29 Cantwell v. Connecticut, 310 U.S. 296 (1940).

30 Palko v. Connecticut, 302 U.S. 319, 326–27 (1937).

31 *Barnette*, 319 U.S. 624, 642 (1943).

32 Cantwell v. Connecticut, 310 U.S. 296 (1940).

33 Everson v. Board of Education, 330 U.S. 1, 15–16, 18 (1947). The Court nonetheless held the public reimbursement of transportation costs for children attending either public or Catholic schools did not violate the First Amendment.

34 Thomas v. Collins, 323 U.S. 516, 529–30 (1945); Murdock v. Pennsylvania, 319 U.S. 105, 111, 115 (1943).

35 Michael K. Brown et al., Whitewashing Race 27–30 (2003) (quoting Houston); Ira Katznelson, When Affirmative Action was White 55–60 (2005); Legislative History of the National Labor Relations Act, 1935, at 1058–59 (1985 Commemorative ed.). Members of other marginalized groups who became fuller democratic participants often did so at a cost. To participate, an individual typically needed to relinquish any strong identification with or markings of their ethnic or religious backgrounds. Many Jews managed to land government jobs in the 1930s, but only if they did not appear to be distinctly Jewish, according to dominant stereotypes. Auerbach, *supra* note 6, at 224–32; Robert A. Burt, Two Jewish Justices: Outcasts in the Promised Land 39 (1988) (Felix Frankfurter minimized his specifically Jewish background to facilitate professional success).

36 305 U.S. 337, 349–52 (1938); Robert J. Cottrol et al., *Brown v. Board of Education*: Caste, Culture, and the Constitution 53–58 (2003); Richard Kluger, Simple Justice 131–37 (1975); Mark Tushnet, The NAACP's Legal Strategy Against Segregated Education, 1925–1950 (1987).

37 339 U.S. 629, 632–34 (1950); *see* McLaurin v. Oklahoma State Regents, 339 U.S. 637 (1950) (also considering intangible factors).

38 317 U.S. 111, 118, 120, 129 (1942).

39 334 U.S. 1, 19 (1948); The Civil Rights Cases, 109 U.S. 3 (1883).

40 347 U.S. 483, 493 (1954); McMahon, *supra* note 1, at 14 (*Brown* manifested President Franklin Roosevelt's efforts to create a "more inclusive democracy"). The Warren Court was part of "the New Deal-Great Society political regime." Terri Jennings Peretti, Partisan Supremacy: How the G.O.P. Enlisted Courts to Rig America's Election Rules 5 (2020).

41 349 U.S. 294, 301 (1955); Griffin v. Cnty. Sch. Bd. of Prince Edward Cnty., 377 U.S. 218, 229 (1964); Ian Haney Lopez, Dog Whistle Politics: How Coded Racial Appeals Have Reinvented Racism and Wrecked the Middle Class 81 (2014) ("fewer than"). On the ineffectiveness of *Brown*: Gerald N. Rosenberg, The Hollow Hope: Can Courts Bring About Social Change? 110–56 (1991); David W. Romero & Francine Sanders Romero, *Precedent, Parity, and Racial Discrimination: A Federal/ State Comparison of the Impact of* Brown v. Board of Education, 37 Law & Soc'y Rev. 809 (2003). On the Civil Rights Movement in general: John Hope Franklin & Alfred A. Moss, Jr., From Slavery to Freedom 492–531 (7th ed. 1994); David J. Garrow, Bearing the Cross: Martin Luther King, Jr., and the Southern Christian Leadership Conference (1986).

42 370 U.S. 421 (1962).

43 Sherbert v. Verner, 374 U.S. 398, 403, 406–08 (1963).

44 Lynch v. Donnelly, 465 U.S. 668 (1984) (upholding constitutionality of public display of a crèche).

45 O'Lone v. Estate of Shabazz, 482 U.S. 342 (1987) (needing to defer to prison officials, Court viewed strict scrutiny as inappropriate); Goldman v. Weinberger,

475 U.S. 503 (1986) (emphasizing context of military, Court did not apply strict scrutiny); United States v. Lee, 455 U.S. 252 (1982) (concluding government satisfied strict scrutiny and did not need to exempt an Old Order Amish employer from collecting and paying Social Security taxes).

46 376 U.S. 254 (1964). A "public official" can recover "damages for a defamatory falsehood relating to his official conduct" only if "he proves that the statement was made with 'actual malice'—that is, with knowledge that it was false or with reckless disregard of whether it was false or not." *Id.* at 279–80.

47 393 U.S. 503 (1969).

48 395 U.S. 444 (1969).

49 376 U.S. at 270. Many of the Warren Court's individual rights decisions involved the criminal process. *E.g.*, Miranda v. Arizona, 384 U.S. 436 (1966) (police must advise suspects in custody of constitutional rights before beginning interrogations); Mapp v. Ohio, 367 U.S. 643 (1961) (applying exclusionary rule in state courts, banning evidence of crime if obtained in violation of Fourth Amendment search-and-seizure requirements); Corinna Barrett Lain, *Countermajoritarian Hero or Zero? Rethinking the Warren Court's Role in the Criminal Procedure Revolution*, 152 U. Pa. L. Rev. 1361 (2004).

50 369 U.S. 186 (1962), *overruling* Colegrove v. Green, 328 U.S. 549 (1946).

51 376 U.S. 1 (1964).

52 377 U.S. 533 (1964).

53 364 U.S. 339, 340–41, 347 (1960).

54 United States v. O'Brien, 391 U.S. 367 (1968) (upholding conviction of Vietnam War protestor); Adderley v. Florida, 385 U.S. 39 (1966) (upholding convictions of civil rights protestors); Civil Rights Act of 1964, 78 Stat. 241; Voting Rights Act of 1965, 79 Stat. 437. On the regime politics understanding of Supreme Court decision-making: Peretti, *supra* note 40, at 5–9; Robert A. Dahl, *Decision-Making in a Democracy: The Supreme Court as a National Policy-Maker*, 6 J. Pub. L. 279 (1957); Lain, *supra* note 49, at 1361–69 (many Warren Court criminal procedure decisions were not countermajoritarian).

55 379 U.S. 241, 252, 254, 257–58, 261–62 (1964).

56 *Id.* at 250; *see id.* at 291–92 (Goldberg, J., concurring) (emphasizing protection of individual dignity).

57 *Id.* at 291–92 (quoting S. Rep. No.872, 88th Cong., 2d Sess., 16).

58 *Id.* at 261–62.

59 Franklin & Moss, *supra* note 41, at 525; Manning Marable, The Great Wells of Democracy 71 (2002). I am not suggesting the nation ever actually achieved a fully inclusive and egalitarian democracy.

60 South Carolina v. Katzenbach, 383 U.S. 301, 327 (1966); Katzenbach v. Morgan, 384 U.S. 641, 652–53 (1966).

61 Allen v. State Bd. of Elections, 393 U.S. 544, 565–67 (1969).

4. CONSERVATIVE REACTIONS TO PLURALIST DEMOCRACY AND THE WARREN COURT

1 Richard W. Steele, Free Speech in the Good War 11 (1999) (quoting Frank Hogan); *see* Grenville Clark, *Conservatism and Civil Liberty*, 24 A.B.A. J. 640, 640–44 (1938) (address to Nassau County Bar Association, June 11, 1938) (urging conservatives to press for civil rights); Annelien De Dijn, Freedom: An Unruly History 3–5 (2020) (page citations to Kindle ed.) (rights to freedom have historically been invoked to counter more widespread democratic participation); Ken I. Kersch, Constructing Civil Liberties: Discontinuities in the Development of American Constitutional Law 112–17 (2004) (judicial protection of civil liberties was conservative reaction to demands for expanded national power). Useful sources on conservatism in general during the late twentieth and early twenty-first centuries include the following: Sara Diamond, Roads to Dominion (1995); Steven Hahn, Illiberal America: A History (2024) (page citations to Kindle ed.); Lisa McGirr, Suburban Warriors: The Origins of the New American Right (2001); George H. Nash, The Conservative Intellectual Movement in America Since 1945 (2008 ed.; 1st ed. 1976); Daniel T. Rodgers, Age of Fracture (2011); Robert O. Self, All in the Family: The Realignment of American Democracy Since the 1960s (2012); Sean Wilentz, The Age of Reagan: A History, 1974–2008 (2008); Peter Berkowitz, *Introduction, in* Varieties of Conservatism in America xiii (2004); Adam Wolfson, *Conservatives and Neoconservatives* (2004), *reprinted in* The Neocon Reader 213 (Irwin Stelzer ed., 2004).

2 Jefferson Cowie, The Great Exception: The New Deal and the Limits of American Politics 183–85 (2016); James T. Patterson, Grand Expectations: The United States, 1945–1974, at 243–75 (1996); *see* Ken I. Kersch, Conservatives and the Constitution x–xi (2019) (emphasizing varied conservative responses during twentieth century).

3 *Roe*, 410 U.S. 113 (1973); Alexander M. Bickel, The Morality of Consent 25–28 (1975); Robert H. Bork, *The Impossibility of Finding Welfare Rights in the Constitution*, 1979 Wash. U.L.Q. 695, 695 [hereinafter Impossibility] (arguing against a right to welfare as being neither a specified right nor a secondary right necessary to government processes); Robert H. Bork, *Neutral Principles and Some First Amendment Problems*, 47 Ind. L.J. 1, 6–11 (1971) [hereinafter Neutral] (arguing that legislatures should choose fundamental values); *see* Ian Millhiser, The Agenda: How a Republican Supreme Court is Reshaping America 10–11 (2021) (quoting Republican presidents on judicial restraint).

4 *E.g.*, Raoul Berger, Government by Judiciary 45, 363–72 (1977); Richard A. Epstein, *The Proper Scope of the Commerce Power*, 73 Va. L. Rev. 1387, 1387–88 (1987); *see* Erwin Chemerinsky, Federal Jurisdiction 823–32 (5th ed. 2007) ("Our Federalism").

5 403 U.S. 602, 612–13 (1971).

6 McCreary County v. ACLU, 545 U.S. 844, 893 (2005) (Scalia, J., dissenting); Wallace v. Jaffree, 472 U.S. 38, 91–114 (1985) (Rehnquist, J., dissenting); Robert H. Bork, Slouching Towards Gomorrah 289 (1996).

7   Lynch v. Donnelly, 465 U.S. 668, 687–88 (O'Connor, J., concurring); *see* County of Allegheny v. ACLU, 492 U.S. 573, 595–97 (1989) (plurality using endorsement test).

8   County of Allegheny v. ACLU, 492 U.S. 573, 659 (1989) (Kennedy, J., concurring and dissenting); *see* Lee v. Weisman, 505 U.S. 577 (1992) (applying coercion test).

9   463 U.S. 783, 786 (1983).

10 Sherbert v. Verner, 374 U.S. 398, 403, 406–08 (1963).

11 494 U.S. 872, 890 (1990); Jamal Greene, *The Age of Scalia*, 130 Harv. L. Rev. 144, 163–64 (2016).

12 Empirical studies of free exercise claims in the lower courts: James C. Brent, *An Agent and Two Principals: U.S. Court of Appeals Responses to* Employment Division, Department of Human Resources v. Smith *and the Religious Freedom Restoration Act*, 27 Am. Pol. Q. 236 (1999); Frank Way & Barbara J. Burt, *Religious Marginality and the Free Exercise Clause*, 77 Am. Pol. Sci. Rev. 652 (1983).

13 *Smith*, 494 U.S. at 888, 890.

14 494 U.S. at 877–78, 882–83.

15 Widmar v. Vincent, 454 U.S. 276 (1981) (combining religious-freedom claim with a free-expression claim).

16 508 U.S. 520, 533 (1993); Daniel O. Conkle, Constitutional Law: The Religion Clauses 91–92 (2003).

17 *See Smith*, 494 U.S. at 877–78 (examples of ways government might purposefully discriminate against or target religion).

18 Clark M. Neily III, Terms of Engagement: How Our Courts Should Enforce the Constitution's Promise of Limited Government 10 (2013); *see* Clint Bollick, David's Hammer: The Case for an Activist Judiciary (2007) (conservative arguing for an aggressive judiciary).

19 Douglas H. Ginsburg, *Delegation Running Riot*, Regulation, No. 1, 1995, at 83, 84; Randy E. Barnett, Restoring the Lost Constitution (2004); Richard A. Epstein, *The Mistakes of 1937*, 11 Geo. Mason U. L. Rev. 5, 20 (1988–1989); United States v. Lopez, 514 U.S. 549, 599 (1995) (Thomas, J., concurring).

20 Walter Berns, The First Amendment and the Future of American Democracy 233 (1976); *see* Walter Berns, Taking the Constitution Seriously (1987); Walter Berns, Freedom, Virtue, and the First Amendment (1957) [hereinafter Berns, Freedom].

21 Berns, Freedom, *supra* note 20, at 47, 72, 126, 242, 251, 255–56.

22 Bickel, *supra* note 3, at 23.

23 Neutral, *supra* note 3, at 8, 20; *see* Impossibility, *supra* note 3, at 695 (advocating for originalism).

24 Robert Bork, The Tempting of America 94–95 (1990); Engel v. Vitale, 370 U.S. 421 (1962).

25 Friedrich A. Hayek, The Road to Serfdom (1944); Russell Kirk, The Conservative Mind: From Burke to Santayana (1953); Nash, *supra* note 1, at 104–15; Wolfson, *supra* note 1, at 216–17, 221; Berkowitz, *supra* note 1, at xiv–xviii.

26 Nash, *supra* note 1, at 197–98, 235–43; Stephen M. Feldman, Neoconservative Politics and the Supreme Court: Law, Power, and Democracy 47–92 (2013) (discussing

neoconservatism); McGirr, *supra* note 1, at 260 (on Reagan); Self, *supra* note 1, at 414 (emphasizing conservative success).

27 The leading history on the emergence of the white power movement was only published in 2018. Kathleen Belew, Bring the War Home (2018). Conservative movements of the latter twentieth century can be categorized in multiple ways. Sara Diamond identifies a New Right, which emphasized anticommunism, a racist Right, a Christian Right, and a neoconservative movement, which initially arose from former liberals. Diamond, *supra* note 1, at 9–10.

28 Useful sources on neoliberalism: David Harvey, A Brief History of Neoliberalism (2005); Daniel Stedman Jones, Masters of the Universe: Hayek, Friedman, and the Birth of Neoliberal Politics (2012) [hereinafter Jones, Masters].

29 Adam Smith, The Wealth of Nations (1776); Stephen M. Feldman, The New Roberts Court, Donald Trump, and Our Failing Constitution 89–96, 167 (2017).

30 Milton Friedman, *Neo-Liberalism and its Prospects*, Farmand, at 89 (Feb. 17, 1951), *reprinted in* The Collected Works of Milton Friedman (Robert Leeson & Charles G. Palm, eds.) <https://miltonfriedman.hoover.org/internal/media/dispatcher/214957/full>; Rodgers, *supra* note 1, at 4–8.

31 Friedrich A. Hayek, The Constitution of Liberty 94–95, 122 (2011 definitive ed.; 1960 1st ed.); Jones, Masters, *supra* note 28, at 109 (on hubris).

32 Milton Friedman, *Adam Smith's Relevance for 1976*, Selected Papers No. 50, at 15–16, 18; *see* Hahn, *supra* note 1, at 282–313 (on neoliberalism as a form of illiberalism and its rise in the late twentieth century).

33 Kenneth Arrow, Social Choice and Individual Values (1951) (seminal work); Daniel A. Farber & Philip P. Frickey, Law and Public Choice (1991); Jones, Masters, *supra* note 28, at 126–32; Mark Kelman, *On Democracy-Bashing: A Skeptical Look at the Theoretical and 'Empirical' Practice of the Public Choice Movement*, 74 Va. L. Rev. 199 (1988) (criticizing public choice). The economist Mancur Olson was a leader in exploring collective action problems in government. Mancur Olson, The Rise and Decline of Nations (1982); Mancur Olson, The Logic of Collective Action (2d ed. 1971).

34 Rodgers, *supra* note 1, at 52 (quoting Friedman); *id.* at 42–44, 55; Jeffry A. Frieden, Global Capitalism 363 (2006) (stagflation); Paul Craig Roberts, *The Breakdown of the Keynesian Model, reprinted in* Supply-Side Economics: A Critical Appraisal 1 (Richard H. Fink ed., 1982).

35 Ronald Reagan, *First Inaugural Address* (Jan. 20, 1981); Rodgers, *supra* note 1, at 75 (quoting Wriston); Thomas Piketty, Capital in the Twenty-first Century 24 (Arthur Goldhammer trans., 2014) (Figure: Income Inequality in the United States, 1910–2010); Joseph E. Stiglitz, The Price of Inequality 8–9, 89 (2013 ed.); Wilentz, *supra* note 1, at 144–50, 194–203; George Gilder, *The Supply-Side, in* Supply-Side Economics: A Critical Appraisal 14 (Richard H. Fink ed., 1982).

5. WHITE CHRISTIAN NATIONALISM ENTERS THE POLITICAL MAINSTREAM

1 Kathleen Belew, Bring the War Home 10–11, 23–24 (2018). Helpful sources on conservatism in general during the latter half of the twentieth century and the early twenty-first century include the following: Jefferson Cowie, Freedom's Dominion: A Saga of White Resistance to Federal Power (2022) (page citations to Kindle ed.); Sara Diamond, Roads to Dominion (1995); Steven Hahn, Illiberal America: A History (2024) (page citations to Kindle ed.); Lisa McGirr, Suburban Warriors: The Origins of the New American Right (2001); Robert O. Self, All in the Family: The Realignment of American Democracy Since the 1960s (2012); Sean Wilentz, The Age of Reagan: A History, 1974–2008 (2008). Helpful sources on white Christian nationalism, whether emphasizing white supremacy or Christianity, include the following: Carol Anderson, White Rage: The Unspoken Truth of Our Racial Divide (2016); Belew, *supra*; Joseph Darda, How White Men Won the Culture Wars (2021); John Fanestil, American Heresy: The Roots and Reach of White Christian Nationalism (2023); Philip S. Gorski & Samuel L. Perry, The Flag and the Cross: White Christian Nationalism and the Threat to American Democracy (2022); Ashley Jardina, White Identity Politics (2019); Robert P. Jones, White Too Long (2020) [hereinafter Jones, Too Long]; Robert P. Jones, The End of White Christian America (2016); Khyati Y. Joshi, White Christian Privilege (2020); Sarah Posner, Unholy (2021); Katherine Stewart, The Power Worshippers (2019); Jemar Tisby, The Color of Compromise: The Truth About the American Church's Complicity in Racism (2019); Andrew L. Whitehead & Samuel L. Perry, Taking America Back for God: Christian Nationalism in the United States (2020); Leonard Zeskind, Blood and Politics: The History of the White Nationalist Movement from the Margins to the Mainstream (2009).

2 Anderson, *supra* note 1; Belew, *supra* note 1; Darda, *supra* note 1; Jardina, *supra* note 1.

3 Jones, End, *supra* note 1; Stewart, *supra* note 1; Whitehead & Perry, *supra* note 1.

4 "White Christian supremacy in America is the product of a centuries-long project in which notions of White racial superiority and Christian religious superiority have augmented and magnified each other." Joshi, *supra* note 1, at 5. "White supremacy lives on today not just in explicitly and consciously held attitudes among white Christians; it has become deeply integrated into the DNA of white Christianity itself." Jones, Too Long, *supra* note 1, at 187.

5 For example, I cite repeatedly Robert P. Jones as a critic of white Christian nationalism, but Jones himself is unequivocally a Christian. Jones, Too Long, *supra* note 1, at 1–6. Similarly, Kristin Kobes Du Mez is a committed Christian who has criticized white Christian nationalism. Kristin Kobes Du Mez, Jesus and John Wayne: How White Evangelicals Corrupted a Faith and Fractured a Nation (2020). On the day after the 2024 presidential election, the presiding bishop of the Episcopal Church wrote: "We are Christians who support the dignity, safety, and equality of

women and LGBTQ+ people as an expression of our faith. I pray that President Trump and his administration will do the same." Elizabeth Dias & Ruth Graham, *Trump's Believers See a Presidency With God on Their Side*, NYTimes (December 7, 2024).

6   Belew, *supra* note 1, at 6–7, 10, 22–24; Hahn, *supra* note 1, at 316–17; Jones, Too Long, *supra* note 1, at 8–9; James T. Patterson, Grand Expectations: The United States, 1945–1974, at 769–70 (1996) [hereinafter Patterson, Grand]; Zeskind, *supra* note 1, at 123–218.

7   Belew, *supra* note 1, at 10; Civil Rights Act of 1964, 78 Stat. 241; John Hope Franklin & Alfred A. Moss, Jr., From Slavery to Freedom 508–10 (7th ed. 1994); Nathan Glazer, Affirmative Discrimination: Ethnic Inequality and Public Policy 168–95 (1978 ed.; 1st ed. 1975) (on white resentment); Ibram X. Kendi, Stamped From the Beginning 384–90, 430 (2016); Patterson, Grand, *supra* note 6, at 442–57, 620–29, 642, 723–24.

8   Michael J. Klarman, *Foreword: The Degradation of American Democracy – And the Court*, 134 Harv. L. Rev. 1, 128 (2020); Kendi, *supra* note 7, at 365–77; Stewart, *supra* note 1, at 190–91.

9   Bob Jones Univ. v. United States, 461 U.S. 574, 604 (1983); *id.* at 577–82, 602–03; Stewart, *supra* note 1, at 54–77; Zahid Shahab Ahmed & Galib Bashirov, *Religious Fundamentalism and Violent Extremism*, in The Difficult Task of Peace 245, 251–52 (Francisco Rojas Aravena ed., 2020); Jane Dailey, *Sex, Segregation, and the Sacred After* Brown, 91 J. of American History 119 (2004); John C. Jeffries, Jr. & James E. Ryan, *A Political History of the Establishment Clause*, 100 Mich. L. Rev. 279, 340 (2001).

10 *Roe*, 410 U.S. 113 (1973); Posner, *supra* note 1, at 100–124; Stewart, *supra* note 1, at 54–77; Klarman, *supra* note 8, at 127–28; Neil A. O'Brian, *Before Reagan: The Development of Abortion's Partisan Divide*, 18 Perspectives on Politics 1031 (2020).

11 Darda, *supra* note 1, at 102–11, 121–26; Glazer, *supra* note 7, at 2, 168–95; James T. Patterson, Restless Giant 206 (2005) [hereinafter Patterson, Giant]; Wilentz, *supra* note 1, at 186; Keeanga-Ymahtta Taylor, *A Culture of Racism*, in A Field Guide to White Supremacy 31, 34–35 (Kathleen Belew & Ramón A. Gutiérrez eds., 2021); Steve Inskeep, *What Does 'Born In The U.S.A.' Really Mean?*, NPR Morning Edition (March 26, 2019) <https://www.npr.org/2019/03/26/706566556/bruce-springsteen-born-in-the-usa-american-anthem>.

12 Belew, *supra* note 1, at 3, 104; Jones, Masters, *supra* note 1, at 19, 263–69; Self, *supra* note 1, at 402–03; Wilentz, *supra* note 1, at 194–203.

13 Zeskind, *supra* note 1, at xvii; Belew, *supra* note 1, at 3–7, 122–26, 135–36, 156–84, 196–97, 219–23; *see* Isabel Wilkerson, Caste: The Origins of Our Discontents (2020) (caste systems in the United States, Nazi Germany, and India).

14 Rousas John Rushdoony, The Nature of the American System 8 (1965) (quoted in Stewart, *supra* note 1, at 113); Stewart, *supra* note 1, at 104, 112–14; Virginia Garrard, *Hidden in Plain Sight: Dominion Theology, Spiritual Warfare, and Violence in Latin America*, 11 Religions 648 (2020).

15 Rousas John Rushdoony, The Institutes of Biblical Law 100 (1973) [hereinafter Rushdoony, Institutes].

16 Stewart, *supra* note 1, at 104.

17 Rousas John Rushdoony, The Politics of Guilt and Pity 19–20 (1970); Rushdoony, Institutes, *supra* note 15, at 586–88; Stewart, *supra* note 1, at 113–14; Molly Worthen, *The Chalcedon Problem: Rousas John Rushdoony and the Origins of Christian Reconstructionism*, 77 Church History 399 (2008); *see* John C. Calhoun, *Speech On the Reception of Abolition Petitions, Delivered in the Senate* (Feb. 6, 1837), *in* 2 The Works of John C. Calhoun 625, 630–31 (1851).

18 Belew, *supra* note 1, at 6, 26, 51; Tanya Telfair Sharpe, *The Identity Christian Movement: Ideology of Domestic Terrorism*, 30 J. of Black Studies 604, 617 (2000); *see* Sydney E. Ahlstrom, A Religious History of the American People 805–16 (1972) (discussing origins of American fundamentalist movement). The definition of fundamentalism is contested. Zahid Shahab Ahmed & Galib Bashirov, *Religious Fundamentalism and Violent Extremism, in* The Difficult Task of Peace 245, 246–49 (Francisco Rojas Aravena ed., 2020); Douglas Pratt, *Religion and Terrorism: Christian Fundamentalism and Extremism*, 22 Terrorism & Political Violence 438, 439–42 (2010); Margaret Bendroth, *Christian Fundamentalism in America*, Oxford Research Encyclopedias: Religion (Feb. 27, 2017) <https://oxfordre.com/religion/view/10.1093/acrefore/9780199340378.001.0001/acrefore-9780199340378-e-419> (explaining contested definitions of fundamentalism and evangelicalism, while also emphasizing the historical background).

19 *Kingdom Identity Ministries Doctrinal Statement of Beliefs* (1999) [hereinafter Kingdom Identity] (quoted in Sharpe, *supra* note 18, at 607); Belew, *supra* note 1, at 6; Louis Jacobs, The Jewish Religion: A Companion 77–78, 273–74 (1995); Paul Johnson, A History of the Jews 3–79 (1987); Deborah E. Lipstadt, Antisemitism: Here and Now 32–33 (2019); Sharpe, *supra* note 18, at 607.

20 Sharpe, *supra* note 18, at 610.

21 Kingdom Identity, *supra* note 19 (quoted in Sharpe, *supra* note 18, at 611).

22 Sharpe, *supra* note 18, at 614.

23 Diamond, *supra* note 1, at 266; Jones, Too Long, *supra* note 1, at 93–94 (comparing pre- and post-millennialism).

24 Belew, *supra* note 1, at 5–7, 26, 51. On the contested definitions of evangelicism: Seth Dowland, *American Evangelicism and the Politics of Whiteness*, The Christian Century (June 19, 2018). It is worth noting that not all evangelicals are fundamentalists (believing in the literal interpretation of the Protestant Bible). On the relationship between fundamentalism and evangelicalism, see the following: Bendroth, *supra* note 18; Steve Waldman & John Green, *Evangelicals v. Fundamentalists*, Frontline: The Jesus Factor <https://www.pbs.org/wgbh/pages/frontline/shows/jesus/evangelicals/vs.html> (accessed: February 1, 2021); *History of American Christian Movements: Evangelicals and Fundamentalists*, Sacred Heart University Library <https://library.sacredheart.edu/c.php?g=29705&p=7013527>

(accessed: February 1, 2021) (emphasizing contested nature of the definitions of evangelicalism and fundamentalism).

25 Ahlstrom, *supra* note 18, at 959; Pew Research Center, *Religion and Public Life* <https://www.pewforum.org/religious-landscape-study/>; Diamond, *supra* note 1, at 267; Sharpe, *supra* note 18, at 619–20; *see* Self, *supra* note 1, at 351–58 (discussing fundamentalists); Tisby, *supra* note 1, at 153 (on racism and evangelicalism). "American evangelicalism became virtually synonymous with the GOP and whiteness." Tisby, *supra* note 1, at 153. White supremacy is "embedded in the DNA of American Christianity." Jones, Too Long, *supra* note 1, at 3.

26 Belew, *supra* note 1, at 7; Leonard Dinnerstein, Antisemitism in America xxii–xxiv, 166–68 (1994); Stephen M. Feldman, Please Don't Wish Me a Merry Christmas: A Critical History of the Separation of Church and State 209–10 (1997) [hereinafter Feldman, Please Don't] (describing *Protocols of the Elders of Zion*); William Nicholls, Christian Antisemitism 355–56, 386–87 (1993); Ahmed & Bashirov, *supra* note 18, at 251.

27 Belew, *supra* note 1, at 111; *see id.* at 4–5, 11, 108–13 (leaderless resistance strategy). Andrew Macdonald, The Turner Diaries (1978). Andrew Macdonald was a pseudonym for William Pierce. For information on *The Turner Diaries*, see Belew, *supra* note 1, at 110–13, 246 n.45, 281 n.37; Hahn, *supra* note 1, at 332–34; *The Turner Diaries*, 10 American Decades Primary Sources 1990 (Cynthia Rose ed., 2004).

28 Louis Beam, *Leaderless Resistance, in* Inter-Klan Newsletter and Survival Alert (1983) (quoted in Belew, *supra* note 1, at 112).

29 Belew, *supra* note 1, at 5 ("the founding"), 113 ("a white"); Zeskind, *supra* note 1, at xviii ("the flag").

30 The Declaration of Independence, *reprinted in* 2 Great Issues in American History 70, 71 (Richard Hofstadter ed., 1958); *id.* at 72–74; Lisa Arellano, Vigilantes and Lynch Mobs 4, 8, 20–21, 38–49 (2012); Cowie, *supra* note 1, at 17–18, 493–95 (freedom and democracy have often been invoked to justify subjugation of others).

31 Arellano, *supra* note 30, at 76 (quoting Coutant); *id.* at 75–78, 137; Franklin E. Zimring, The Contradictions of American Capital Punishment (2003) (vigilantism is central to understanding American attitudes toward capital punishment); Farah Peterson, *Constitutionalism in Unexpected Places*, 106 Va. L. Rev. 559 (2020) (mob violence as part of American constitutional traditions).

32 Kendi, *supra* note 7, at 259; Franklin & Moss, *supra* note 7, at 312–17; Jones, Too Long, *supra* note 1, at 28–32; Wilkerson, *supra* note 13, at 92–94.

33 Belew, *supra* note 1, at 10. A 2016 survey showed that while white evangelicals generally did not view race to be a problem, they viewed themselves as victims of reverse discrimination. Tisby, *supra* note 1, at 183.

34 Orlandrew E. Danzell & Lisandra M. Maisonet Montañez, *Understanding the Lone Wolf Terror Phenomena: Assessing Current Profiles*, 8 Behavioral Sciences of Terrorism and Political Aggression 135 (2015); Edwin Bakker & Beatrice de Graaf, *Preventing Lone Wolf Terrorism*, 5 Perspectives on Terrorism 43 (2011); International Center for the Study of Terrorism, *Tracing the Motivations and Antecedent*

Behaviors of Lone-Actor Terrorism 16–22 (Aug. 2012) <https://www.dhs.gov/sites/default/files/publications/OPSR_TP_ARC-Lone-Actor-Routine-Activity-Analysis-Report_Aug2012-508.pdf>.

35 Belew, *supra* note 1, at 1–16, 210–11, 236–39; Hahn, *supra* note 1, at 333–34; Zeskind, *supra* note 1, at xi–xxiv.

36 On events that might mark the end of the Cold War, possibilities include: The destruction of the Berlin wall, the banning of the communist party in Russia, and a declaration by Russian president Boris Yeltsin that the Cold War had ended. Patterson, Giant, supra note 11, at 194–95; Wilentz, *supra* note 1, at 313.

37 Francis Fukuyama, *The End of History?*, 16 The National Interest 3–18 (Summer 1989).

38 Sheldon S. Wolin, Politics and Vision 596 (Expanded ed. 2004).

39 Jones, Masters, *supra* note 1, at 332. On Clinton's shift rightward: Self, *supra* note 1, at 411–12. On privatization: Joel Bakan, The Corporation 113–38 (2004); Randy Barnett, The Structure of Liberty 179–80, 261 (1998).

40 Jeffry A. Frieden, Global Capitalism 430–32 (2006); John Micklethwait & Adrian Wooldridge, The Company: A Short History of a Revolutionary Idea 173–74 (2003); Alfred D. Chandler & Bruce Mazlish, *Introduction, in* Leviathans 1, 2 (Alfred D. Chandler & Bruce Mazlish eds., 2005).

41 David S. Allen, Democracy, Inc.: The Press and Law in the Corporate Rationalization of the Public Sphere (2005); Sheldon S. Wolin, Democracy Incorporated (2008).

42 Arthur Brooks, *Why the Stimulus Failed*, National Review (Sept. 25, 2012); Jacob S. Hacker & Paul Pierson, Winner-Take-All Politics 118–19 (2010) (corporate political power); Dara Strolovitch, Affirmative Advocacy 209–10 (2007) (corporations and businesses dominate lobbying).

43 Thomas Bailey et al., 2 The American Pageant 1017 (11th ed. 1998); Belew, *supra* note 1, at 6–7, 187–90, 196–200, 206–07.

44 Patrick Joseph Buchanan, *Culture War Speech: Address to the Republican National Convention* ¶¶ 23, 39 (Aug. 17, 1992), *in* Voices of Democracy <https://voicesofdemocracy.umd.edu/buchanan-culture-war-speech-speech-text/> [hereinafter Buchanan, Speech]; *see* Darda, *supra* note 1, at 20.

45 Self, *supra* note 1, at 402–03; Ahlstrom, *supra* note 18, at 925; Belew, *supra* note 1, at 35–36; Feldman, Please Don't, *supra* note 26, at 119–20, 223–24; Zeskind, *supra* note 1, at xxi–xxii.

46 Patterson, Giant, *supra* note 11, at 251; *id.* at 266–67; Self, *supra* note 1, at 402–03.

47 Daniel Schlozman & Sam Rosenfeld, *The Long New Right and the World It Made*, Paper Prepared for the American Political Science Association Meeting 4 (Boston, MA, Aug. 31, 2018) (Jan. 2019 version) <https://static1.squarespace.com/static/540f1546e4b0ca60699c8f73/t/5c3e694321c67c3d28e992ba/1547594053027/Long+New+Right+Jan+2019.pdf>.

48 John Dillin, *Buchanan Zeroes In on 'Illegals'*, The Christian Science Monitor (May 15, 1992) (quoting Buchanan); William F. Buckley, Jr., In Search of Anti-Semitism (1992); Diamond, *supra* note 1, at 293–94.

49 Patterson, Giant, *supra* note 11, at 292 (quoting Buchanan).

50 Buchanan, Speech, *supra* note 44, at ¶ 49.

51 Diamond, *supra* note 1, at 226, 293.

52 Romer v. Evans, 517 U.S. 620, 623–24, 631–35 (1996); McGirr, *supra* note 1, at 257; Self, *supra* note 1, at 10–11, 400–404.

53 George W. Bush, *Islam is Peace*, Remarks by the President at Islamic Center of Washington, D.C. (Sept. 17, 2001) <https://georgewbush-whitehouse.archives.gov/news/releases/2001/09/20010917-11.html>; Wilentz, *supra* note 1, at 433–34.

54 George W. Bush, *President Bush Delivers Graduation Speech at West Point* (June 1, 2002) <https://georgewbush-whitehouse.archives.gov/news/releases/2002/06/20020601-3.html>.

55 Kendi, *supra* note 7, at 477–78; Zeskind, *supra* note 1, at 516–20.

56 Steven Levitsky & Daniel Ziblatt, Tyranny of the Minority: Why American Democracy Reached the Breaking Point 101–2 (2023).

57 Kyle Cheney, *No, Clinton Didn't Start the Birther Thing. This Guy Did*, Politico (Sept. 16, 2016); U.S. Const. art. II, § 1, cl. 5 (only natural born citizens eligible for presidency); Hahn, *supra* note 1, at 337–39; Kendi, *supra* note 7, at 498; Levitsky & Ziblatt, *supra* note 56, at 107, 112–15; Wilkerson, *supra* note 13, at 318; Russell Berman, *Gallup: Tea Party's Top Concerns Are Debt, Size of Government*, The Hill (July 5, 2010); Jeremy W. Peters, *The Tea Party Didn't Get What It Wanted, but It Did Unleash the Politics of Anger*, NYTimes (Aug. 28, 2019).

58 Kendi, *supra* note 7, at 494; Algernon Austin, America Is Not Post-Racial: Xenophobia, Islamophobia, Racism, and the 44th President (2015); Hahn, *supra* note 1, at 314–17, 339–40.

59 Wilkerson, *supra* note 13, at 318–19.

60 Thomas B. Edsall, *Is Rush Limbaugh's Country Gone?*, NYTimes (Nov. 18, 2012) (quoting Limbaugh); Hahn, *supra* note 1, at 338–39; Perry Bacon, Jr., *Foes Use Obama's Muslim Ties to Fuel Rumors About Him*, washingtonpost.com, Nov. 29, 2007 <http://www.washingtonpost.com/wp-dyn/content/article/2007/11/28/AR2007112802757.html>.

61 Hahn, *supra* note 1, at 339–46; Levitsky & Ziblatt, *supra* note 56, at 112–17; Tehama Lopez Bunyasi, *The Role of Whiteness in the 2016 Presidential Primaries*, 17 Perspectives on Politics 679 (2019); Diana C. Mutz, *Status Threat, Not Economic Hardship, Explains the 2016 Presidential Vote*, 115 Proceedings of the National Academy of Sciences 4330 (April 23, 2018); Marc Hooghe & Ruth Dassonneville, *Explaining the Trump Vote: The Effect of Racist Resentment and Anti-Immigrant Sentiments*, 51 PS: Political Science & Politics 528 (2018).

62 Christopher H. Achen & Larry M. Bartels, Democracy for Realists: Why Elections Do Not Produce Responsive Government 267, 313 (2016).

63 Tisby, *supra* note 1, at 187–89; Alton Frye, *A Christian's Questions for Trump's Evangelical Voters*, The Globalist: Rethinking Globalization (May 31, 2020); *see* Ta-Nehisi Coates, We Were Eight Years in Power xvi (2017) (white fear of Obama's success infused Trump and his symbols of racism with the potency to win); Wilkerson, *supra* note 13, at 329 (white evangelicals are the Republican base); Lilliana Mason et al., *Activating Animus: The Uniquely Social Roots of Trump Support*, Am. Pol. Sci. Rev. First View 1 (June 30, 2021) (political support for Trump could be predicted based on animus toward minority groups from years before).

64 Jessica Martinez & Gregory A. Smith, *How the Faithful Voted: A Preliminary 2016 Analysis*, Pew Research Center (Nov. 9, 2016); Janelle Wong, *The Evangelical Vote and Race in the 2016 Presidential Election*, 3 J. Race, Ethnicity, and Politics 81, 82 (2018).

65 Gregory A. Smith, *Among White Evangelicals, Regular Churchgoers Are the Most Supportive of Trump*, Pew Research Center (April 26, 2017).

66 Wong, *supra* note 64, at 95; *id.* at 81–82, 94–101.

67 Dowland, *supra* note 24.

68 Gregory A. Smith, *More White Americans Adopted Than Shed Evangelical Label During Trump Presidency, Especially His Supporters*, Pewresearch.com (Sept. 15, 2021).

69 Wilkerson, *supra* note 13, at 331; Rogers M. Smith & Desmond King, *White Protectionism in America*, 19 Perspectives on Politics 460 (2021).

70 Amber Phillips, *'They're Rapists.' President Trump's Campaign Launch Speech Two Years Later, Annotated*, Washington Post (June 16, 2017).

71 Yair Rosenberg, *'Jews Will Not Replace Us': Why White Supremacists Go After Jews*, Washington Post (Aug. 14, 2017). The white, Christian, nationalist marchers also chanted a Nazi slogan, "Blood and Soil," suggesting that "only those people with 'pure' or 'white' bloodlines can be true citizens of the nation. Only they are rooted to the soil. Jews, on the other hand, are 'cosmopolitans,' not nationalists, and as such are interlopers and threats to the well-being of the nation." Lipstadt, *supra* note 19, at 31.

72 Jane Coaston, *Trump's New Defense of his Charlottesville Comments is Incredibly False*, Vox.com (April 26, 2019); Neil MacFarquhar, *Victims of Charlottesville Rally Argue the Violence Was Planned*, NYTimes (Oct. 24, 2021).

73 Dana M. Moss, *Enter a New Regime? Lessons From the Study of Authoritarianism for US Politics*, 51 PS: Political Science & Politics 20, 21 (2018); Daniel Byman, *The Security Threat Hiding in Plain Sight*, Foreign Affairs (Jan. 7, 2021).

74 Belew, *supra* note 1, at 238–39; Tim Elfrink, *After Electoral College Backs Biden, Trump Continues Falsely Insisting He Won: 'This Fake Election Can No Longer Stand'*, Washington Post (December 15, 2020).

75 PRRI, *Support for Christian Nationalism in All 50 States: Findings from PRRI's 2023 American Values Atlas* (Feb. 28, 2024).

76 Department of Homeland Security, *Homeland Threat Assessment* 17–18 (Oct. 2020); Joseph E. Lowndes, *From Pat Buchanan to Donald Trump: The Nativist Turn in Right-Wing Populism*, in A Field Guide to White Supremacy 265 (Kathleen Belew & Ramón A. Gutiérrez eds., 2021); Posner, *supra* note 1, at xiv, 74; Rebecca Ulam Weiner, *The Growing White Supremacist Menace*, Foreign Affairs (June 23, 2020).

77 Zolan Kanno-Youngs & Nicholas Fandos, *D.H.S. Downplayed Threats From Russia and White Supremacists, Whistle-Blower Says*, NYTimes (Sept. 9, 2020). On events in Michigan: Kathleen Gray, *In Michigan, a Dress Rehearsal for the Chaos at the Capitol on Wednesday*, NYTimes (Jan. 9, 2021); Pema Levy, *Attack on Michigan Capitol Was a "Preview" of January 6, Impeachment Prosecutors Argue*, Mother Jones (Feb. 11, 2021).

78 Belew, *supra* note 1, at 6–7; Bob Woodward & Robert Costa, Peril 209–12, 224–27, 234–58 (2021); Laura E. Adkins & Emily Burack, *Capitol Riots: What Far-Right Hate Symbols Were on Display?*, Jerusalem Post (Jan. 8, 2021); Nick Corasaniti et al., *The Times Called Officials in Every State: No Evidence of Voter Fraud*, NYTimes (Nov. 10, 2020); Jodi Kantor et al., *Another Provocative Flag Was Flown at Another Alito Home*, NYTimes (May 22, 2024); Michael J. Mooney, *The Boogaloo Bois Prepare for Civil War*, The Atlantic (Jan. 15, 2021); Matthew Rosenberg & Ainara Tiefenthäler, *Decoding the Far-Right Symbols at the Capitol Riot*, NYTimes (Jan. 13, 2021); *see* Thomas Mockaitis, Violent Extremists, chapter 4 (2019) (summarizing views of white, Christian, nationalist groups).

79 CBS Baltimore Staff, *'We Love You, You're Very Special': President Trump Tweets Message, Later Removed, To Rioters Storming The U.S. Capitol*, Baltimore CBS (Jan. 6, 2021); Kevin Breuninger & Dan Mangan, *Two More Police Officers Die by Suicide After Defending Capitol During Riot by Pro-Trump Mob, Tally Now 4*, CNBC (Aug. 2, 2021); Jack Healy, *These Are the 5 People Who Died in the Capitol Riot*, NYTimes (Jan. 11, 2021); Peter Hermann & Julie Zauzmer, *Beaten, Sprayed with Mace and Hit with Stun Guns: Police Describe Injuries to Dozens of Officers During Assault on U.S. Capitol*, Washington Post (Jan. 11, 2021).

80 Courtney Subramanian, *A Minute-by-minute Timeline of Trump's Day as the Capitol Siege Unfolded on Jan. 6*, USA Today (Feb. 11, 2021); Jamie Gangel et al., *New Details About Trump-McCarthy Shouting Match Show Trump Refused to Call Off the Rioters*, CNN.com (Feb. 12, 2021); Michael McConnell, *How Democrats Could Have Made Republicans Squirm*, NYTimes (Feb. 14, 2021); *see* Cowie, *supra* note 1, at 493–95 (the Capitol insurrection resonated with an American tradition of whites insisting on their freedom to subjugate others).

81 Ben Leonard, *'Practically and Morally Responsible': McConnell Scorches Trump—But Votes to Acquit*, Politico (Feb. 13, 2021) (quoting McConnell); U.S. Const. art. I, § 3, cl. 6; Jonathan Bernstein, *Is the Republican Party Headed for a Schism?*, Bloomberg.com (Feb. 11, 2021); Weiyi Cai, *Impeachment Results: How Democrats and Republicans Voted*, NYTimes (Jan. 13, 2021); Weiyi Cai, *Trump's Second Impeachment: How the Senate Voted*, NYTimes (Feb. 13, 2021); Evie Fordham, *Republicans Who Voted to Convict Trump Face Backlash at Home*, Foxnews.com (Feb. 14, 2021); Sarah Mimms, *These 7 Republicans Voted to Convict Donald Trump for Inciting the Deadly Capitol Riot*, Buzzfeednews.com (Feb. 13, 2021); Domenico Montanaro, *These Are The 10 Republicans Who Voted To Impeach Trump*, NPR.org (Jan. 14, 2021); Harry Stevens et al., *How Members of Congress Voted on Counting the Electoral College Vote*, Washington Post (Jan. 7, 2021).

82 Bernstein, *supra* note 81; Thomas B. Edsall, *The QAnon Delusion has not Loosened Its Grip*, NYTimes (Feb. 3, 2021); *see* Jardina, *supra* note 1, at 8 (many whites strongly align their politics with white identity but do not openly approve of white nationalism); Smith & King, *supra* note 69, at 460 (Trump is a "white nationalist" who has remade "the modern Republican Party in his image").

83 Rachel M. Blum & Christopher Sebastian Parker, *Panel Study of the MAGA Movement* (surveys conducted in late December 2020 and late January 2021) <https://sites.uw.edu/magastudy/>: section on *The Pandemic and Paranoia* <https://sites.uw.edu/magastudy/the-pandemic-and-paranoia/>; *id.* at section on *Demographics & Group Affinities* <https://sites.uw.edu/magastudy/demographics-group-affinities/>.

84 Michael Humphrey, *I Analyzed All of Trump's Tweets to Find Out What He was Really Saying*, The Conversation (Feb. 8, 2021); Thomas B. Edsall, *The Capitol Insurrection was as Christian Nationalist as it Gets*, NYTimes (Jan. 28, 2021).

85 Schlozman & Rosenfeld, *supra* note 47, at 76; Hahn, *supra* note 1, at 317–18 (Republican party pivoting from neoliberalism to white Christian nationalism); Jeff D. Colgan, *Trump Wants to Impose a Whopping 35% Tariff on Businesses that Move Jobs Overseas. This Is Why*, Washington Post (December 4, 2016); Tim Dickinson, *How Trump Took the Middle Class to the Cleaners*, Rolling Stone (Oct. 26, 2020).

86 Lisa McGirr, *Trump Is the Republican Party's Past and Its Future*, NYTimes (Jan. 13, 2021); Hahn, *supra* note 1, at 341–46.

87 Zeskind, *supra* note 1, at xvii–xviii.

88 *See* Whitehead & Perry, *supra* note 1, at 4–5, 153–54 (Christian nationalism is about political power and imposing a particular social order).

89 Population Projections Tables (2017), Census.gov <https://www.census.gov/programs-surveys/popproj/data/tables.html>; Jones, End, *supra* note 1, at 40–41, 47–56; Zachary Baron Shemtob, *The Catholic and Jewish Court: Explaining the Absence of Protestants on the Nation's Highest Judicial Body*, 27 J. Law & Religion 359 (2011); Marci A. Hamilton & Leslie C. Griffin, *How Did Six Conservative Catholics Become Supreme Court Justices Together?*, Verdict (Justia) (May 3, 2023); Daniel Burke, *What is Neil Gorsuch's religion? It's complicated*, CNN Politics (March 22, 2017); *Religious Identity and Supreme Court Justices—A Brief History*, The Conversation (Oct. 19, 2020). Tensions between conservative Protestants and conservative Catholics are much less than in prior American history. Rod Dreher can thus claim to be talking to Protestants, Catholics, and Eastern Orthodox Christians. Rod Dreher, The Benedict Option 4–5 (2017) [hereinafter Dreher, Option].

90 Joshi, *supra* note 1, at 1, 57, 129–30, 158–59; *see* Leora Batnitzky, How Judaism Became a Religion 1–5 (2011) (Judaism needed to fit within the concept of a Protestant religion); Jones, Too Long, *supra* note 1, at 5–6 (white Christian churches have actively sought to construct and protect white supremacy).

91 Joshi, *supra* note 1, at 46; Jardina, *supra* note 1, at 7, 105–07; Jones, End, *supra* note 1, at 41–42; Whitehead & Perry, *supra* note 1, at 4–5.

92 Fanestil, *supra* note 1, at 2–7; Gorski & Perry, *supra* note 1, at 13–45 (empirical data demonstrating extent of white, Christian, nationalist attitudes in United States). Examples of Christian grievance: Rod Dreher, Live Not By Lies (2020) [hereinafter Dreher, Lies]; Erwin W. Lutzer, We Will Not Be Silenced (2020).

93 Dreher, Option, *supra* note 89, at 9; *id.* at 36–37; Lutzer, *supra* note 92, at 20; Stephen Wolfe, The Case for Christian Nationalism 398 (2022) (Americans were to be "a Christian people").

94 Michael J. Mooney, *Trump's Apostle*, Texas Monthly (Aug. 2019).

95 Robert Jeffress, Not All Roads Lead to Heaven 26–27 (2016) [hereinafter Jeffress, Roads]. I will also cite Robert Jeffress, What Every Christian Should Know (2023) [hereinafter Jeffress, Know].

96 Dreher, Option, *supra* note 89, at 17, 99; Dreher, Lies, *supra* note 92, at 210–14; Wolfe, *supra* note 93, at 5 (criticizing "theologies that exclude Christianity from public institutions"); *see* Smith & King, *supra* note 69, at 460–61 (Trump portrayed whites as victims).

97 Lutzer, *supra* note 92, at 121, 249, 254; *see* Dreher, Option, *supra* note 89, at 9–11 (Christians need to aggressively promote traditional Christianity).

98 Dreher, Option, *supra* note 89, at 195; Jeffress, Roads, *supra* note 95, at 19–20; 135 S. Ct. 2584 (2015).

99 Dreher, Lies, *supra* note 92, at xiii, 212–13; *see* Dreher, Option, *supra* note 89, at 2–9 (hostility against Christians); Lutzer, *supra* note 92, at 78–87, 177–206 (capitalism and CRT).

100 Lutzer, *supra* note 92, at 118; *see id.* at 214–16 (worrying about schools); Dreher, Lies, *supra* note 92, at 210–12 (living Christian life).

101 Jeffress, Roads, *supra* note 95, at 14.

102 Lutzer, *supra* note 92, at 77.

103 Jeffress, Roads, *supra* note 95, at 14, 21–22, 88, 110–11; Jeffress, Know, *supra* note 95, at 128; *see* Jeffress, Roads, *supra* note 95, at 116–17 (blaming Jews); Feldman, Please Don't, *supra* note 26, at 10–21 (Christian significance of falsely blaming Jews for Jesus's death).

104 Dreher, Lies, *supra* note 92, at xiv–xv, 89; *see id.* at ix–xv; Dreher, Option, *supra* note 89, at 88–99; Gorski & Perry, *supra* note 1, at 8.

105 Jeffress, Roads, *supra* note 95, at 87.

106 Garrard, *supra* note 14; Rushdoony, Institutes, *supra* note 15, at 100.

107 Paul Rosenberg, *Meet the New Apostolic Reformation, Cutting Edge of the Christian Right*, Salon.com (Jan. 2, 2024) (quoting White-Cain). White-Cain is part of a Dominion movement called the New Apostolic Reformation. Southern Poverty Law Center, *Christian Supremacy and U.S. Politics: An Interview with Theologian André Gagné*, SPLCenter.org (May 31, 2024).

108 Jeffress, Roads, *supra* note 95, at 14; Jeffress, Know, *supra* note 95, at 125.

109 Stewart, *supra* note 1, at 56; *see* Jardina, *supra* note 1, at 5, 105–07; Jones, Too Long, *supra* note 1, at 239–40; Stewart, *supra* note 1, at 5–8, 276–77; Larry M. Bartels,

Ethnic Antagonism Erodes Republicans' Commitment to Democracy, 117 Proceedings National Academy of Sciences (Aug. 2020).

110 Zack Beauchamp, *The Anti-American Right*, Vox.com (Aug. 3, 2021) (quoting Noem and Glenn Elmers); Pew Research Center, Cultural Issues and the 2024 Election (June 6, 2024).

111 Darda, *supra* note 1, at 190–91; Jones, End, *supra* note 1, at 246; Jones, Too Long, *supra* note 1, at 13–15; Joshi, *supra* note 1, at 59, 85, 203–04; Posner, *supra* note 1, at 157–58; Stewart, *supra* note 1, at 31, 244–45; Smith & King, *supra* note 69, at 467–68 (Trump administration policies); Mary Ellen Flannery, *Anti-DEI Laws Take Aim at Students of Color and LGBTQ+ Students*, National Education Association (Feb. 14, 2024) <https://www.nea.org/nea-today/all-news-articles/anti-dei-laws-take-aim-students-color-and-lgbtq-students>.

112 John Haltiwanger, *Nearly Half of Republicans Say 'A Time Will Come When Patriotic Americans Have to Take the Law into Their Own Hands,' New Poll Shows*, BusinessInsider.com (July 29, 2021) <https://www.businessinsider.com/47-percent-gop-voters-patriots-take-law-own-hands-poll-2021-7>; Jones, Too Long, *supra* note 1, at 237–42; Joshi, *supra* note 1, at 91.

113 Beauchamp, *supra* note 110.

114 Michael Gold & Maggie Haberman, *Trump's Newest Venture? A $60 Bible*, NYTimes (March 26, 2024).

115 Philip Bump, *An All-American Bible—With a Cut of the Sales Going to Trump*, Washington Post (March 26, 2024).

6. THE ROBERTS COURT'S DISDAIN FOR PLURALIST DEMOCRACY

1 Between 1937 and the early 1990s, the Court upheld every challenged congressional exercise of its commerce power—*e.g.*, United States v. Carolene Products Co., 304 U.S. 144 (1938) (upholding Filled Milk Act); NLRB v. Jones & Laughlin Steel Corp., 301 U.S. 1 (1937) (upholding National Labor Relations Act)—with the sole exception of a 1976 case, which the Court soon overruled. National League of Cities v. Usery, 426 U.S. 833 (1976), *overruled by* Garcia v. San Antonio Metro. Transit Auth., 469 U.S. 528 (1985).

2 The Court initiated this formalist turn in a decision invalidating congressional action but focusing more on the Tenth Amendment. New York v. United States, 505 U.S. 144 (1992). On the Court's anti-democracy view: Ian Millhiser, The Agenda: How a Republican Supreme Court is Reshaping America 31–52 (2021); Aziz Z. Huq, *The Counterdemocratic Difficulty*, 117 Nw. U. L. Rev. 1099, 1100–07 (2023); Michael J. Klarman, *Foreword: The Degradation of American Democracy – And the Court*, 134 Harv. L. Rev. 1, 4–11 (2020).

3 514 U.S. 549, 558–59, 561 (1995); *see* Perez v. United States, 402 U.S. 146, 150 (1971) (articulating the three categories).

4 514 U.S. at 567–68; Hammer v. Dagenhart, 247 U.S. 251, 274, 276 (1918).

5 132 S. Ct. 2566 (2012); 26 U.S.C. §§5000A, (c), (g)(1).

6 132 S. Ct. at 2586–87; *id.* at 2644, 2647–49 (joint dissent) (conservative justices agreeing with Roberts). Roberts nonetheless upheld the individual mandate pursuant to Congress's taxing power. *Id.* at 2599–600.

7 South Dakota v. Dole, 483 U.S. 203 (1987); *see* Oklahoma v. Civil Service Commission, 330 U.S. 127 (1947).

8 132 S. Ct. at 2603.

9 *Id.* at 2604; *id.* at 2662 (joint dissent).

10 *Lopez*, 514 U.S. at 562–63. By asking Congress to make findings, the Court reintroduced another doctrinal mechanism that had facilitated judicial limiting of congressional power during the pre-1937 era. Hill v. Wallace, 259 U.S. 44, 68–69 (1922); *see* A. Christopher Bryant & Timothy J. Simeone, *Remanding to Congress: The Supreme Court's New "On the Record" Constitutional Review of Federal Statutes*, 86 Cornell L. Rev. 328, 356 (2001). The Rehnquist Court questioned congressional findings in other cases. United States v. Morrison, 529 U.S. 598, 615 (2000) (invalidating Violence Against Women Act); City of Boerne v. Flores, 521 U.S. 527, 530 (1997) (invalidating Religious Freedom Restoration Act).

11 133 S. Ct. 2612, 2627 (2013); *id.* at 2620–22, 2628, 2631; VRA, § 4(b), 79 Stat. 438.

12 133 S. Ct. at 2632 (Ginsburg, J., dissenting); *id.* at 2635–36, 2642–44 (Ginsburg, J., dissenting).

13 Brennan Center for Justice, *Summary of Voter ID Laws Passed Since 2011*, at 13–14 (Nov. 12, 2013); Jonathan Brater et al., Purges: A Growing Threat to the Right to Vote (Brennan Center for Justice 2018); Carol Anderson, White Rage: The Unspoken Truth of Our Racial Divide 148–54 (2016); Zachary Roth, The Great Suppression: Voting Rights, Corporate Cash, and the Conservative Assault on Democracy (2016); Ari Berman, *Texas's Jim Crow Voting Laws*, The Nation 14 (Oct. 31, 2016).

14 Shelby County v. Holder, 133 S. Ct. 2612 (2013) (Fifteenth Amendment power); National Federation of Independent Business v. Sebelius, 132 S. Ct. 2566 (2012) (commerce and spending powers). The Court has not similarly limited Congress's taxing power. Moore v. United States, 144 S. Ct. 1680 (2024) (upholding tax in an explicitly narrow ruling in which Court emphasized following precedents and avoided a decision that could otherwise lead to a "fiscal calamity").

15 Fischer v. United States, 144 S. Ct. 2176 (2024) (in a case involving numerous prosecutions arising from the January 6, 2021, insurrection and storming of the Capitol—including the prosecution of former President Trump—the Court narrowly interpreted a federal criminal statute, holding that for obstruction of an official proceeding to be within the statutory prohibition, the government must prove the defendant impaired the integrity of physical evidence); Garland v. Cargill, 144 S. Ct. 1613 (2024) (held federal agency exceeded statutory authority in defining bump stocks as machine guns); Biden v. Nebraska, 143 S. Ct. 2355 (2023) (invoking major questions doctrine to interpret statute narrowly and invalidate loan forgiveness program).

16 Loper Bright Enterprises v. Raimondo, 144 S. Ct. 2244 (2024), *overruling* Chevron v. NRDC, 467 U.S. 837 (1984) (in a strike against federal administrative power,

Court overruled *Chevron* doctrine, which required courts to defer to any reasonable agency interpretations of ambiguous statutes; courts must independently interpret statutes regardless of technicality of questions); Securities and Exchange Commission v. Jarkesy, 144 S. Ct. 2117 (2024) (in a decision that will diminish the power of numerous federal agencies, the Court held that the SEC's routine imposition of fines in administrative proceedings—to penalize securities fraud—violates Seventh Amendment right to a jury trial in suits at common law); Ohio v. Environmental Protection Agency, 144 S. Ct. 2040 (2024) (grants temporary stay preventing EPA from enforcing its "good neighbor" plan under the Clean Air Act, which would prevent uncooperative states from allowing ozone pollution to drift downwind into other states); Garland v. Cargill, 144 S. Ct. 1613 (2024) (held federal agency exceeded statutory authority in defining bump stocks as machine guns); Biden v. Nebraska, 143 S. Ct. 2355 (2023) (invalidating loan forgiveness program).

17 Citizens United v. FEC, 558 U.S. 310 (2010) (invalidating campaign finance restrictions on corporations).

18 Rucho v. Common Cause, 139 S. Ct. 2484 (2019) (holding political gerrymandering nonjusticiable).

19 Alexander v. S.C. State Conf. of the NAACP, 144 S. Ct. 1221 (2024).

20 American Tradition Partnership, Inc. v. Bullock, 132 S. Ct. 2490 (2012) (invalidating state law restricting corporate political campaign expenditures); Brown v. Entertainment Merchants Association, 131 S. Ct. 2729, 2732 (2011) (invalidating state law prohibiting "the sale or rental of 'violent video games' to minors"); Sorrell v. IMS Health Inc., 131 S. Ct. 2653 (2011) (invalidating state law restricting the sale of medical data); Mark A. Lemley, *The Imperial Supreme Court*, 136 Harv. L. Rev. F. 97, 108–10 (2022) (imperial Court unconcerned with protecting state sovereignty).

21 558 U.S. 310 (2010); Pub. L. No. 107–155, 116 Stat. 81.

22 558 U.S. at 336–41 (*citing* Buckley v. Valeo, 424 U.S. 1 (1976)).

23 *Id.* at 340–42 (*citing* First National Bank of Boston v. Bellotti, 435 U.S. 765 (1978)).

24 558 U.S. at 339. On the self-governance rationale and its development: Stephen M. Feldman, Free Expression and Democracy in America: A History 395–401 (2008); Alexander Meiklejohn, Free Speech: And its Relation to Self-Government 18, 26 (1948); Frederick Schauer, *Free Speech and the Argument from Democracy, in* Liberal Democracy: Nomos XXV 241 (J. Roland Pennock & John W. Chapman, eds., 1983); G. Edward White, *The First Amendment Comes of Age: The Emergence of Free Speech In Twentieth-century America*, 95 Mich. L. Rev. 299, 300–301 (1996) (free speech becomes constitutional lodestar).

25 558 U.S. at 354; *id.* at 340.

26 *Id.* at 356–60. On congressional and social science findings: *Id.* at 452 (Stevens, J., concurring in part and dissenting in part); Larry M. Bartels et al., *Inequality and American Governance, in* Inequality and American Democracy 88, 113–17 (Lawrence R. Jacobs & Theda Skocpol eds., 2005).

27 558 U.S. 353; *id.* at 354–55 (quoting The Federalist No. 10 (James Madison)).

28 Stephen M. Feldman, The New Roberts Court, Donald Trump, and Our Failing Constitution 180–81, 204–15 (2017); Thomas Piketty, Capital in the Twenty-first Century (Arthur Goldhammer trans., 2014); Jedediah Purdy, *Beyond the Bosses' Constitution: The First Amendment and Class Entrenchment*, 118 Colum. L. Rev. 2161, 2166–70 (2018).

29 131 S. Ct. 2806, 2813, 2818, 2821 (2011); *id.* at 2833 (Kagan, J., dissenting).

30 132 S. Ct. 2490, 2491 (2012); Mont. Code Ann. §13-35-227(1) (2011). On Montana history: 132 S. Ct. at 2491–92 (Breyer, J., dissenting).

31 *Citizens United*, in theory, applied equally to corporations and unions. But *Knox v. Service Employees International Union* considered whether a public employee union imposing a special assessment fee to support political advocacy had satisfied free-speech requirements when it failed to allow non-members to opt out of the fee. 132 S. Ct. 2277 (2012). The conservative bloc held that even if the union had provided an opt-out for the non-members, it would have been insufficient to satisfy the First Amendment. Subsequently, union efforts to raise money for political campaigns would face obstacles beyond those faced by corporations. To compound problems facing unions, *Janus v. Am. Fed'n of State, Cty., & Mun. Employees, Council 31* held that workers cannot be forced to pay public employee union fees related solely to collective bargaining representation even though the workers benefit from the representation. 138 S. Ct. 2448 (2018).

32 On the undermining of pluralist democracy, *Allen v. Milligan*, 143 S. Ct. 1487 (2023), is the exception that proves the rule. Many have emphasized that the Court saved a key provision of the VRA because Roberts and Kavanaugh joined the progressive justices in refusing to reinterpret section 2 as requiring only race-neutral actions. Roberts, though, reasoned Alabama had not presented good reasons for reinterpreting section 2 in that particular case. *Id.* at 1510–11. Kavanaugh invited a future similar challenge while adding that any race-based considerations, even if constitutional in 1982 when this statutory section was enacted, would have to be time-limited. *Id.* at 1519 (Kavanaugh, J., concurring).

33 FEC v. Cruz, 596 U.S. 289, 305–07, 312–13 (2022) (invalidating campaign finance restriction and refusing to defer to Congress).

7. RELIGIOUS FREEDOM AT THE EARLY ROBERTS COURT

1 *Religious Freedom: What's at Stake If We Lose It*, Heritage.org (no date); *see* Tom Gjelten, *How The Fight For Religious Freedom Has Fallen Victim To The Culture Wars*, NPR.org (May 23, 2019) (discussing religious freedom disagreement between Republicans and Democrats).

2 Ken I. Kersch, Conservatives and the Constitution 372–74 (2019) (conservative Christian theology is significant to much current constitutional thought despite how many leading constitutional scholars prominently focus on originalism).

3 572 U.S. 565 (2014).

4 Engel v. Vitale, 370 U.S. 421 (1962).

5 Wallace v. Jaffree, 472 U.S. 38 (1985).

6 McCreary County v. American Civil Liberties Union of Kentucky, 545 U.S. 844 (2005).
7 572 U.S. at 575–76; *id.* at 586–91 (plurality); *see* Lee v. Weisman, 505 U.S. 577, 636–44 (1992) (Scalia, J., dissenting) (applying coercion test).
8 572 U.S. at 577; *id.* at 618 (Kagan, J., dissenting).
9 *Id.* at 579; *id.* at 595 (Alito, J., concurring).
10 139 S. Ct. 2067, 2080–81 (2019) (plurality), *reversing* Am. Humanist Ass'n v. Maryland-Nat'l Capital Park & Planning Comm'n, 874 F.3d 195, 206–12 (4th Cir. 2017).
11 139 S. Ct. at 2074 (part of Alito's introduction, unidentified as majority or plurality). In another case, the Court invalidated on procedural grounds an injunction that, if allowed to stand, would have prevented the continuing display of a large Christian cross. Salazar v. Buono, 559 U.S. 700 (2010). Kennedy's plurality opinion explained that a Christian cross could universally honor all fallen soldiers, regardless of their religious beliefs. *Id.* at 715; *see id.* at 725 (Alito, J., concurring in part and concurring in the judgment) (cross was appropriate symbol "to commemorate American war dead").
12 139 S. Ct. at 2104 (Ginsburg, J., dissenting).
13 *Id.* at 2091 (Breyer, J., concurring); *id.* at 2094 (Kagan, J., concurring in part).
14 *Id.* at 2096–97 (Thomas, J., concurring in the judgment). For Thomas, arguing the original meaning of the Establishment Clause precludes applying it against state and local governments: Elk Grove Unified School District v. Newdow, 542 U.S. 1, 50 (2004) (Thomas, J., concurring in the judgment); Rosenberger v. Rectors and Visitors of the University of Virginia, 515 U.S. 819, 852–55 (1995) (Thomas, J., concurring).
15 139 S. Ct. at 2101–02 (Gorsuch, J., concurring in the judgment); *id.* at 2093 (Kavanaugh, J., concurring).
16 The Court held that free speech prevented the government from requiring family planning clinics to provide information about abortion, though the Court had previously upheld laws requiring pro-life (anti-abortion) statements. Nat'l Inst. of Family & Life Advocates v. Becerra, 138 S. Ct. 2361 (2018); *see id.* at 2384–86 (Breyer, J., dissenting) (emphasizing inconsistency of Court's decisions).
17 Warth v. Seldin, 422 U.S. 490, 508–10 (1975); Frothingham v. Mellon, 262 U.S. 447 (1923).
18 392 U.S. 83 (1968).
19 551 U.S. 587, 592 (2007); *id.* at 603–09 (plurality); *id.* at 618 (Scalia, J., concurring in the judgment); *id.* at 637 (Souter, J., dissenting).
20 563 U.S. 125, 142 (2011).
21 *American Legion*, 139 S. Ct. 2067, 2098–2103 (2019) (Gorsuch, J., concurring in the judgment) (those offended by religious displays lack standing to raise Establishment Clause challenges). In a free speech case brought by an evangelical Christian, however, the Court concluded that a claim for nominal damages was sufficient to establish constitutional standing. Uzuegbunam v. Preczewski, 141 S. Ct. 792 (2021).

22 The large majority of private schools are Christian. National Center for Education Statistics, *The Condition of Education: Private School Enrollment*; National Center for Education Statistics, *School Choice in the United States: 2019*; Council for American Private Education, *Private School FAQs*. In 2006, of the total number of hospital beds owned by religiously affiliated organizations, 70 percent were Catholic. Martha A. Boden, *Compassion Inaction: Why President Bush's Faith-Based Initiatives Violate the Establishment Clause*, 29 Seattle U. L. Rev. 991, 1022 (2006).

23 563 U.S. at 148 (Kagan, J., dissenting).

24 140 S. Ct. 2246, 2254 (2020).

25 Lamb's Chapel v. Ctr. Moriches Union Free Sch. Dist., 508 U.S. 384, 398 (1993) (Scalia, J., concurring in the judgment).

26 *American Legion*, 139 S. Ct. at 2085 (majority).

27 565 U.S. 171, 188, 190 (2012); *see id.* at 188–89 (also discussing Establishment Clause); Americans with Disabilities Act of 1990, 104 Stat. 327, 42 U.S.C. § 12101 et seq.

28 140 S. Ct. 2049, 2071 (2020) (Thomas, J., concurring).

29 *Id.* at 2055, 2063–66; *see id.* at 2060–61 (also discussing Establishment Clause); Age Discrimination in Employment Act of 1967, 81 Stat. 602, as amended, 29 U.S.C. § 621 et seq.

30 140 S. Ct. at 2071–72 (Sotomayor, J., dissenting).

31 *Id.* at 2082 (Sotomayor, J., dissenting).

32 137 S. Ct. 2012, 2024 (2017); *see id.* at 2020–24.

33 138 S. Ct. 1719, 1724 (2018); Colo. Rev. Stat. § 24-34-601(2)(a) (2017).

34 138 S. Ct. at 1729. The Warren Court did not interpret the Free Exercise Clause to require religious exemptions from antidiscrimination laws. Newman v. Piggie Park Enterprises, Inc., 390 U.S. 400, 403 n.5 (1968) (dismissing as frivolous a claim that free exercise should protect racial discrimination).

35 138 S. Ct. at 1724, 1731.

36 *Id.* at 1732.

37 Paul Johnson, A History of the Jews 169–310 (1987); *see That Jews Should be Distinguished From Christians in Dress*, *reprinted in* The Jew in the Medieval World: A Source Book, 315–1791, at 138 (Jacob R. Marcus ed., 1938) (thirteenth-century decree requiring Jews to wear conical hats or yellow patches).

38 Drew Gilpin Faust, *A Southern Stewardship: The Intellectual and the Proslavery Argument*, *reprinted in* Proslavery Thought, Ideology, and Politics 129, 137–39 (Paul Finkelman ed., 1989); *see* Thornton Stringfellow, *The Bible Argument: Or, Slavery in the Light of Divine Revelation*, *in* Cotton is King and Pro-Slavery Arguments 460 (E. N. Elliott, ed., Augusta: Pritchard, Abbot and Loomis, 1860) (1968 reprint ed.).

39 Jane Dailey, *Sex, Segregation, and the Sacred after Brown*, 91 J. Am. Hist. 119, 121, 125–26 (2004).

40 138 S. Ct. at 1751 (Ginsburg, J., dissenting).

41 *Id.* at 1738 (Gorsuch, J., concurring); *see* Obergefell v. Hodges, 135 S. Ct. 2584, 2642–43 (2015) (Alito, J. dissenting) (worrying the Court's constitutional protection of same-sex marriage would demean the religiously faithful).

42 Stephen I. Vladeck, *The Solicitor General and the Shadow Docket,* 133 Harv. L. Rev. 123 (2019). On the standards for relief: Trump v. Int'l Refugee Assistance Project, 137 S. Ct. 2080 (2017); Philip Morris USA v. Patricia Henley, 2004 WL 2386754 (U.S.).

43 140 S. Ct. 1613 (2020); *id.* at 1613–14 (Roberts, C.J., concurring); *id.* at 1614 (Kavanaugh, J., dissenting).

44 140 S. Ct. 2246, 2151–53 (2020).

45 *Id.* at 2254; *see id.* at 2261–63.

46 *Id.* at 2279 (Ginsburg, J., dissenting).

47 *Id.* at 2297 (Sotomayor, J., dissenting).

48 *Id.* at 2256.

49 Adam Liptak, *Supreme Court Gives Religious Schools More Access to State Aid,* NYTimes (June 30, 2020); Private School Review, *Top Montana Religiously Affiliated Schools.*

50 140 S. Ct. 2603, 2603–06 (2020) (Alito, J., dissenting).

51 Roman Catholic Diocese of Brooklyn v. Cuomo, 141 S. Ct. 63 (2020); Espinoza v. Montana Dep't of Revenue, 140 S. Ct. 2246 (2020); Masterpiece Cakeshop, Ltd. v. Colorado Civil Rights Commission, 138 S. Ct. 1719 (2018); Trinity Lutheran Church of Columbia, Inc. v. Comer, 137 S. Ct. 2012 (2017).

52 Lee Epstein & Eric A. Posner, *The Roberts Court and the Transformation of Constitutional Protections for Religion: A Statistical Portrait,* 2021 Sup. Ct. Rev. 315 (2021); Michael J. Klarman, *Foreword: The Degradation of American Democracy – And the Court,* 134 Harv. L. Rev. 1, 125–35 (2020).

8. NON-CHRISTIANS DO NOT FULLY BELONG

1 Calvary Chapel Dayton Valley v. Sisolak, 140 S. Ct. 2603 (2020); S. Bay United Pentecostal Church v. Newsom, 140 S. Ct. 1613 (2020).

2 141 S. Ct. 63, 66–67 (2020).

3 *Id.* at 69 (Gorsuch, J., concurring).

4 *Id.* at 73 (Kavanaugh, J., concurring).

5 *Id.* at 80 & n.2 (Sotomayor, J., dissenting). Roberts dissented because New York had already changed its restrictions on religious services, so he viewed the case as effectively moot. *Id.* at 75 (Roberts, C.J., dissenting). Breyer dissented, largely emphasizing that the granting of an injunction should be limited to extraordinary circumstances. *Id.* at 77–78 (Breyer, J., dissenting).

6 141 S. Ct. 527 (2020).

7 141 S. Ct. 972 (2020).

8 141 S. Ct. 527 (2020); *id.* at 529 (Gorsuch, J., dissenting).

9 140 S. Ct. 1613 (2020).

10 141 S. Ct. 716 (2021).

11 *Id.* at 717 (Roberts, C.J., concurring).
12 *Id.* at 717 (Gorsuch, J., statement). Gorsuch's opinion is labeled as a "statement" rather than a concurrence or dissent, though it appears to be concurring in part and dissenting in part. *Id.* at 717–20 (Gorsuch, J., statement).
13 *Id.* at 717–19 (Gorsuch, J., statement).
14 *Id.* at 720–22 (Kagan, J., dissenting); Douglas Laycock, *The Remnants of Free Exercise*, 1990 Sup. Ct. Rev. 1, 49 (1990) (one way to read *Smith* was that it, in effect, granted religion "most-favored nation status").
15 141 S. Ct. at 720, 722 (Kagan, J., dissenting).
16 141 S. Ct. 1294, 1296 (2021). The Court also granted an injunction against California in *Gateway City Church v. Newsom*, 141 S. Ct. 1460 (2021), justifying the decision by referring to *S. Bay United Pentecostal Church v. Newsom*, 141 S. Ct. 716 (2021).
17 141 S. Ct. at 1298–99 (Kagan, J., dissenting).
18 Oral argument was on November 4, 2020. Supreme Court of the United States, No. 19–123, Fulton v. City of Philadelphia.
19 140 S. Ct. 1104 (2020) (granting petition for certiorari). Petition for Certiorari, Fulton v. City of Philadelphia, 2019 WL 3380520 (U.S.); Ian Millhiser, *The Fight Over Whether Religion is a License to Discriminate is Back Before the Supreme Court*, Vox (Feb. 25, 2020).
20 141 S. Ct. 1868, 1875–76 (2021). CSS also raised a free speech claim. *Id.* at 1876.
21 *Id.* at 1883 (Alito, J., concurring in the judgment); *id.* at 1926 (Gorsuch, J., concurring in the judgment); *id.* at 1882–83 (Barrett, J., concurring).
22 *Id.* at 1880; *see id.* at 1879–81 (disposing of the Fair Practices Ordinance issue).
23 *Id.* at 1877.
24 *Id.*
25 *Id.* (quoting *Sherbert*, 374 U.S. 398, 401 (1963)); *see* Laycock, *supra* note 14, at 47–53 (suggesting different possible readings of *Smith*).
26 141 S. Ct. at 1878.
27 *Id.* at 1881.
28 *Id.* at 1877–82.
29 *Id.* at 1883–1926 (Alito, J., concurring in the judgment); *see id.* at 1931 (Gorsuch, J., concurring in the judgment) ("*Smith* has been criticized since the day it was decided").
30 *Tandon*, 141 S. Ct. 1294 (2021); *South Bay II*, 141 S. Ct. 716 (2021); *Roman Catholic Diocese of Brooklyn*, 141 S. Ct. 63 (2020); *Espinoza*, 140 S. Ct. 2246 (2020).
31 *Fulton*, 141 S. Ct. at 1877, 1881–82.
32 *Id.* at 1915–17 (Alito, J., concurring in the judgment).
33 *Id.* at 1894 (quoting Antonin Scalia, A Matter of Interpretation 38 (1997)); *see* Bruce Allen Murphy, Scalia: A Court of One (2014); Stephen M. Feldman, *Justice Scalia and the Originalist Fallacy, in* The Conservative Revolution of Antonin Scalia 189 (Howard Schweber & David A. Schultz eds., Lexington Books, 2018).
34 Murphy, *supra* note 33, at 385.
35 *Fulton*, 141 S. Ct. at 1895 (Alito, J., concurring in the judgment) (quoting District of Columbia v. Heller, 554 U.S. 570, 576 (2008)).

36 141 S. Ct. at 1894 (Alito, J., concurring in the judgment).
37 *Id.* at 1896–97 (Alito, J., concurring in the judgment); *see id.* at 1917; *id.* at 1931 (Gorsuch, J., concurring in the judgment) (agreeing with Alito's originalist interpretation of free exercise).
38 *Id.* at 1924 (Alito, J., concurring in the judgment). Alito acknowledged this test might need to be "rephrased or supplemented" in the future. *Id.* (Alito, J., concurring in the judgment).
39 *Id.* at 1899 (Alito, J., concurring in the judgment).
40 *Id.* at 1896 n.28 (Alito, J., concurring in the judgment).
41 *Id.* at 1908 (Alito, J., concurring in the judgment); *see* Stephen M. Feldman, Please Don't Wish Me a Merry Christmas: A Critical History of the Separation of Church and State 145–74.
42 141 S. Ct. at 1896 n.29 (Alito, J., concurring in the judgment).
43 Neil Gorsuch, A Republic, If You Can Keep It 10, 107, 110 (2019) (explaining originalism). Historians criticizing originalism: Jack N. Rakove, Original Meanings 6–8 (1996); Saul Cornell, *Meaning and Understanding in the History of Constitutional Ideas: The Intellectual History Alternative to Originalism*, 82 Fordham L. Rev. 721, 733–40 (2013). On religious history: Feldman, Please Don't, *supra* note 41, at 145–74; Ira C. Lupu & Robert W. Tuttle, *The Radical Uncertainty of Free Exercise Principles: A Comment on* Fulton v. City of Philadelphia, American Constitution Society, Supreme Court Rev. (5th ed. 2020–2021) (Alito misinterprets history of free exercise as encompassing all religiously motivated conduct).
44 In at least two ways, one might criticize a supposedly originalist interpretation of the First Amendment that endorses de facto Christianity as determining the meaning of religious freedom. First, the originalist claim to discern apolitical, fixed, and determinate constitutional meaning is highly questionable. Saul Cornell, *Reading the Constitution, 1787–91: History, Originalism, and Constitutional Meaning*, 37 Law & Hist. Rev. 821 (2019); Stephen M. Feldman, *Constitutional Interpretation and History: New Originalism or Eclecticism?*, 28 B.Y.U. J. Pub. L. 283 (2014). Thus, for example, during the early national years, the meaning of freedom in general was contested, and in particular, freedom might have been more widely understood to mean freedom to participate in self-government rather than freedom to subjugate or discriminate against others. Annelien De Dijn, Freedom: An Unruly History 341–43 (2020) (page citations to Kindle ed.). Second, the adoption of the Fourteenth Amendment might change the constitutional meaning of religious freedom. Kurt T. Lash, *The Second Adoption of the Free Exercise Clause: Religious Exemptions Under the Fourteenth Amendment*, 88 Nw. U. L. Rev. 1106 (1994).
45 *Fulton*, 141 S. Ct. at 1881; *id.* at 1924–26 (Alito, J., concurring in the judgment); Gerald Gunther, *Foreword: In Search of Evolving Doctrine on a Changing Court: A Model For a Newer Equal Protection*, 86 Harv. L. Rev. 1, 8 (1972) (introducing terminology of strict in theory, fatal in fact).
46 *Tandon*, 141 S. Ct. 1294, 1298 (2021) (per curiam); *see South Bay II*, 141 S. Ct. 716, 717–20 (2021) (statement of Justice Gorsuch, with whom Justices Thomas and

Alito join); Does 1–3 v. Mills, No. 21A90, 2021 WL 5027177 (U.S. Oct. 29, 2021)
(Gorsuch, J., dissenting).

47 *Fulton*, 141 S. Ct. at 1881–82; *id.* at 1924 (Alito, J., concurring in the judgment);
Obergefell, 576 U.S. 644 (2015).

48 141 S. Ct. at 1881–82.

49 *Id.* at 1924–25 (Alito, J., concurring in the judgment).

50 *Id.* at 1925 (Alito, J., concurring in the judgment); *id.* at 1875.

51 *Id.* at 1886, 1924 (Alito, J., concurring in the judgment).

52 Shelley v. Kraemer, 334 U.S. 1 (1948) (enforcement of racially restrictive covenants
violated equal protection).

53 *Id.* at 1883–1926 (Alito, J., concurring in the judgment).

54 *Brown*, 347 U.S. 483, 493–96 (1954); *Plessy*, 163 U.S. 537 (1896).

55 *Boerne*, 521 U.S. 507 (1997); *Katzenbach*, 384 U.S. 641 (1966).

56 Trump v. Hawaii, 138 S. Ct. 2392, 2434 (2018) (Sotomayor, J., dissenting) (quoting
Larson v. Valente, 456 U.S. 228. 244 (1982)); 138 S. Ct. at 2417.

57 Also, the Roberts Court has occasionally interpreted statutes so that non-
Christians win and Christians lose. The Court has interpreted RFRA to protect
the practices of a religious sect that originated in the Amazon rainforest. Gonzales
v. O Centro Espirita Beneficente Uniao do Vegetal, 546 U.S. 418 (2006). The sect,
though, had some connection to Christianity. *Id.* at 425. The Court has also held
that state sovereign immunity precluded a Christian prisoner from suing under
RLUIPA. Sossamon v. Texas, 563 U.S. 277 (2011). In a subsequent case, the Court
held that a state could not satisfy strict scrutiny under RLUIPA, thus allowing a
Muslim to win his claim. Holt v. Hobbs, 574 U.S. 352 (2015). Of course, the Court
has also interpreted statutes to benefit Christians. Little Sisters of the Poor v.
Pennsylvania, 140 S. Ct. 2367 (2020) (upholding agency interpretation of ACA
allowing employers to avoid paying for insurance coverage for contraceptives
based on religious or moral objections; favoring a Christian employer); Burwell
v. Hobby Lobby Stores, Inc., 573 U.S. 682 (2014) (interpreting RFRA to allow
religiously-motivated corporations—specifically a Christian-oriented corporation—to avoid compliance with the ACA provision requiring corporations to
provide health insurance coverage to employees for contraceptives).

58 140 S. Ct. 2603, 2609 (2020) (Gorsuch, J., dissenting); *see id.* at 2615 ("churches,
synagogues, temples, and mosques") (Kavanaugh, J., dissenting); *id.* at 2604
("church, synagogue, or mosque") (Alito, J., dissenting).

59 141 S. Ct. 716, 720 (2021) (Gorsuch, J., statement).

60 141 S. Ct. 63, 66 (2020).

61 On interest-convergence principle: Derrick Bell, Brown v. Board of Education *and
the Interest-Convergence Dilemma*, 93 Harv. L. Rev. 518 (1980); Stephen M. Feldman, *Do the Right Thing: Understanding the Interest-Convergence Thesis*, 106 Nw.
U. L. Rev. Colloquy 248 (2012).

62 139 S. Ct. 661 (2019); *see id.* at 662 (Kagan, J., dissenting); Ray v. Comm'r, Alabama
Dep't of Corr., 915 F.3d 689 (11th Cir. 2019). This decision generated controversy.

Adam Liptak, *Justices Allow Execution of Muslim Death Row Inmate Who Sought Imam*, NYTimes (Feb. 7, 2019). Perhaps because of the media attention, the Court granted a stay for a Buddhist in a similar case arising less than 2 months later, though Alito, Thomas, and Gorsuch dissented, asserting that the request for a stay had been filed in an untimely manner. Murphy v. Collier, 139 S. Ct. 1475 (2019). The Court subsequently enjoined an execution for a Christian prisoner pursuant to the Religious Land Use and Institutionalized Persons Act of 2000 (RLUIPA). Ramirez v. Collier, 595 U.S. 411 (2022). The prisoner sought to have his pastor sing and say prayers and lay hands on him as he died.

63 138 S. Ct. 2392, 2405 (2018). The dispute was twice at the Court before returning for this final resolution. Trump v. IRAP, 138 S. Ct. 353 (2017); Trump v. Hawaii, 138 S. Ct. 377 (2017). The final ban was Presidential Proclamation No. 9645, 82 Fed. Reg. 45161 (2017).

64 138 S. Ct. at 2438–39, 2442 (Sotomayor, J., dissenting).

65 *Id.* at 2442 (Sotomayor, J., dissenting).

66 *Id.* at 2418, 2420.

67 *Id.* at 2433 (Sotomayor, J., dissenting).

68 555 U.S. 460 (2009).

69 Good News Club v. Milford Central School, 533 U.S. 98 (2001); Rosenberger v. Rectors and Visitors of the University of Virginia, 515 U.S. 819 (1995).

70 Perry Education Assn. v. Perry Local Educators' Assn., 460 U.S. 37, 45 (1983).

71 555 U.S. at 464; *id.* at 481 (Stevens, J., concurring) ("recently minted").

72 142 S. Ct. 1583, 1587–88 (2022); *see id.* at 1592–93.

73 *Id.* at 1595 (Kavanaugh, J., concurring).

74 *Id.* at 1589–90 (flexible standard); *id.* at 1598 (Alito, J., concurring in the judgment) (rule); *see* Stephen M. Feldman, *Free-Speech Formalism Is Not Formal*, 12 Drexel L. Rev. 723, 739–45 (2020) (explaining the political tilt of formal rules); Stephen M. Feldman, *Free-Speech Formalism and Social Injustice*, 26 Wm. & Mary J. Race, Gender & Social Justice 47, 55–73 (2019) (explaining why conservative justices prefer formalism). For an example of the conservative and progressive justices disagreeing about the usefulness of formal rules, see *City of Austin, Texas v. Reagan Nat'l Advert. of Austin, LLC*, 142 S. Ct. 1464 (2022) (discussing whether a law regulating expression is content-based or content-neutral); *see id.* at 1475 (Sotomayor, J., majority opinion) (arguing for commonsense approach); *id.* at 1476, 1478 (Breyer, J., concurring) (favoring rules of thumb and commonsense over bright-line rules); *id.* at 1481–82 (Thomas, J., dissenting) (arguing for rigid approach).

75 For what it's worth, neither the Court nor American society in general has ever strayed far from an interpretation of religious freedom commensurate with Christian interests and values. Feldman, Please Don't, *supra* note 41, at 175–254.

76 142 S. Ct. 2407 (2022). Daniel Silliman, *Praying Football Coach Wins at Supreme Court*, Christianitytoday.com (June 27, 2022). Kennedy explained that he was "inspired to start holding midfield prayers with students after he saw an evangelical

Christian movie." Danny Westneat, *The Myth at the Heart of the Praying Bremerton Coach Case*, Seattletimes.com (June 29, 2022).

77 142 S. Ct. at 2417, 2433.

78 *Id.* at 2435–40 (Sotomayor, J., dissenting).

79 *Id.* at 2417–18; *see* Santa Fe Independent School Dist. v. Doe, 530 U.S. 290 (2000) (student-led prayers at school football games violated Establishment Clause); Lee v. Weisman, 505 U.S. 577 (1992) (recitation of a prayer at a public school graduation violated the Establishment Clause); Engel v. Vitale, 370 U.S. 421, 425 (1962) (invalidating recitation of supposedly nondenominational prayer in public school classrooms).

80 142 S. Ct. at 2432–33. The case also involved a free-speech claim. *Id.* at 2423–26.

81 *Id.* at 2421–22.

82 Carson v. Makin, 142 S. Ct. 1987, 1996–98 (2022); *Fulton*, 141 S. Ct. at 1876–82.

83 This precise language is from Douglas Laycock. Laycock, *supra* note 14, at 49; *see* Andrew Koppelman, *The Increasingly Dangerous Variants of the "Most-Favored-Nation" Theory of Religious Liberty*, 108 Iowa L. Rev. 2237, 2238 (2023).

84 Carson v. Makin, 142 S. Ct. 1987, 2013–15 (2022) (Sotomayor, J., dissenting) (Court is forcing Maine to fund religious schools if it funds public schools); *South Bay II*, 141 S. Ct. 716, 720–22 (2021) (Kagan, J., dissenting) (Court was forcing the state to treat unlike cases as if they were the same).

85 142 S. Ct. at 2426–27. The Court also repudiated the endorsement test. *Id.*

86 *Id.* at 2428. The Court did not repudiate the coercion test, which had long been favored by conservative justices. Stephen M. Feldman, Neoconservative Politics and the Supreme Court: Law, Power, and Democracy 163–64 (2013). The Court, though, narrowed its conception of coercion—reasoning that coercion must be understood pursuant to "the original meaning of the Establishment Clause," *Kennedy*, 142 S. Ct. at 2429—and found that Kennedy had not coerced student participation in the prayers. *Id.* at 2428–32.

87 142 S. Ct. at 2426.

88 *Id.* at 2447 (Sotomayor, J., dissenting).

89 *Id.* at 2426.

90 Morton Borden, Jews, Turks, and Infidels 111–25 (1984); Naomi W. Cohen, Jews in Christian America: The Pursuit of Religious Equality 110–11, 266 n.52 (1992); Lawrence M. Friedman, A History of American Law 587 (2d ed. 1985); Irving Howe, World of Our Fathers 362 (1976).

91 142 S. Ct. at 2432–33.

92 142 S. Ct. 1987, 1998 (2022); *see id.* at 1996–97.

93 *Id.* at 2005–06 (Breyer, J., dissenting).

94 *Kennedy*, 142 S. Ct. at 2430.

95 *Carson*, 142 S. Ct. at 1996–98; *Fulton*, 141 S. Ct. at 1876–82.

96 *Kennedy*, 142 S. Ct. at 2422.

97 *Masterpiece Cakeshop*, 138 S. Ct. 1719 (2018).

98 *Fulton*, 141 S. Ct. 1868 (2021).

9. WHO FULLY BELONGS?

1 347 U.S. 483, 495 (1954).

2 Cox v. Louisiana, 379 U.S. 536 (1965); Edwards v. South Carolina, 372 U.S. 229 (1963). For a case where the Court did not protect protesters, see *Adderley v. Florida*, 385 U.S. 39 (1966); Stephen M. Feldman, Free Expression and Democracy in America: A History 413–19 (2008) (explaining these cases).

3 376 U.S. 254, 279–80 (1964); Lucas A. Powe, Jr., The Warren Court and American Politics 309–10 (2000).

4 379 U.S. 241 (1964).

5 Thomas J. Sugrue, Sweet Land of Liberty 449 (2008); Ibram X. Kendi, Stamped From the Beginning 365–77 (2016) (discussing massive resistance to desegregation after *Brown*).

6 418 U.S. 717 (1974); John Hope Franklin & Alfred A. Moss, Jr., From Slavery to Freedom 517 (7th ed. 1994) (on the difficulty of achieving desegregation).

7 426 U.S. 229, 232–34, 239, 242, 246–48 (1976); *see* McCleskey v. Kemp, 481 U.S. 279 (1987) (upholding capital-sentencing scheme despite strong statistical evidence of discriminatory effects).

8 438 U.S. 265, 317 (1978) (Powell, J.); *id.* at 311–18 (Powell, J.).

9 539 U.S. 306, 343 (2003); Gratz v. Bollinger, 539 U.S. 244 (2003) (invalidating University of Michigan undergraduate, affirmative action program that quantified the plus).

10 579 U.S. 365, 375 (2016).

11 Theodore Shaw, *Justice Anthony Kennedy's Race Jurisprudence*, Scotusblog (June 29, 2018).

12 *Fisher II*, 579 U.S. at 389–90 (Alito, J., dissenting); *Grutter*, 539 U.S. at 394 (Thomas, J., concurring and dissenting); *id.* at 380 (Rehnquist, C.J., dissenting); *id.* at 347 (Scalia, J., concurring and dissenting).

13 Nathan Glazer, Affirmative Discrimination: Ethnic Inequality and Public Policy ix, 67–68, 168 (1978 ed.; 1st ed. 1975); *see* Stephen M. Feldman, Neoconservative Politics and the Supreme Court: Law, Power, and Democracy 47–92 (2013) (explaining neoconservatism); Charles Krauthammer, *Lott Fiasco Exposes Conservative Split*, Jewish World Review, Dec. 19, 2002 (neoconservatism and colorblindness).

14 515 U.S. 200, 237–38 (1995).

15 *Id.* at 239 (Scalia, J., concurring in part and concurring in the judgment).

16 *Id.* at 241 (Thomas, J., concurring in part and concurring in the judgment).

17 551 U.S. 701, 748 (2007) (Roberts, C.J., plurality opinion).

18 *Id.* at 748 (Thomas, J., concurring).

19 *Brown*, 347 U.S. 483 (1954); Reva B. Siegel, *Equality Talk: Antisubordination and Anticlassification Values in Constitutional Struggles Over* Brown, 117 Harv. L. Rev. 1470, 1470–78, 1532–34 (2004).

20 Michael Eric Dyson, Tears We Cannot Stop 53 (2017). Other useful sources on structural racism and white privilege: Carol Anderson, White Rage: The Unspo-

ken Truth of Our Racial Divide (2016); Eduardo Bonilla-Silva, Racism Without
Racists: Color-Blind Racism and the Persistence of Racial Inequality in the United
States (5th ed. 2018); Robin DiAngelo, White Fragility (2018); Ian Haney Lopez,
Dog Whistle Politics: How Coded Racial Appeals Have Reinvented Racism and
Wrecked the Middle Class (2014); Charles W. Mills, The Racial Contract 93 (1997);
Khiara M. Bridges, *White Privilege and White Disadvantage*, 105 Va. L. Rev. 449
(2019); Osagie K. Obasogie, *Reflections on Bell's Hate Thy Neighbor*, 42 Law &
Soc. Inquiry 566, 568 (2017); Angela Onwuachi-Willig, *Policing the Boundaries of
Whiteness: The Tragedy of Being "Out of Place" from Emmett Till to Trayvon Mar-
tin*, 102 Iowa L. Rev. 1113 (2017). "[B]eing white offers you benefits, understanding,
forgiveness where needed." Dyson, *supra*, at 79.

21 Eugene Scott, *Sen. John Cornyn's Distorted Interpretation of 'Systemic Racism'
Displayed What a Lot of Americans Don't Get About It*, Washington Post (June
17, 2020); Sanford Nowlin, *In Hearing, Both of Texas' Republican Senators Deny
Systemic Racism Exists*, San Antonio Current (June 17, 2020).

22 *See* Mills, *supra* note 20, at 93–94 (connecting structural racism with white cogni-
tion); Anthony G. Greenwald & Linda Hamilton Krieger, *Implicit Bias: Scientific
Foundations*, 94 Cal. L. Rev. 945 (2006) (discussing implicit racial biases).

23 Bonilla-Silva, *supra* note 20, at 87–89; DiAngelo, *supra* note 20, at 41, 107–9.

24 Kerri Ullucci, *Book Review*, 41 Urban Education 533, 538 (2006). People of color "find
that race is, paradoxically, both everywhere and nowhere, structuring their lives but
not formally recognized in political/moral theory." Mills, *supra* note 20, at 76.

25 Ali Michael & Eleonora Bartoli, *What White Children Need to Know About Race*,
National Association of Independent Schools Magazine (Summer 2014); Dyson,
supra note 20, at 65; *see* Bonilla-Silva, *supra* note 20, at 7, 53–76; Lopez, *supra* note
20, at 78–79; Eleonora Bartoli et al., *Training for Colour-Blindness: White Racial
Socialisation*, 1 Whiteness & Education 125 (2016) (explaining implications of
racial socialization in white families).

26 Mills, *supra* note 20, at 93; Adolph L. Reed, Jr., *The Puzzle of Black Republicans*,
NY Times, December 18, 2012; Lopez, *supra* note 20, at 141; Marissa Jackson,
*Neo-Colonialism, Same Old Racism: A Critical Analysis of the United States' Shift
Toward Colorblindness As A Tool for the Protection of the American Colonial Em-
pire and White Supremacy*, 11 Berkeley J. Afr.-Am. L. & Pol'y 156 (2009).

27 Bonilla-Silva, *supra* note 20, at 2, 204–5; Monique W. Morris, Black Stats: African
Americans By the Numbers in the Twenty-First Century 74, 102 (2014); Tami
Luhby, *US Black-White Inequality in 6 Stark Charts*, CNN (June 3, 2020).

28 Kendi, Stamped, *supra* note 5, at 2; *id.* at 4–9; Bonilla-Silva, *supra* note 20, at 1–4,
240–42.

29 Paul Krugman, *Republicans and Race*, New York Times, Nov. 19, 2007; *The Men-
dacity Index*, Washington Monthly, Sept. 2003 (Reagan wildly exaggerated facts).

30 Lopez, *supra* note 20, at 3, 177–79; Joel Olson, *Whiteness and the Polarization of American Politics*, 61 Pol. Res. Q. 1, 1–2 (2008) (emphasizing norms against overt racism).

31 *Parents Involved*, 551 U.S. at 799 (Stevens, J., dissenting).

32 Ta-Nehisi Coates, We Were Eight Years in Power 73–74 (2017) (the nation tries to evade the centrality of slavery even in telling the story of the Civil War); William E. Connolly, Identity/Difference: Democratic Negotiations of Political Paradox 101–2 (1991) (colorblindness pressures people of color to assimilate to the mainstream while denying their differences); Osamudia R. James, *Valuing Identity*, 102 Minn. L. Rev. 127 (2017) (arguing against colorblindness).

33 Anderson, *supra* note 20, at 144–54; Jonathan Brater et al., Purges: A Growing Threat to the Right to Vote 1 (Brennan Center for Justice 2018); Brennan Center for Justice, *The Effects of* Shelby County v. Holder (Aug. 6, 2018); Lawrence Goldstone, *America's Relentless Suppression of Black Voters*, New Republic (Oct. 24, 2018).

34 Pew Center on the States, *Inaccurate, Costly, and Inefficient: Evidence that America's Voter Registration System Needs an Upgrade* 1–2 (Feb. 14, 2012); Ben Jealous & Ryan P. Haygood, Center for American Progress, *The Battle to Protect the Vote: Voter Suppression Efforts in Five States and Their Effect on the 2014 Midterm Elections* (Dec. 2014).

35 138 S. Ct. 2305 (2018). Lower court decisions: Perez v. Abbott, 274 F. Supp. 3d 624 (W.D. Tex. 2017); Perez v. Abbott, 267 F. Supp. 3d 750 (W.D. Tex. 2017).

36 138 S. Ct. at 2313; *see id.* at 2324–27.

37 *Id.* at 2345–46 (Sotomayor, J., dissenting) (citing *Arlington Heights*, 429 U.S. 252, 266–68 (1977)).

38 138 S. Ct. at 2336, 2360 (Sotomayor, J., dissenting). The Court has allowed other discriminatory gerrymandering schemes to stand. Gill v. Whitford, 138 S. Ct. 1916 (2018) (lower court held that gerrymandered districting scheme violated equal protection and First Amendment, but Supreme Court reversed for lack of standing); Husted v. A. Philip Randolph Inst., 138 S. Ct. 1833 (2018) (upholding, in a statutory decision, aggressive state program for purging individuals from voter rolls); *cf.* North Carolina v. Covington, 138 S. Ct. 2548 (U.S. 2018) (summarily affirming in part and reversing in part District Court order for redrawing legislative districts because of racial gerrymandering); Benisek v. Lamone, 138 S. Ct. 1942 (2018) (affirming lower court order denying a preliminary injunction in a political gerrymandering case).

39 143 S. Ct. 2141, 2161 (2023). *SFFA* combined two cases, one challenging Harvard's program and one challenging the University of North Carolina's program. Technically, the Equal Protection Clause would not apply against Harvard because it is a private institution. Hence, Harvard's program was challenged under Title VI, but the Court interpreted Title VI to be commensurate with the scope of equal protection. *Id.* at 2156–57 n.2. The Court's discussion consequently focused on equal protection. For descriptions of the affirmative action programs at Harvard and North Carolina, see *id.* at 2154–56.

40 *Id.* at 2175 (quoting *Brown*, 347 U.S. at 495; & *Plessy*, 163 U.S. at 559 (Harlan, J., dissenting)).

41 *Id.* at 2163–67.

42 *Id.* at 2173.

43 *Id.* at 2257 (Sotomayor, J., dissenting).

44 *Id.* at 2234 (Sotomayor, J., dissenting); *see id.* at 2274–75 (Jackson, J., dissenting); Khiara M. Bridges, *Foreword: Race in the Roberts Court*, 136 Harv. L. Rev. 23, 25 (2022) (Roberts Court is doing "nothing to destabilize and disestablish the country's existing racial hierarchy").

45 143 S. Ct. at 2263 (Brown, J., dissenting); *see* Bonilla-Silva, *supra* note 20, at xv, 2, 7–9, 240–42 (discussing structural or systemic racism); Stephen M. Feldman, Please Don't Wish Me a Merry Christmas: A Critical History of the Separation of Church and State 265–70 (1997) (explaining structural power).

46 *Id.* at 2235–36 (Sotomayor, J., dissenting); *see id.* at 2263–64, 2268–70 (Jackson, J., dissenting) (elaborating structures and history of racism).

47 *Id.* at 2251–52 (Sotomayor, J., dissenting).

48 *Id.* at 2169–70. It is worth noting that Asian Americans were among the plaintiff class in *SFFA*. Regardless, while Roberts's majority opinion discussed Asian Americans in the university admissions processes, it did not focus on their status in its holding or reasoning. *Id.* at 2154–55, 2167–68. Thomas, in a concurrence joined by no other justices, argued that the affirmative action programs explicitly discriminated against Asian Americans, *id.* at 2199–2200 (Thomas, J., concurring), but Sotomayor's dissent underscored that the trial court actually found otherwise. *Id.* at 2256–58 (Sotomayor, J., dissenting). Indeed, one can reasonably argue that the SFFA organization included Asian Americans as named plaintiffs partly for cynical political reasons, to avoid casting the case as solely a white-versus-Black confrontation. Kali Holloway, *Inside the Cynical Campaign to Claim that Affirmative Action Hurts Asian Americans*, The Nation (Aug. 9, 2023).

49 143 S. Ct. at 2271 (Jackson, J., dissenting).

50 *Id.* at 2225–26, 2236–37, 2263 (Sotomayor, J., dissenting).

51 *E.g.*, McCleskey v. Kemp, 481 U.S. 279 (1987) (upholding capital-sentencing scheme despite strong statistical evidence of discriminatory effects).

52 Bonilla-Silva, *supra* note 20, at 52, 56, 59; Ian Haney-Lopez, *Intentional Blindness*, 87 N.Y.U. L. Rev. 1779, 1781–89 (2012).

53 144 S. Ct. 1221, 1233–34 (2024).

54 *Id.* at 1268–69 (Kagan, J., dissenting).

55 *Id.* at 1233, 1236, 1240; *id.* at 1269 (Kagan, J., dissenting) (criticizing majority for changing law).

56 *Id.* at 1235; *Shelby County*, 133 S. Ct. 2612 (2013).

57 *Id.* at 1235.

58 *Id.* at 1269 (Kagan, J., dissenting). Kagan also underscored that the Court had, seven years earlier, found an equal protection violation in a similar case, resolved without the two legal twists. Cooper v. Harris, 581 U.S. 285 (2017) (cited in *Alexander*, 144 S. Ct. at 1269 (Kagan, J., dissenting)). The key difference between the cases was the Court's new personnel. "Today, for all practical purposes, the *Cooper* dissent becomes the law." 144 S. Ct. at 1269 (Kagan, J., dissenting).

59 144 S. Ct. at 1270 (Kagan, J., dissenting). Alito tried to distinguish this racial gerry-
    mandering claim from a vote-dilution claim. He reasoned that a vote-dilution claim
    would be even more difficult to prove because the challenger would need to prove in-
    tentional or purposeful racial discrimination. *Id.* at 1252. But it is difficult to see how
    a challenger could overcome the good faith presumption in a racial gerrymandering
    case without, in effect, proving intentional or purposeful racial discrimination.

60 *Id.* at 1236 (citing *SFFA*, 600 U.S. 181, 206 (2023)). Thomas's concurrence in part
    emphasized colorblindness. *Id.* at 152–53 (Thomas, concurring in part).

61 *Id.* at 1260, 1264–65 (Thomas, concurring in part). Among the conservative jus-
    tices, Gorsuch's treatment of Native Americans stands out as an exception to the
    justices' usual treatment of people of color. *E.g.*, Haaland v. Brackeen, 599 U.S. 255,
    297 (2023) (Gorsuch, J., concurring) (upholding constitutionality of Indian Child
    Welfare Act, thus allowing tribes to raise their children with less state interfer-
    ence). Gorsuch's sympathy for Native American claims has been attributed to his
    youth spent in Colorado (he is a westerner), to his experience as a judge on the
    Tenth Circuit (again, he is a westerner), and to his ostensible focus on original
    meaning (treating tribes as sovereign). *Id.* at 307–08 (Gorsuch, J., concurring);
    Adam Liptak, *Justice Neil Gorsuch Is a Committed Defender of Tribal Rights*, NY-
    Times (June 15, 2023); Mark Joseph Stern, *The Surprising Reason Neil Gorsuch Has
    Been So Good on Native Rights*, Slate.com (June 15, 2023).

62 *Roe*, 410 U.S. 113, 152–53 (1973); Stephen M. Feldman, Pack the Court! A Defense
    of Supreme Court Expansion 145–48 (2021) (Roberts Court abortion cases de-
    cided before *Dobbs*).

63 505 U.S. 833, 846, 853, 870 (1992).

64 410 U.S. at 153, 164.

65 Obergefell v. Hodges, 576 U.S. 644 (2015) (protecting same-sex marriage); Gris-
    wold v. Connecticut, 381 U.S. 479 (1965) (emphasizing marital relationship).

66 *Casey*, 505 U.S. 833, 851 (1992); *see* Eisenstadt v. Baird, 405 U.S. 438, 453 (1972)
    (important decisions are within the right of privacy).

67 Roberts v. U.S. Jaycees, 468 U.S. 609, 619–20 (1984) (elaborating protected rela-
    tionships).

68 *Obergefell*, 576 U.S. at 659–66 (changing notions of marriage); Lawrence v. Texas,
    539 U.S. 558, 578–79 (2003) (meaning of due process can change over time); *see
    Dobbs*, 142 S. Ct. at 2325 (Breyer, J., Sotomayor, J., & Kagan, J., jointly dissenting)
    (constitutional meaning should evolve).

69 Washington v. Glucksberg, 521 U.S. 702, 720–21 (1997).

70 Bowers v. Hardwick, 478 U.S. 186 (1986) (holding that state could proscribe ho-
    mosexual sodomy), *overruled by* Lawrence v. Texas, 539 U.S. 558 (2003).

71 410 U.S. at 152–53.

72 142 S. Ct. 2228, 2260 (2022); *id.* at 2246.

73 *See id.* at 2257–58 (undermining *Casey* and "the freedom to make 'intimate and
    personal choices' that are 'central to personal dignity and autonomy'").

74 *Id.* at 2243, 2258, 2265, 2277, 2280.

75 *Id.* at 2248–49, 2252–54; *Kennedy*, 142 S. Ct. 2407, 2428 (2022).

76 *See* U.S. Const. amend. XIX (prohibiting denial of vote based on sex, but ratified in 1920); U.S. Const. amend. XIV, § 2 (expressly distinguishing rights of male and female citizens for purposes of representation). Aspects of coverture laws remained in effect into the twentieth century. Allison A. Tait, *The Return of Coverture*, 114 Mich. L. Rev. First Impressions 99, 101 & n.7 (2016).

77 142 S. Ct. at 2248–54; *id.* at 2324–25, 2333 (Breyer, J., Sotomayor, J., & Kagan, J., jointly dissenting) (criticizing the Court's reliance on history and originalism).

78 *Id.* at 2317, 2323, 2343 (Breyer, J., Sotomayor, J., & Kagan, J., jointly dissenting).

79 *Id.* at 2253–54, 2279–80.

80 *Id.* at 2345 (Breyer, J., Sotomayor, J., & Kagan, J., jointly dissenting).

81 *Id.* at 2284. State legislators enacting restrictions on women's reproductive rights often claim to be concerned about women's health, but these restrictive laws tend to increase health risks for women. Michelle Goodwin, Policing the Womb 6–7 (2020).

82 142 S. Ct. at 2246–48.

83 *Id.* at 2256; *see id.* at 2248–56.

84 Dorothy Sue Gobble, Linda Gordon, & Astrid Henry, Feminism Unfinished 112–13 (2014); Reva B. Siegel, *Memory Games: Dobbs's Originalism As Anti-Democratic Living Constitutionalism—and Some Pathways for Resistance*, 101 Tex. L. Rev. 1127, 1169–93 (2023); *see* Ari Berman, Minority Rule: The Right-Wing Attack on the Will of the People 301–03 (2024) (page citations to Kindle ed.) (summarizing Alito's misreading of history).

85 142 S. Ct. at 2243; *id.* at 2259, 2279, 2284.

86 *Shelby County*, 133 S. Ct. 2612 (2013) (invalidating section of VRA); NFIB v. Sebelius, 132 S. Ct. 2566 (2012) (invalidating parts of the ACA). So far, the Court has not limited Congress's taxing power as it has other congressional powers. Moore v. United States, 144 S. Ct. 1680 (2024) (upholding tax in an explicitly narrow ruling in which Court emphasized following precedents and avoided a decision that could otherwise lead to a "fiscal calamity").

87 Fischer v. United States, 144 S. Ct. 2176 (2024) (in a case involving numerous prosecutions arising from the January 6, 2021, insurrection and storming of the Capitol—including the prosecution of former President Trump—the Court narrowly interpreted a federal criminal statute, holding that for obstruction of an official proceeding to be within the statutory prohibition, the government must prove the defendant impaired the integrity of physical evidence); Garland v. Cargill, 144 S. Ct. 1613 (2024) (held federal agency exceeded statutory authority in defining bump stocks as machine guns); Biden v. Nebraska, 143 S. Ct. 2355 (2023) (invoking major questions doctrine to interpret statute narrowly and invalidate loan forgiveness program).

88 Loper Bright Enterprises v. Raimondo, 144 S. Ct. 2244 (2024), *overruling* Chevron v. NRDC, 467 U.S. 837 (1984) (in a strike against federal administrative power, Court overruled *Chevron* doctrine, which required courts to defer to any reason-

able agency interpretations of ambiguous statutes; courts must independently interpret statutes regardless of technicality of questions); Securities and Exchange Commission v. Jarkesy, 144 S. Ct. 2117 (2024) (in a decision that will diminish the power of numerous federal agencies, the Court held that the SEC's routine imposition of fines in administrative proceedings—to penalize securities fraud— violates Seventh Amendment right to a jury trial in suits at common law); Ohio v. Environmental Protection Agency, 144 S. Ct. 2040 (2024) (grants temporary stay preventing EPA from enforcing its "good neighbor" plan under the Clean Air Act, which would prevent uncooperative states from allowing ozone pollution to drift downwind into other states); Garland v. Cargill, 144 S. Ct. 1613 (2024) (held federal agency exceeded statutory authority in defining bump stocks as machine guns); Biden v. Nebraska, 143 S. Ct. 2355 (2023) (invalidating loan forgiveness program).

89 *Shelby County*, 133 S. Ct. 2612 (2013).

90 Citizens United v. FEC, 558 U.S. 310 (2010) (invalidating campaign finance restrictions on corporations).

91 Rucho v. Common Cause, 139 S. Ct. 2484 (2019) (political gerrymandering is nonjusticiable).

92 Alexander v. S.C. State Conf. of the NAACP, 144 S. Ct. 1221 (2024).

93 Mark A. Lemley, *The Imperial Supreme Court*, 136 Harv. L. Rev. F. 97, 108–10 (2022); *e.g.*, American Tradition Partnership, Inc. v. Bullock, 132 S. Ct. 2490 (2012) (invalidating state law restricting corporate political campaign expenditures); Brown v. Entertainment Merchants Association, 131 S. Ct. 2729, 2732 (2011) (invalidating state law prohibiting "the sale or rental of 'violent video games' to minors"); Sorrell v. IMS Health Inc., 131 S. Ct. 2653 (2011) (invalidating state law restricting the sale of medical data).

94 142 S. Ct. at 2344 (Breyer, J., Sotomayor, J., & Kagan, J., jointly dissenting); *see* Melissa Murray & Katherine Shaw, Dobbs *and Democracy*, 137 Harv. L. Rev. 728 (2024) (criticizing the Court's claim to bolster democracy in *Dobbs*). "The ability of women to participate equally in the economic and social life of the Nation has been facilitated by their ability to control their reproductive lives." Planned Parenthood of Pennsylvania v. Casey, 505 U.S. 833, 856, (1992). "Reproductive freedom is a matter of social justice, not individual choice." Dorothy Roberts, Killing the Black Body: Race, Reproduction, and the Meaning of Liberty 6 (1997). Legislation "that chips away at reproductive rights and encroaches on women's reproductive healthcare is about more than abortion. Rather, it is about a fundamental respect for the humanity, dignity, and citizenship of girls and women." Goodwin, *supra* note 81, at 11.

95 142 S. Ct. at 2276. The Court also dismissed an equal-protection claim with barely any discussion. *Id.* at 2245–46.

96 The Court subsequently held that anti-abortion doctors and medical associations lacked standing to challenge the Food and Drug Administration's approval of mifepristone, an abortion-inducing medication. FDA v. Alliance for Hippocratic

Medicine, 144 S. Ct. 1540 (2024). Such a procedural decision, grounded on a lack of standing, does not preclude other potential parties, including state governments, from challenging the FDA's action in the future. Moreover, a Republican-controlled Congress or administration could override or change the FDA approval. Abbie VanSickle, *The Supreme Court, For Now, Upholds Access to a Widely Available Abortion Pill*, NYTimes (June 13, 2024). Subsequently, with a brief per curiam opinion, the Court dismissed another abortion case as improvidently granted writs of certiorari. Moyle v. United States, 603 U.S. 324 (2024). The issue in the case was whether a federal statute, the Emergency Medical Treatment and Labor Act (EMTALA), preempts state laws, such as Idaho's Defense of Life Act, which prohibit abortions. The effect of this dismissal is to delay: The substantive issue remains and is likely to arise in conservative states banning abortion. In a case involving marriage and immigration, the Court applied the substantive due process approach from *Dobbs*, though the Court cited an earlier decision, *Washington v. Glucksberg*, 521 U.S. 702 (1997), rather than *Dobbs*. The Court refused to find a constitutionally protected substantive due process right. Dep't of State v. Munoz, 602 U.S. 899 (2024). Sotomayor's dissent, however, emphasized that the Court was following *Dobbs* and that the *Munoz* decision demonstrates the narrowing of substantive due process rights unrelated to abortion. The Roberts Court has decided other cases, unrelated to abortion, that have diminished women's rights. *E.g.*, Ledbetter v. Goodyear Tire & Rubber Co., 550 U.S. 618 (2007) (interpreting Title VII so that it is difficult for women to recover for unequal pay). On the abortion front, some Jewish women, along with other non-Christians and even some Christians, have initiated lawsuits claiming that abortion restrictions violate their free exercise rights. Alice Miranda Ollstein, *The Sleeper Legal Strategy that Could Topple Abortion Bans*, Politico (June 21, 2023); Abby Vesoulis, *Meet the Religious Crusaders Fighting for Abortion Rights*, Mother Jones (Feb. 17, 2023).

97 Jordan Blair Woods, *LGBT Identity and Crime*, 105 Calif. L. Rev. 667, 679–80 (2017).

98 539 U.S. 558, 578–79 (2003).

99 576 U.S. 644 (2015).

100 *Obergefell*: decided five-to-four. 576 U.S. at 648–50. *Lawrence*: decided six-to-three, though O'Connor concurred in the judgment without joining Kennedy's opinion. 539 U.S. at 561–62.

101 138 S. Ct. 1719, 1724, 1731–32 (2018).

102 141 S. Ct. 1868, 1881–82 (2021).

103 576 U.S. 644 (2015).

104 141 S. Ct. at 1882; *id.* at 1924 (Alito, J., concurring in the judgment).

105 143 S. Ct. 2298, 2308 (2023).

106 *Id.* at 2312; *see* Boy Scouts of America v. Dale, 530 U.S. at 640 (2000) (emphasizing expressive association).

107 143 S. Ct. at 2303, 2312, 2320.

108 The stipulated facts included the statement that the business owner's "belief that marriage is a union between one man and one woman is a sincerely held religious

conviction." *Id.* at 2309; *see* Katie Yoder, *Meet Lorie Smith, the Christian Artist with a Supreme Court Free Speech Case*, Catholic News Agency (December 2, 2022) (describing the website designer's Christian journey of faith).

109 The business owner had engaged in "status-based discrimination, plain and simple [but] the majority insists that petitioners discriminate based on message, not status." 143 S. Ct. at 2338–39 (Sotomayor, J., dissenting). Gorsuch's majority opinion reasoned that the stipulated facts limited the decision, but the opinion also admitted that defining "expressive activity" or conduct would be difficult. *Id.* at 2319; *see id.* at 2339 (Sotomayor, J., dissenting) (questioning Court's logic in relying on the stipulated facts).

110 Netta Barak-Corren, *A License to Discriminate? The Market Response to* Masterpiece Cakeshop, 56 Harv. C.R.-C.L. L. Rev. 315 (2021) (empirical study showing *Masterpiece Cakeshop* effectively increased discrimination against same-sex couples).

111 143 S. Ct. at 2325, 2343 (Sotomayor, J., dissenting).

112 *Dobbs*, 142 S. Ct. at 2257–58, 2277, 2280; *see Obergefell*, 576 U.S. 644, 672 (2015); *Lawrence*, 539 U.S. 558, 567 (2003).

113 142 S. Ct. at 2246, 2260.

114 *Id.* at 2301 (Thomas, J., concurring). *Dep't of State v. Munoz*, 602 U.S. 899 (2024), discussed *supra* note 96, suggests that the conservative justices will apply the *Dobbs* approach in subsequent substantive due process cases.

115 *Plessy*, 163 U.S. 537, 544 (1896).

116 *Id.* at 560 (Harlan, J., dissenting).

10. TOWARD A FULLY REALIZED DEMOCRACY

1 United States v. Lopez, 514 U.S. 549, 599 (1995) (Thomas, J., concurring).

2 Jefferson Cowie, The Great Exception: The New Deal and the Limits of American Politics 9–28 (2016).

3 Steven Levitsky & Daniel Ziblatt, Tyranny of the Minority: Why American Democracy Reached the Breaking Point 101–2 (2023).

4 Steven Hahn, Illiberal America: A History 314–17, 337–40 (2024) (page citations to Kindle ed.); Levitsky & Ziblatt, *supra* note 3, at 107, 112–17; Tehama Lopez Bunyasi, *The Role of Whiteness in the 2016 Presidential Primaries*, 17 Perspectives on Politics 679 (2019); Marc Hooghe & Ruth Dassonneville, *Explaining the Trump Vote: The Effect of Racist Resentment and Anti-Immigrant Sentiments*, 51 PS: Political Science & Politics 528 (2018).

5 Levitsky & Ziblatt, *supra* note 3, at 172–77; Stephen Jessee et al., *A Decade-long Longitudinal Survey Shows that the Supreme Court is Now Much More Conservative than the Public*, 119 PNAS (June 6, 2022). Trump's winning a plurality (not a majority) of the popular vote in 2024 does not change these conclusions. Amy Walter, *2024 National Popular Vote Tracker*, The Cook Political Report <https://www.cookpolitical.com/vote-tracker/2024/electoral-college>.

6 John Fanestil, American Heresy: The Roots and Reach of White Christian Nationalism 3 (2023) (white, Christian, nationalist attitudes are present in all

Christian denominations); *see* Ken I. Kersch, Conservatives and the Constitution 372–74 (2019) (arguing for significance of conservative Christian theology
to much current constitutional thought despite how many leading constitutional
scholars prominently focus on originalism). In this chapter, I will cite the following sources on Christianity: Rod Dreher, The Benedict Option (2017) [hereinafter
Dreher, Option]; Rod Dreher, Live Not By Lies (2020) [hereinafter Dreher, Lies];
Erwin W. Lutzer, We Will Not Be Silenced (2020); Stephen Wolfe, The Case for
Christian Nationalism (2022); Kevin Deyoung, *The Rise of Right-Wing Wokeism*,
The Gospel Coalition (thegospelcoalition.org) (Nov. 28, 2022).

7　Deyoung, *supra* note 6; *see* Dreher, Option, *supra* note 6, at 36–37; Lutzer, *supra*
note 6, at 20; Wolfe, *supra* note 6, at 398.

8　Dreher, Lies, *supra* note 6, at xiii; Fanestil, *supra* note 6, at 2–3, 6; Wolfe, *supra*
note 6, at 5; Deyoung, *supra* note 6.

9　Dreher, Lies, *supra* note 6, at 212–13; Deyoung, *supra* note 6; *see* Dreher, Option,
supra note 6, at 2–9 (emphasizing hostility against Christians).

10　*See* Isabel Wilkerson, Caste: The Origins of Our Discontents (2020) (on caste
systems).

11　Adam Liptak, *Alito Refuses Calls for Recusal Over Display of Provocative Flags*,
NYTimes (May 29, 2024); Jodi Kantor et al., *Another Provocative Flag Was Flown
at Another Alito Home*, NYTimes (May 22, 2024); Jodi Kantor, *At Justice Alito's
House, a 'Stop the Steal' Symbol on Display*, NYTimes (May 16, 2024).

12　Abbie VanSickle, *In Secret Recordings, Alito Endorses Nation of 'Godliness.' Roberts
Talks of Pluralism*, NYTimes (June 10, 2024).

13　Alito has also made public speeches where he has articulated views arguably
consistent with white Christian nationalism. In a speech to the Federalist Society,
he lamented: "You can't say that marriage is the union between one man and one
woman. Until very recently, that's what the vast majority of Americans thought.
Now it's considered bigotry." Josh Blackman, *Video and Transcript of Justice Alito's
Keynote Address to the Federalist Society*, The Volokh Conspiracy (Nov. 12, 2020).

14　PRRI, *Support for Christian Nationalism in All 50 States: Findings from PRRI's 2023
American Values Atlas* (Feb. 28, 2024).

15　The Heritage Foundation, *Mandate for Leadership: The Conservative Promise* xiv,
561–62 (2023) <//efaidnbmnnnibpcajpcglclefindmkaj/https://static.project2025.
org/2025_MandateForLeadership_FULL.pdf>; *see id.* at 4, 453, 560–61, 581.

16　Maggie Astor, *Heritage Foundation Head Refers to 'Second American Revolution'*,
NYTimes (July 3, 2024).

17　Population Projections Tables (2017), Census.gov <https://www.census.gov/programs-
surveys/popproj/data/tables.html>; *see* Annelien De Dijn, Freedom: An Unruly
History 341–43 (2020) (page citations to Kindle ed.) (the meaning of freedom is
historically contingent, and the Roberts Court's conception of freedom, as including a
right to discriminate, does not perhaps fit with the most widespread understanding of
freedom in the early national years—a freedom to participate in self-government).

18　U.S. Const. pmbl.

19 To be sure, many other forces, historical and current, contribute to the subordination of these groups. *See SFFA*, 143 S. Ct. 2141, 2235–36 (2023) (Sotomayor, J., dissenting) (discussing structural racism); *id.* at 2263–64, 2268–70 (Jackson, J., dissenting) (elaborating structures and history of racism).

20 141 S. Ct. 1868, 1925 (2021) (Alito, J., concurring in the judgment).

21 Jeremy Waldron, The Harm in Hate Speech 33, 47, 95 (2012).

22 143 S. Ct. at 2271 (Jackson, J., dissenting).

23 143 S. Ct. at 2325 (Sotomayor, J., dissenting).

24 142 S. Ct. at 2344 (Breyer, J., Sotomayor, J., & Kagan, J., jointly dissenting); *see* Dorothy Roberts, Killing the Black Body: Race, Reproduction, and the Meaning of Liberty 6 (1997).

25 Fanestil, *supra* note 6, at 2–7 (widespread belief in white Christian nationalism); Heather Cox Richardson, Democracy Awakening: Notes on the State of America xvi (2023) (critics of democracy emphasize nation's religious history at time of founding).

26 Stephen M. Feldman, Pack the Court! A Defense of Supreme Court Expansion (2021) [hereinafter Feldman, Pack] (arguing for Democrats to expand the Court and add progressive justices).

27 Wilfred E. Binkley & Malcolm C. Moos, A Grammar of American Politics 8–11 (1949); Robert A. Dahl, A Preface to Democratic Theory (1956) [hereinafter Preface]; John Dewey, Freedom and Culture 176 (1939).

28 Robert A. Dahl, Democracy and its Critics 109 (1989) [hereinafter Democracy]. On rights integral to the democratic process: *Id.* at 169–75; Preface, *supra* note 27, at 67; Robert A. Dahl, A Preface to Economic Democracy 59–60 (1985) [hereinafter Economic Democracy].

29 John Rawls, Political Liberalism xvi–xvii, xxvii, 10, 29–35 (1996 ed.) (articulating the philosophy of political liberalism); Michael J. Sandel, Democracy's Discontent 3–24, 28, 250–73 (1996) (explaining procedural republic).

30 Steven Levitsky & Daniel Ziblatt, How Democracies Die 97–100, 231 (2018) [hereinafter Levitsky & Ziblatt, How] (importance of preserving democratic norms); *see* Benjamin Barber, Strong Democracy 143–44 (1984) ("pluralist democracy" is inherently deficient because it is built on substantive premises undermining a stronger form of democracy).

31 Democracy, *supra* note 28, at 172; Economic Democracy, *supra* note 28, at 48–49; Preface, *supra* note 27, at 4, 143; *see* Daniel J. Boorstin, The Genius of American Politics 1, 162 (1953) ("genuine community of our values"); David B. Truman, The Governmental Process 129, 138, 512–13 (2d ed. 1971; 1st ed. 1951) (rules of the game for democracy).

32 Robert A. Dahl, How Democratic Is the American Constitution? 150–52 (2d ed. 2003) [hereinafter How Democratic]; Economic Democracy, *supra* note 28, at 46 (emphasizing relative economic well-being); Rawls, *supra* note 29, at 7 (assuming citizens' basic needs are met if those citizens are to exercise basic rights and liberties "fruitfully").

33 Gomillion v. Lightfoot, 364 U.S. 339 (1960) (invalidating law changing city boundaries to eliminate most African American voters).

34 Waldron, *supra* note 21, at 5, 61 (discussing relation between hate speech and being a citizen in good standing); Christopher R. Leslie, *The Geography of Equal Protection*, 101 Minn. L. Rev. 1579, 1579–83 (2017) (laws discriminating against LGBTQ individuals should be subject to heightened scrutiny in equal protection challenges).

35 John H. Ely, Democracy and Distrust 101–2, 181 (1980). For criticisms, see Daniel R. Ortiz, *Pursuing A Perfect Politics: The Allure and Failure of Process Theory*, 77 Va. L. Rev. 721 (1991); Richard D. Parker, *The Past of Constitutional Theory—And Its Future*, 42 Ohio St. L.J. 223 (1981); Paul Brest, *The Substance of Process*, 42 Ohio St. L.J. 131 (1981); Mark Tushnet, *Darkness on the Edge of Town: The Contributions of John Hart Ely to Constitutional Theory*, 89 Yale L.J. 1037 (1980).

36 Ely, *supra* note 35, at 106; *see id.* at 73–104 (emphasizing representation-reinforcement theory as process-based).

37 *Id.* at 120.

38 *Id.* at 105–34.

39 *Id.* at 103, 117.

40 *Id.* at 74, 135; *see id.* at 135–79.

41 *Id.* at 101, 117.

42 *Id.* at 151–53.

43 Brest, *supra* note 35, at 140; Ortiz, *supra* note 35, at 735–41; Parker, *supra* note 35, at 234–35.

44 Brest, *supra* note 35, at 142.

45 *See* Levitsky & Ziblatt, How, *supra* note 30, at 97–100 (emphasizing need to enhance and protect democratic norms in order to protect democratic government); Sandel, *supra* note 29, at 274–316 (emphasizing difficulties of a procedural republic).

46 How Democratic, *supra* note 32, at 132–33.

47 Waldron, *supra* note 21, at 33.

48 Ronald Dworkin, Freedom's Law 73 (1996); *see* Rawls, *supra* note 29, at 30 ("a conception of equal citizenship . . . goes with that of a democratic society of free and equal citizens"). "In strong democracy, politics is something done by, not to, citizens." Barber, *supra* note 30, at 133; *see* Benjamin I. Page & Martin Gilens, Democracy in America? 5–6 (2020 ed.) (emphasizing an equal voice for all citizens). "The demos must include all adult members except transients and persons proven to be mentally defective." Economic Democracy, *supra* note 28, 59–60.

49 Waldron, *supra* note 21, at 219–20; *see* Douglas Nejaime & Reva B. Siegel, *Conscience Wars: Complicity-Based Conscience Claims in Religion and Politics*, 124 Yale L.J. 2516 (2015) (allowing religious believers to discriminate inflicts harm on others); Clifford Rosky, *Anti-Gay Curriculum Laws*, 117 Colum. L. Rev. 1461 (2017) (harms inflicted on LGBTQ individuals by anti-gay curriculum laws).

50 Carole Pateman, Participation and Democratic Theory 108–10 (1970) (linking democratic equality in public and private spheres); Nancy Fraser, *Recognition*

Without Ethics?, 18 Theory, Culture & Society 21, 27–29 (2001) (emphasizing "participatory parity").

51 Sigal R. Ben-Porath, Free Speech on Campus 43 (2017) (potential for silencing outsiders on campus); William E. Connolly, Identity/Difference: Democratic Negotiations of Political Paradox 100–102 (1991) (members of targeted groups sometimes seek assimilation to avoid degradation); Waldron, *supra* note 21, at 96–97 (concern about legitimating debate over hate speech); Catriona Mackenzie, *Three Dimensions of Autonomy: A Relational Analysis, in* Autonomy, Oppression, and Gender 15, 21–23 (Andrea Veltman & Mark Piper eds., 2014) (importance of protecting opportunities in social environments).

52 Waldron, *supra* note 21, at 33.

53 Natalie Stoljar, *Autonomy and Adaptive Preference Formation, in* Autonomy, Oppression, and Gender 227 (Andrea Veltman & Mark Piper eds., 2014) (effects of discrimination).

54 Waldron, *supra* note 21, at 95; *see* Kwame Anthony Appiah, The Ethics of Identity 193 (2005) (a dignified and autonomous existence requires full access to public spaces).

55 Waldron, *supra* note 21, at 47. On the importance of free expression to democracy: Thornhill v. Alabama, 310 U.S. 88, 96 (1940); Alexander Meiklejohn, Free Speech: And its Relation to Self-Government 18, 26 (1948); Harry Kalven, Jr., *The New York Times Case*, 1964 Sup. Ct. Rev. 191, 208.

56 In his historical study of freedom and democracy, Jefferson Cowie concludes that "what was necessary to make democracy work [is] protecting—equally, aggressively, unflinchingly, and martially when necessary—the rights of all people." Jefferson Cowie, Freedom's Dominion: A Saga of White Resistance to Federal Power 485–86 (2022) (page citations to Kindle ed.). "[C]ries of freedom to the contrary be damned," he emphasizes. *Id.* at 497. "We need a way of rethinking the meaning of liberty so that it protects all citizens equally." Roberts, *supra* note 24, at 294; *see* Newman v. Piggie Park Enterprises, Inc., 390 U.S. 400, 403 n.5 (1968) (Warren Court dismissed as frivolous a claim that free exercise should protect racial discrimination).

57 142 S. Ct. at 2243, 2259, 2279, 2284.

58 Waldron, *supra* note 21, at 219–20.

59 *Dobbs*, 142 S. Ct. at 2344 (Breyer, J., Sotomayor, J., & Kagan, J., jointly dissenting).

60 My argument bypasses potential problems arising from the state-action doctrine, which emphasizes that most constitutional limitations apply only against traditional state actors. San Francisco Arts & Athletics, Inc. v. U.S. Olympic Committee, 483 U.S. 522 (1987) (applying state-action doctrine); Terri Peretti, *Constructing the State Action Doctrine, 1940–1990,* 35 Law & Soc. Inquiry 273 (2010) (discussing evolution of state-action doctrine). I do not argue that private conduct or discrimination, in general, violates the Constitution. Rather, I argue that such non-government conduct has no constitutional value. For that reason, the Court should not extend constitutional protections to such conduct. Moreover, along the same lines, I do not argue that the Court itself has violated the Constitution by shielding private discriminatory conduct,

though *Shelley v. Kraemer* suggests judicial action can sometimes amount to state action. 344 U.S. 1 (1948). Instead, I present a normative argument: that the Court should not interpret the Constitution to protect discriminatory conduct.

61 Dworkin, *supra* note 48, at 73.

62 Waldron, *supra* note 21, at 219–20.

63 *See* Stephen M. Feldman, Free Expression and Democracy in America: A History 411–12 (2008) (cases where Court upheld free-speech rights allowing the targeting of marginalized groups); Feldman, Pack, *supra* note 26, at 156 (examples of invocations of Christian Bible in pro-slavery arguments); Drew Gilpin Faust, *A Southern Stewardship: The Intellectual and the Proslavery Argument, reprinted in* Proslavery Thought, Ideology, and Politics 129, 137–39 (Paul Finkelman ed., 1989) (pro-slavery reliance on Bible and Christianity).

64 *See* Rogers M. Smith, Civic Ideals 12 (1997) (egalitarians need "to give up conceiving of good governments as bloodless neutral umpires of private activities and preexisting rights"); Mark E. Warren, *A Problem-Based Approach to Democratic Theory*, 111 Am. Pol. Sci. Rev. 39 (2017) (democratic governments should empower inclusion in democratic decision-making).

65 Religious freedom therefore should not trump a right to full and equal standing in the democratic polity. Jennifer Nedelsky, Law's Relations 232–36 (2011) (arguing constitutional rights should not be understood as trumps).

66 As of December 5, 2024, the Cook Report showed Trump with 49.7% and Harris with 48.31% of the total popular vote. Amy Walter, *2024 National Popular Vote Tracker*, The Cook Political Report <https://www.cookpolitical.com/vote-tracker/2024/electoral-college>; Domenico Montanaro, *Trump Falls Just Below 50% in Popular Vote, But Gets More than in Past Elections*, NPR (December 3, 2024) <https://www.npr.org/2024/12/03/nx-s1-5213810/2024-presidential-election-popular-vote-trump-kamala-harris>. Elsewhere, I have argued extensively for the legitimacy and necessity of Democratic Supreme Court expansion. Feldman, Pack, *supra* note 26, at 171–85.

67 H.R.1, *For the People Act of 2021*, 117th Congress (2021–2022) <https://www.congress.gov/bill/117th-congress/house-bill/1/text>.

68 Stephen M. Feldman, *Justice Scalia and the Originalist Fallacy, in* The Conservative Revolution of Antonin Scalia 189 (Howard Schweber & David A. Schultz eds., Lexington Books, 2018) (criticizing originalist claim to discern apolitical, fixed, and determinate constitutional meanings).

69 While the phrase "Blood and Soil" predated the Nazis, it became a Nazi slogan suggesting that "only those people with 'pure' or 'white' bloodlines can be true citizens." Deborah E. Lipstadt, Antisemitism: Here and Now 31 (2019); U.S. Holocaust Memorial Museum, *Origins of Neo-Nazi and White Supremacist Terms and Symbols: A Glossary; see* Joseph Fishkin & William E. Forbath, The Anti-Oligarchy Constitution: Reconstructing the Economic Foundations of American Democracy 4–5 (2022) (contrasting European nations with the United States).

70 The Federalist No. 1 (Alexander Hamilton).

INDEX

Abbott v. Perez, 158–59, 162

abortion, 3–4, 10, 60, 73, 82–83, 94, 165–69, 176; becomes key issue, 72; full and equal citizenship, 178–79, 185–86; historical explanations for nineteenth-century anti-abortion laws, 168; medication abortions, 177; Roberts Court saying unique, 166, 171–72

ACA. *See* Affordable Care Act

actual malice standard, 56

ADA. *See* Americans with Disabilities Act

Adams, John, 22, 26

Adams, John Quincy, 26

Adarand Constructors, Inc. v. Pena, 152–53

ADEA. *See* Age Discrimination in Employment Act

affirmative action, 9, 151–54, 157, 159–62, 165, 178–79; 25-25 year expectation of O'Connor, 151, 159; quotas, 151–52; race-plus programs, 151, 159; white resentment, 71–72

Affordable Care Act (ACA), 8, 85, 102–4

Afghanistan, 83

African Methodism, 146

Age Discrimination in Employment Act (ADEA), 118

agrarian economy, 36–37, 42; sense of equality, 18

Agricultural Adjustment Act, 43, 53

Agudath Israel of America, 125

Alabama, 32, 41, 56, 138

Alexander v. South Carolina State Conference of the NAACP, 162–65

Alfred P. Murrah Federal Building, 79

Alito, Samuel, 4–5, 113–15, 117–18, 121, 123, 125, 127, 130–37, 141–42, 158, 163–64, 166–69, 171, 177–79; criticism of Scalia, 132; de facto Christianity, 133–34; on flags on home, 177; white Christian nationalism, 177

Allgeyer v. Louisiana, 37–38, 45

America First, 82

American Enterprise Institute, 81

American Legion v. American Humanist Association, 113–15, 117

American Political Science Association, 34

Americans with Disabilities Act (ADA), 117–18

American Tradition Partnership, Inc. v. Bullock, 109

anti-Catholicism, 33, 44, 82, 84, 93, 145

anticlassification principle, 154, 159–60

anti-elitism, 27

Antifederalism, 22

anti-Muslim bias, 22, 83, 85–87, 95, 138–39, 145; fundamentalists, 75

antisemitism, 12, 22, 26, 44, 73, 75–76, 78–79, 81, 84, 87, 89, 120, 145; blaming Jews for Christ's death, 95; blood libel, 76; Buchanan and, 82; Christian Identity ideology, 74–75; conspiracy theories, 76; fundamentalists, 75; New World Order, 76; of Rushdoony, 74; South Carolina, 23; structures of Christian privilege, 93, 148; Trump and, 88, 97; ZOG, 76

antisubordination principle, 154, 159–60

Arizona, 108, 116

Arizona Christian School Tuition Organization v. Winn, 116
Arizona Free Enterprise Club's Freedom Club PAC v. Bennett, 108–9
Arlington Heights v. Metropolitan Housing Development Corporation, 158
Articles of Confederation, 18
Asian Americans, 84

bad tendency test. *See* free expression
Baker v. Carr, 56
balancing tests (judicial), 50
Baptists, 8, 94, 146
Barnett, Randy, 64
Barrett, Amy Coney, 5, 9, 109, 124–25, 130, 137, 142, 159, 165, 170, 178; as changing free exercise cases, 125
BCRA. *See* Bipartisan Campaign Reform Act of 2002
Beam, Louis, 74, 76, 79, 91
Belew, Kathleen, 76
Berns, Walter, 64–65, 109
Bickel, Alexander, 65, 109
Biden, Joe, 87–88, 90, 96, 177
Bill of Rights, 12, 50, 97
Bipartisan Campaign Reform Act of 2002 (BCRA), 106–7
birtherism, 84–85
Bituminous Coal Conservation Act, 46
Black, Hugo, 48–49
Black Americans, 22, 28–33, 36, 38, 40–41, 43, 49, 51–53, 57–58, 71, 73, 76, 84–85, 92, 97, 151, 154–57, 162, 165, 175. *See also* people of color; Black evangelicals, 86; disfranchisement, 17, 29, 31–33, 57–58; lynchings, 78, 89; New Deal, 52; personal identity, 161; racial covenants, 54, 136; Rushdoony on, 74
Black Codes, 29
Black Lives Matter, 92
Blackmun, Harry, 60
Black power movement, 71

Bladensburg (Christian) cross, 8, 113–15, 117, 124
blasphemy, 22–23, 36, 145, 186
Blood and Soil, 188
Blue Laws, 145
Blum, Rachel M., 90
Bob Jones University, 71–72
Bork, Robert, 65, 109
Born in the U.S.A., 72
Brain Trust, 45
Branch Davidians, 81
Brandeis, Louis, 93
Brandenburg v. Ohio, 56
Brest, Paul, 182
Breyer, Stephen, 114, 127, 129, 141, 146, 167
Brooks, Arthur, 81
Brown v. Board of Education (Brown I), 54–55, 71, 136, 149; anticlassification or antisubordination, 154–55, 159–60; Roberts Court, 153–54, 157, 159–61, 165
Brown v. Board of Education (Brown II), 55, 149, 165
Buchanan, Pat, 81–83, 91; America First slogan of, 82
Buddhism, 146
Burger, Warren, 60
Burger Court, 8, 11, 61, 150
Burkean conservatism, 66
Bush, George H. W., 69, 81–82
Bush, George W., 80, 83; Faith-Based and Community Initiatives of, 115

CADA. *See* Colorado Anti-Discrimination Act
Calhoun, John C., 74
California, 121, 127–28, 137
Calvary Chapel Dayton Valley v. Sisolak, 122, 125, 137
Capitol insurrection, 88–90, 97, 177
Cardozo, Benjamin, 51
Carolene Products. *See United States v. Carolene Products Company*

Carson v. Makin, 145
Carter v. Carter Coal Company, 46
caste system, 10, 73, 91–92, 148, 154, 159, 171, 176
Catholic Americans, 20, 33, 63, 82, 84, 118, 125, 129, 133, 137, 145, 170, 177–78; judges, 44; on Supreme Court, 93; Trump and, 86
Catholic Social Services (CSS), 129–31, 133–36, 170, 178
Centers for Disease Control and Prevention (CDC), 177
Chad, 138
Charlottesville, Virginia, 87
chattel slavery. *See* slavery
Cherokee Nation v. Georgia, 196n34
choice. *See* abortion
Christian fundamentalism, 75
Christian Identity, 74–75
Christianity. *See also* Catholic Americans; de facto Christianity; Protestantism: Christian flag, 140–41; Christian writers, 94; criticizing critical race theory, 94; defending capitalism, 94; Dreher on, 94–95; evangelicalism (Christian), 75, 85–86, 94, 96, 219n24; fundamentalism (Christian), 71, 74, 75, 82, 219n24; Jeffress on, 8, 94–96; Lutzer on, 94–95; marriage, 5, 10, 94, 119, 129, 135–36, 171; percentage of United States, 84, 92; purported tension with democracy, 74, 77–80, 95–96, 176, 178; structures of privilege, 93, 148.; White-Cain on, 96
Christian nation, 39
Christian privilege and power, 70, 93, 97, 148. *See also* white Christian nationalism; as without awareness, 96
Christian Reconstruction, 74
Church of Jesus Christ of Latter-Day Saints, 39, 145; Trump and, 86
Church of the Lukumi Babalu Aye, Inc. v. City of Hialeah, 63, 118–19, 121–23, 125–

27, 131–32, 135; as most important free exercise precedent, 120
Citibank, 69
Citizens United v. Federal Election Commission, 8, 12–13, 106–9
City of Boerne v. Flores, 136–37
Civilian Conservation Corps, 43
Civil Rights Act of 1875, 33
Civil Rights Act of 1964, 57–58, 71
Civil Rights Movement, 57, 71, 149
Civil War, 30, 33, 36–37
Claremont Institute, 96
class legislation, 34, 38–39, 46–47; taking from A and giving to B, 35
Clinton, Bill, 80, 82, 90
Clinton, Hillary Rodham, 82, 90
coercion test, 61, 112, 124
Cold War, end of, 80–81
Colegrove v. Green, 49; overruled, 56
Colorado, 83, 121, 127; Colorado Civil Rights Commission, 119, 170
Colorado Anti-Discrimination Act (CADA), 119–21
colorblindness, 9, 152–57, 159–62, 165, 177; epistemology of ignorance, 155; racial status quo, 154–55, 160, 162
commerce power, 46–47, 57, 106, 150. See also *United States v. Lopez*; deference to democracy, 101–3
common good, 1, 3, 13, 17, 34–35, 39–41, 43–44, 50, 52, 64–65, 175, 183; as changing, 27; exclusion, 21; laissez faire, 37, 46; moral values of white Christian men, 35; as mythical or duplicitous, 45; as objective, 26; political parties, 28
Confederacy, 29–30, 74, 89
congressional findings, 57, 104–5, 107
congressional power, 46–47, 57, 59, 101–3, 136, 150; deference to democracy, 101–3
Connecticut, 24, 35
conservatism (political), 7, 10. *See also* Republican Party; changes relative to Supreme Court, 6, 13, 101, 111, 123, 175

constitutional framing, 1, 6, 9, 11, 17–23, 34, 112, 144, 146; commitment to democracy, 20; excessive democracy, 19–20; exclusion, 21–26; forces pressing for more democracy, 26; framers as elitists, 1, 19–20, 26; framers as virtuous elite, 20, 26; moral condemnation of slavery, 24; sense of equality, 18; slave owning delegates, 25; small farmers, 18–20; word "slave" omitted in text of, 24

constitutional interpretation, 4, 11

constitutional ratification, 1, 10–11, 19, 21–22, 29–30, 33, 134, 146, 167; Bill of Rights, 12; Fifteenth Amendment, 12; Fourteenth Amendment, 12; Nineteenth Amendment, 12; percentage of population voting, 22

Continental Congress, 18

Cooley, Thomas, 65

Cornyn, John, 154–55

coronavirus. *See* Covid-19 (coronavirus) pandemic

corporations: democracy, 81; in the early national years, 12; going multinational, 81; spending on political campaigns, 8, 12–13, 106–9, 168

cotton gin, 25

court packing. *See* Supreme Court expansion

Coutant, Charles, 77

coverture, 22, 186

Covid-19 (coronavirus) pandemic, 88, 121, 123, 125–28, 137–38; first free exercise case with Barrett rather than Ginsburg, 125

critical race theory, 94

crosses (Christian). *See* Bladensburg cross

CSS. *See* Catholic Social Services

Dahl, Robert A., 180, 183

Dallas, Texas, 94

Danville Christian Academy, Inc. v. Beshear, 127

Declaration of Independence, 17–18, 77, 97

de facto Christianity, 6, 22–24, 39, 92–93, 114–17, 136–39, 141–46. *See also* Protestantism; Christianity as part of common law, 23; Roberts Court, 8–9, 111–15, 117, 124, 133–34, 136–38, 142–48, 167

deference to democracy. *See* judicial restraint

DEI (diversity, equity, and inclusion), 97

Delaware, 23

democracy. *See also* fully realized pluralist democracy; pluralist democracy; republican democracy: as exclusive, inegalitarian, and hierarchical, 1, 3, 6, 8, 10, 12, 36, 98, 110, 157–59, 168, 172, 175, 179; as inclusive, egalitarian, and participatory, 1–2, 6–7, 26, 43–44, 47, 52–53, 55, 58–59, 84, 101, 171, 175–76, 188; purported tension with Christianity, 74, 77–80, 95–96, 176, 178; self-governance rationale (for free expression) and, 56, 107–8; tension with white Christian nationalism, 77–80, 95–96, 176, 178

Democracy, Inc., 81

Democratic Party, 30, 66, 82, 187–88; New Deal, 44–45, 52; Obama and, 84; Progressivism (early-twentieth century), 37; recent presidential elections, 5; southern Democrats, 32; Trump and, 90

Department of Homeland Security, 88

Department of Justice, 177

depression (economic), 19. *See also* Great Depression

desegregation, 149. *See also* with all deliberate speed; rendered practically impossible, 150; resistance, 55; school district lines, 150; segregated private religious schools, 71, 150

Detroit, 150

discrete and insular minority, 182; origins in footnote four, 49

discrimination: appearing to legitimate further political debate, 184; based on LGBTQ+ status, 10–11, 83, 170–72, 178, 181, 183–86; based on race, 11, 31–33, 39–41, 49, 52, 54, 56–58, 71–72, 86, 105, 162–65, 181–82, 184–86; based on religion, 11, 63, 86, 181, 184–86; based on sex, 11, 181, 184–86; against Christians, 8–9, 86, 111, 120, 124, 128, 134, 136, 139, 145, 148, 164, 170, 176, 185–86; by Christians, 9, 120–21, 124, 134–36, 145, 148, 170–72, 176, 178, 185–86; disability, 117; facially neutral laws with discriminatory effects, 150–51, 158, 162; free expression, 184–85; proving intentional discrimination, 151, 158, 162–63; relation to democracy, 179–88; religious freedom, 184–86; warping political community, 183–84

District of Columbia v. Heller, 132, 197n46

diversity, equity, and inclusion. *See* DEI

Dobbs v. Jackson Women's Health Organization, 3, 9–10, 178–79, 185; democracy, 168–69; ignoring women's interests and autonomy, 167–69; implicitly undermining LGBTQ+ rights, 171–72; originalism, 167; overruling five decades of precedents, 168; supposedly about abortion only, 166, 171–72

dog whistling, 156

domestic dependent nations, 196n34

Domestic Violent Extremists, 88

Dominion theology, 95

Douglas, William O., 49

Dowland, Seth, 86

Dred Scott v. Sandford, 28; Fourteenth Amendment, 29

Dreher, Rod, 94–95

due process, 5, 10, 29, 46, 59, 165–69, 171–72, 175, 185; flexible and evolving, 166; liberty, 38–39, 50, 166, 172; narrow and rigid, 166; originalism, 166–67; Roberts Court rejecting two protected interests, 166; tradition and history, 166; two protected interests, 166, 171

Due Process Clause, U.S. Constitution, 10, 165–66

Duke, David, 82

Dunn v. Ray, 138

Eastman, John, 88

economic solidarity, 43, 60

Edmunds, George F., 31

Edwards, Bela Bates, 24

1866 Civil Rights Act, 29

Eisenhower, Dwight D., 60

Electoral College, 20, 176, 188; three-fifths rule, 25

Ely, John Hart, 181–82

Emergency Banking Act, 43

Employment Division, Department of Human Resources v. Smith, 62–64, 111, 123; exceptions to rational basis, 63, 118–20, 126, 130–32; undermined, 117–20, 122, 124, 126–33, 136–37, 143

endorsement test, 61, 112, 124

Engel v. Vitale, 55, 65

environmental movement, 71

epistemology of ignorance, colorblindness, 155

Epstein, Richard, 64

equal protection, 2–3, 7, 29, 50–51, 53–55, 59, 64, 109, 150–64, 172, 175, 185. *See also* affirmative action; colorblindness; formal equality, 9, 152–54, 160–61; little protection during republican democratic era, 39–40; proving intentional discrimination, 151, 158, 162–63; racial gerrymanders, 32, 57, 106, 163–65, 168, 187; rational basis review, 150, 162; separate but equal doctrine, 33, 39–41, 52–53, 55, 136, 149, 154, 159; strict scrutiny, 150–55, 159, 161–62, 165; turned upside down, 155, 160–62, 165; who belongs, 161

Equal Protection Clause, U.S. Constitution, 161

Espinoza v. Montana Department of Revenue, 116, 121–22

Establishment Clause, U.S. Constitution, 7–8, 39, 55, 111–13, 123, 137–39, 142, 144–46. See also religious freedom; history and tradition, 61, 112–15, 117, 124, 144, 146; incorporated against state and local governments, 51; taxpayer standing, 115–16

evangelicalism (Christian), 219n24; conservative, 75; defined, 75; fundamentalists, 75; percentage of United States, 75; proselytizing non-Christians, 95; Trump and, 85–86, 94, 96

exile (of true Constitution), 3, 7, 64–66, 101, 172, 175

Fair Practices Ordinance, 129–30

Faith-Based and Community Initiatives program, 115

FDR. See Roosevelt, Franklin D.

Federal Emergency Relief Administration, 43

federalism, 61, 63, 124

Federalist Essays, 19; No. 10, 107; No. 22, 21; No. 37, 21; No. 45, 21

Fifteenth Amendment, U.S. Constitution, 30–33; failure, 31–32; narrow, 31; ratification, 12; section two power, 59, 105

filibuster, 187

First Amendment, U.S. Constitution, 128. See also free expression; religious freedom; LGBTQ+ rights, 171; originalism, 144; Rushdoony on, 74

Fisher v. University of Texas at Austin (Fisher II), 152, 159

five-fifths (unwritten) clause, 33

Flast v. Cohen, 115–16

Florida, 96

Ford, Betty, 72

formalism (judicial), 38–39, 101–4, 107–8, 152–54, 160–61; being questioned,

46–47, 54, 57, 101; conservative justices prefer, 141; equality, 9; France on, 157; protecting power, 46, 141

forty acres and a mule, 30

Fourteenth Amendment, U.S. Constitution, 12, 40, 54, 149, 162, 165. See also due process; equal protection; business, 38; Dred Scott v. Sandford, 29; failure, 30, 32; framing, 29; ratification, 10, 29, 167; section five power, 59, 136

Fox News, 94

framing. See constitutional framing

France, Anatole, 157

Frankfurter, Felix, 49

Franklin, Benjamin, 21

free exercise, 8, 10, 39, 51, 71, 111, 116–33, 135–38, 142–47, 170–71, 178; exceptions to rational basis test, 63, 118–20, 126, 130–32; first case with Barrett rather than Ginsburg, 125; ministerial exception, 117–18, 124; neutrality, 63, 117, 120, 122–23, 125–26, 130, 132, 143, 147; originalism, 132–34; purposeful discrimination, 63, 120, 130, 143; rational basis test, 62–63, 117, 119–20, 123–24, 128, 130–32, 143; state antiestablishment principles, 122, 145; strict scrutiny, 55, 62–63, 118–20, 123–24, 126–27, 129–35, 143, 145, 147, 170; unemployment compensation, 63, 130–31

Free Exercise Clause, U.S. Constitution, 8. See also religious freedom; incorporated against state and local governments, 51

free expression (free speech), 2, 7, 12, 50–52, 63–65, 107, 109, 177, 180, 185. See also self-governance rationale (for free expression); bad tendency test, 40, 65; discrimination, 170–71, 179, 184–85; fixed star, 51; government speech, 140–41; LGBTQ+ rights, 170–72, 175, 178; little protection during republican democratic era, 39–40; matrix,

51; prior restraints, 40; protected after 1937, 51; public forums, 140–41; religious speech, 114, 140–41; Roberts Court, 8, 10, 106, 108–9, 140–41, 170–71, 184; viewpoint discrimination, 141; Warren Court, 56

Frelinghuysen, Frederick, 31

Friedman, Milton, 67–69

Fukuyama, Francis, 80

fully realized pluralist democracy, 10, 179–88; certain issues off the table, 181, 184–86; fantasy, 179, 187; full and equal citizenship, 182–86; how to achieve, 187–88; neutrality, 186; prohibition of discrimination, 180; tension with Roberts Court, 183–85, 187–88; of white Christian heterosexual men, 185–86; who belongs, 183–86

Fulton v. City of Philadelphia, Pennsylvania, 129–36, 170, 178, 184

fundamentalism (Christian), 71, 82, 219n24; antisemitism, 75; Christian Identity, 75; conservative, 75; defined, 74; evangelicals, 75; racism, 75

Gaines, Lloyd, 53

Garrard, Virginia, 95

Georgia, 18, 25, 32

Gerry, Elbridge, 19

gerrymandering: political gerrymandering, 106, 163–64, 168, 187; racial gerrymandering, 32, 57, 106, 163–64, 168, 187

Gilded Age, 36

Ginsburg, Douglas, 64

Ginsburg, Ruth Bader, 9, 105, 114, 120, 127, 137, 159; her death, 5, 124–25; her final free exercise case, 122

Glazer, Nathan, 152

Goldwater, Barry, 72

Gomillion v. Lightfoot, 56

Gorsuch, Neil, 5, 114–15, 121, 123, 125–27, 130–31, 137, 141–44; his religion, 93

government speech, 140–41

Graham, Billy, 72

Grant, Ulysses S., 32

Great Depression, 6; collapse of European democracies, 42; collective economic rights, 43; Supreme Court, 46

Great Society program, 57–58

Grutter v. Bollinger, 151–52, 159

Gun-Free School Zones Act, 102

Gupta, Vanita, 154–55

Hamilton, Alexander, 19, 21, 188

Hammond, James, 23–24

Harlan, John Marshall, 40, 159, 172

Harvard University, 151, 159

Hayek, Friedrich, 66–67

Heart of Atlanta Motel, Inc. v. United States, 57–58, 150

Hein v. Freedom From Religion Foundation, Inc., 115–16

Heller. See District of Columbia v. Heller

Heritage Foundation, 177–78

High Plains Harvest Church v. Polis, 127

Hispanic Americans, 84

Hosanna-Tabor Evangelical Lutheran Church & School v. Equal Employment Opportunity Commission, 117–18

Hosmer, Stephen, 35

House of Representatives, 20, 31, 56, 105, 187–88; Trump impeachment and, 89–90

Houston, Charles Hamilton, 52

Howard University, 52

Humanism, 146

Humphrey, Michael, 90

immigration, 41–42; Buchanan and, 82; industrialization, 36; naturalization, 28; New Deal, 43; racism, 33; restrictions on, 33–34, 42, 86–87, 92; scapegoats, 92; travel ban, 138–39; Trump and, 87; voting, 34; white evangelicals, 86

individualism, 27, 60; Great Depression, 43–44; neoliberalism, 67 industrialization, 25, 36–37, 41–42

Institutes of Biblical Law, 74

interest convergence, 137–38, 140–42, 147, 236n61

Internal Revenue Service, 102

#IONSFFA#IOFF. See *Students for Fair Admissions, Inc. (or SFFA) v. President & Fellows of Harvard College*

Iran, 138

Iraq, 83, 138

Iredell, James, 22

Islam, 22–23, 75, 83, 85–87, 95, 138–39, 145. See also anti-Muslim bias

Jackson, Andrew, 26–28; national bank veto, 27

Jackson, Ketanji Brown, 160–61; full and equal citizenship, 179

Jackson, Robert, 50–51

Jaffe, Louis L., 45

January 6. See Capitol insurrection

Jefferson, Thomas, 18, 52, 124

Jeffress, Robert, 94–96; Trump's apostle, 8, 94

Jehovah's Witnesses, 51

Jesus. See evangelicalism (Christian)

Jewish Americans, 12, 22, 44, 73, 75–76, 78–79, 81, 84, 87, 95, 97, 120, 125–26, 137, 145, 155; Christian Identity ideology, 74–75; immigration, 33; Rosh Hashanah and Yom Kippur, 93; Rushdoony on, 74; in South Carolina, 23; on Supreme Court, 93

Jim Crow, 54, 73, 92, 120, 150, 153–54, 157, 160, 186. See also antisemitism; non-Christians

Johnson, Andrew, 30

Johnson, Lyndon B., 57

Jones & Laughlin. See *NLRB v. Jones & Laughlin Steel Corporation*

Joshi, Khyati Y., 93

judicial engagement, 64

judicial restraint, 6–7, 48–50, 57–58, 60–62, 101, 103, 123–24; rejected for judicial engagement, 64; religious freedom, 61–63, 117; waning interest, 6, 13, 64, 111, 175

Kagan, Elena, 108, 114, 116, 122, 127–29, 143, 152, 163–64, 167

Katzenbach v. Morgan, 59, 136–37

Kavanaugh, Brett, 5

Kennedy, Anthony, 4–5, 12, 61, 102, 106–7, 112, 120, 152, 169

Kennedy, Joseph, 142, 144

Kennedy v. Bremerton School District, 142–46, 166

Kent, James, 23, 35, 64

Kentucky, 127

King, Martin Luther, Jr., 150

King Cotton, 25

Kingdom Identity Ministries Doctrinal Statement of Beliefs, 74–75

King James Bible, 97

Kirk, Russell, 66

KKK. See Ku Klux Klan

Korematsu v. United States, 51

Ku Klux Klan, 31, 70, 73, 82

labor unions. See unionization

laissez faire, 67, 101–2; emergence post-Civil War, 37, 46; neoliberalism, 67–68; not predominant before Civil War, 35

law-politics dynamic, 3–5

law professors, Supreme Court decision making, 3–4

Lawrence v. Texas, 5, 169, 171

LDS. See Church of Jesus Christ of Latter-Day Saints

Leadership Conference on Civil and Human Rights, 154

Lemon test: doctrinal alternatives, 61, 111; a ghoul, 117; ignored, 62, 112; repudiated, 113–15, 123, 141, 144

Lemon v. Kurtzman, 61. See also *Lemon* test

Lent, 137

LGBTQ+, 1, 3, 5, 10–13, 83, 88, 92, 94, 96–97, 110, 121, 136, 148–49, 155, 169–72, 175–78, 180–81, 183–86; First Amendment, 171; free expression, 170–72, 175, 178

liberalism. *See* progressive politics

libertarianism, 66, 89. *See also* neoliberalism

liberty to contract, 38–39, 172. See also *Lochner*-era

Libya, 138

Limbaugh, Rush, 85

Lincoln, Abraham, 28, 37

Lochner Court, 2

Lochner-era, 37–40, 45–47, 101–2, 104. See also *Lochner v. New York*; number of laws invalidated, 39

Lochner v. New York, 38, 46. See also *Lochner*-era

Lopez. See *United States v. Lopez*

Lopez, Ian Haney, 156

Louisiana, 32

Lukumi. See *Church of the Lukumi Babalu Aye, Inc. v. City of Hialeah*

Lutzer, Erwin W., 94–95

lynchings, 78

Madison, James, 12, 19, 21, 107

Maine, 145

marriage, 94, 129, 166; same-sex marriage, 5, 10, 119, 129, 135–36, 171

Marshall, John, 57

Marshall, Thurgood, 4–6, 64, 102

Marsh v. Chambers, 61, 112

Martin, Luther, 24

Maryland, 18, 24, 113

Mason, George, 21, 24

Massachusetts, 18, 20, 35

Masterpiece Cakeshop, Ltd. v. Colorado Civil Rights Commission, 119–21, 123, 139, 170, 184

McGirr, Lisa, 91–92

McVeigh, Timothy, 79, 91

Medicaid, 103–4

mercantilism, 13

Mexico, 82, 87

Michigan, 88

Milliken v. Bradley, 150

minority rule, Roberts Court (as favoring exclusive, inegalitarian, and hierarchical democracy), 1, 3, 6, 8–10, 13, 110–11, 134, 147–49, 157–59, 162–64, 168, 172, 175–79, 184–85, 187–88

Mississippi, 41, 58

Missouri, 119

Missouri ex rel. Gaines v. Canada, 53

Moley, Raymond, 45

Montana, 109, 121–22

Mormonism. *See* Church of Jesus Christ of Latter-Day Saints

Morris, Gouverneur, 18, 24

Moss, Dana M., 87

most-favored nation status, 143

Munro, William B., 34

Murphy, Frank, 49

Muslim Americans. *See* Islam

Muslims. *See* Islam

National Association for the Advancement of Colored People (NAACP), 52–53, 162–64

National Federation of Independent Business v. Sebelius, 8, 102–4

National Industrial Recovery Act, 44

National Labor Relations Act, 44, 47–48; exclusion of many Black Americans, 52

national security, 138–39

Native Americans, 19, 62, 84, 195n34, 243n61. *See also* people of color

naturalization, 28–29

neoconservatism, 66, 80, 152

neoliberalism, 7, 66–70, 73–74, 79–80, 83, 91–92, 102. *See also* public choice theory; laissez faire, 67–68; privatization, 80; Republican Party, 80; Roberts Court, 104, 108; Tea Party, 84; Trump and, 91

neo-Nazis, 73
Nevada, 122–23, 137
New Deal, 2, 42–48, 52, 59, 101, 175; voter
  turnout, 45
New Jersey, 17, 127
New York, 34, 36, 83, 125–26, 137
New York Times v. Sullivan, 56, 149
New York v. United States, 227n2
Nichols, Terry, 79
9/11 terrorist attacks, 80, 83–84
1937 transition, 46–54, 103; conservative
  criticisms of, 2–3, 7, 64–66, 101, 172,
  175
Nineteenth Amendment, U.S. Constitution, 33; ratification, 12
Nixon, Richard, 60
NLRA. *See* National Labor Relations Act
*NLRB v. Jones & Laughlin Steel Corpora-
  tion*, 47–48
Noem, Kristi, 96
non-Christians, 1, 3, 11–13, 35–36, 62, 72–
  73, 75, 77–79, 81, 86–88, 92, 95–97, 110–
  11, 113–14, 125, 145–47, 149, 155, 170, 172,
  175–76, 178, 180–81, 184–86. *See also*
  Islam; Jewish Americans; interest convergence, 137–38, 140–42, 147; office
  holding, 12, 18, 22–23; Roberts Court,
  137–42; Roberts Court's ecumenical
  language, 9, 137, 141, 147
nonpreferentialism, 61, 115, 124
North Carolina, 22, 25, 32, 159
North Korea, 138–39

Obama, Barack, 7–8, 80, 84–86, 92, 102,
  175–76; inclusive, egalitarian, participatory democracy of, 84
Obama, Michelle, 85
Obergefell v. Hodges, 5, 94, 135–36, 169–72
O'Connor, Sandra Day, 4–5, 61, 102, 153;
  25-25 year affirmative action expectation, 151, 159
office holding, restrictions, 12, 18, 21–23,
  29, 31, 78

Oklahoma City, 79, 81
one person, one vote, 56
Oregon, 83
originalism, 1, 3, 9, 61, 64–65, 146, 166–68,
  188; corporate campaign spending,
  107; criticisms of, 11–13, 46, 197nn43;
  due process, 166–67; First Amendment, 144; free exercise, 132–34; freez-
  ing constitutional meaning, 9, 144, 167;
  history and tradition, 144, 166
*Our Lady of Guadalupe School v.
  Morrissey-Berru*, 118

*Parents Involved in Community Schools
  v. Seattle School District No. 1*, 153–54,
  157, 161
Parker, Christopher Sebastian, 90
Passover, 137
Patient Protection and Affordable Care
  Act. *See* Affordable Care Act
Pence, Mike, 88–89
Pennsylvania, 22, 24, 36
People, the. *See* We the People
people of color, 1, 3, 9–13, 22, 35–36, 71–73,
  75–76, 78, 81, 84, 86–88, 92, 96–97, 106,
  110, 147–65, 172, 175–76, 178, 180–81,
  184–86. *See also* Black Americans;
  Native Americans; Christian Identity
  condemnation as mud people, 75; per-
  sonal identity, 161; white flight, 150
Perich, Cheryl, 117
Perkins, Frances, 43
Pew Research Center, 86, 96
Philadelphia, 32, 129
Phillips, Jack, 119–21
Pinckney, Charles, 18
Pinckney, Charles Cotesworth, 25
Planned Parenthood v. Casey, 4, 165, 168
Pleasant Grove City v. Summum, 140–41
Pledge of Allegiance, 97
Plessy v. Ferguson, 33, 39–40, 52, 136, 149,
  159, 172. *See also* separate but equal
  doctrine

pluralist democracy, 2–3, 6–8, 42–60; conservative justices resist, 45–46; conservative reactions to, 59–70, 101; fully realized, 10, 179–88; lobbying, 44; process, 180; substantive norms and conditions, 180–86; theory, 45, 52, 58

pluralist democratic judicial review, 46–60; balancing tests, 50; focus on democracy, 48–50; rejecting focus on common good, 47; rejecting formalism, 46–47, 54, 57, 101; rejecting laissez faire, 46

police power (state and local), 35

political parties. *See also specific political parties*: accepted for common good, 28; factions, 27

political science, in Supreme Court decision making, 3–4

post-millennialism, 75

Powell, Lewis, 151

prayers in public meetings, 9, 111–13, 115, 124, 147

prayers in public schools, 55, 65, 112, 142–47

preferred freedoms, 52

Pritchett, C. Herman, 48

private religious schools, 118

private schools, 121–22, 145; predominantly Christian, 116, 118, 122; racial segregation, 55

progressive justices, 4, 114, 123, 125, 127–28, 154; of 1930s, 46; full and equal citizenship, 179, 185

progressive politics, 4, 6, 46, 102, 111, 114–15, 123, 125, 127–29, 138, 156, 158, 163, 165, 179–80, 185, 187–88

Progressivism (early-twentieth century), 37–39, 43

Project 2025, Mandate for Leadership, 177–78

Protestantism, 6, 18, 22–24, 33–34, 39, 43–44, 74–75, 82, 84, 112, 133, 144–45. *See*

also Christianity; de facto Christianity; evangelicalism (Christian); fundamentalism; constitutional framers, 20; Protestants on Supreme Court, 93; racially segregated schools, 71

public choice theory, 68

public forum, free expression, 140–41

Public Religion Research Institute, 177

public schools, 59, 145–46, 186; affirmative action, 151–54, 157; firearms, 102; free speech, 56, 140; holiday parties, 93; moments of silence, 112; prayers, 7, 9, 55–56, 65, 112, 142–45, 147, 166; privatization, 71, 80; racial segregation, 7, 29, 41, 53–55, 71–72, 150; religion, 95

public sphere and private sphere relationship, 2, 22, 26–27, 40–41, 53–54, 58, 83, 108–9, 141, 169, 171, 179

QAnon, 90

racial discrimination. *See* discrimination, based on race; racism

racial segregation. *See* racism

racism, 6, 21–22, 24–26, 36, 73, 75, 78, 135. *See also* discrimination, based on race; slavery; Buchanan and, 82; directed at Obama, 85; dog whistles, 156; facially neutral laws with discriminatory effects, 150–51, 158, 162; identity, 161; naturalization, 28–29; racist structures, 92–93, 154–57, 160; in relation to New Deal, 52; statistics, 156, 158, 160–62; Trump and, 87–88, 97; who belongs, 161

railroads, 36–37

Ramadan, 137

Rambo, 72–73

Randolph, Edmund, 19

ratification. *See* constitutional ratification

rational basis review. *See* equal protection

rational basis test. *See* free exercise

Ray, Domineque, 138

Reagan, Ronald, 66, 69, 72–73, 81, 156; conservative disenchantment with, 73

Reconstruction, 9, 28–31, 52, 106, 161, 165; readmission of Confederate states, 30

Reconstruction Amendments, U.S. Constitution, 28, 106. *See also* Fifteenth Amendment; Fourteenth Amendment

Rehnquist, William, 4, 102, 104

Rehnquist Court, 4, 8, 63, 101–4, 111, 118, 123, 140, 150, 165, 169; affirmative action, 151–52; anti-democracy, 101; formalism, 102

religion clauses. *See* religious freedom

religious freedom, 2–3, 7–9, 23–24, 50–52, 55, 64–65, 109, 172, 175, 177, 180, 185. *See also* Establishment Clause; Free Exercise Clause; coercion test, 61, 112, 124; convergence of interests, 137–38, 140–42, 147; de facto Christianity, 23; discrimination, 184–86; the early Roberts Court, 111–24; endorsement test, 61, 112, 124; history and tradition, 61, 112–15, 117, 124, 144, 146; intersection of Free Exercise and Establishment Clauses, 142–46; judicial restraint, 61–63; the later Roberts Court, 125–39, 141–48; *Lemon* test, 61–62, 111–15, 117, 123, 141, 144; little protection during republican democratic era, 39–40; moments of silence, 112; most-favored nation status, 143; neutrality, 63, 116–17, 120, 122–23, 125–26, 130, 132, 143, 147; religion clauses being complementary, 144; religious speech, 114, 140–41; religious strife, 146; tension between religion clauses, 144; understood from distinctly Christian perspective, 95; wall of separation, 51–52, 55–56, 61, 65, 123–24; Warren Court, 55–56; white Christian nationalism, 111, 134, 147–49, 179

religious test or oath, 22

representation reinforcement, 49–50, 181–82. *See also* *United States v. Carolene Products Company*

republican democracy, 1, 6–7, 17–20, 30–42, 44–45, 48, 51, 64–65, 147, 172. *See also* common good; republican democratic judicial review; collapse, 44; exclusion, 21–26; political parties as accepted, 28; political parties as factions, 27; release of economic energy, 35; as rural, agrarian, and relatively homogenous, 36–37, 42; virtue (civic), 17, 21–22, 27, 34–35, 39–41, 43–44, 65, 175, 183, 201n22; well ordered society, 35

republican democratic judicial review, 34, 36, 38–41, 45, 48, 64–65, 147, 172, 175; laissez faire, 37, 102; *Lochner*-era, 37–40, 45–47, 101–2, 104; moral values, 35; taking from A and giving to B, 35

Republican Party, 7, 28–31, 37, 60, 96, 187. *See also* conservatism (political); neoliberalism, 80; Progressivism (early-twentieth century), 37; white Christian nationalism, 80, 88–97, 177

Revolutionary War, 12, 18–19, 24, 178; vigilantism, 77

Reynolds v. Sims, 56

Reynolds v. United States, 39

right to choose. *See* abortion

Road to Serfdom, 66

Roberts, John, 4, 102–5, 116, 119, 121–23, 125, 127, 129–31, 134–35, 137–39, 142, 153, 157, 159. *See also* Roberts Court

Roberts, Owen, 46

Roberts Court: administrative agencies, 106; affirmative action, 9, 152–54, 156, 159–62, 165, 179; aggrandizing power, 106; anti-democracy, 3, 8, 101–6, 108–10, 168, 178, 188; *Brown v. Board*, 153–54, 157, 159–61, 165; conservative justices, 4–5, 101, 176; de facto Christianity, 8–9, 111–15, 117, 124, 133–34, 136–38, 142–48, 167; due process,

166–69, 171–72, 175; free expression, 8, 10, 106–9, 140–41, 170–71, 184; hostility to Congress, 3, 102–6, 110, 168, 178; later Roberts Court distinguished from early Roberts Court, 5; LGBTQ+ rights, 169–72, 175, 178; minority rule (as favoring exclusive, inegalitarian, and hierarchical democracy), 1, 3, 6, 8–10, 13, 110–11, 134, 147–49, 157–59, 162–64, 168, 172, 175–79, 184–85, 187–88; national security, 139; non-Christians, 137–42; *Plessy v. Ferguson*, 172; protection of wealth and economic marketplace, 106, 108–9; religion clauses being complementary, 144; religious makeup, 93; state sovereignty, 106, 124, 168; taxpayer standing, 115–16; white Christian nationalism, 1, 3, 6, 8–10, 13, 110–11, 134, 147–49, 157–59, 163–64, 172, 175–79, 184–85, 188

Robinson v. Murphy, 127

Roe v. Wade, 3, 60, 72, 165–66, 168, 178, 185

Roman Catholic Diocese of Brooklyn v. Cuomo, 125–29, 137

Romer v. Evans, 222n52

Roosevelt, Franklin D., 42–46, 48, 52; big business, 45; Brain Trust, 45; court-packing plan, 2, 46; first '100 days', 43

Roosevelt Court, 48

Rostow, Eugene V., 48

Ruby Ridge, Idaho, 81

Rucho v. Common Cause, 163, 165

rural and agarian, 36–37, 42, 44

rural school districts, 145

Rushdoony, Rousas John (RJ), 74

Rutledge, John, 25

same-sex marriage, 5, 10, 119, 129, 135–36, 171. *See also* LGBTQ+

Santeria religion, 63

Scalia, Antonin, 4–5, 12, 102, 112, 115, 152–53; criticizing *Lemon* test, 117; his judicial magnum opus, 132; Roberts Court conservatives criticize *Smith* opinion, 132; *Smith* free exercise opinion, 62

segregation. *See* racism

self-governance rationale (for free expression), 56, 107–8

Senate, 5, 20, 31, 52, 58, 88–89, 154–55, 158, 176, 187–88; FDR's court-packing plan, 46; trial of Trump, 89–90

separate but equal doctrine, 33, 39–41, 52–53, 55, 136, 149, 154, 159. *See also Plessy v. Ferguson*

Seven Aphorisms, 140

sexism, 10, 26, 73, 97, 149, 165–69. *See also* women; coverture, 22, 186; women's traditional roles, 168

shadow docket, 121–22, 125–29

sharecropping, 30

Shaw, Lemuel, 35

Shays' Rebellion, 20

Shelby County v. Holder, 8, 105–6, 108, 157, 159, 164

Shelley v. Kraemer, 54

Sherbert v. Verner, 131

Sherman, Roger, 24

Sherman, William Tecumseh (General), 30

Shurtleff, Harold, 140–41

Shurtleff v. City of Boston, Massachusetts, 140–41

slavery, 6, 20, 27, 29–30, 33, 97, 154, 186. *See also* racism; argument that positive good, 74; Christianity, 120; constitutional framing, 24–26; Declaration of Independence, 18; development of capitalism, 25; moral condemnation at constitutional framing, 24; population at time of constitutional framing, 24; Presidents, 26; Rushdoony on, 74; slave labor *versus* free labor, 37; slave owning delegates at constitutional framing, 25; Thirteenth Amendment, 28; three-fifths rule, 25; voting, 18; word "slave" not in constitutional text and, 24

Smith, Adam, 67–68

Smith free exercise case. See Employment Division, Department of Human Resources v. Smith

Social Darwinism, 37

Social Security Act, 44, 60; exclusion of many Black Americans, 52

Sotomayor, Sonia, 118, 126–27, 129, 137–39, 142–44, 158, 160–61, 167; on full and equal citizenship, 171, 179

Souter, David, 4

South Bay II, 127, 129, 131, 137

South Bay United Pentecostal Church v. Newsom, 121–23, 125, 127

South Carolina, 18, 23, 25, 32, 41

South Dakota, 96

Soviet Union, 80–81, 94

spending power, 103–4, 106; deference to democracy and, 103

Springsteen, Bruce, 72–73

Stallone, Sylvester, 72

Star of David, 114

Stevens, Thaddeus, 30

Stone, Harlan F., 48–50

Story, Joseph, 23, 64; Commentaries on the Constitution of, 40

strict scrutiny. *See also* equal protection; free exercise: denying that strict in theory but fatal in fact, 151; proving intentional discrimination, 151, 158, 162–63; strict in theory but fatal in fact, 134–35, 147, 151–52, 161

strict scrutiny lite, 134, 152

Students for Fair Admissions, Inc. (or SFFA) v. President & Fellows of Harvard College, 159–61, 165, 179, 185

substantive due process. *See* due process

suffrage. *See* voting rights

Summum, 140. See also *Pleasant Grove City v. Summum*

Sumner, William Graham, 37

Sunday laws, 22, 36, 145

Supreme Court, U.S. *See also* republican democratic judicial review; Roberts Court; Warren Court: conservative justices, 4–6, 101, 176; law professors, 3–4; number of Republican and Democrat appointees, 5; pluralist democratic judicial review, 46–60, 101; political science, 3–4; religion of justices, 93

Supreme Court expansion (court packing), 46, 187

Sweatt, Herman Marion, 53

Sweatt v. Painter, 53

Syria, 138

Tandon v. Newsom, 128, 131

Taney, Roger, 93

taxpayer standing, 115–16

Tea Party, 84

Ten Commandments, 112, 140

Tennessee Valley Authority, 44

Tenth Amendment, U.S. Constitution, 227n2

Texas, 106, 154, 158

Thayer, Martin, 29

Thirteenth Amendment, U.S. Constitution, 28

Thomas, Clarence, 2, 4–6, 64, 88, 102, 112, 114–15, 121, 123, 125, 127, 130, 137, 141–42, 153–54, 157, 165, 171, 175

303 Creative LLC v. Elenis, 170–71, 179, 184–85

Tinker v. Des Moines Independent Community School District, 56

Tocqueville, Alexis de: on Christianity, 24; on individualism, 27

Town of Greece v. Galloway, 111–13, 115

traditionalist conservatism: moral clarity, 66, 74, 83; in relation to white Christian nationalism, 74

travel ban under Trump, 138–39

treat like cases alike, 128–29

tribes. *See* Native Americans

Trinity Lutheran Church of Columbia, Inc. v. Comer, 119, 122
Trumbull, Lyman, 29
Trump, Donald, 5, 7–8, 80, 82, 121, 176–77; 2024 election, 187; birtherism, 84; evangelicals, 85–86, 94, 96; impeachment, 89–90; peddling innocence, 96; selling Christian Bible, 97; support of white Christians, 85–86; travel ban, 138; tweets, 90; white Christian nationalism, 88, 90–91
Trump v. Hawaii, 138–39, 141
Tugwell, Rex, 43
Turner Diaries: Beam in, 76; McVeigh in, 79
Tuskegee, Alabama, 56
Twin Towers, 80, 83
2024 presidential election, 5, 90, 187

unionization, 36, 47; free expression, 40, 51; Roosevelt and, 45
United States v. Carolene Products Company, 48, 50. *See also* representation reinforcement
United States v. Lopez, 102–4, 108
Unite the Right rally, 87
University of California Regents v. Bakke, 151–52, 159
University of Texas, 53, 152
urbanization, 36, 41–42
U.S. Constitution. *See specific Amendments*; *specific Clauses*; *specific topics*

Van Devanter, Willis, 48
Venezuela, 138–39
Vermont, 31
Vietnam War, 7, 70, 72–74, 80; protests against, 56–57, 71
vigilantism, 31–32, 77–78, 97
Virginia, 24, 32; Unite the Right rally in, 87
virtue (civic), 1, 3, 17, 19–22, 34–35, 39–41, 43–44, 50, 52, 64–65, 175, 183; as chang-
ing, 27; framers as virtuous elite, 20, 26; inconsistent with partisanship, 27; moral values of white Christian men, 35; mythical or duplicitous, 45
voter identification law, 106
voting rights, 8, 43, 45, 49, 68, 105, 150, 158–59, 183; immigrants, 34; Native Americans, 195n34, 199n6; need for greater protections, 187; non-Christian, 12, 18; political parties, 27; race, 12, 17, 28–32, 57, 157–58; recent restrictions, 106, 157; Reconstruction, 30–32; sex, 12, 17, 33–34; wealth, 18, 21, 27
Voting Rights Act (VRA), 8, 57, 59, 105–6, 157–58, 164, 168; effective, 58
VRA. *See* Voting Rights Act

Waco, Texas, 81
Waldron, Jeremy, 184
wall of separation, 51–52, 55–56; criticism of, 65; *Lemon* test, 61; rejection of, 124; retreat from, 61, 123; Supreme Court rejection, 61, 123–24
Warren, Earl, 2, 5, 60
Warren Court, 7–8; criticisms of, 2, 7, 11, 59–66, 101; as favoring inclusive, egalitarian, participatory democracy, 2, 7, 54–60, 101, 175, 179, 188; free exercise, 55, 62; free expression, 56, 149; racial discrimination, 149–50; religious freedom, 55–56; taxpayer standing, 115
Washington, D.C., 69, 150
Washington, George, 26
Washington v. Davis, 150–51, 158, 162–63
wealth, 1–2, 12, 18–21, 26–27, 32, 36–37, 39–40, 60, 69, 81, 91, 101, 106, 108–9, 141, 156, 160, 168
well ordered society, 35
Wesberry v. Sanders, 56
West Coast Hotel Company v. Parrish, 46, 48
We the People, 1–3, 10, 78, 97–98, 147, 149, 178

Wharton, Francis, 38
White, Edward Douglass, 93
White-Cain, Paula, 96
white Christian heterosexual men, 1–3, 6, 8, 10, 12–13, 18–21, 26–28, 73, 78, 90, 92, 97, 109–10, 172, 175–76, 178–79, 188; as full and equal citizens, 185–86; moral values, 35; as privileged without awareness, 96
white Christian nationalism, 6–10, 66, 69–70, 72–76, 97, 102; abortion, 176; Alito and, 177; caste system, 10, 73, 91–92, 98, 148, 176; explained, 92–93; going deeper into political mainstream, 79–86, 88–90; independent of Trump, 177; innocence, 96; its origins, 70–72; LGBTQ+ rights, 176; lone wolves, 79; non-Christians, 176; not anti-Catholic, 82; Project 2025, 177; relationship with democracy, 77–79; religious freedom, 111, 134, 147–49, 179; Republican conservatism, 91–97; Republican Party, 80, 88–97, 177; resentment or grievance, 9, 71–73, 79, 82, 85–88, 92, 94, 111, 117, 124, 147, 176; Roberts Court, 1, 3, 6, 8–10, 13, 110–11, 134, 147–49, 157–59, 163–64, 172, 175–79, 184–85, 188; traditional family roles, 176; Trump and, 88, 90–91; white Christian women and, 74; widespread in American conservatism, 177
white flight, 150
white supremacy and privilege, 70–71, 73, 87–89. *See also* white Christian nationalism
Whitmer, Gretchen, 88
Whitney, Eli, 25
Wickard v. Filburn, 53
Wilson, Henry, 31
Wilson, James, 22
with all deliberate speed, 55, 71, 149. *See also* desegregation
women, 1, 3–4, 9, 11–13, 17, 22, 27–28, 33, 35–36, 43, 46, 71, 73, 78, 82, 86, 97, 110, 148–49, 155, 165–69, 172, 175, 178–81, 184–86. *See also* sexism
Wortman, Tunis, 27
Wriston, Walter, 69

Wyoming, 77

Yale University, 37, 48, 65
Yemen, 138
Yoruba religion, 63

ABOUT THE AUTHOR

STEPHEN M. FELDMAN is the Jerry W. Housel/Carl F. Arnold Distinguished Professor of Law and Adjunct Professor of Political Science at the University of Wyoming. He is the author of *Please Don't Wish Me a Merry Christmas: A Critical History of the Separation of Church and State* (New York University Press, 1997); *Free Expression and Democracy in America: A History* (University of Chicago Press, 2008); and *Pack the Court! A Defense of Supreme Court Expansion* (Temple University Press, 2021), among other titles. He also writes fiction and has published several short stories.